Critical Concepts™ Series . . .

Walleye Presentation

*Core Techniques—
Livebait Rigging, Jigging,
and Traditional Systems*

Critical Concepts™ Series . . .

Walleye Presentation

Core Techniques—
Livebait Rigging, Jigging, and Traditional Systems

Expert Advice from North America's
Leading Authority on Freshwater Fishing

THE IN-FISHERMAN STAFF

In-Fisherman

A PRIMEDIA Company

Critical Concepts™ Series . . .
Walleye Presentation: Core Techniques—Livebait Rigging, Jigging, and Traditional Systems

Editor In Chief *Doug Stange*
Editors *Steve Quinn, Matt Straw*
Staff Writer *Jeff Simpson*
Contributing Staff Members *Al Lindner, Mark Dorn, Jim Kalkofen, Dan Sura, Jim Lindner, Joann Phipps*
Founders *Al Lindner, Ron Lindner*
Project Coordinator *Scott Lawrence*
Copy Editor *J.Z. Grover*
Cover *Nelson Graphic Design*
Layout & Design *Scott Lawrence with Jim Pfaff, Brian Lindberg, and Ron Schrader*

Acknowledgments

Keith Kavajecz, *rod design, Ch. 2*; Tom Irwin, *superline trolling Ch. 3*; Jeff Murray, *leech rigging Ch. 4*; Ron Anlauf, *bottom bouncers, Ch. 6*; Larry Porter, *jigging spoons, Ch. 7*; Terry Wickstrom and Tom Bruno, *jigging spoons, Ch. 7*; Ron Boggs, *bladebaits, Ch. 7*; Jim Fofrich Sr., *weight-forward spinners, Ch. 7*; Ron Boggs, *supertuning crankbaits, Ch. 8*; Tom Neustrom, *crawfish pattern crankbaits, Ch. 8*; Jeff Murray and Harry Stiles, *crankbaits in rivers, Ch. 8*; Mark Strand, *slipfloats, Ch. 9*; Greg Bohn and Ray Hansen, *slip floats at night, Ch. 9*; Dick Sternberg, *slipsfloats during mayfly hatches, Ch. 9*.

Walleye Presentation: Core Techniques—Livebait Rigging, Jigging, and Traditional Systems

Printing Edition   11 10 9 8 7 6 5 4 3

First Edition

Library of Congress Cataloging-in-Publication Data
ISBN: 1-892947-06-4

Introduction

From the Editors—
All About This Book

Among walleye anglers, the words "fishing" and "trolling" tend to be synonymous. Historically speaking, most walleye presentations have evolved from a trolling perspective, as opposed to those incorporated by bass anglers, who tend to cast toward submerged cover or flooded objects an overwhelming amount of the time. Walleyes, by comparison, often tend to be deeper, somewhat less cover-oriented (at times), and more migratory than bass. In such instances, trolling merely maximizes the amount of time your lure or bait is in front of or searching for fish. This doesn't mean that you should never cast for walleyes, because there are many situations where walleyes use shallow water and casting provides a decided advantage over trolling; just that the public perception is that trolling rules the waves where walleyes are concerned. In actuality, the ability to both cast and troll is essential to consistent walleye fishing success.

This book delves into traditional walleye fishing systems: livebait rigs, jigs, slipbobbers, spinners, backtrolling, bottom bouncing, three-way rigging, structure fishing, and a host of techniques richly rooted in walleye legend and lore.

With trolling foremost in the minds of walleye anglers, however, presentations have been described as two-stage systems: 1) you position the boat via various boat control maneuvers, taking into account factors like wind, current, and trolling speed, while 2) boat movement correspondingly positions lines, lures, and baits. Trolling—the walleye two-step. Lines and lures follow the boat around, so you must effectively maneuver the boat to position your offerings. Boat control therefore becomes paramount to success.

Walleye trolling systems can also be divided into two broad classifications: precision and coverage systems. In general terms, precision tactics like livebait rigging and vertical jigging tend to saturate limited areas with slow, meticulous, teasing presentations designed to tempt bites. At the opposite end of the trolling spectrum, coverage presentations like open water crankbait or spinner trolling quickly and systematically search large areas, perhaps sacrificing a bit of local precision in exchange for quickly locating fish and triggering strikes, though a good troller can specifically target depth levels wherever fish are present.

This book, the third in our series on walleye fishing, chiefly focuses on precision presentation tactics, be they accomplished by casting or trolling. Hands-on systems that enable you to tease and extract fish along distinct structural edges, from within cover, and along shallow shorelines at night. The fourth installment in our walleye series will conclude with traditional boat control methods, multi-rod coverage systems, and advanced use of electronics for exploring the vast potential of open water, be it for suspended or basin-hugging walleyes. A full complement of versatile techniques that can be matched to any fishing conditions. Armed with such an array of angling options, walleyes can swim, but they no longer have anywhere to hide.

Or think of it another way. This book delves into traditional walleye fishing systems: livebait rigs, jigs, slipbobbers, spinners, backtrolling, bottom bouncing, three-way rigging, structure fishing, and a host of techniques richly rooted in walleye legend and lore. The following book will explore both traditional boat control methods and the brave new world of walleye fishing—the open water frontier—primarily via systems, equipment, and techniques that did not exist 10 or 15 years ago. An effective blend of old and new, propelling a traditional outdoor heritage into the 21st century.

Basics, or Essentials?

H ow difficult it must be to start from scratch and become familiar, much less comfortable, with today's vast array of fishing tackle, techniques, equipment, and electronics. Unlike those of us who learned to fish from parents and grandparents in less technique-happy times, some of today's newcomers are understandably overwhelmed by the sport's complexity and options. Keeping up with product introductions and innovations and staying abreast of trends, particularly on the electronics end, is just about limitless.

The new breed of GPS mapping and plotter units parallels products in the ever-changing computer industry: as soon as you buy something, it's already being pushed aside by the next generation on the drawing board. Unless you're an electronics buff (nerd?), you quickly realize you don't have a clue and had better get some knowledgeable help from people who speak plain English. Tech heads fluent in computerese and technobabble often assume that everyone else speaks the same language, so they lose you in the first thirty seconds of conversation. It's a pleasant relief to locate someone who can explain equipment options and functions in layman's terms.

Even the basics are important because they provide the foundation for expanding anglers' knowledge and growth.

Is the fishing business becoming as guilty of this as the computer industry? In-Fisherman's editorial philosophy has always been to cater to the upper echelon of anglers by reporting on state-of-the-art developments, from sophisticated presentation systems to the latest gadgets and gizmos. The problem inherent in this, however, lies in assuming that everyone's already aware of the basics and that there's little call for publishing features like *Hooking on a Worm 101*. Yet that's simply not the case, particularly with walleyes.

Walleye fishing is expanding across North America, with new anglers coming into the fold every day. Often they're experienced in fishing for other species, just new to walleyes. In other cases, they truly are newcomers to the sport. Even the basics are important because they provide the foundation for expanding anglers' knowledge and growth.

While we continually seek the most timely and updated information on walleyes and walleye fishing, we haven't forgotten our roots and what it's like to be hungry for knowledge, even of the most basic kind. The challenge becomes providing a mix of the old and the new, the traditional and the trends, so we can inform new readers without alienating veterans who think they're past the basics.

New wrinkles aren't always of an earth-shaking variety, like a crash course in GPS mapping. Most often, they're little rigging tips, equipment ideas, or unusual fish locations that are vital—things that help anglers progress by degrees long after they've become familiar with the so-called basics.

These are good lessons for everyone. We all have weaknesses in our knowledge, and none of us learns everything by ourselves. It's an ongoing, sharing process. If you reach a point where you stop learning, you stop growing. When you put yourself in position to discover something new, your experience keeps expanding. Knowledge is the total of your experiences, little and big. And little things can add up to a big difference. So we should never assume that the basics are beneath us, even though they are the actual base beneath us, providing that all-important foundation upon which we build our skills.

So, for you old timers who may scoff at basic features on rigging tips, matching tackle to conditions, or something as simple as tying knots, think again. Is this stuff all fresh in your memory and firmly at the forefront of your thought processes? Or mightn't the occasional gentle reminder be a good thing for all of us? Reviews of basics help us reevaluate what we may otherwise take for granted. And maybe they'll encourage us to try a new tactic occasionally, instead of automatically repeating the same approaches.

You frequently update your tackle; why not update your thinking as well? As for us, we won't tell you about a GPS unit without making sure you also know how to tie on a hook.

Dave Csanda
Senior Editor

Contents

Chapter		Page

1. *From Humble Beginnings*
Walleye Fishing Yesterday, Today... and Tomorrow 1

2. *Spinning, Casting, Trolling*
Effective Rod & Reel Combos. 15

3. *A Fine Line Between Success and Stress*
Monofilament, Superlines, Knots, and More 37

4. *Hook, Line, & Sinker*
Balanced Livebait Rigs and Components 59

5. *The World's Most Versatile Lures*
Jigs & Dressings 89

6. *Flashin' Passion*
Spinners and Bouncers. 111

7. *Heavy Metal Magic*
Spoons, Blades, Weight-Forwards, and Variations 143

8. *Crankin' and Spankin'*
Casting and Longline Trolling Crankbaits 165

9. *Bob, Bob, Bobbin' Along*
Slipfloat Setups & Strategies. 193

10. *Organized and Accessible*
Tackle Boxes and Storage 217

11. *Technology 2000*
State-of-the-Art Systems—A Preview 237

Index 241

From Humble Beginnings

WALLEYE FISHING YESTERDAY, TODAY . . . AND TOMORROW

" *Those who cannot remember the past are condemned to repeat it.*"

—George Santayana

Walleye fishing lay dormant until about the mid-1950s. Minor regional developments occurred, but no national movement focused them and harnessed their collective energies. But an avalanche of new ideas and technology lay on the horizon. As it began to break, the combination of elements propelled walleye fishing into the modern age.

GOLDEN YEARS—THE MODERN WALLEYE ERA

Walleye fishing remained relatively unsophisticated in the mid-1950s. Most anglers fished from 12- to 16-foot wooden rental boats powered by 5- to 10-hp motors. Tubular steel casting rods were just giving way to fiberglass spinning rods—long flexible shafts with soft tips capable of detecting light bites.

Times were changing, but the process was slow. Heavy-hardware spinners were perhaps the most popular walleye equipment. A sucker minnow threaded on the wire shaft of a Strip On, Prescott, or True Spin spinner was considered the most advanced presentation.

Timing is everything. A good idea implemented at the wrong time goes unrewarded if the proper environment doesn't exist to encourage or foster its development. Unharvested innovation shrivels on the vine, never achieving its potential until or unless the climate changes.

Braided Dacron line was popular, although anglers also began trying earlier versions of braided nylon introduced by Du Pont shortly after World War II. The mono of that era was stiff and kinky compared to today's supple lines; it was difficult to handle when rigged on a revolving-spool casting reel like the Pflueger Supreme. (The Ambassadeur 5000, forerunner of modern casting reels, had just been introduced.) European spinning reels, like the Mitchell and Luxor (France) and Quick (Germany), however, encouraged the use of light monofilament by American fishermen.

Walleye anglers fished with minnows on large snelled hooks, using round bobbers or weighted lines. Hooks were snelled on catgut, a thick, stiff, brittle substance resembling the material used to string tennis racquets. Catgut was also used on some inline spinner rigs, but it quickly wore out from abrasion.

Multiple-hook rigs and lures were also in fashion. Flatfish-type lures, with treble-gang hooks to increase hooking percentages for light-biting walleyes, were drifted or rowed (seldom motor trolled) on weighted lines or three-way rigs. Some anglers tipped the hooks with pieces of nightcrawler. Others preferred a "natural" approach. Fishermen returning from Canadian wilderness trips swore they needed only a Dardevle spoon. Hardware was key.

The Modern Walleye Era

Events or Significant Products*	Signs of the Times

Post
World
War II
	• primitive monofilament (Du Pont '46)
	• wooden rental boats with 5- to 10-hp outboards
	• hardware—Flatfish, Strip-Ons, True Spins,
	  Prescott Spinners, Dardevles, snelled hooks on
	  catgut, fiberglass rods, spinning reels

1955	Buck Perry introduces structure fishing	
1957	Lowrance Lo-K-Tor	
1958	Stren, Trilene; Barracuda Jigs, Upperman Bucktail Jigs	
1959		• 3-hook crawler harnesses
1961	Little Joe Red Devil Spinner	• gradual shift to privately owned aluminum boats
1962	Rapala arrives on American scene	
1967	Bill Binkelman's *Nightcrawler Secrets*; Lindy Rig	

1968	Lindners innovate backtrolling, deep water
	  walleye fishing
		• Lund 315, 25-hp Johnson, rubber truck-flap
		  splashguards

1969	Walleyes Unlimited USA formed	

1970	Ban on commercial fishing in Ohio waters of Lake Erie	
1971	Silverline Walleye Tournament, Hastings, MN; Vexilar 155A graph	
1972	Leeches as bait (Mille Lacs); graphite rods appear	• light tackle dominates walleye market
1973	Bobbers at night (Mille Lacs)	
1974	Bobbers during day on deep mudflats (Mille Lacs)	
1975	*In-Fisherman* Study Reports; Vexilar 555 graph; discovery of Lake Erie suspended walleye schools	
1976	Waterdogs as bait	

1978	Daytime bobbers on shallow rocks (Mille Lacs);
	  first Mercury Marine National Walleye Tournament;
	  First Lund pike boat designed by Gary Roach;
	  Erie Dearie
		• mid South walleyes popularized

1980		• spinners and bottom bouncers on Plains states reservoirs
1981		• jigging spoons producing walleyes in the South
1982	Seasonal night-fishing ban on Mille Lacs (10 p.m. to 6 a.m.)	• scent products • trolling boards popularized for walleyes
1983	Columbia River walleyes popularized	• downriggers for walleyes
1984	first national walleye circuit fails; Humminbird LCR technology	• 50-hp outboards, larger trolling motors • shallow water walleye patterns acknowledged
1985	MWC walleye circuit begins	• mobile ice fishing technology
1986		• expanding popularity of bottom bouncers and spinners
1987		• shift toward big water console walleye boats
1988		• LORAN technology becoming accepted by walleye anglers
1989	first PWT tournament (Mille Lacs); In-Fisherman *Walleye In-Sider* tabloid introduced	

1990	Professional Walleye Trail circuit begins	• fiberglass walleye boat designs emerging
1991	spring open water crankbait trolling on Lake Erie	
1992	GPS technology available	• powerful bowmount electrics encourage bow presentations
1994	In-Fisherman *Walleye In-Sider* switches to magazine format; Spiderwire superbraid	• handheld GPS units
1995		• GPS mapping technology
1996		• walleye-specific soft plastics and crankbaits
1997		• underwater videocameras
1998	In-Fisherman *Ice Fishing Guide* debuts	• 200-hp outboards and 18- to 20-foot boats
1999		

*Early innovations often date back to specific introductions or persons. Later trends often are the by-products of many anglers' efforts and cannot be tied to exact dates or individuals. By the 1980s, information began to spread so fast that "new" became "common" within a single season.

REVOLUTION

Revolutions are like glowing coals fanned into sudden flame by a catalyzing event. In the case of walleye fishing, several spontaneous and simultaneous factors awakened walleye fishing, and American angling in general.

In the mid-1950s, a voice altering the course of fishing history rose from the South. E. L. "Buck" Perry of North Carolina preached a new theory called *structure fishing*. He spoke of drop-offs, edges, and deep-to-shallow-water fish movements. He backed his claims with record catches of all freshwater species. Anglers began to visualize what lay beneath the surface of the waters they fished.

Closely following this concept was Carl Lowrance's 1957 introduction of the Fish Lo-K-Tor. Lowrance called it his "eyes to the bottom." Early devotees grasped it's significance, particularly when teamed with Perry's structure concept. The avalanche had begun to move.

In 1957 and 1958, Berkley introduced Trilene monofilament, and Du Pont unveiled its new premium line, Stren—high-quality monofilament lines that allowed unheard-of presentation options. Prior to this, the finesse techniques so critical to the walleye scene today would have been difficult, if not impossible. Braided black Dacron didn't lend itself to the manufacture of livebait rigs and harnesses. But now, lighter and smaller artificial lures, natural livebait presentations, and effective deep water techniques became possible. A flurry of innovative tackle introductions followed.

One of the first significant innovations was the introduction of saltwater jigs to the freshwater market in about 1958. Barracuda jigs and Upperman Bucktails tipped with minnows produced walleyes. Smaller wire-shaft spinner rigs were teamed with long monofilament leaders and tipped with crawlers (Joe Fellegy—Mille Lacs Lake, Minnesota). The first three-hook nightcrawler harnesses appeared.

The next major innovation occurred in 1961 with the introduction of the Little Joe Red Devil spinner. Unlike its wire-shaft predecessors, the Red Devil featured an Indiana blade, a single or double hook, and beads and a clevis, which revolved on a lightweight monofilament leader. It became the foundation for future spinner rigs and the power trolling concept.

The Rapala minnow (introduced in 1960) struck the American angling scene like a thunderbolt when a 1962 issue of *Life* magazine described it as a lure that fish couldn't resist. It forever changed the way fishermen fish with lures. The subtle swimming action of the balsa minnow produced monumental catches of all species, spurring a host of wood and plastic imitations. Tremendous growth in tackle sales followed.

Walleyes had previously been considered a primarily spring fish because most significant catches occurred when fish were grouped in shallow water during the spawning cycle. During summer, catches were poor or sporadic. And during fall, few fishermen were fishing. Granted, though, some good catches were made during winter through the ice. But cold weather walleye fishing was confined to regional pockets in the North, where ice fishing was a tradition.

But the face of walleye fishing was changing. The combination of sonar, structure fishing, and light monofilament line brought a new era of angling effectiveness. Anglers began catching walleyes all year long. A gradual shift toward

private ownership of trailerable aluminum boats heralded an end to the "good old days" of wooden rental boats. Anglers were becoming sophisticated, and they wanted to fish from their own personalized and effective equipment.

In 1967, several milestone introductions to the walleye world occurred, the fruition of light-line experimentation by leading walleye pioneers. Bill Binkelman, founding editor of *Fishing Facts* magazine, published *Nightcrawler Secrets*. Ever the champion of slow, subtle techniques, Binkelman espoused the virtues of a fat, juicy, conditioned nightcrawler hooked lightly through the nose and presented on 4-pound-test line along with a simple lead shot and a #10 hook.

Al and Ron Lindner, meanwhile, formally introduced the Lindy Rig. This first packaged concept consisted of an assembled snell, hook, swivel clip, and sliding,

"walking" sinker, complete with instructions.

Earlier versions used by the Lindners and friends like guide Harry Van Dorn had relied on an egg sinker. Ron's shoe-shaped sinker design was touted as walking across rocks and minimizing snags while presenting livebait naturally. When a walleye struck, you gave it time to swallow the bait before setting the hook. The walleye felt no resistance because the line slid through the walking sinker. Lindy Tackle surged to the forefront of the walleye world.

The following year, the Lindners developed and popularized backtrolling, bringing together the central elements of walleye fishing—structure fishing, natural bait presentation, and boat control—into a neat package. When they drifted off

a point and caught a walleye in 80 feet of water on Lake Okoboji, Iowa, the Lindners broke the depth barrier and introduced deep water fishing to the walleye world.

State-of-the-art equipment included a 15-foot fiberglass Lund 315 tri-hull, a 25-hp Johnson outboard with an on-tiller gearshift, a Lowrance depthfinder, a Minn Kota or Shakespeare transom electric trolling motor, and rubber truck flaps bolted to the transom to deflect the waves that buffeted the transom when the angler trolled slowly in reverse. Moving backwards reduced trolling speed and allowed maximum boat control, a dynamic combination.

Never before had walleye fishing been so effective. And never before had the public been so involved in the change. Binkelman continued to publish his ideas. And the Lindners and their promotional crew barnstormed the country, promoting education and their own tackle line. Finesse techniques using light line became the rage. "Hardware" techniques—spinners and spoons—were buried in a sea of tiny hooks and light line. Of course, the effectiveness of spinners would be rediscovered years later—the rebirth of a walleye standby. But the late 1960s and the 1970s belonged to the light line brigade.

THE 1970S

By the 1970s, TV anglers like the Lindners, Gadabout Gaddis, Jerry McKinnis, Virgil Ward, and other pioneers were bringing fishing into living rooms across America, demonstrating how much fun and how effective fishing could be. Educational fishing articles pioneered by *Fishing Facts* magazine began to replace "me-and-Joe-went-fishing" stories, drawing more converts into the walleye game.

Early instructional fishing clubs like Walleyes Unlimited USA (1969) were established. Walleye competitions like the 1971 Silverline Tournament on the Mississippi River at Hastings, Minnesota, pitted walleye anglers against each other in a test of skill. (The Lindners won it— on Ron's secret spot, or so he claims.)

In 1972, Lindy-rigged leeches began making

their mark on the deep-lying mudflats of Minnesota's famous Mille Lacs Lake. In the spring of 1973, shoreline anglers discovered the incredible effectiveness of leeches bobber-fished in shallow water at night. By 1974, anglers were catching fish with slipbobbers and leeches on the deep (20- to 30-foot) mudflats. Leeches were the "in" bait for walleyes.

Meanwhile, on the Great Lakes, few people outside Ohio noticed when Erie Dearie-style weight-forward spinners were introduced to the Lake Erie market in 1968. The walleye population was so depressed by a combination of pollution-caused eutrophication and commercial exploitation that few folks bothered to fish there.

But the 1970 ban on commercial fishing for walleye in Ohio and the cleanup of Lake Erie brought astonishing results. In 1975, anglers discovered schools of walleyes suspended in open water. Mother Nature had replenished her stores. Over the next few years, Lake Erie became the focus of walleye fishermen in the East. Varieties of weight-forward spinners appeared, charter captains began guiding along the Ohio shore, and thousands of new walleye converts flocked to the former "Dead Sea." In 1971, Vexilar quietly introduced Japan Radio Company's 155A graph to the Great Lakes market. Four years later, introduction of the Vexilar 555 paper graph caused controversy. Righteous environmentalists led a "ban the graph" movement in Minnesota, trying to take it off the market before it decimated fish populations. Their protests failed. Fish populations survived. And the graph became a popular and effective tool.

The early 1970s also brought graphite rods. Graphite, lightweight and sensitive, helped anglers fish more comfortably. Graphite also made it possible to feel lighter bites from walleyes. Traditional "strike and set techniques" (feel a strike and set instantly) gave way to feeding line to walleyes before setting the hook, in conjunction with popularization of the Lindy Rig.

By 1975, the Lindners had sold their interest in Lindy Tackle and were in the process of launching a consulting and product evaluation service, a fishing promotional service offering seminars and television, plus a host of other services. Nearly lost amidst the hoopla was a series of educational study reports issued without advertising in order to keep the evaluations bias free. Those educational study reports were the beginning of *In-Fisherman* magazine, today the heart of the In-Fisherman Communications Network. The study reports taught the Fish + Location + Presentation = Success formula, defined Calendar Periods of seasonal fish behavior, and offered a Lake, River, and Reservoir Classification System.

From humble roots, a force arose that has changed the course of fishing history. During the next years, a solid staff of leading fishermen and educators (Al Lindner, Ron Lindner, Dave Csanda, Doug Stange, Jim Lindner, and others)

pioneered new directions in teaching anglers about walleyes. The staff did more than document change via TV shows and magazine articles—they played a major role in shaping that change. Most important, perhaps, In-Fisherman began to serve as a resource center uniting the disparate worlds of fisheries science, fishing industry, fishing communicators, and fishing public.

The year 1978 witnessed several milestones. Mille Lacs, Minnesota, anglers discovered the daytime effectiveness of slipbobbers and leeches on shallow, windswept rocks. The first Mercury Marine National Walleye Tournament was held on Lake Winnebago, Wisconsin. And Lund Boats designed the first "pike boat." This walleye rig sported a flat floor, storage compartments, and prerigged electronic hookups.

Anglers were experimenting, improving, innovating. They scoured bait shops for waterdogs, the "ultimate" livebait introduced by Carl Lowrance in 1976. "Dogs" were in short supply, however. Minnows, crawlers, and leeches were still the staple walleye producers. "Shad baits"—evolved models of "alphabet" plugs like the Big 0, Balsa B, and Little N introduced several years earlier—also captured angler attention.

THE 1980S

In the interest of brevity, we'll pass by all but a few names and focus only briefly on events as we move through the 1980s and into the 1990s. Early in the 1980s, larger, more seaworthy boats allowed exploration of offshore waters on big, windswept lakes. In late winter, North Country anglers headed south to Arkansas and Tennessee to catch giant reservoir 'eyes on upriver spawning runs.

Fishery management agencies had to alter walleye management programs when the fishes' popularity increased with anglers and when research studies revealed more about the biology of the species. Walleyes were introduced outside their native range as additional predators in reservoirs that had surplus shad or other preyfish.

Stocking was once the backbone of walleye management, but in some cases, other strategies have become more valuable. Through computer modeling and other analytical techniques, managers can now select size and bag limits to change the abundance and size distribution of a population.

Many of these concepts, such as slot limits, were developed in the 1980s for largemouth bass. Managers applied them with some modification to walleye fisheries in the 1990s.

In planning stocking allocations, biologists can now use data on lake type, watershed, and prey abundance to fine-tune annual plants. And recent findings on walleye genetics have helped managers stock the most suitable fish.

Habitat constraints on walleye survival, growth, and reproduction have also been identified. In some cases, pollution and construction of dams have reduced good-quality walleye habitat. These problems may be alleviated in the future.

Where habitat seemed unsuitable for walleyes, managers in some states tried saugeyes, a fast-growing hybrid of the walleye and sauger. Saugeyes often prosper in waters deemed too warm, shallow, and turbid for walleyes. Notable saugeye fisheries today add to angling opportunities in Ohio, Tennessee, Oklahoma, Colorado, and other states.

Many of the developments in walleye management became possible because of passage of the Wallop-Breaux amendment to the Dingell-Johnson fund, which imposed a user fee on fishing tackle. The Sport Fish Restoration Act annually provides nearly $200 million for fishery work, education, and boating access projects in all 50 states. Without this program, our nation's fisheries would be in a dismal state as we approach the 21st century.

In 1982, in-line planer boards were introduced as tools for walleye fishing on small lakes and later in the western basin of Lake Erie. The downrigging craze for salmon and trout on lakes Michigan and Huron also touched walleye fishing. Anglers began to use 18-foot inland-style boats on the Great Lakes. By the late 1980s, downriggers would become standard walleye fare in the central and eastern basins of Lake Erie and on Lake Ontario. Trolling boards are now widely used, their popularity spurred by the success of tournament anglers.

The first national walleye circuit was attempted in 1984, and it failed. The next year, the Manufacturer's Walleye Council (MWC) circuit instituted a series of 2-angler team qualifying events with an annual championship. MWC, later renamed the Masters Walleye Circuit, paved the way for tournament competition on a national level.

In 1984, Hummingbird introduced LCR (liquid crystal readout) technology, creating a trend that would dominate the electronics scene. By the late 1980s, most flasher depthfinders were discontinued. Many seasoned anglers continue to rely on their old units, however, preferring instantaneous readouts and precise signal interpretations to less-detailed pixel readouts.

Ah, the 1980s—so many refinements, discoveries, and innovations that in most cases it's difficult to pinpoint who discovered what and exactly what was introduced where and when! Anglers began to jig for walleyes in weeds. A shift toward effective, mobile ice fishing techniques, using portable depthfinders and ice shacks, snowmobiles, custom-designed rods, power augers, and a host of spoons and jigs, began to revolutionize the winter sport. Myriad innovations appeared in jig styles—head shapes and colors; plastic bodies in varying shapes and colors, some scented or imprinted with fish triggering scents (Berkley Power Worms, Johnson Chumm'n Lures); the scent craze—Dr. Juice, Fish Formula, and the like. Rod actions changed. Reels changed. It was the most competitive time in the history of the fishing tackle manufacturing world.

It was the most competitive time in the history of the fishing tackle manufacturing world.

Tournament fishermen spurred refinements and discoveries. Spinner rigs evolved—larger, smaller, multicolored blades. Anglers discovered they could catch walleyes in shallow water, in weeds, and on windswept rocks. They tried everything to gain a competitive edge.

Crankbait trolling systems were devised for open water, using in-line trolling boards; masts, tow lines, planer boards (skis), and line releases; leadcore line. Competition demanded repeatable trolling accuracy. Commercial fishermen had long known that walleyes suspended. The rest of the walleye angling world was learning to work effectively at those same depths.

Discoveries were accompanied by the rebirth of old techniques. Bottom bouncers and spinners, a staple Missouri River reservoir technique, expanded to the Great Lakes and inland waters. Jigging spoons, commonly used in ice fishing, were applied successfully to open water.

The potential of western reservoirs and rivers began to unfold. Huge fish resided in the Columbia River along the Oregon-Washington border. Reservoirs in Montana, Wyoming, and Colorado, impoundments on the Plains of Nebraska and Kansas, and those in the highlands of Texas produced tremendous fishing.

Typical walleye water was a thing of the past. Walleyes swam in a variety of environments—deep, shallow, suspended, in weeds, wood, and on the flats. Buck Perry's adage that the fish are "deep, shallow, or in between" took on new meaning. In many environments, walleyes simultaneously exhibited several location patterns, each requiring a different presentation for maximum effectiveness.

Today's walleye frontiers lie on big waters: Lake Erie, Bay de Noc, Saginaw Bay, Lake of the Woods, and sprawling western reservoirs. Boat manufacturers have responded by producing high-tech fishing boats for long-distance pursuit of walleyes on huge, windswept waters. Not 30-foot launches for 10 to 20 anglers, but 2-man rigs, 18 to 20 feet long, designed to troll, backtroll, drift, fish small lakes and rivers, and handle heavy seas. Boats with 150-hp outboard motors backed by 15-hp "kicker" outboards and 45-pound thrust, 24-volt electrics maneuver and troll at slow speed.

LORAN navigation for inland waters in the late 1980s removed much of the anxiety attached to fishing huge waters. Anglers could find and relocate offshore spots consistently despite fog, darkness, and most bad weather. LORAN reception in the central Plains west of the Mississippi River was poor, however, due to a lack of radio towers. But GPS (Global Positioning System) satellite navigation units introduced in the early '90s filled the gap. You can return to a spot the size of your boat, anywhere on earth, as long as you have the coordinates. Who would have predicted we'd be fishing walleyes by latitude and longitude?

The growing popularity of walleye fishing spurred the introduction of new publications. In-Fisherman introduced the *Walleye Guide* in 1983, the most-read single-species newsstand publication in history. The expanding popularity of walleyes touched even East Coast publishers based on fishing's "Big Three." Where walleyes once got covered only in passing or only in yearly fishing guides, they began to be covered in many issues. One magazine placed a walleye on the cover for the first time in over 50 years.

THE 1990S

Recognizing that walleye anglers needed even more coverage of what was happening in the world of walleyes, in 1990 In-Fisherman introduced the *Walleye In-Sider* to coincide with the establishment of a big-money walleye circuit for professional walleye anglers. The Professional Walleye Trail premiered a draw-for-partner, individual competition format with qualifying tournaments and a national championship. The biggest names in walleye fishing shortly elevated the level of competition to that of B.A.S.S. events. By the mid '90s, the PWT switched to a Pro-Am format to enable a growing number of anglers to participate and to learn from competitive walleye fishing events.

Wherever walleye pros go—tournaments, seminars, or sport shows—they draw crowds of anglers seeking information on how to catch their favorite fish. The *Walleye In-Sider* responds by covering what's happening on the cutting edge of the walleye world, behind the scenes, at tournaments, and among tournament pros. Tournaments, after all, play an important role in shaping trends in angling. Tournaments refine and define fishing techniques, products, equipment, and knowledge.

In the 1990s, walleyes remained a popular item on restaurant menus, although nontribal commercial walleye fishing has been phased out in all United States waters. The impetus for this switch has been two-fold: the growing recreational walleye fishery, and recognition by fishery management agencies and state legislatures that sportfishing has huge economic and social importance. In most Canadian waters, where angling pressure is lower, biologists have felt that some waters can sustain both commercial and sport fisheries. These resource allocation decisions have not, however, been without controversy.

Walleyes made the transaction from food fish to sportfish, despite their reputation for providing a tasty meal. Today, more anglers are voluntarily releasing walleyes. Many anglers practice selective harvest, keeping a meal or two of a size or a species that doesn't harm the fishery, and releasing the rest. Fish are a valuable resource that can be enjoyed more than once. This applies as much to walleyes as to other species.

Where is walleye fishing heading? The '90s witnessed the continuing introduction of bigger, faster, safer boats capable of traveling long distances on big water. High performance hulls sporting 200-plus horsepower, 4-stroke kicker outboards, and a wealth of high-tech electronics make anglers more effective and mobile.

GPS technology evolved into split-screen mapping systems, allowing visual representation of position and destination. Stored waypoints, plotter screens, and computer technology now permit anglers to pinpoint locations and destinations, plot fish movement, and repeat trolling passes with previously unheard-of accuracy. They also provide instant orientation, instill confidence, and increase safety on large waters, thanks to permanently mounted units in boats and handheld units for use afloat, afoot, or on the ice. Nice to know you can get there and back again in rain, snow, sleet, and dark of night.

Liquid crystal technology now dominates the depthfinder business, with traditional flasher units and paper graphs taking a distant backseat to LCRs, or, in some cases, even disappearing from the market. (Flashers are still popular among ice anglers.) Today's units offer a mind-boggling array of features and displays. Some old hands refuse to let loose of their old equipment, however, having become accustomed to interpreting signals during many years of use. Others adapt to the new technology, even going so far as to adopt videosonar from companies like Genetron.

Those searching for even greater information now apply the fast developing underwater camera technology introduced in the late '90s by companies like Fish Eye and Aqua-Vu. Basically, a towed underwater camera attaches via a cable to a portable, battery-powered TV screen, providing an underwater image. Loads of fun to explore with, but it's a bit difficult to fish, run the boat, and watch your electronics and camera all at the same time. Most folks find it easiest to watch and not fish, or to watch and fish from a still position, like through the ice. Watching is learning. Seeing is believing.

Ice fishing truly came of age in the '90s, incorporating the mobile Trap Attack system and portable shelters and electronics pioneered by ice fishing legend Dave Genz. Ice angling was popularized in the pages of In-Fisherman publications, including the annual *Ice Fishing Guide*, a first-of-its-kind magazine dedicated to hard water angling, which treats ice fishing with the same professionalism as open water angling.

Continued improvements and innovations in rods, reels, rigs, and lines occurred. Superlines hit the walleye market, first in the form of braided Spectra, later in thermally fused Micro Dyneema versions that were easier to tie knots with. Spiderwire and Fire Line topped the super charts, with a number of similar lines swelling the market. Not about to be replaced by super competitors, however, new versions of monofilament lines held market share via specialized formulations for strength, abrasion resistance, limpness, and other factors. These provided walleye anglers with a wide selection of specialized lines to match fishing conditions.

At every turn, fishing equipment continues to improve. There's a new generation of sharper, razor-laser-chemically sharpened hooks for better hooking and holding power. Modular tackle storage systems. More manufacturers catering to the walleye market, not just with relabeled bass lures but with designs specifically tailored to walleyes. Everything from soft plastic shapes and tails to hardbaits for trolling applications, to snap weights and refined planer board systems for open water pursuit.

A better understanding of how, why, and where fish suspend has grown from frequent explorations for Great Lakes walleyes. Anglers now apply the same technology and open water systems to inland waters, unlocking the secrets of suspended walleyes in smaller waters.

2000—AND BEYOND

So where do we go from here? Certainly, more people will fish for walleyes in the 21st Century. The rebirth of Great Lakes walleye fisheries, the growing popularity of walleyes in western reservoirs, the accessibility of Canadian waters, and the continued productivity of traditional walleye waters ensure continued interest and growth in walleye fishing. And a wealth of new technology makes anglers more effective, more comfortable, more mobile, and more versatile than ever before.

Where will the next big breakthroughs in walleye fishing come from? It seems we've already broken every barrier, explored every option there is to explore, refined every aspect to a finer degree. Yet that's the way it's always been. Just when you think you know everything there is to know and have explored the topic from every angle, some new development explodes on the scene and causes you to rethink past chapter and verse and begin exploring new directions.

That's part of our job—staying on top of trends and bringing them to you, so you can increase your fishing success and enjoyment. As the new century dawns, we'll continue to be there with you, as we have been for almost three decades, helping to define trends and always doing our best to keep you a step ahead of the rest of the crowd.

Spinning, Casting, Trolling

EFFECTIVE ROD &
REEL COMBOS

Rods are like any other tools—they have different weights, lengths, shapes, and perform different functions. You wouldn't putt with a driver or pound a nail with a big wrench, and you wouldn't go after walleyes with a panfish rod. Rods are tools designed for specific jobs, and unless you select the appropriate one for the job, you can end up with a fishing experience that's unpleasant, inefficient, and somewhat dangerous. Better to select the proper tool for the job to begin with.

The key to any fishing situation, tacklewise, is to balance rod, reel, line, and lure to conditions. Which rod to choose? You'll find a bewildering array on the market, and even manufacturers don't agree on rod action and terminology. So we need common ground, a frame of reference, to be able to discuss what's what and who's who. Let's begin with a bit of historical foundation for understanding modern rod design and development.

HISTORICAL PERSPECTIVE

The first Skyline graphite rods hit the market in the early '70s, revolutionizing the rod business. The lightweight, thin-diameter blanks felt like toys but were sensitive and powerful compared to the fiberglass rods of the era. Graphite gained rapid acceptance and popularity among serious anglers. By the late '70s, graphite or graphite composite rods dominated the industry. Since then, rod makers have experimented with more expensive products like boron, but they've kept coming back to graphite as the backbone of the rod manufacturing process. The combination of graphite properties is tough to beat.

Graphite fibers provide the sensitivity that allows you to feel changes through the line and rod—strikes, bites, rocks, soft bottom, weeds—everything. You don't have to see a rod tip bend to detect a walleye bite, though it's always a good idea to watch the tip.

Today's rods offer high-modulus (stiffness), state-of-the-art technology, but design properties must be balanced in order for rods to be effective and durable.

Handling Different Conditions

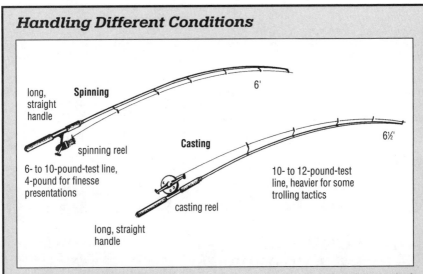

long, straight handle

Spinning

6'

spinning reel

6- to 10-pound-test line, 4-pound for finesse presentations

Casting

6½'

casting reel

10- to 12-pound-test line, heavier for some trolling tactics

long, straight handle

Spinning rods generally are less powerful than casting rods and are better suited to finesse techniques using line of 10-pound test or less. Rodmakers space their guides for peak performance based on rod action. Standard long, straight handles tuck under your arm to improve hooksetting, take the strain off your forearm while trolling, and pop with ease into a rod holder. Spinning reels with dependable drags provide control and prevent light line from breaking.

Casting rods generally are more powerful than spinning rods and are best suited to trolling and heavy casting techniques with line of about 10-pound test and heavier. Long, straight handles are preferred. Casting reels provide line capacity for trolling tactics and cranking power for pulling fish out of cover.

Versatile anglers own several of each to cover most conditions.

Too stiff, too thin, too lightweight, and they shatter when overloaded or fail under the cumulative punishment of hard fishing. Rods must have a blend of characteristics, not only ultimate strength. Light, flexible rods for light line presentations. Powerful rods for casting large lures and setting hooks with heavy monofilament, taking out inherent line stretch and burying steel.

Rods are again on the brink of revolution. Superlines with near-zero stretch have shaken the market. Existing rod designs are geared chiefly to monofilament that stretches up to 30 percent. Take the same rods and powerful sweeping hooksets, and rig them with superline that only stretches 3 percent, and the rods may shatter or at least overwork the lures or bait. Anglers using superlines must adjust their hooksets to compensate.

A new generation of fishing rods and reels designed to be fished with superlines is appearing on the market. Ironically, to compensate for the lack of line stretch, these rods are softer and more flexible than traditional rod designs—an apparent throwback to those glorious days of yesteryear and their soft-tipped rods. Difference is, they're still highly sensitive graphite, just with softer actions to match ultrasensitive, no-stretch line. What's going on underwater is transmitted via the line, whichever rod you use.

Superlines have led many anglers to dig around in their garages to relocate castoff rods considered too soft or not sensitive enough for mono. They might perform surprisingly well with no-stretch line.

ROD DESIGN—SENSITIVE MUSCLE

You'd think terminology would exist for a product that's been around a long time. But it seems that no two manufacturers can agree on what a medium-action rod is. Theoretically, it's some blend of strength and bend, but no industry standard is in place, and rod makers continue to foster confusion based on personal or company philosophy.

Permit a generalization: companies that cater heavily to trout anglers and flyfishers seem to offer medium-action noodles in their spinning and casting series; their rod designers have dainty finesse instead of sensitive muscle on the brain. To keep it plain and simple, their rods tend to be too soft, bending at mid-length instead of at the tip.

Companies catering more to bass and walleye anglers usually offer more oomph in their medium-action rods. Since terminology is confusing, *oomph* is as good a word as anything else, though *sensitive muscle* has a nice ring to it. Let's try to describe it better.

Action—Other than heavy trolling conditions, most good walleye rods offer a fast action or taper. They remain rigid in the butt and midsection and bend in the upper third near the rod tip. A fast tip loads up quickly to cast lightweight lures, bends when a livebait rig or jig is lifted, and betrays light bites by flexing. They also have sufficient beef to set the hook and fight the fish while performing well with 4- to 10-pound-test line. A moderate-action rod, by comparison, tends to bend into the midsection and is perhaps better for casting or trolling heavier lures like crankbaits. Action, therefore, best describes the bend in the rod. The term *action* commonly designates different models.

Power—Power, on the other hand, describes the strength of the rod, ultralight being a limber rod for tiny lures, heavy being a rod for heavy lures. Problem is, it's easy to confuse these terms with ultralight action or heavy action. An ultralight rod doesn't have to display a slow bend. Action and power aren't necessarily interchangeable.

Medium Schmedium, Just Tell Me What Works

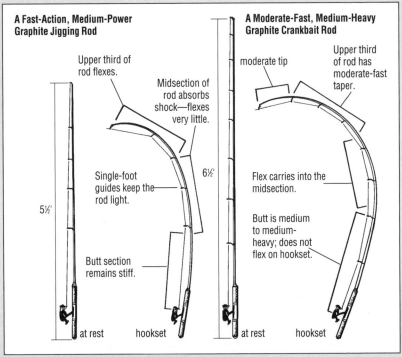

A Fast-Action, Medium-Power Graphite Jigging Rod

Upper third of rod flexes.

Midsection of rod absorbs shock—flexes very little.

Single-foot guides keep the rod light.

5½'

6½'

Butt section remains stiff.

at rest   hookset

A Moderate-Fast, Medium-Heavy Graphite Crankbait Rod

moderate tip

Upper third of rod has moderate-fast taper.

Flex carries into the midsection.

Butt is medium to medium-heavy; does not flex on hookset.

at rest   hookset

The difference between action and power: action is the bend of the rod, power the strength of the rod. They're related, but not necessarily the same. Most walleye rods for finesse techniques have fast tips and medium-power blanks. For heavier lures or trolling techniques, rods with moderate-fast medium-heavy characteristics are more appropriate.

The word *power* is seldom used to describe rods, but we'll use it here.

The best description for a good finesse walleye rod would probably be a fast-action, moderate-power spinning rod. Good luck finding that description on a rod blank or in a catalog. What you will find instead is something like "6-foot medium-action, 4-10 lb. line, 1/8- to 3/8-ounce lures." This approximate line weight and lure size designation is a tip-off for medium power, but it's no guarantee. Thereafter, you need to pick up the rod and use your own judgment. Don't just read the label, or you're destined for disappointment.

Power trolling with bottom bouncers, three-ways, or planer boards generally calls for longer, heavier casting rods with straight handles that fit into rod holders or tuck under your forearm to take the strain off your wrist while you're trolling. We'll risk a generalization: 6- to 6½-foot medium to medium-heavy rods for bouncers and three-ways, 7- to 8-foot medium-heavy rods for trolling planer boards.

Check the designation on the label. If it's something like 3/8- to 1-ounce lures, you're more on target than with lighter rods, assuming you like the way it bends and feels. You'll be able to troll 3-ounce sinkers, even though the rod supposedly tops out at 1 ounce (recommended maximum casting weight). Just don't try *casting* 3-ounce sinkers!

Other options? Spinning rods for casting slipfloats tend to be longer (7 feet) and offer moderate action so they can toss featherweight floats on 4-pound line. Downrigger rods are at the opposite end of the power scale: 8-foot heavy rods with medium-fast tapers that bend dramatically under tension and spring upward on the strike to help set hooks.

And now, superlines enter the field, turning the whole design process topsy-turvy. Rod design categories are in a quandary, a state of flux. Years ago, most designers felt superlines would be a passing fad, so they tailored few products to them. Now, with fused superlines like FireLine and SpiderWire Fusion gaining popularity, some companies are finally designing rods specifically for superline use.

Mono is far from dead, and superlines are far from taking over the market. Mono will always be important, while superlines are likely to occupy more than just a niche. How rodmakers will designate rods in the future is anybody's guess. The question now: how far should you go to equip yourself for the new lines?

Guide Specifics

Top-flight spinning rods sport high frame, single-foot guides. High frame guides reduce line slap.

Tall, single-foot stainless steel guides used to bend like butter. New titanium-alloy guides are "40 percent lighter and three times stronger than steel," says Carl Haber, national sales representative for Fuji.

The most important part of the guide is the ring the line passes through. These are all made from some kind of ceramic. Most are aluminum-oxide based; some are silicon based.

Silicon carbide is the hardest ring material. It's efficient at dissipating heat—something a tarpon fisherman would be interested in. A walleye fisherman is more interested in longevity, and silicon carbide rings are durable. Don't be surprised, however, if the rod you choose has some variation of aluminum oxide guides, which are much less expensive. A full set of silicone carbide guides can cost

more than a finished rod.

Better rods may have fewer guides than you're used to seeing. Wraps stiffen the blank at each guide. "We try to get away with the fewest possible guides," says Gary Schaeffer, rod building engineer at G. Loomis.

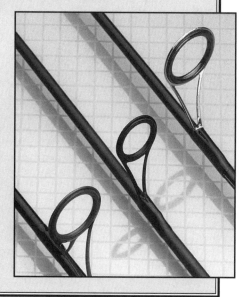

Get A Handle On It

Good rods were sporting cork handles before the Revolutionary War. Then, in the blink of an eye in historical terms, most jigging blanks were adorned with EVA (rubberized foam) handles in the late '70s and early '80s. Most returned to cork because customers preferred it.

Material isn't the only feature of the handle that you have to live with. The length and style of a handle determine how pleasurable or annoying a rod may be.

Handles come in three basic styles. Plain cork Tennessee grips are popular with anglers who like to find their own balancing points and who attach their reels with vinyl electrical tape. Handles with sliding rings accomplish the same thing, but make it easy to find the balancing point before taping. Handles with locking reels seats are the most convenient.

Some locking seats have a twisting foregrip that screws down over the reel foot; others have a simpler design employing two locking rings that turn on external threads. Both are adequate, but beware of overtightening and wrenching the cork free on some twisting foregrip models. You'll have a rod that swivels around in your hand.

Jigging rod handles serve other functions besides holding reels. Shorter rods need shorter handles that won't interfere with the fluid motions used to pitch jigs short distances to brushy banks or along riprap shorelines. On 7-foot rods, you need a long handle for two-hand power casts into the wind or for going an extra yard.

Handle styling and jigging style should match, too. Anglers who like to pin the line against the blank with their forefinger prefer a bullet taper where the handle meets the blank. Others who touch the line at the reel or against the handle may prefer handles that flair. If you love a rod but its handle is too bulky, trim it with sandpaper.

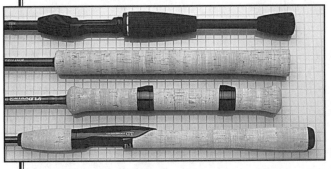

The answer depends on you. Best advice is to walk before you run, dog-paddle before you freestyle. Chances are you may already own rods you can use for testing these new waters. And ironically, those manufacturers we characterized as marketing too-soft-for-bass-and-walleye noodle rods may have, in fact, unwittingly carved a niche in the superline rod market by offering products with more flex and less oomph—technically speaking.

Quick rod tips—One-piece rods typically increase sensitivity. Two-piece rods are easier to transport, but they sacrifice a bit of feel in their ferrule-to-ferrule connection. Cork or foam handles are comfortable in cold weather, and cold metal isn't.

Long, straight casting rod handles are great for two-handed casting, fit in rod holders, and reduce arm fatigue while you're trolling. Pistol grips have limited use and popularity. Spinning handles should be long enough to fit in a rod holder.

Single-foot ceramic oxide guides, typically found on high-end rods, usually cost a bit more but reduce line wear by providing a smoother surface. Frayed or broken lines indicate guide trouble somewhere, however, even with ceramic oxides. Visually check guides for chips or cracks. Swish a cottonball through suspect guides and replace any that snag threads of cotton. Carry ferrule cement, Fishin' Glue, or an equivalent for quick repairs on the water.

Selection—It's impossible to list every rod and reel combo from every manufacturer that can be used for walleye fishing. Livebait rigging rods are considerably different from longer, stouter planer board trolling rods. Light jigging rods may double as good livebait rigging rods, but they probably won't work for trolling three-way rigs or bottom bouncers. So a few different combos are needed to cover various presentations—different tools for different jobs. The number and type of rods you need depends on how you fish most of the time. The rest of the time, make do.

How to choose? Look at catalogs. Read magazines and ads. Ask your buddies for references. Try their rods for a day. Hands-on experience has no substitute. Solicit the advice of experienced anglers, tempering their suggestions with the promotional dollars they may receive. Visit a tackle shop or attend sport shows and pick up rods to get a feel for their characteristics. How does it feel in your hand, balanced with a reel, with a lure on the end? Flex it. Powerful enough? Too stiff? Too wimpy? Bounce a lure on the floor with it. Sensitive or senseless? What blend of characteristics do you get for the price?

Expect to pay at least $50 for a good walleye rod, perhaps as much as $100.

Expect to pay at least $50 for a good walleye rod, perhaps as much as $100. But do you really need to spend $200? Probably not, unless you feel it's worth the extra investment.

Selecting a rod and reel combo is not a relationship to be entered into lightly, because you're hoping for a long-term commitment, not a tumultuous weekend fling that ends in a shattered romance. Examine the big picture. Choose carefully and wisely. You may enter a few mismatched partnerships along the way, but once you settle on a winning combo, you'll have the satisfaction of knowing it'll be there for you, deep water or shallow, offering all the sensitivity you deserve.

BALANCED TACKLE FOR BEST PERFORMANCE

Compare rod catalogs from ten years ago with the one that just came in the mail, and the most striking difference is probably specialization. A decade ago, every catalog listed a 6-foot medium-action rod. Today they list 6-foot Lindy-Rig rods or 6-foot jig rods.

The number of specialized walleye rods on the market has soared, making it possible to buy a rod specifically manufactured for each walleye angling presentation. This may seem as if it would simplify things for the buyer, but not necessarily so. One manufacturer's rigging rod may feel and fish exactly like another's jigging rod. And some manufacturers make rods or reels designed for bass that work perfectly for walleyes. So catalog purchases can be confusing without a solid tip or some experience with the manufacturer's product to back them up.

How Stiff Is Stiff Enough, Without Getting Stiffed on Price?

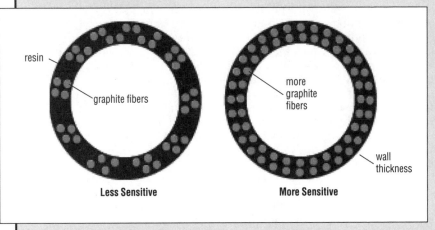

resin

graphite fibers

more graphite fibers

wall thickness

Less Sensitive   **More Sensitive**

Modulus is an engineering term defining a material's stiffness or resistance to bending. The higher the modulus, theoretically, the thinner, lighter, and more sensitive the rod blank. Different kinds of graphite offer differing moduli. But there are practical limits—a rod has to bend. If the combination of properties isn't correct, an expensive high-modulus graphite rod could shatter.

Less expensive composite rods are formed from mixtures of graphite, fiberglass, and resin. Durability and toughness increase and so does weight. Sensitivity generally decreases, due to the nonhomogeneous blend of materials transmitting signals to your hand.

In between lie a host of graphite materials like IMX, IM6, IM7, HMG from which most top rods are constructed. Average modulus is somewhere in the 40-million range. Material and construction techniques provide excellent blends of all properties, forming graphite rods that are dependable, sensitive, strong, and fun to fish with.

All rod blanks are formed by weaving materials around a tapered shaft called a mandril, using different shaped mandrils to create different tapers. Rods formed from seemingly similar graphite materials aren't necessarily equal, however. Construction processes—design and quality control—vary among manufacturers. Amount and orientation of graphite fibers also vary. Various resins hold together varying graphite fibers. Wall thicknesses vary along the length of the blank. To the layman, it's Advil time.

There's no surer way to differentiate quality between manufacturers, and between series of rods from the same manufacturer, than to pick up the rods and try them. Most anglers eventually determine a preferred manufacturer and models based on rod performance, budget, service, and availability.

But it's getting harder to go wrong.

Let's discuss spinning gear in simple terms; later, we'll get more specific.

In principle, 6-foot spinning rods double as tools for vertical jigging and for rigging. Six-and-a-half-foot models work overtime as crankbait rods, trolling rods, and rigging rods, while 7-footers can also be used to present bait below floats, to rig, and to drift bait.

The shortest rods—5 feet 9 inches—are precision short-range instruments for over-the-bow vertical jigging and pitching light jigs out to about 50 feet from the boat. Their taper and action should match the 6-foot rods in this category.

Like the 5-foot 9-inch rod, the 6-foot jigging rod is designed for short casts and vertical to near-vertical jigging. It must balance well with 1/16-, 1/8-, and 1/4-ounce jigs. The optimum jigging range is from below the boat to about 70 feet out. The taper should be fast to extra fast. When a walleye picks up your jig, 1/4 of the rod—the tip—gives to the fish, then locks at a point where the rest of the rod refuses to budge, allowing you to set with a simple wrist or forearm movement. It must balance well with limp, small-diameter 6-pound line.

A 6½-footer designed for midrange casting works baits at distances out to 100 feet. About 1/4 to 1/3 of this rod flexes, slightly softening the launch for longer casts with tipped jigs. Then it stiffens abruptly. The backbone gives lift for manipulating a jig at increased distances, and the tip is better for loading against the pull of a crankbait. Mid- to high-modulus graphite is both light and stiff, accentuating sensitivity. The action and length are also perfect for casting blades and spoons, and they're close to ideal for crankbaits. This rod needs a slightly longer handle for two-fisting baits on the cast.

Long casts with heavy baits are best achieved with longer rods. Power casting with 1/4- to 3/8-ounce (sometimes 1/2-ounce) jigs, crankbaits, and blades is best accomplished with a 7-foot rod. The taper is much the same as on the 6½-foot model, but the rod is slightly heavier. This rod works with slipfloats and will handle small bouncers. But mainly it's a power casting tool.

Don't know about you, but it sounds like that most-appropriate-tool thing again. Subtle differences in shape and construction make a difference in performance. What about price? Is there a difference? Are expensive rods worth the investment?

QUALITY

When it comes to quality, rod makers describe what they believe is the critical difference between an adequate jigging rod and an excellent jigging rod. The term that pops up most often isn't *sensitivity*, or *modulus*, or even *weight*. It's *recovery time*.

"Recovery time," explains Dale Barnes of Fenwick, "is the amount of time it takes the rod to stop vibrating—to stop wiggling after a cast or jigging motion. A better rod returns to its original configuration quicker. The more time you spend in contact with the lure, the better the rod feels, and the more successful you'll be."

Bruce Holt of G. Loomis emphasizes that weight and recovery time are related. *Primary factors,* he calls them. "The less weight in conjunction with fine design, the better the recovery. Better graphite fibers create a lighter rod that recovers faster. The less interference the better between fisherman and jig and ultimately a fish eating the jig."

> "Recovery time is the amount of time it takes the rod to stop vibrating—to stop wiggling after a cast or jigging motion."

But how to compare recovery time? Try holding two rods of equal length side by side, tips against the floor. Flex them, then let them snap back unrestricted. The one with the faster recovery time stops vibrating first. Compare power and action. You'll feel the heavier resistance from a more powerful rod.

Why does it cost more to manufacture a fine-quality rod? Components, for one thing. Cheap rods cut corners with pot-metal guides, rickety reel seats, and gonzo graphite composited with fiberglass scrim.

Wayne Nelsen, rod buyer and designer for Cabela's, says the expense goes beyond components. "The mandrels used to wrap graphite patterns, the resins that hold the patterns, the heating tables and other tools used to make state-of-the-art rods cost more than run-of-the-mill equipment."

Evidence of growth in rod building's high-end niche was the ensuing modulus war beginning about 1990. Suddenly rod makers were leapfrogging each other to the latest high-modulus mark. The higher the modulus, the stiffer the graphite fiber and the thinner the rod blank. The current modulus mark to beat is about 80 million.

"I'm not convinced that high modulus is the answer," Nelsen says. "It gets stiff, brittle, hard to work with. It's lighter, but you have to strike a balance."

G. Loomis started the modulus muddle with IM6 (38 million modulus). "We don't even use the term *modulus* anymore," Holt continues. "It only confuses people. The race for high modulus is superficial. It doesn't mean you're getting a better rod because one modulus rates higher than the next. Above a certain point, high graphite content becomes counterproductive."

The patented Loomis IMX fiber is around 49 million modulus, which is apparently where Loomis strikes its balance (for now, anyway). As we've said, the higher the modulus, the thinner and lighter a blank can be. But as Nelsen warns, there's a fine line between "light and sensitive" and "thin and brittle."

WALLEYE RODS BY DESIGN

Open the rod lockers on a walleye boat, and you're likely to see a pile of fishing rods: trolling rods with line counter reels, various sizes of spinning rods, and a handful of baitcasters. The reason? A good angler must be versatile to catch walleyes consistently. The right rod makes each technique easier and more efficient.

Earlier we briefly discussed the principal differences in popular spinning rods. Here are some tips for selecting a balanced complement of rods to handle all conditions. We'll discuss design characteristics rather than model numbers, because manufacturers seem to change models and designations faster than cold fronts roar across the waters.

Jigging—Jigging is vertical jigging; pitching jigs to shallow rocks, weeds, or wood; tossing jigs middle distances on shallow to middepth flats; vertical jigging in current; pitching and drifting jigs in current; snapjigging; and power casting jigs and plastics long distances. Three spinning rods can handle it all, though adding several specialty rods through the years improves the arsenal.

A 6-foot rod rated for 4- to 8-pound test handles light pitching in shallow water with 1/16- to 1/8-ounce jigs. A medium-power rod with a fast tip is optimum. It handles most vertical jigging duties well, though many expert anglers prefer a 5-foot 9-inch stick for that duty.

A 6½-foot rod rated for 6- to 10-pound line with a fast action and a medium-power rating handles middle-distance casting and some deep vertical jigging, though a 5½- to 6-foot rod with a fast action and medium-heavy power is a better choice for jigging vertically with heavy jigs or in heavy current. This slightly heavier rod makes a better ripjigging tool and works well with jigging spoons in current.

Finally, a 7-foot graphite with a fast action and medium- to medium-heavy power rating is required for power casting 1/4- to 3/8-ounce hair jigs or jig-and-plastic combos from shore or along deep weedlines. Power is needed to lift moderately heavy jigs aggressively for long sweeping hops. This rod's rating should include lines in the 8- to 12-pound-test range.

The main distinction between a jigging rod and other walleye spinning rods is the speed of the tip. Jigging tools require faster tips for better feel and better jig control.

About Rod Materials

Questions about the materials used to construct rods remain foremost in the minds of anglers trying to make a buying decision. Should the rod in question be of fiberglass, graphite, or composite fiberglass and graphite design? No simple answer exists, but In-Fisherman editors offer hints to help you make up your mind.

Graphite is lighter than fiberglass, although fiberglass tends to be more durable. The lightness of graphite also is a factor in increasing sensitivity, although the quality of the rod construction process is just as significant in producing a sensitive rod. Still, a finely constructed graphite rod will be more sensitive than a finely constructed fiberglass rod. And a finely constructed fiberglass rod likely is more durable than a finely constructed graphite rod.

We suggest that you study the entire product line from a firmly established company in order to get an idea about the basic difference in rod material (and overall construction) versus price. One need only pick up a St. Croix catalog, for example, to see that their finest rod series, the Avid series, is made of their best grade of graphite, which they call SCIII. Most Avid rods retail in the $150 range. The Premier series, meanwhile, is constructed from SCII graphite. Most Premier rods retail for around $80. Finally, St. Croix offers a limited series of Pro-Glass rods (SCI fiberglass) retailing for around $75.

Some anglers prefer fiberglass (or composite material) for reasons beyond durability. Fiberglass is slower reacting than graphite, more forgiving so fish don't easily detect the lure-to-line-to-rod connection

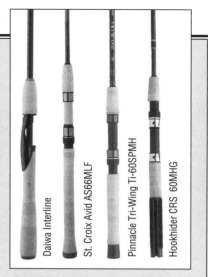

Daiwa Interline — St. Croix Avid AS66MLF — Pinnacle Tri-Wing Ti-60SPMH — Hookhider CRS 60MHG

when they inhale a bait like a spinner and bottom bouncer. Few anglers, though, would choose to fish jigs with anything less than graphite, except as a factor of price.

The question of price versus ultimate sensitivity becomes more difficult when one grade of graphite is pitted against a slightly lesser grade. Even a novice angler can feel the weight difference between the St. Croix Avid series and the St. Croix Premier series. It becomes highly subjective, though, even for moderately experienced anglers, to determine a difference in performance, one rod material versus another, when not compared in an actual fishing situation. Such a difference usually is noticed only by highly experienced anglers.

Beyond rod material, the first criterion in choosing a fishing rod is what the rod will be used for. A few rod designs approach being all-purpose, but for most anglers, as their skill level increases, so does their preference for specific designs that perform best in certain situations. In-Fisherman editors routinely recommend specific designs within articles about certain types of fishing.

Livebait rigging—The most basic needs in a rigging rod are met by the same 6½-foot spinning rod used for intermediate jigging. Options or specialty purchases include going with a little lighter power in a rod rated for 4-pound test to finesse walleyes with long, light leaders, or going slightly longer for better control and better sweepsets. Having a fast tip isn't always a plus. A more moderate action allows you to feel the fish without it feeling you.

The longer the stick, the more balance between properties. A 7½-foot rod has plenty of room for a long, limber tip section so you can feed line to fish with the rod partially loaded and keep track of the fish without alerting it. It also permits more powerful hooksetting because its butt section is longer than on shorter rods. This tool also doubles nicely as a slipfloat rod. The main drawback is that the long rod may become tip heavy when you hold it level while backtrolling for hours on end. If so, add a counterbalance to the handle end, or opt for a shorter version (around 6½ feet). Experience is the best teacher.

Three-way rigging and bottom bouncing—Baitcasting tackle is prime for bottom bouncing and three-way rigging. Casting reels allow quicker depth adjustments. Just hit the thumb bar to follow sharp drops. One-handed operation frees the other hand to work the tiller or a sandwich. Weights for these two systems are comparable, generally 1/2 to 3 ounces. The main difference? A three-way rod often presents lures, so the tip can be faster. Bottom bouncers usually present bait, so a slightly softer tip may be a plus.

Baitcasting tackle is prime for bottom bouncing and three-way rigging.

Casting rods stand up well to heavier bouncers. Choose a 6½-foot rod with medium tip action (a fast tip with heavy weight can snap leaders on big fish) and a medium-heavy power rating to set hooks and fight fish through the weight of the bouncer. That one's for holding. For rod holder duty, select a 7- to 7½-foot rod with a slightly softer action that yields to the fish and won't alert them before the rod can be reached. This rod should be rated to handle 10- to 17-pound-test line, with 12-pound the optimum choice in most situations. These rods are also good for casting crankbaits into timber.

Reels should be on the small side. A low-profile casting reel, with a flippin' switch or special thumb bar that allows the reel to engage when pressure is released so depth adjustments can be made with one hand, is optimum. Some casting reels actually reel backwards (direct drive), a concession to walleye fishermen who still like to backreel a big fish.

Crankbaits—A crankbait rod needs a limber tip to achieve casting distance while minimizing stress on knots. A limber tip should load to about 40 percent of maximum from the resistance provided by the lip of the lure working through the water. This means the backbone of the rod should be instantly brought to bear on a hookset. Could be casting or spinning tackle. Your call.

That 6½-foot intermediate jigging rod makes a fair crankbait rod, but the optimum length is 7 to 7½ feet. Longer rods with the right action cast slightly farther, allowing more room for that perfect balance of properties. A longer rod can be dipped into the water for that extra foot or so of depth on the retrieve. It's possible to hold a longer rod in more positions and remain ready to make a good hookset because of the longer sweep it affords. Minnowbaits and other shallow divers that work better on 6-pound test can, at times, be thrown on the same rod, but discriminating anglers may want a tool with a faster tip for quicker hooksets.

Most walleye cranking calls for 6- to 12-pound test, the heavier lines being required around rocks and wood. Since light line performs best on spinning reels, most walleye cranking is done with spinning gear. Situations calling for 10-pound or heavier line can be handled with casting rods of the same length and action with a medium-heavy power. (The same sticks also assume bottom-bouncer duty.) These rods also handle trolling chores other than aids like boards, divers, or downriggers. For longlining Shad Raps or minnowbaits, the same 7- to 7½-foot spinning rod is optimum. For speed trolling or pulling wide wobblers like Hot'N Tots, opt for the casting gear mentioned above. Spinning reels should have a quick-retrieve ratio and a large line capacity. Bigger spools allow more and easier casting distance with 8- to 10-pound line.

For trolling with in-line planer boards, a 7-foot 6-inch trigger-grip casting rod rated for 8- to 20-pound test is optimum. A range of line strengths suggests a relatively limber tip, but this rod will need backbone to stand up to the pull of a board. Reels need more line capacity for trolling with boards because of the distances involved in getting the board out with the lure far back or way down to the proper depth.

Slipbobbers—Slipbobber rods should protect light line with shock absorption and make long casts in tough conditions. One good example is the 7-foot crankbait rod already discussed. Slipbobber rods should be longer than 6 feet. To control line and drift in breezy conditions, longer is better. Length, coupled with a fast tip, helps set the hook through the weight of the rigging and the 90-degree angle of the dangle.

At times, 4-pound test and light 1/32-ounce jigs are needed to fool finicky walleyes. Slipfloats can present small jigs at a distance. And the way to throw, control, and fish with floats and light line is with a medium-fast spinning blank rated for 4- to 10-pound line.

Planer-diver trolling rods—Trolling with level wind line counter reels has become popular with walleye fishermen on big waters, as evidenced by the number of line counter reels appearing over the past few years. Counting passes of the line-gathering bar or using digital line counters offers precise distance and depth control, especially with planer-divers like Dipsy Divers because knowing how far out they are translates into knowing how deep they run. Planer-diver trolling rods and line counter reels work well with leadcore and wire line. Clicker systems on reels allow an even payout of line when letting out boards or Dipsy Divers, and they also alert you quickly to a big fish or a snag.

Planer board rods typically run from 7½ to 8½ feet in length, with telescoping handles that easily fit into rod lockers. Long rods help hold lines off the water, increase the spread of planer boards, and absorb the shock of trolling in waves. Most walleye anglers troll with 10-pound-test mono when using boards.

A Dipsy Diver produces an exceptional amount of pull, requiring a medium-heavy action casting rod 8 to 9 feet long. The added length and limber tip absorbs shock. These rods should be rated for

17- to 25-pound test. A stout butt retains control of equipment and a hooked fish. EVA handles are best because foam is more durable than cork when rods get ripped out of holders a lot.

Downrigger—Line from a downrigger rod shoots down at a sharp angle toward the cannonball, then out at almost a 90-degree angle to the lure. After a release, the rod has to pull up a lot of slack to establish a straight line to the fish. This requires length and strength coupled with high flexibility. To maintain tension through this maneuver, the rod must be fully loaded into a big bend right from the start.

No need for sensitivity here. Primary considerations are durability and proper action. Choose rods in the 8- to 9-foot range in standard graphite, fiberglass, or composite materials. Action is activity specific, which in this case means the top half of the rod must bend evenly (parabolic), while the butt needs backbone for picking up line and moving big fish at trolling speeds. No other rod bends quite like a good downrigger rod for walleyes. Line counting level winds are the reels of choice.

In most walleye areas other than the Great Lakes, downriggers are considered to be of limited use, though they often have untapped potential as part of a legitimate deep water system.

Superline duty—For all-around duty, a superline combo is a logical addition for increasing sensitivity and hooksetting power in heavy wind or in other conditions where those abilities may be compromised. Walleye anglers like superlines, such as SpiderWire Fusion or Berkley FireLine, for longline trolling with crankbaits, casting jigs, rigging, and for casting crankbaits if—and only if—a 3- to 5-foot segment of monofilament leader is tied directly to the end of the fused line with back-to-back uni-knots. The less visible mono tends to increase the number of bites with jigs or bait, especially in clear water, because superlines are opaque and easier for walleyes to see. Superlines don't stretch, and the mono also acts as a shock leader for hammering bigger fish without having the hooks rip free on a short line near the boat.

Superline takes crankbaits deeper, improves feel in some circumstances, and improves hooksetting power.

Superline takes crankbaits deeper, improves feel in some circumstances, and improves hooksetting power. Superline rods need slightly softer tips with a shade more parabolic action to perform the same function as other rods in each category. (Even with the perfect rod, hooksets should be reduced to something slightly stronger than a wrist snap.) And reels designed for superlines should have a better record against line cinch, binding, loops, and other problems sometimes associated with polyethylene braids.

Noodles—Spinning rods exceeding 9 or 10 feet in length, nicknamed noodles, enjoyed a flurry of popularity with the Great Lakes trout and salmon crowd as a challenging means for catching large powerful fish on light line. Walleye anglers sometimes use noodle rods for their combination of light line finesse and coverage, though they're generally considered limited use items.

Noodle rods chiefly are placed in rod holders and used to drift or backtroll livebait. Waves causing a subtle lift-rise of the soft rod tip impart a lively action to the crawler without overdoing the motion. And light 4-pound-test line won't spook fish in a crowd. Even the most tentative biter tends to inhale and hold the bait rather than dropping it because the soft rod bends so easily that no unnatural resistance spooks 'em.

Noodling

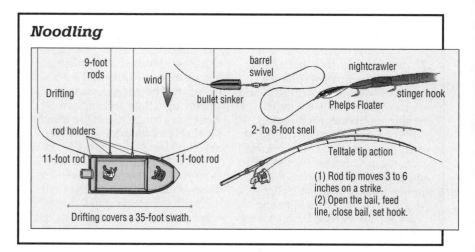

Drifting — 9-foot rods, wind, barrel swivel, bullet sinker, nightcrawler, Phelps Floater, stinger hook, 2- to 8-foot snell

rod holders — 11-foot rod — 11-foot rod

Drifting covers a 35-foot swath.

Telltale tip action
(1) Rod tip moves 3 to 6 inches on a strike.
(2) Open the bail, feed line, close bail, set hook.

Watch for the rod tip to move about 3 to 6 inches on the initial bite, stop, and then begin to bend again. A snag, by comparison, bends the rod without interruption. When fish are aggressive and run with the bait, set the hook immediately. When fish are fussy, open the bail and feed a little line to give them time to swallow the bait. It's a judgment call based on what's happening on any particular day.

The extended time it takes for the long rod to bend gives you time to react and grab the rod out of the holder before the fish feels pressure, spooks, and drops the bait. Then either set the hook or feed line, depending on walleye activity that particular day.

Because these light-action rods are so limber, it's necessary to set the hook hard, instead of expecting walleyes to hook themselves. And you can't horse 'em. Be patient, and slowly pump the fish to the boat. Enjoy the fight, confident in knowing that the soft rod will absorb shock and prevent breaking even the lightest line. As a walleye approaches the boat, don't reel your sinker up to the rod tip; stop reeling when it's 3 or 4 feet below the tip. Then bring the rod tip as high over your head as possible to compensate for the exaggerated bend in the rod, allowing you to net the fish.

REEL EXCITEMENT, REEL CONFUSION

Reels have undergone changes that make choices more difficult, but as technology strives to finally beat line twist, oscillation, and other minor irritations, products have improved. Infinite antireverse, previously a feature found only on the most expensive spinning reels, is common on reels priced in the midrange. Drags on low-profile casting reels have never been better. And more reels from more companies are available than ever before, including several baitcasters designed with walleyes in mind.

Matching reel performance with today's fine rods ensures a sweeter feel and better performance than anything available in the past. Most reel companies offer many lines of reels with features and prices geared to trigger mass merchandising sales. Quality differences can't be detected with a simple glance but require close examination.

Pick up a reel and spin it. How smooth does it feel? How long does a spinning

Evaluating Spinning Reels for Walleyes: Shop & Compare

Line capacity: Most manufacturers offer a series of spinning reels with various capacities. Walleye models generally fall into the medium-light category, holding 100 yards of 8-pound line, perhaps 130 yards of 6-pound test. They're adequate for most finesse walleye situations like livebait rigging, jigging, slipbobbering, even casting lightweight crankbaits with light line.

Smooth operation: Smooth is relative. You want a reel that doesn't vibrate or click on retrieve and that allows you to feel the motion of your lure and detect light bites or strikes. Inexpensive reels don't feel like premium models. Intermediate

to high-end reels starting at around $50 are more sensitive and are built to last. Ball bearings increase smooth operation and minimize vibration, though more than about 5 bearings probably doesn't noticeably improve performance.

Drag: Multi-disc drags outperform single-disc and especially felt drags; multi-discs shed water and maintain even tension in rain or when dunked overboard. Rear versus front drag is a matter of personal preference. A rear drag is adjustable under tension when a big fish moves away, and its spool can be changed without having to readjust the drag. A front drag probably

Spool Dynamics

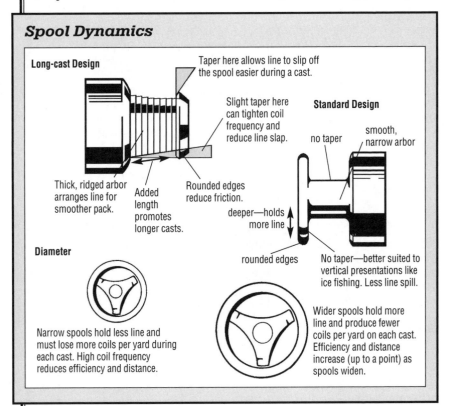

Long-cast Design

Taper here allows line to slip off the spool easier during a cast.

Slight taper here can tighten coil frequency and reduce line slap.

Thick, ridged arbor arranges line for smoother pack.

Added length promotes longer casts.

Rounded edges reduce friction.

Standard Design

no taper

smooth, narrow arbor

deeper—holds more line

rounded edges

No taper—better suited to vertical presentations like ice fishing. Less line spill.

Diameter

Narrow spools hold less line and must lose more coils per yard during each cast. High coil frequency reduces efficiency and distance.

Wider spools hold more line and produce fewer coils per yard on each cast. Efficiency and distance increase (up to a point) as spools widen.

offers more precise tension adjustment because it uses more washers.

Antireverse: Infinite antireverse prevents the bail from spinning backward when you let go of the handle—a common cause of loops and tangles when rigging or jigging. It won't slip when setting the hook with the reel locked, either.

Retrieve ratio: Most spinning reels offer ratios in the range from 1:4.4 to 1:5.4. Lower gear ratios are for power cranking with larger crankbaits. Higher ratios accompany reels with smaller spools in order to maintain line pickup speed.

Twist reduction: Twist reduction bail designs help alleviate (though not eliminate) line twist. Roller guides and spool lips coated with titanium or other durable substances reduce line friction and wear.

Long cast: Long-cast spool designs lengthen the spool, increasing line capacity and making long-distance casting easier. More line flies off the spool with each layer, so fewer layers are needed to achieve equal distance. This minimizes digging down into the spool on each cast and pulling off underlying layers of ever more tightly coiled, stiffer line, which diminishes casting ability. Shorter spools would have to be wide and bulky to achieve similar casting characteristics. Short spools are fine for vertical jigging, rigging, and ice fishing.

Overall perspective: Manufacturers offer different model lines with inexpensive to premium components designed to compete pricewise with other manufacturers targeting the same segment of the market. Thus the bewildering concept of three or four different model lines, each with the same size reels, from each manufacturer.

Pick up different models, open and close the bails, feel the retrieve, shop price, note features. Several ball bearings, ball-bearing roller guides, multi-disc drags, infinite antireverse, twist reduction, and other performance features are worthwhile investments. Graphite spools and frames offer reductions in weight. Right-left handles adjust to your personal style. Nebulous features like casting triggers and handle shapes are matters of personal choice. Fancy paint jobs should be more than just eye-catching because superior coatings and premium components can stand up to years of abuse in the elements.

Pinnacle PKF25

Anti-Twist Mechanisms

Instant Antireverse

Retrieve Ratio

Drag

Line Capacity

Handles

reel spin when you let go of the handle? How smooth is the drag? In general, you get what you pay for, though many midpriced reels are well suited to the recreational walleye angler. For many walleye presentations, the reel is basically a storage device that doesn't need to be fancy. With others, fine features are at a premium.

You may choose to go for extra ball bearings and high-tech features and spending big bucks. Otherwise, shop wisely, but don't cut corners. Also, don't get caught up in "more is obviously better." Use the following guidelines to select reels that meet your needs and enhance your fishing pleasure and success.

SPINNING

Light line (6- to 8-pound test) walleye presentations often work best with medium-light spinning reels. Reel packages may not say that, so instead look for a line capacity of about 200 to 240 yards of 6-pound mono and a reel that weighs between 7.5 and 9 ounces. That should indicate which reel in a manufacturer's line fits the bill. For lighter line like 4-pound test, consider a reel one size smaller, often called a *light* or even *ultralight*. For heavier casting applications with 10- to 12-pound line, the next larger-sized reel, often called a medium,

---

Evaluating Baitcasting Reels : Shop & Compare

*R*etrieve Ratio: Fast retrieve ratios (6:1 or higher) retrieve baits rapidly after fishing them almost vertically. Burning rattle-baits or shallow-running cranks call for fast reels, though walleye anglers seldom fish in this manner. Medium ratios (about 4.8: to 5.8:1) match most situations.

Line capacity: Small-capacity reels (holding, say, 100 yards of 12-pound test) cast well with 10- or 12-pound line at relatively close ranges and hold sufficient line for bottom bouncing, three-way rigs, or vertical jigging with bladebaits or jigging spoons. Seldom are larger reels needed for walleyes.

Magnetic brake: Many of today's premium reels offer this feature that allows fine-tuning casting control. Many reels, though, cast well without magnetic brakes.

Ball bearings: Bearings add smoothness to a reel's moving parts. More than about 5 bearings, however, probably doesn't noticeably improve performance.

Instant antireverse: This desirable feature promotes improved sensitivity and solid hooksets, and all top-line baitcasters offer it.

Thumb bar: Allows releasing the spool with your casting hand just prior to casting, instead of reaching with the opposite hand. Handy, but not absolutely necessary.

Flippin' switch: One of the best casting reel applications for walleyes is using small flippin' reels for bottom bouncing, three-way rigging, and vertical fishing with jigging spoons and bladebaits. The flippin' feature allows a heavy rig to drop to bottom simply by depressing the button. Once the lure or sinker makes contact, lift your thumb, and the reel's engaged. No changing hands, no turning the handle to engage the reel. This enhances control when holding a rod in each hand, or keeping one hand on the electric or outboard while trolling.

Drag: The best drags are multi-disc as opposed to single-disc. Some drags click as they're

---

may handle heavier line and achieve greater casting distance. In a pinch, however, one intermediate model should cover all bases.

In general, if you use gelspun thin-diameter superlines, downsize one model. Use plenty of monofilament backing to fill the spool, no matter what size spinning reel you use. Connect the two lines with a double nail knot. Superlines often come in short spool lengths of about 100 to 150 yards, so backing is needed to maintain outer spool diameter for peak performance.

Thin-diameter superlines may require changes in future reel categories, such as line-capacity designations for mono versus superline. Spinning reels usually considered ultralight may perform as well as or better than traditional sizes that require mono backing beneath a 100-yard outer layer of skinny superline. Superlines cast beautifully on spinning reels, have little memory, and their performance isn't affected by small spool diameter.

Long-cast or similarly named spools are longer and thinner than traditional wider spools. They excel with light line used in most finesse walleye presentations. Heavier monofilament line coils tightly around the narrow diameter, however, increasing line twist.

adjusted, providing a measure of how much the drag moves. Most new baitcasters have star drags.

Handles: Larger handles make grasping easier and also increase cranking power and reduce winding speed.

Weight: Few baitcasters weigh over 12 ounces. Bearings, metal frames, and large spools add weight.

One-piece frame: One-piece metal frames create a solid reel. Typically offered on round-style reels, some new low-profile baitcasters also offer this composition.

Trolling reels and line counters: Trolling reels excel for longline trolling applications. While not designed for casting, they store line and enable letting out precise lengths for controlling lure depth. Count the passes of line across the spool of the reel to estimate line length, or select a line counter reel

that precisely indicates line length.

Small saltwater or standard freshwater reels minimize weight while providing adequate line storage—perhaps 250 yards of 10- to 12-pound line. That's more capacity than you need for mono or superline, but sufficient for bulkier leadcore.

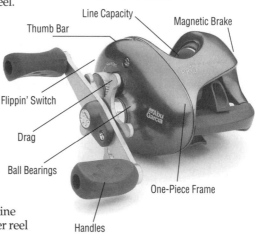

Abu Garcia TP3000C

Line Capacity

Magnetic Brake

Thumb Bar

Flippin' Switch

Drag

Ball Bearings

One-Piece Frame

Handles

Many spinning reels come with extra spools that pop on or screw on. Extra spools are handy for backup line or for line weight change. Some casting reels feature replaceable line spools for quick changes, but most don't.

Most spinning reels today sport roller guides on the bail where line bends 90 degrees before spooling. The guide spins, reducing line twist and wear.

Gear mechanism is one feature where differences can be detected. Inexpensive reels have cheap gears that grind and vibrate, reducing sensitivity. And their durability is questionable. Premium reels, however, have smooth brass, bronze, or other premium pinion and gear mechanisms for long life and peak performance. Read the label and compare.

Gear ratio determines performance. High-speed retrieve ratios of about 5 to 1 or 6 to 1 pick up more line per turn of the reel handle—5 or 6 circumferences of the spool. Lower gear ratios may be only 4 to 1, retrieving less line per crank. Use low-speed reels for slow, subtle retrieves when you don't want to overwork a lure—for example, a slow swimming crankbait. Use high-speed reels for fast retrieves like spinners. In general, walleye anglers opt for a fairly high retrieve, disciplining themselves to turn the handle slower when conditions call for slow lure motion. In general, high gear ratio is more important with casting or trolling reels to move a lure fast or to retrieve long lengths of line quickly.

How many ball bearings are enough? More bearings, more money, perhaps smoother operation. Pick up the reel and spin it. Is it smoother than the manufacturer's other three reels in the same product line, which appear identical except for paint job, model name, number of bearings, and price tag? You make the call.

Choice of drag depends on angler preference. Rear drags feature more washers for a theoretically more adjustable drag system. Consequently, they're a bit more expensive and bulkier because of the extra knob. Drag can be reset while a fish is running, and reels generally feature easy-to-pop-off, push-button spools.

Front drags twist-tighten to attach the spool and set the drag. Drag must be reset each time you change spools, and the drag can't be reset while a fish is running. Proponents say front drags use larger washers with a direct twist-set connection for smoother operation. Front drags dominated the last decade, though rear drags are making a comeback.

Many spinning reels feature right-left retrieve, equally suited for right or left-handed operation or for two-fisted jigging—a reel handle on opposite sides of each rod. Handles fold or screw in and out for transport.

Infinite antireverse doesn't mean you can't backreel, but that the bail won't spin backwards and tangle line when you remove your hand from the reel. This is handy when backtrolling, because even a quarter turn backwards as the bail centers itself creates a loop of line that can catch on the bail mechanism. With detachable antireverse, you can turn it off and backreel. This feature is also available on some casting reels.

CASTING-TROLLING

Generally, smaller low-profile baitcasting reels are most suited for bottom-bouncer, three-way, jigging spoon, or heavy crankbait walleye applications. Ten-pound-test line doesn't require much line capacity, and besides, such reels are lighter and less tiring to hold. Typical reels hold about 125 yards of 12-pound-test mono and weigh 8 to 9½ ounces. Round reels with more line capacity are tailored to trolling presentations, while line capacity and more weight aren't needed for handheld applications. Trolling reels generally are offshoots of salmon or salt-water markets with large line capacity for longline trolling. Seven or eight manufacturers offer smaller models suitable for walleyes that feature line counters for precision control.

Palm-sized reels with a flippin' feature facilitate handheld trolling applications like bottom bouncing. Punch the button, lower the bottom bouncer or three-way, and once it's on bottom, simply lift your thumb. The reel re-engages without having to turn the reel handle with your other hand. It's nice to be able to keep one hand on the motor and one on the rod without interruption.

Some reels have traditional disengage switches on one side of the reel. Others have a thumb bar in the center that disengages easily for casting or releasing line. Flippin' reels have thumb bars.

A select few casting reels have a direct drive option: you can backreel a big fish on light line. Most lack this feature, and it isn't advertised because reel manufacturers build casting reels for bass and don't understand how valuable direct drive is for walleyes. Find a direct drive thumb bar with a flippin' switch, and you have a walleye gem. And these aren't usually the most expensive reels in a product line, either.

Modern low-profile casting reels have an adjustable magnetic brake system to slow the spool at the end of a cast, decreasing spool overrun and backlash. Some have detachable line guides that disengage for casting to reduce friction and increase distance. A few feature detachable spools for quick line replacement. Some come with left hand retrieves.

QUICK TIPS

When spooling line, avoid line twist as much as possible by winding on line under tension, especially superline. On casting reels, wind spool-to-spool in a direct path, with one spool turning in the direction opposite to the other, line following the same curvature onto the reel as it leaves the filler spool. Fill almost to the edge of the rotating spool.

On some spinning reels, twist is unavoidable because there's no perfect filling method. The best you can do is to point the reel toward the ground, hold the filler spool so the line follows the curvature off the filler spool onto the reel, then lay the filler spool on the ground, winding line onto the spool under tension. Fill spools to within 1/8-inch of the lip.

Chances are, no matter what you do, you'll get some line twist with mono. To remove line twist, drag 100 feet of line (no lure attached) behind the boat at moderate speed for several minutes, slowly winding it in under tension.

When spooling line, avoid line twist as much as possible by winding on line under tension, especially superline.

Setting drags on mono versus superline: drags are usually set by grabbing the monofilament line just above the reel, pulling, and adjusting until tension feels right. That's fine, but a more realistic feel of what will happen under pressure is to tie the line to a tree, back off, simulate setting the hook,

then set the drag. With superlines, be conservative. They offer no stretch. On casting reels, line can bury back into the spool if the drag doesn't slip, so set drags lighter than with mono. Also, back off drags when your reel's not in use for a time to prevent memory in the drag mechanism.

Check instructions for lubrication. Hit key points with either oil or grease, but avoid thick grease in cold weather. Graphite and molybdenum perform best in cold temperatures.

REEL CONFUSING?

You bet. Manufacturers offer many lines of similar-looking spinning reels with different features in a wide range of prices, attempting to provide reels for everyone from bargain-seeking occasional anglers to professionals. Do your homework. Examine features on different models and brands. More ball bearings mean more money. Pick up a reel and spin it. Is there a difference between a 3- and 5-bearing model? Less vibration improves feel. Do you prefer front or rear drag? How smooth are they? Long-cast spools? Extra spools? Line capacity and reel weight should be minimized for finesse spinning presentations. Consider flippin' features on small casting reels for handheld trolling applications. Consider line counters for planer board and crankbait trolling.

Shop for quality and features, not just price. An inexpensive reel may cost you fish in the long run. A premier reel requires money up-front but provides a long-term return on your investment. And that's a "reel" deal.

Chapter 3

Balanced Tackle

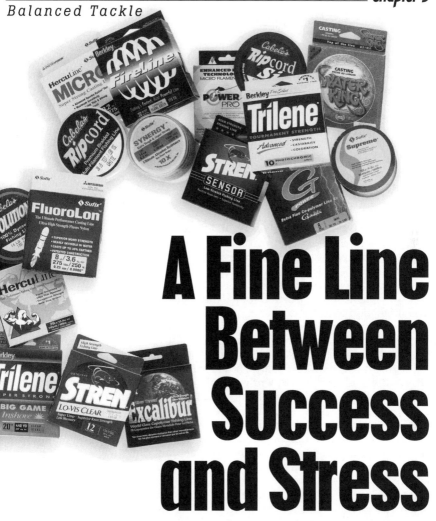

A Fine Line Between Success and Stress

MONOFILAMENT, SUPERLINES, KNOTS, AND MORE

E very skill requires tools. The artist has tiny brushes and brushes wider than the hand. The architect uses pencil leads of various thickness to trace lines along rulers, squares, shapes, and angles. The photographer carries a lens to match each purpose, a filter for every effect.

Line is a tool. Using the same line for every job is like an artist trying to do everything with one brush. Imagine painting details like buttons on a shirt with a brush bigger than your thumb, or laying on background colors with six horse hairs.

Imagine fighting trophy walleyes out of boulders in current with a soft line that nicks easily. Might get lucky once, even twice. But successful fishing, like other sports, is a matter of putting the percentages in your favor.

Techniques like line watching, practiced over time, become skills. Seeing the line jump or move on a strike is an advantage. The right tool for the job may be a high-vis line, but other considerations must always be factored in. In very clear, shallow water, high-vis may turn some walleyes away from a bait. Such judgments come with experience.

Good fishermen match high-vis characteristics to conditions. Dark, windy days may call for bright line. Berkley Trilene XT Solar, for instance, jumps out against almost any background. Bright, calm days invite applications of downscale colors like DuPont's aqua-fluorescent Magnathin.

All lines are not equal. In most instances, matching line characteristics to fishing conditions will make you more effective, make fishing more productive and pleasurable, and result in a better day on the water.

TRADITIONAL LINE BY DESIGN

Nylon lines are designed to do specific things or to cover a range of applications. About ten basic nylon polymers offer properties considered desirable in monofilament fishing lines. Most lines are made of one (homopolymers) or two (copolymers) of these nylons.

The nylons are melted, then extruded through a dye, and stretched. The nylons in combination with the extrusion process determine line characteristics. Maxima, for instance, uses the same polymer in four different lines. Each line is different, though, because each is extruded differently.

Line choice is determined by technique. Open water trolling, the fastest-growing segment of the walleye world, is an example. Trolling lures behind planer boards, diver-planers, and downrigger balls demands that hooks set themselves. Rods are in holders, and if everything isn't in sync, fish routinely escape. The system works best with low-stretch lines that can withstand shock.

Thin, high tensile-strength copolymers work well with certain systems, especially flatlining and trolling with small, in-line planer boards. But these lines are seldom abrasion resistant, nor are they very shock proof.

Thin lines cast well and also help you make the most of vertical presentations in current and wind. Smaller diameters mean less line is affected by moving air and water. Lighter jigs reach bottom quicker. Added tensile strength allows you to cut back on diameter while retaining the hooksetting power of thicker lines with the same pound test.

Abrasion-resistant lines withstand the stress and shock of trolling with things like Dipsy Divers and Fish Seekers. These lines stretch less than lines in most other categories. The primary function of these lines is to present baits and to haul heavy fish out of dense wood or rock cover. Abrasion-resistant lines include Ande Premium, Berkley Trilene XT, Stren Super Tough, and PRADCO Super Silver Thread.

Limp, castable lines have qualities you can't get in tough abrasion-resistant monofilaments. With these lines, you can at times throw a lure 5 to 10 percent farther—important when casting jigs or lures along weedlines or reefs. Most fishermen also use such lines to present livebait. But most anglers prefer nick-proof line for presenting spinner rigs; limp line grooves where the clevis revolves on the line. Limp lines include Ande Tournament, Berkley Trilene XL, Stren Easy Cast, and PRADCO Silver Thread AN-40.

Life and Times of Fishing Line

Braided linen, silk, and cotton lines.	
DuPont invents nylon.	1938
Dow Corning attempts "saran line."	
Nylon lines available, but research chiefly devoted to war effort.	World War II
DuPont begins manufacturing and supplying monofilament lines.	1946
Berkley introduces Trilene.	1958
DuPont introduces Stren.	
DuPont introduces fluorescent Stren.	1962
Chemical additives and colors introduced.	1968
Berkley switches to copolymers.	1980
Cofilaments introduced.	1990
Angler using Spectra kite string wins B.A.S.S. tournament.	1993
Spiderwire (braided polyethylene lines) introduced.	1994
Berkley introduces FireLine, the first fused superline.	1995
Flurocarbon lines introduced.	1999

Most companies offer an all-purpose line with some abrasion resistance and some supple characteristics as well. Might seem like the answer to all your problems. And for most fishermen, these lines perform well in all but the most extreme conditions. Technicians, though, do better with lines designed for specific purposes.

Sometimes you must sacrifice one line characteristic and make do. In very cold weather, low stretch, thin diameter, high tensile-strength lines become wiry. Abrasion-resistant lines develop coil memory. You need limp line, even for working cover. Remove the tail-end section of line often throughout a day of fishing. And respool frequently.

THE CHAIN CONCEPT

Everything in the chain, from the point of the hook to the butt of the rod, has to work together. A 6-pound line on a rod rated for 12- to 17-pound test is a weak link. You'll get by when walleyes are under 3 pounds. Hook an 8 or 10, and you're in trouble.

Match your line to the job, then match rods, reels, hooks, and lures to the line. If walleyes are active near bottom on the edge of a huge mudflat 30 feet down, you might troll the area, using spinner rigs on crawler harnesses behind 3-ounce bottom bouncers.

This isn't a finesse situation. Use 12- or 14-pound test on a casting reel. Seventeen's starting to get just too thick to easily keep the rig down. The leader can be 10- or 12-pound test. The main line also determines hook sturdiness. Hooks should be heavy-gauge steel to withstand 12-pound line.

Line's part of a system. What systems will you use this year? Eventually you'll want line spooled and marked and ready to handle those systems. If most of your fishing is with livebait rigs coupled with light sinkers or with jigs around clean bottom, a limp 6- or 8-pound rather than a stiff abrasion-resistant line may bring more fish to the bait.

If you're casting to shallow cover, line color is important. Fluorescent lines let you see more strikes. But if you're on spooky fish in clear water, maybe go low-vis in smoke gray or green. Will you be making lots of long-distance casts? A supple castable line will get you 10, even 15 feet more on each cast—if your spool's full and the line's fresh.

Monofilament is the last thing you should have to worry about when walleye fishing. And you won't have to worry if you do your homework before you leave the dock.

Basic Characteristics of Monofilament Line

Stiff Lines
1. transmit vibration better
2. set hooks faster
3. set larger hooks better
4. coil in cold weather
5. abraid less
6. increase bottom feel
7. move less freely in current
8. tend to accept less shock
9. allow fish to feel you quicker with livebait rigs
10. free you from tying more knots

Limp Lines
1. present livebaits more naturally
2. require thinner hooks
3. cast farther
4. remain supple in cold weather
5. abraid more easily
6. slightly reduce bottom feel and lure action
7. allow current to move a bait freely
8. buffer shock better
9. allow slightly more time before fish feel rod pressure
10. force you to check knots and line often

General-purpose lines have a blend of characteristics lying somewhere between stiff and limp lines.

EVOLUTION OF NEW LINES

After years of creeping along at impulse speed, line makers suddenly kicked into warp speed and leapt forward into hyperspace, leaving old line concepts spinning in their confused and turbulent wake.

The next generation of fishing lines has arrived, complete with new technology, terminology, and psychology of use. It's difficult, however, to choose and apply new lines properly without background information on recent changes.

FLUOROCARBON LINES

The recent introduction of fluorocarbon lines and leaders for minimizing visibility in ultraclear saltwater conditions is beginning to carry over into the freshwater market. Because of their cost, early versions were limited to small spools of leader material noted for being tough, invisible, and a bit on the stiff side. In 1999, both Stren and Berkley offered consumers full-spool fluorocarbon lines for the first time.

When tying knots with fluorocarbon lines, wet both your line and hookeye, then slowly draw the knot tight to minimize heat buildup, which might damage the line. Fluorocarbon has about the same stretch as nylon line, but is denser—good for keeping light jigs on bottom.

Line Categories

Line Type	Abbreviation	Market Examples
Abrasion-Resistant	AR	Ande Premium, Berkley XT, Berkley Big Game Inshore, Cortland Camo, Maxima Ultragreen, Super Silver Thread, Stren Super Tough, Triple Fish
Copolymers	C	Berkley Trilene Ultrathin, Cabela's Platinum, Damyl Tectan, Stren Magnathin
Limp, Castable	L	Ande Tournament, Berkley XL, Bass Pro Shops Excel, Fenwick Flexline, Silver Thread Excalibur, Stren Easy Cast
Superbraids	SB	Berkley Gorilla Braid, Cabela's Ripcord, Spiderwire, Suffix Herculine
Fused Braids	FB	Berkley FireLine, Spiderwire Fusion, Cabela's Ripcord SI, Suffix Micro
High Vis	HV	Chartreuse Ande, Berkley XT Solar, yellow Stren, any fluorescent line
Low Vis	LV	Cortland Camo, Fin-Nor Fluorocarbon, Suffix Fluorolon, Triple Fish Camo Escent, VMC Water King, any green or smoke-colored line
Low-Stretch Mono	LS	Gamakatsu G-Power, Spiderwire Mono, Stren Sensor
UV Resistant	UV	Fenwick Flexline, Fenwick Riverline, Silver Thread Excalibur, VMC Water King

Matching Line to Conditions

Conditions	Obvious Choices	Compromises
Ice	L, LV	AR, SB, FB
Cold	L, SB	AR, FB
Heat	AR, C, UV	any
Muddy water	HV	any
Clear water	LV	most
Deep	SB, FB, C	most
Shallow	LV, L, AR	any
Rocks	AR	none
Weeds	AR	C, SB, FB
Wood	AR	LS
Current	SB, FB, C	AR, L
Bright light	LV, UV, C	AR, L
Low light	any	any
Trolling lures (main)	LS, SB, FB, AR	C, L
Trolling bait (leader)	L, C	AR
Casting lures	C, SB, FB	AR, L, LS
Hooksets difficult	SB, FB, LS	C, AR

SUPERLINES

Original no-stretch or low-stretch superlines were gel-spun polyethylene braids made from Spectra or other space-age fibers. They boasted high tensile strength and minimal stretch, combined durability and performance, and possessed diameters a fraction of the thickness of equivalent mono lines. Sounds like the best of all worlds, especially where light line finesse presentations excel for fussy fish. But the initial claims triggering I-can't-wait-to-try-it sales did not result in the abandonment of traditional monofilament line. Braided superlines weren't necessarily too good to be true; instead, they required much more adaptation than most anglers expected.

The braiding technology used to weave superlines was slow and expensive: $20 for a 100-yard spool wasn't unusual. Lines proved so thin that knots were difficult to tie. Many knots failed; anglers generally accepted the palomar knot as most effective. With superline's minor inherent stretch, anglers using traditional rod tip movements overworked lures and broke line or ripped the hook from a fish's mouth on the hookset. Skinny lines also buried into casting reel spools on the hookset or became caught behind revolving spools that had been designed to accommodate thicker diameter lines.

In effect, braided superlines required adjustment and a period of orientation to use properly. Many anglers who tried braided superlines experienced various difficulties and returned to mono because it offered them a better all-around blend of fishable properties.

Fused superlines entered the market in mid-1995. They're a bit thicker than the original braided superlines, but much easier to handle. Formed by fusing a bundle of super fibers rather than braiding them, fused lines are cheaper and quicker to manufacture, and they behave more like monofilament.

Most knots are easy to tie, and the line feels and acts like thin mono instead of some unfamiliar and intimidating fibrous braid. Yet there's very little stretch—perhaps 3 percent, compared to 20 percent with monofilament—which puts performance back in the super category.

In essence, you're dealing with a hybrid product that teams some of the best features of both. Not problem free, but certainly more familiar and less imposing to use. Fused superline offers a faster learning curve for achieving an acceptable level of comfort and confidence. Use a softer rod, a more subtle rod tip motion, and a looser drag setting to move up to super performance.

Among fused superlines, SpiderWire Fusion and Berkley FireLine dominated the early introductions of mid-1995. Walleye anglers initially applied the new fused superlines to big water trolling and deep water applications with noteworthy success. Clearly, fused superlines helped rejuvenate confidence in the entire spectrum of superlines, leading anglers to experiment with other applications.

If you're going to try superlines, begin with one of the fused ones—they're easier to handle. Then, for ultrafinesse and ultrathin technology, try a superbraid.

MATCHING 21ST-CENTURY LINE TO FISHING CONDITIONS

A few years ago, several companies declared that the new superbraids would make monofilament lines obsolete. Fishermen suffered a brief chill of doubt, the same chill that walks your spine when your new computer is declared out-of-date before you even plug it in. Ads showing mono being bombed out of existence by the new polyethylene braids rekindled memories of those old record players stored in the attic.

Years later, those same line companies are introducing new monofilaments. The question today is not, "Will mono survive?" but rather, "Will we finally see a mono that incorporates all the positive qualities we want (limpness and abrasion resistance) and fewer of the negatives (memory), in one line?" And, "Will we finally see a mono with truly low stretch that doesn't fish like wire? Or a mono that doesn't absorb water?" Well, yes. Maybe.

Mono isn't going anywhere—except ahead. Quietly, in the background of the ongoing din around the braid revolution, great things are happening to monofilament.

LOW-STRETCH MONO WITH BRAID CHARACTERISTICS

Michael Fine, former press relations manager for Stren Fishing Lines, describes Stren Sensor as a kind of halfway point between superbraids and monofilament. "It offers superbraid characteristics without the negatives," Fine says. "It handles like mono because it is mono. But normal mono stretches from 22 to 30 percent. Sensor stretches about half that much."

The big knock on low-stretch monofilaments in the past has been lack of castability. In fact, most are marketed as trolling lines. Not so with Sensor, according to Fine. "It's memory free, yet strong, with easy castability. To get a strong, abrasion-resistant line in the past, castability and small diameter had to be sacrificed. If you wanted castability, you sacrificed abrasion resistance. This new patented process, while not reducing diameter, reduces stretch by half. The new superlines wrap around rod tips and guides, bind up in spools, and generally just don't stretch quite enough. This will be a more versatile line—a halfway point between superlines and mono in terms of stretch."

Quietly, in the background of the ongoing din around the braid revolution, great things are happening to monofilament.

Sometimes both stealth and stretch are needed. Acknowledging that lines sometimes need to stretch or hide better than braid, Johnson Worldwide Associates surprised everyone with the introduction of SpiderWire Super Mono. John Morlan, product manager for Spider-Wire, says, "the focus is on low stretch, strength, and abrasion resistance. In this first year we're offering it only in clear, but we plan to add colors. Super Mono stretches 15 to 20 percent less than other premium monofilaments, and its tensile strength runs 15 to 20 percent stronger, with diameters comparable to other premium lines. It's tough, but we've been able to make this a relatively limp line for easier casting.

"Basically, certain applications call for a clear line for stealth, or good abrasion resistance, or a little stretch. Or all three. Super Mono offers better abrasion resistance than SpiderWire. We want a line that satisfies every basic fishing application."

BRAID EVOLUTION

The superbraids, composed of thin polyethylene fibers with much stronger strength-to-thickness ratios than nylon monofilaments, are available in original sleeve-like (hollow), and *flat* versions like Berkley's Gorilla Braid, or fused versions like FireLine. A lot of fishermen are still asking, "Why have both?" and, "Which should I buy?"

Fused lines were developed to satisfy the demand for a braid that fishes more like mono and doesn't unbraid as easily. Fused lines tend to be less shock resistant and slightly weaker.

Line Perspectives from Al Lindner

Certain techniques really demand certain lines. When Al Lindner is livebait rigging, he uses Berkley XT, an abrasion-resistant line, on his spool, but he uses Berkley XL, a limp line, for leaders. "That way I get better movement out of the bait, yet better sensitivity and stronger hooksets," he says. "Best of both worlds."

Casting jigs to riprap, trees, or rockpiles is ridiculous with limp lines. Nicks happen much faster, even with much less pressure applied. For trolling bottom bouncers with spinner rigs, the line on your baitcasting reel should be abrasion resistant; the leader, too, especially with a steel clevis that wears on line as the blade spins.

High-stretch lines like Berkley Ice Line work fine for ice fishing, but in warm weather, they make hooksets difficult, and sensitivity goes out the window. The stiffer the line, the higher the sensitivity, but limp lines tend to work better for ice fishing than abrasion-resistant lines because coils and memory are encouraged by cold.

What about color? As a rule, choose the least visible line. "I believe there's something to that," Al Lindner says. "I note the color of the water and try to use a line that blends in. Most of the time, it's green. A green line blends into the largest number of water conditions."

That goes for line diameter, too. When using slipbobbers, for instance, walleyes have lots of time to ogle a bait. And they're ogling the line, too. Most days, an observable difference in catch rates can be seen between 6- and 4-pound lines, with 4-pound catching more walleyes. Use the smallest diameter possible in a line that blends in. That advice may seem to endorse superbraids, but on the other hand, they're also opaque and therefore highly visible to fish. Most anglers tend to use braids only with lures like crankbaits and spinners, where the fish is focused on the presentation and has less time to view the line.

Al Lindner fishes hard, and he experiments more than almost anyone. He likes superlines in some situations, but not in others. "The lines are one of the best things that ever happened to trolling," he observes. "For contour trolling, for flatline trolling, for pulling three-ways and spinners, you just can't beat fused superline, for all the reasons that I'm sure have already been outlined by others."

"SpiderWire braid is still the strongest, most sensitive line in the world, and it does get deeper than Fusion," Morlan says. "Fusion is basically a user-friendly superline, a little of the best of both worlds. It's easier to tie knots with and feels more like mono to the average fisherman."

All this, yet some of the best anglers we know still contend they could fish without difficulty today with the same premium lines they used in 1980—say, with Berkley XL or original Stren. On the other hand, some of the best anglers we know fish braids about 80 percent of the time. There's little question the fishing world has moved a long way toward solving many of the specific problems anglers face in dealing with the common problem of connecting directly to the fish.

"For several years I spent a ton of time working with wire line for walleyes. The wire allowed pin-point trolling precision in tight corners. But the fused lines make wire obsolete. Fused lines are so much easier to work with. Last season, I had fused line on every one of my trolling rods.

"But I don't like superlines for jigging," he continues. "And I've spent a ton of time trying it. Deep water. Shallow water. In weeds and along weedlines. In timber. You name it, I just don't see any advantage. The sensitivity factor just isn't that critical at the short distances at which we jig. But the no-stretch factor is a big drawback for me.

"If you can feel the fish that well, they can feel you. I like the slight forgiveness in mono at close range. I like that taut-but-never-quite-tight feeling that goes with a jig bite. I like being able to monitor the fish—to feel the fish—when they can't quite monitor me. This has all been part of my fishing for almost thirty years.

"I just miss too many fish when I jig with superline. I roll fish on the hookset. I straighten hooks. Of course, I'm just super-tuned into fishing with monofilament. Fused line casts like a dream on spinning gear. I know that I should just lift and not set when a fish takes a jig. But I just don't feel like deprogramming myself after all these years when the advantages in the situations I've outlined aren't that great.

"I've done plenty of testing with two jigging rods, too. I'd tie a jig direct to fused line on one rod and add an 18-inch mono leader to the fused line on the other rod. I've never been comfortable with opaque line, and I'm pretty sure walleyes prefer to eat the mono-rigged jig over the jig tied direct. But of course I'll keep experimenting. For now, though, I'm just going to run mono on my jigging rods, while my trolling rods are rigged with superline."

'EYES ON FIRE—THE CASE FOR SUPERLINES

In mid-1995, fused superlines rocked the fishing industry like an earthquake registering 8.0 on the Richter scale. Initial reports were that the second generation of superlines would be easier to use than the original braided superlines introduced in 1993.

Yet despite waves of optimism, overriding feelings of caution surfaced, too. "Looks great, but we'll see . . . " Some folks felt the line industry had cried *Wolf!* with the first generation of braided superlines. Initial excitement was followed by skeptical disillusionment once it became evident how much adjusting was sometimes required to use the new lines. Fool me once, shame on you. Fool me twice, well. Many anglers would approach superlines a bit more cautiously the second time around.

Fishing with superlines definitely requires adjustments, but they allow you to accomplish things you can't do with mono. Here are some superline tips from top walleye anglers who helped pioneer the use of superlines for walleyes.

FIREMEN

Gary Parsons and Keith Kavajecz are a hot duo in competitive walleye fishing and partners in business promotions and fishing savvy. Considered among the premier walleye trollers in the world today, Parsons and Kavajecz have fallen bow-over-transom in love with Berkley's new FireLine, championing its cause.

Gary: "I believe FireLine provided a big step in the evolution of walleye trolling systems. It has revolutionized our fishing. First and foremost, the hair-thin diameter cuts water like a knife, allowing baits to dive much deeper than on mono. Also, baits achieve their maximum natural rolling action. The combination is too good for walleyes to resist."

Keith: "Trolling with FireLine lets us troll unweighted crankbaits into much deeper water. Many lures now run down to the 25-foot range, and some deeper. This puts them at the thermocline in many natural lakes—a natural fish-holding zone in summer. But perhaps more important, FireLine enhances finesse by minimizing spooking.

"We've talked a lot about adding snap weights 50 feet ahead of a crankbait to minimize spooking walleyes. But in some instances, particularly in ultra-clear Great Lakes' waters, 50 feet isn't enough. Walleyes spot the sinker and are alerted to something unnatural. But by trolling with FireLine, the bait gets deeper without a sinker. Nothing to spook fish."

Gary: "And think about this: it's not necessary to add sinkers and change weights. Instead, just use line length to make cranks dive to a certain depth. Anybody can do it. All of a sudden, we have a bunch of instant experts on the water, guides and weekend anglers. This line takes the intimidation out of trolling."

Keith: "Not that there aren't aspects to learn and adjustments to make. For one thing, it's easy to lose fish when you're fighting them too hard on mono; and it's easier to lose them with no-stretch line. Even after years of learning to baby fish, winding them in slowly without pumping the rod tip, letting the rod tip maintain tension, we still lost walleyes during our introduction to FireLine trolling when hooks ripped out. Using Premium Triple Grip trebles helped alleviate the problem."

Gary: "The line by itself didn't do it. Nor did premium hooks. The combination of several products available for the first time, plus a lot of experimentation, made the system click. I can't imagine going back to mono for open water trolling and loads of other uses, too."

Keith: "At a PWT tournament at Lake Oahe, South Dakota, Gary discovered a super pattern for contour-trolling crankbaits at about the 25-foot level. It worked so well that we abandoned all ideas of rigging or jigging and instead longline trolled diving shad baits on 250 to 300 feet of FireLine. Baits that normally ran at 16 feet on mono cruised just above bottom at 25. By following points and contours, we eliminated lots of unproductive water, zeroing in on pods of fish that most anglers missed."

Gary: "The no-stretch aspect of fused superline adds another dimension to crankbait trolling—precision depth control. We used to think our baits were at a certain level when actually they were more in an approximate range. Now, with FireLine, we can predict within a foot or so exactly how deep our baits are running. Shorter line lengths, no stretch, precision control."

SPIDERMEN

Scott and Marty Glorvigen, fishing twins from Grand Rapids, Minnesota, lend perspective to the superline story. Besides being PWT pros, fishing guides, and manufacturers within the fishing tackle industry, the Glorvi-guys are "spider guys" sponsored by the folks at SpiderWire. When Spiderwire first hit the market, the twins avoided using mono in order to maintain sponsor allegiance. They competed head-to-head with the best walleye anglers in the business, using not only the new fused superlines but also the original superbraids that drove so many anglers to distraction. When you're forced to use something, you learn its strengths and weaknesses.

Attack of the Spidermen: Scott and Marty Glorvigen. Or is it Marty and Scott?

Marty: "Scott and I have used both the original SpiderWire superbraid and SpiderWire Fusion under a variety of conditions. The consistency of Fusion—what you feel when you hold it between your fingers—is a lot like mono and therefore isn't so intimidating. I believe that SpiderWire is actually more sensitive than Fusion, but both are much more sensitive than mono."

Scott: "Fusion is much easier to tie knots with. We both like to use a triple palomar for superlines, but most knots work well with Fusion. A triple palomar increases line surface area against the hook eye and prevents slippage with SpiderWire. With superbraids, most other knots begin to slip at about 30 percent line strength. It's important to use the proper knot."

Marty: "Fusion's larger diameter is more suited to trolling boards. It clamps between releases better than thinner SpiderWire. We put two releases on the front of our trolling boards and one on the back to increase the amount of surface area gripping line. Using this system with no-stretch line, we can run boards much farther out than with mono."

Scott: "The true value of superlines lies in their combination of characteristics. We always wanted lines with small diameter, zero stretch, and maximum feel. So what happened? Technology leapfrogged us. The industry came out with ultrathin superbraids that everyone found difficult to use. Next, they came out with fused superlines that anyone can use with a bit of effort."

Marty: "To try a superline, go at it backwards. First try fused superlines, which are easier to handle and gain confidence in. Then, if you want to go for ultrafinesse and ultrathin technology, try a superbraid. Get your toe in the door before jumping in with both feet."

Scott: "Because of all the steelhead fishing we've done, we select lines for sensitivity and small diameter to minimize spooking and maximize the natural action of bait. The same applies to walleyes. Both superbraids and fused superlines offer more sensitivity, but braids do it with an even smaller diameter."

Marty: "When selecting which superline to use for walleyes, don't get caught up in the idea of adding more strength at an equivalent mono diameter, like a

30-pound line with the same 8- or 10-pound diameter. Instead, think equivalent strength with thinner line. You're matching, not compensating.

"Bass fishermen might want to maintain line diameter and go up to a line with more strength, but walleye and panfishermen should do the opposite and select a fused superline with the same pound-test rating as the mono they usually use, decreasing line diameter and adding more finesse to presentations. Then, when the bite is really tough, consider switching to a braided superline for an even thinner diameter and maximum finesse. Fish 6- or 8-pound test with the equivalent diameter of 1- or 2-pound mono. At times, this really makes a difference."

Scott: "When's the last time you tried tying knots with 1- or 2-pound mono? That's the equivalent of what you're trying to do. The only anglers accomplished at tying knots with such light line are panfish anglers, chiefly for ice fishing. It takes practice. Most folks won't make the effort and are more comfortable using a fused superline."

Marty: "If you're going to use superlines, match equipment to line strength, not to line diameter. Using 30-pound-test line on a rod designed to fish 8-pound test could result in the rod breaking on a hookset. Remember, there's no stretch. Hooksets should be done with the wrist, not the arms."

"If you're going to use superlines, match equipment to line strength, not to line diameter."

—Marty Glorvigen

Scott: "Choosing the finest graphite rod versus a softer fiberglass is no longer so easy. High-modulus graphite rods were developed to compensate for mono's loss in sensitivity and to remove stretch when setting hooks. But superlines don't stretch and are inherently more sensitive than mono. A good superline rod is still sensitive, but it's softer to compensate for lack of line stretch."

Marty: "And with additional strength at low diameter, it's not necessary to fish a baitcasting reel for most walleye applications. Spinning reels accommodate superlines heavy enough for most walleye presentations. With the possible exception of longline trolling, where it's necessary to accurately measure the amount of line out with a line counter trolling reel, spinning gear works just fine."

Scott: "Superlines tend to dig into the spool and backlash with most casting reels unless you run a light drag. They're so thin, they slip between parallel layers of line."

Marty: "With any casting reel, use plenty of mono backing to prevent slippage on the arbor. Then fill the reel to capacity with a thin outer layer of superline. And wind line on under firm tension to ensure it lies in tight layers. I use a leather glove to grip the line just above the reel before it enters the spool, nice and tight."

Scott: "Sense of feel is amazing with superlines, and they make me more efficient and productive. Superlines telegraph exactly what's going on underwater, what the bait's doing, and what bottom is like. Visualizing changes from sand to gravel makes it possible to fish them better.

"Most people can't read a change on electronics from big rock to small rock, but with superlines, it's possible to feel changes. Hang a tiny piece of sandgrass on your crankbait, and you can feel the change in lure vibration. Feel spinners rotate. Feel the change in bottom composition from hard pack to silt along the deep edge of a drop-off. Feel fish hit, instead of the line just getting heavy. This helps gauge level of fish aggressiveness and to set the hook accordingly. Feel minnow movement on the end of a line. There's no end to the things you can detect."

Marty: "With their thin diameter and no stretch, superlines cut the water, forcing crankbaits to dig deep—much deeper and quicker than stretchy mono. At some point, mono stretches and extra speed makes lures run shallower, which doesn't happen with superline. It's possible to cast and retrieve crankbaits deeper or troll them deeper and faster without added weight. So long as the bait can operate at the higher speed, it'll continue to run deeper."

Scott: "At a recent Lake Erie tournament, the water was so clear that clip-on sinkers spooked fish. But unweighted superline trolling had no negative effect, producing most of the top finishes."

Marty: "When you work a lure, it's necessary to consider lack of stretch. With mono, move your rod tip a few feet, and the lure doesn't move that far. With superline, it moves a few feet. Downsize the amount of rod tip motion to fish traditional tactics like snapjigging: used to be we swept our rod tips 4 or 5 feet to take stretch out of mono and make the jig dance. If we did that with Spider-Wire or Fusion, the jig would move the same distance. Now, we just move it a few inches. Same for deep water jigging. It's necessary to learn a cadence or rhythm, because every rod tip motion seems to impart an exaggerated motion to a bait or lure."

Scott: "We achieve different things with SpiderWire or Fusion. For example, we used to fish shallow coontail edges with jigs. Was it because active fish were only on edges, or was it too hard to work inside thick clumps? Now we can pitch a 1/8-ounce jig on 6-pound line into coontail clumps and rip it out with a twitch of the wrist. We can fish a crankbait over the top and feel when it just ticks weeds or run it between clumps, deeper into weeds than ever before."

Marty: "Avoid sweeping hooksets. A little wrist action is all it takes. Most of the time, walleyes hook themselves. When you hook a fish, don't pump the rod, or you'll tear out the hook. Don't fight 'em as with mono. If they're hooked, they're hooked. Reel slowly and let them take drag, if needed. Maintain tension, but don't horse 'em."

Scott: "Misconceptions! I'm not afraid of the opaque color, and I don't add a mono leader between the superline and lure or bait. About the only time I use mono is as a livebait rig snell, not for decreased visibility, but because mono is stiffer than SpiderWire and will maintain some distance between the sinker and bait when the sinker hits bottom and the bait continues forward."

"Superlines won't affect beginners as much as they will experienced fishermen, because beginners don't have preconceived notions about what line should feel like and how it should perform."

—Scott Glorvigen

Marty: "Learn to use superline properly, and its advantages far outweigh its difficulties. Its sensitivity really opens your eyes to the underwater world. And when you're night-fishing, relying on feel of the lure to tell you what's happening, it's awesome. Like seeing in the dark."

Scott: "Superlines won't affect beginners as much as they will experienced fishermen, because beginners don't have preconceived notions about what line should feel like and how it should perform. Once a veteran angler learns to use a superline, however, it's hard to return to mono. It's necessary to go through a learning curve, however, to begin achieving its true potential."

Marty: "Don't be afraid of change. Think how much your fishing has changed over the course of learning to fish. You've experienced levels of change. Where would we be if we still used typewriters instead of computers? If we still fished for walleyes as we did when we first started fishing tournaments, we'd be trailing the pack. Change is good. But change isn't easy."

DAY AND NIGHT

Gary Roach, past PWT Angler of the Year, has jigged, rigged, and trolled up a few hundred thousand walleyes over the course of his fishing career. Guess that's why he's known coast-to-coast as Mr. Walleye. His business and promotional fishing partner, Mark Martin, 1990 PWT Champion, nighttime trolling specialist, and guide, has less gray in his considerably younger beard, but a nevertheless impressive history of catching big 'eyes on finesse tactics, especially after dark.

Gary: "Superline is so sensitive that I can feel bait, bottom, and fish. But remember, if you can feel the fish, the fish can also feel you. Put any extra pressure on them with a livebait rig, and they're gone. With FireLine, I usually set right away rather than risk spooking fish.

"I like Berkley's FireLine in the 20/8 size—20-pound test with an equivalent 8-pound mono diameter—for trolling cranks like Shad Raps. Strikes take getting used to; they're shockers. *Bam!* With bottom bouncers, I can feel #3 spinner blades rotating.

"For livebait rigging, I like 6/2 FireLine on an ultralight or light spinning rod. I designed a Gary Roach Signature series of rods for Berkley, with soft tips perfect for fishing superlines. I like spinning better than baitcasting because the line comes off the spool so much better. I still like Trilene XT for a lot of walleye applications, but the fact is, FireLine gives me an advantage and helps me catch fish in certain situations."

Martin: "I echo most of what Gary says, plus I can add some pertinent information about crankbaits. For many years, I've longline trolled minnow-imitators on mono line with guide clients for giant walleyes after dark, particularly in harbors or lakes attached to the Great Lakes. We'd lose a few baits a week. Then the zebra mussels invaded our waters, and we lost up to 150 baits a year. Ouch! We'd just tick a zebra mussel and the bait was gone, just as if a pike had bitten it off.

"Now, however, trolling with 20/8 FireLine has cut our losses back to the levels of the pre-zeeb days. It fishes much like 10-pound-test Trilene XT, only without the stretch. I use it for bottom bouncing, too, in areas of the Great Lakes where zebra mussels eat bouncers like crazy. With superline, they don't.

"I never liked the original superbraids. They'd catch water and tend to float, requiring more line to get baits down, thereby defeating the purpose. But the new fused superline is wonderful. So sensitive. My clients now feel ticks indicating that a fish bumped or brushed their lure when they used to say that maybe they'd had a hit. And when I used to try to feel ticks, now I can feel the line tighten as the fish inhales the lure.

"Superline lets me feel a blade of grass or a leaf fouling my lure. I just snap the rod tip hard to clear the debris and keep on trolling. Then I use a simple wrist twitch to set the hook. I fight the fish slow and easy."

CRUX OF THE BISCUIT

The crux of the biscuit, as In-Fisherman TV producer James Lindner is fond of saying, is that the choice between using superline or not, between fused and braided superline, between manufacturers, and your style of application depends on personal preference, comfort, and confidence. No one can make you use superline, and no one can make you like it.

Many anglers will never get past the initial learning curve described by the Glorvigens; it's not worth their time and effort. But for those who explore the possibilities, diligently learning the in's and out's of fishing with no-stretch superlines, the possibilities are many indeed.

In-Fisherman Staff Consensus About Superlines

"What about superlines? Are they really super?" The answer, after several years of In-Fisherman staff testing, is that they certainly are, used in the right context. None of the staff, however, use superlines exclusively, that is, for every aspect of fishing.

Monofilament is still the predominant choice for most jigging and rigging. Ditto for most casting, whether crankbaits or jigs. The staff, however, is split about evenly on superline for longline trolling with crankbaits in shallow water. Meanwhile, we all concede the superiority of superlines for trolling crankbaits in deep water and at long distances. In short, most of us rely on superlines anytime longlines are needed for trolling with three-way rigs, bottom bouncers, or dropweights. Many of us also use superlines for long casts with jigging spoons or bladebaits, or for presenting baits vertically in water over 50 feet deep.

Superlines fall into two categories. Braids like SpiderWire Spectra 2000 and Berkley Whiplash offer tiny diameter with high break strength. Second-generation fused superlines like SpiderWire Fusion and Berkley FireLine are larger in diameter and offer less break strength than the original braids. Companies suggest that fused lines are easier to tie knots in and to cast.

The most significant misinformation about superlines versus monofilament involves comparative stretch. Monofilament is said to have a stretch factor of about 25 percent, while superlines have a stretch factor of about 4 percent—thus the superior sensitivity of superline. But the stretch characteristics of monofilament have been exaggerated. A 10-inch section of monofilament doesn't stretch 2.5 inches (25 percent) in most instances, nor does a 100-foot section stretch 25 feet.

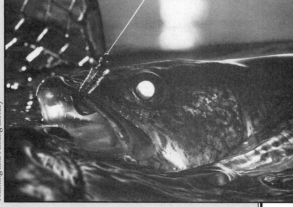

Hunting and Fishing Library

Actually, monofilament doesn't stretch at all until it's put under pressure. So when a fish sucks in a jig on monofilament 25 feet below the boat, the monofilament stretches no more than a superline until after the hookset, when significant pressure is exerted on the mono. Stiffer monofilaments transfer vibrations better than softer monofilaments, just as the material qualities of superline transfer vibrations better than even the stiffest monofilament. Given the short distances at which most presentations are performed, however, the difference in sensitivity isn't the significant factor it becomes at long distances.

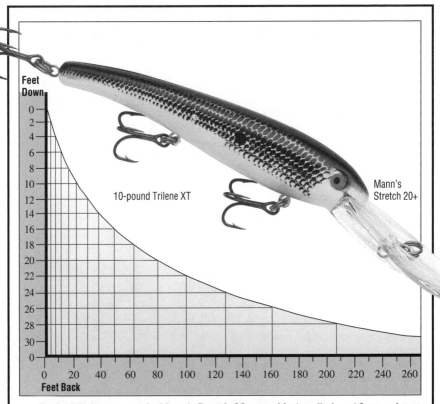

Typical diving range of a Mann's Stretch 20+ crankbait trolled on 10-pound-test Berkley Trilene XT. The same lure trolled on similar lengths of Berkley FireLine reaches about 25 percent deeper; on 375 feet of 10-pound FireLine, it reaches approximately 45 feet—150 percent of the maximum depth attainable with 10-pound mono.

Chart from *Precision Trolling*.

Fused superlines are the next generation of fishing lines, and they're here to stay, leading us into the next century. Monofilament is far from dead and will continue to dominate the line market for the foreseeable future. Where the future leads to is anyone's guess. We believe the increased use of superlines will spawn new techniques and new dimensions of fishing finesse and success, as the follow example reveals.

REACHING SUPER DEPTHS WITH TROLLED CRANKBAITS

Fused superlines are gaining acceptance in the professional fishing world. They combine the advantages of the original superbraids (low stretch, high strength, fine diameter, superior abrasion resistance) with the easier handling of mono-filament (good knot strength and compatibility with most rods and reels).

Anglers using fused lines like Berkley FireLine and SpiderWire Fusion find they can troll floating-diving crankbait presentations to depths unattainable or impractical with monofilament. The combination of small diameter, high break strength, and ability to use longer trolling leads due to the lower stretch factor makes this possible.

When trolling floating-diving crankbaits, two opposing variables are at work: (1) water pressure against the diving lip of the bait makes the crankbait dive, and (2) the upward force of water resistance against the fishing line prevents a trolled crankbait from continuing its descent. With smaller-diameter line minimizing water resistance, however, superlines can achieve increased depth.

DOCUMENTATION

While assembling data for an updated version of their book detailing the trolling depths of popular crankbaits, the *Crankbaits "In-Depth"* staff studied the diving depth of crankbaits trolled on fused superlines. The standard for previous dive curve data for crankbaits was 10-pound-test Berkley Trilene XT. For purposes of continuity, they chose Berkley FireLine to study fusion lines, which they tested with a variety of crankbaits, from shallow to deep divers, using 6-, 10-, and 14-pound FireLine.

The diameter of 10-pound FireLine approximates the diameter of 4-pound monofilament. Compared to 10-pound Trilene XT mono, crankbaits trolled on equal lead lengths of 10-pound FireLine ran about 25 percent deeper than those trolled on 10-pound XT.

As an example, Mann's Stretch 20+ crankbait reached a depth of 20 feet with an 80-foot lead length of 10-pound Trilene XT. Running on 80 feet of 10-pound FireLine, the same bait reached 25 feet. A 5-foot increase can make a difference when you're targeting fish on bottom or fish suspended in the water column. The difference becomes even greater with diving crankbaits or longer leads.

The comparison between monofilament and fusion lines doesn't end there. When they conducted their original crankbait dive studies using monofilament, it was pointless to test lures trolled on more than 240 to 260 feet of line. Deep divers continued to dive if more line was let out, but because of the stretch properties of monofilament, longer lines were impractical.

With fusion lines, however, stretch is no longer a problem. While hauling in a fish from a football field away may seem extreme, it is possible on fused line. A longline approach using fused lines gives us the capability of sending cranks to depths previously impossible without adding weight.

While using weight for gaining additional depth with trolled crankbaits is always an option, the presentation becomes speed dependent. As trolling speed increases, the presentation loses depth; as speed decreases, a lure sinks deeper. Trolling floating-diving crankbaits on super long leads is much less speed dependent and allows greater accuracy in depth.

Researchers trolled crankbaits on fusion lines as far back as 375 feet. Even on these long trolling leads, the lack of stretch in fused lines allowed them to feel the subtle vibrations of the lure. Depths achieved with these super long leads surprised everyone: as a rule, on a 375-foot lead of 10-pound FireLine, crankbait running depth was 150 percent of the maximum depth on the monofilament dive curve.

Look at the dive curve for the Stretch 20+ again, and you see that it approaches the 30-foot mark when trolled on 260 feet of 10-pound Trilene XT. By multiplying this 30-foot maximum by 150 percent (30 x 1.5 = 45), this bait will run approximately 45 feet deep with a 375-foot lead of 10-pound FireLine—deep enough to reach the thermocline in many trolling situations. It is possible to take super-deep divers like the Mann's Stretch 25+, Luhr Jensen Power Dive Minnow, or the 3/4-ounce Hot Lips Express to depths below 60 feet without additional weight.

One would think that if 10-pound FireLine could reach such extreme depths, smaller-diameter 6-pound FireLine should really get baits down there. The *Crankbaits* staff could not, however, demonstrate any significant difference between lures trolled on 6- and 10-pound FireLine. While 6-pound exhibited a slight tendency to run deeper, no statistical difference could be measured between the two.

Because monofilament is still popular with most trollers, the gold standard continues to be the crankbait data collected using 10-pound XT. The best way to introduce the dive data of fusion lines to the fishing public seems to be with a comprehensive, easy-to-use conversion table.

All the data from *Crankbaits "In-Depth"* are included in the updated publication, *Precision Trolling.* By referencing standard dive curves for 10-pound XT, you can easily target specific depths with a variety of monofilaments of different diameters, as well as with 6-, 10-, and 14-pound FireLine.

KNOTS OH FACT OH

To old -isms like "It ain't worth the paper it's printed on" and "Look before you leap," we add, "You're only as good as your knot." Knots are the final connection between hook and line—critical intersections along the shortest, straightest line between fish and angler. If your knot's not up to snuff, fishin's gonna be tough—perhaps truer now than ever before.

Trilene Knot

Mono or fused superline to hooks, lures, swivels, snaps, split rings.

1. Thread the eye of the hook with the line.

2. Make an extra wrap.

3. Then wrap the tag around the main line from three to five times. The heavier the line, the fewer number of wraps; the lighter the line, the more wraps up to five.

4. Complete the knot by passing the tag back through the first two wraps before pulling the knot tight. The best result is achieved when the loops through the eye of the hook retain their wrapping sequence and don't spring apart.

Uni-Knot

Any line to hooks, lures, swivels, snaps, split rings. A good knot for superline.

1. Run at least six inches of line through the eye of the hook, swivel, or lure, and fold to make two parallel lines. Bring the tag end of the line back in a circle toward the hook or lure.

Improved Clinch

Mono or fused superline to hooks, lures, swivels, snaps, split rings.

1. Pass the line through the eye of the hook, swivel, or lure. Double back, and make five turns around the standing line for lines testing 14 pounds or more, seven turns for lighter line.

2. Holding the coils in place, thread the tag end of the line through the first loop above the eye, then through the big loop.

3. Hold the tag end and standing line while pulling up the coils. Make sure the coils are in a spiral, not lapping over each other. Slide tight against the eye.

4. Clip the tag end.

2. Make five or six turns with the tag end around the double line and through the circle.

3. Hold the double line at the point where it passes through the eye, and pull the tag end to snug up the turns.

4. To create a loop connection, adjust the loop size by sliding the knot up or down the standing line. Then pull the tag end with pliers to maximize tightness.

Palomar

Any line to hooks, lures, swivels, snaps, split rings; perhaps the best knot for superbraids.

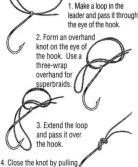

1. Make a loop in the leader and pass it through the eye of the hook.

2. Form an overhand knot on the eye of the hook. Use a three-wrap overhand for superbraids.

3. Extend the loop and pass it over the hook.

4. Close the knot by pulling tag and leader. Trim tag end when complete.

5. To create a snugged knot, pull the standing line to slide the knot up against the eye. Then continue pulling until the knot is tight.

6. Trim the tag end flush with the closest coil on the knot.

Back-To-Back Uni-Knots

Any line to any line, particularly good for joining superlines and mono, although the thinnest superlines often must be doubled at the end to cinch up properly to the mono.

1. Overlap about 12 inches of the ends of two lines. Form a uni-knot circle with the tag end of one line.

2. Wrap the first line five times to form a uni-knot around the second line. Snug the knot by gently pulling on both ends of the first line with enough tension to close the wraps, but not so tight that it actually grips the second line.

3. Form a new uni-knot circle with the tag end of the second line and wrap it five times to form a uni-knot around the original line.

4. Gently pull each line with either hand to slide the two uni-knots together until they jam—then pull tight. Tighten the wraps around the standing lines by firmly pulling the tag ends of each uni-knot.

5. Snip the tag ends.

Uni-Knot Snell Knot

Any line to hook. The uni-knot is also a quick, easy way to a snell a hook.

1. Thread six inches of line through the hook eye.

2. Hold the line against the hook shank, and form a uni-knot circle.

3. Make five to seven turns through the loop and around the standing line and hook shank.

4. Tighten by pulling the standing line in one direction and the tag end in the other.

Snell Knot

Any line to hook. Originally introduced for hooks with spatulate eyes. The snell is appropriate for hooks with up-turned or down-turned eyes when the leader needs to be aligned along the shank of the hook. This knot is most important in many two-hook rigs. The eye of the hook need not be threaded.

1. Make this configuration in the line against the hook. The eye may be threaded, but not with spatulate, knobbed, or flattened eyes.

A - tag
C - loop
B - main line

2. Roll Loop C over so that Loop D is formed and begin wrapping the shank of the hook and the tag.

3. Your snell should begin to look something like this.

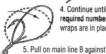

4. Continue until the **required number** of wraps are in place.

5. Pull on main line B against tag A until the knot is formed on the shank. When the eye of the hook is threaded, the snell should be formed down a little from the eye so the chances of a separation occurring from a roughly turned or sharp eye are reduced.

Simple Loop Knot

Mono to hooks, lures, swivels, snaps.

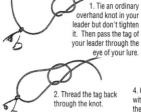

1. Tie an ordinary overhand knot in your leader but don't tighten it. Then pass the tag of your leader through the eye of your lure.

2. Thread the tag back through the knot.

3. Now comes the tricky part: the tag has to bend back, go over the main line, up through the crossover forming the overhand knot, then up through the gap between where the tag was passed through the knot in Step 2.

4. Close the knot with pressure on the loop against the main line.

Surgeon's Knot

Mono to mono; superlines to superlines; one line type to another. The surgeon's knot is used for building fly-fishing leaders and multihook bait-catching rigs. It can also be used for attaching a short dropper near the end of your main line. Its chief advantage over other similar knots are simplicity and speed.

1. Shown is the main line (gray) and the tippet or dropper (black). Lay them alongside each other as shown with an overlap of at least 6 inches.

2. Tie an overhand knot in the main line and the dropper.

3. Make a second wrap in your overhand knot to form four wraps and five crossovers.

4. With equal pressure on each strand, pull the knot tight. Should the knot fail to close properly, pull gently on each end in turn until the knot is closed before trimming the tag end of the dropper. Large loops are easier to work with when tying this knot, so dropper or tippet sections should be cut somewhat longer than with other joins.

Surgeon's Loop

Forming loop end in any line.

1. Bend the line over and back on itself to form a loop.

2. Tie an overhand knot in the loop.

3. Then add an extra wrap to form a double overhand knot in the loop.

4. Close the knot to form a permanent loop.

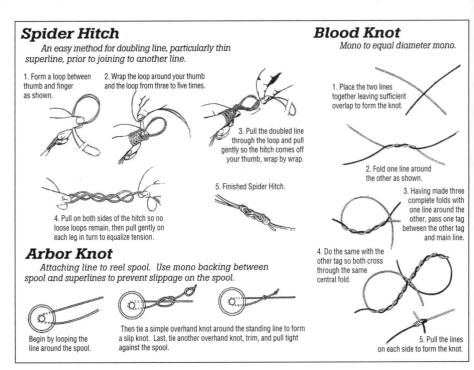

Spider Hitch

An easy method for doubling line, particularly thin superline, prior to joining to another line.

1. Form a loop between thumb and finger as shown.

2. Wrap the loop around your thumb and the loop from three to five times.

3. Pull the doubled line through the loop and pull gently so the hitch comes off your thumb, wrap by wrap.

4. Pull on both sides of the hitch so no loose loops remain, then pull gently on each leg in turn to equalize tension.

5. Finished Spider Hitch.

Arbor Knot

Attaching line to reel spool. Use mono backing between spool and superlines to prevent slippage on the spool.

Begin by looping the line around the spool.

Then tie a simple overhand knot around the standing line to form a slip knot. Last, tie another overhand knot, trim, and pull tight against the spool.

Blood Knot

Mono to equal diameter mono.

1. Place the two lines together leaving sufficient overlap to form the knot.

2. Fold one line around the other as shown.

3. Having made three complete folds with one line around the other, pass one tag between the other tag and main line.

4. Do the same with the other tag so both cross through the same central fold.

5. Pull the lines on each side to form the knot.

When the fishing world was dominated by nylon monofilament and braided Dacron, knots were important but not quite the critical link ushered in by the recent arrival of gel-spun polyethylene. Many good, easy-to-tie knots provide 80 to 95 percent efficiency with mono. Only a handful make the grade with the new breed of skinny superlines. Tying effective knots is essential to using them; a poorly tied or incorrectly chosen knot quickly becomes a slipknot. Success slides through your fingers and right off the end of your line.

A quick review of basic knots designed for monofilament is therefore joined by a close-up look at knots that make the grade for use with superlines. Master their use, and walleyes will follow. And that is worth the paper it's printed on.

THE WIND UP, THE PITCH . . . IT'S A HIT!

Bass fishermen using heavy line can usually get away with worn line—at least for a while. But walleye fishermen using 6- or 8-pound test can't afford to take chances. The slightest nick, fray, or rub quickly reduces 6-pound to 4- or even 2-. No room for error with the line, or with the way you spool it.

Pass line from the bulk spool through the line guides down to the reel. The best knot for attachment is the arbor knot, though an improved clinch or Trilene knot is usually OK.

Casting tackle is easiest to spool. Put a pencil or screwdriver through the bulk spool and have someone hold it in place. Position the reel spool so line winds off the bulk spool onto the reel without twisting; the curvature of the line coming off the bulk spool should match the curvature of the reel spool. Pass the line under tension between your fingertips, or have your partner place a little drag on the bulk spool, so the line winds on tightly.

Spooling line on spinning gear isn't foolproof. Try one of several methods:

1. Lay the bulk spool flat on the floor, label up or down, depending on the way your spinning reel rotates. The curvature of the line coming off the bulk spool should follow the curvature of your reel spool. Done properly, you'll minimize line twist and casting will be easiest. Get it wrong, and line springs off the reel when you open the bail. If you're unsure, wind line on one spool and try casting. If it's a disaster, do the opposite. One word of warning: even done right, expect some twist.

Grasp the rod shaft above the reel with your right hand, let the line pass between your thumb and forefinger under some tension while spooling, and wind with your left. Some anglers like to wind 10 or 20 revolutions, stop, flip the bulk spool over, and do another 20. This probably isn't good, because the line doesn't follow the curvature of the bulk spool.

Another option is to put the bulk spool on a pencil or screwdriver. This causes line twist on spinning reels, however.

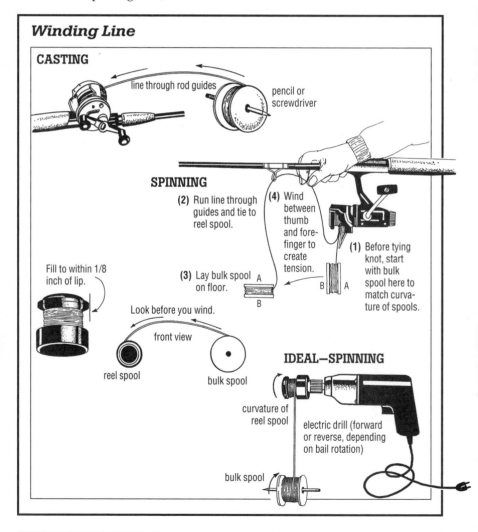

Winding Line

CASTING

line through rod guides

pencil or screwdriver

SPINNING

(2) Run line through guides and tie to reel spool.

(4) Wind between thumb and forefinger to create tension.

(1) Before tying knot, start with bulk spool here to match curvature of spools.

Fill to within 1/8 inch of lip.

(3) Lay bulk spool on floor.

A
B

B A

Look before you wind.

front view

reel spool

bulk spool

IDEAL—SPINNING

curvature of reel spool

electric drill (forward or reverse, depending on bail rotation)

bulk spool

2. A better plan is to clamp a commercially available bracket onto the rod a foot above the reel and hold the bulk spool in place, adjusting tension on the bulk spool to ensure tight layering. This minimizes line twist by allowing the bulk spool to rotate while the bail turns.

3. The best method is to use a commercial line winder or to place an extra spinning reel shaft (spindle) in an electric drill. Install the spinning reel spool on the machine or drill, then wind line off the bulk spool onto the reel spool, as you would on a reel-to-reel tape recorder, making sure the curvature of the line follows the curvature of the spool. Move the line up and down slightly during the process so it winds on in even layers rather than bunching up at the top or bottom of the spool.

Even under the best circumstances, some line twist occurs when you use a new spool of line, line that has been wound on a spool for an extended period, or line that's been twisted by lures that spin. A good trick is to drag your line. Cut off lures or rigs, and as you motor along at modest speed, open the bail and dip the last 6 or 8 feet of line into the water. Surface tension will begin pulling line off the spool. Let out 50 yards, close the bail, and drag it for a minute. Then wind it in under tension. Dragging removes twist and leaves line as limp as spaghetti.

Fifty yards is about all the line anyone ever needs. To conserve line, replace only the top 50 yards. Tie the ends together with a blood knot. Replace the top section frequently.

When spooling superlines, the best advice is to spool tightly. Begin with an underlayer of bulk monofilament line wound onto the spool under strong tension, filling the spool until there is just enough room for a top layer of superline. Mono properly grips the arbor or spool; superline seldom does. If you attach superline directly to the spool or arbor, the slippery stuff usually spins on the shaft or spool, preventing you from retrieving line.

Splice the mono underlayer to the superline with a double nail knot. Trim the excess. Then wind the superline onto the reel under strong tension. Whether spinning or casting, make every layer of coils as tight as possible to prevent the upper layers from digging down into the lower ones under tension, such as hooksets, thereby jamming the reel. Attention to detail when spooling up makes all the difference.

All line eventually wears out. Abrasion, stretch, sunlight, nicks, knots, and peels take a toll. Old line is undependable and difficult to fish with. Kinked line reduces casting distance and lure performance. Match your line type and weight to the methods and tackle you use, and respool often. Invest a bit of time in a bit of line. New line in time may save a 9- or 10-pounder.

Hook, Line, & Sinker

BALANCED LIVEBAIT RIGS AND COMPONENTS

Livebait rigging for walleyes is filled with little details and small components which, when properly balanced and assembled, add up to big differences in your catch. Don't skimp! Little things mean a lot.

THE FINE POINTS OF HOOKS FOR WALLEYES

If you've been fishing walleyes awhile, chances are your tackle boxes are stuffed with small plastic bags and boxes of miscellaneous hooks in various states of corrosion. Not bad if the rust isn't bad; bad news if the orange crud has taken over. May be time for an early spring cleaning and revamping of your selection and collection.

Today's premium hooks are thinner, lighter, and stronger than those of yesteryear. State-of-the-art manufacturing, tempering, and sharpening turned hook points into touch-at-your-own-risk, razor-sharp weapons. Some are even coated with Teflon or other slick substances to penetrate easily.

Take a normal hook off the pegs at the tackle shop. Now grab a pack of laser or chemically sharpened hooks and compare the points. Pull out one of each and push them into your fingertip, scratch them across your fingernail, or do whatever it is you do to test hooks.

Case closed.

The big advantages to superhooks are on the bite and during the hookset. When a walleye bites and gets one of those sticky, supersharp premium hooks in its mouth, the point penetrates with the least pressure.

The new breed of ultrasharp hooks is certainly more expensive. Imagine dropping a quarter apiece for a #8 crawler hook. But for serious anglers willing to invest in the best to maximize their hookup-to-bite ratio, at least a partial upgrade may be in order. If fishing time is precious, a walleye falling off the hook halfway to the boat is like a sudden plummet in the stock market—you'll eventually recover from that sinking feeling in your stomach, but the short-term return on investment suffers big-time. A couple of bucks in hook insurance isn't out of line, because skimping on hooks can easily cheat the buyer out of a dozen walleyes per pack.

Fortunately, walleye fishermen require only a modest assortment of tiny hooks for livebait presentations. For leeches and crawlers, most anglers prefer octopus or baitholder (barbed shank) hooks, either turned-up (common) or turned-down eye (harder to obtain, but nevertheless excellent) for snelling rigs and harnesses. For small livebaits, #6 and #8 are most popular, with larger #4 and #2 for big fish spinner snells, or for lip-hooking most minnows. If you prefer to tie directly to the eye instead of snelling livebait rigs, a straight-shank (eye turned neither up nor down) version is fine. Some are even available in colors—bronze, black, gold, silver, red, blue, green—

Parts of a Hook

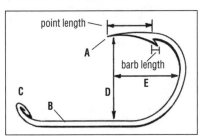

(A) The Point—Must be very sharp. The longer the point, the longer it takes to penetrate. Reduce barbs with a file to ensure quick penetration.

(B) The Bend and Shank—Shank wire gauge and weight and hook size must match line weight. A thick-shanked #1 won't sink past the barb if the hookset is fueled by a light-action rod and 4-pound line. Some steel shanks have less torque or bend during

a hookset. Others bend easily. Which you choose depends on the situation.

(C) The Eye—Eyes are straight, turned down, or turned up. The design determines the knot you use and the rigging application. Turned-up eyes are used for livebait snells, straight eyes for pitching bait coupled with a lead shot. Turned-down eyes are used with crawler rigs.

(D) Hook Gap—Critical. Small gaps don't grab and hold as quickly or efficiently as large gaps. Use the largest gap you can get away with. Bending the base of the shank of a hook out 5 to 10 degrees opens the gap enough on some hooks to improve hookups.

(E) The Throat—It must be just deep enough to allow flesh to pass the barb. Short's better than long for most walleye applications.

for added attraction or reduced visibility, depending on the finish.

Light line aficionados may prefer light wire Aberdeen (O. Mustad's terminology) hooks for finesse presentations with slipbobber or split shot casting rigs. A larger Aberdeen (1/0 or 2/0) makes a good main hook for a spinner-minnow rig. Some slipbobber experts prefer wide-bend Kahle hooks for leeches and crawlers; some riggers like 'em, too, for big minnows. Still, they're in the minority compared to fans of standard octopus bend and baitholder hooks.

The Eagle Claw L787 circle hook is manufactured in sizes #1 through #12 and is useful in baitfishing for walleyes. Similar to Kahles, circle hooks call for no hookset; just start reeling to hook a fish in the corner of the mouth, thereby eliminating fatal deep throat hooking, a common problem when livebait rigging. Circle hooks haven't been used much for walleyes yet, but anglers are obtaining hooksets on up to 95 percent of other freshwater fish. The L787 (sizes 8 to 12) may be an option for bottom bouncer and deadstick tactics, plus fishing with slipfloats.

If you troll open water with crankbaits, you'll see an appreciable difference in landing percentage if you switch from old style thicker, blunter trebles to modern, sticky-sharp trebles like Mustad Triple Grips, Eagle Claw Kahle trebles, VMC Barbarians, or PRADCO Excaliburs, generally #6 or #4 on most walleye crankbaits. One casual touch and they're in to stay, be it a walleye's lip or your finger. Warning! Exercise extreme caution when reaching into your tackle box for a ball of tangled crankbaits or when tossing one crossboat to your buddy. They're painful to the touch. Unhook fish with pliers, and avoid touching hook points, intentionally or unintentionally. They also make good jig stingers in #10 or #8, spinner-crawler harness stingers in #8, #6 or #4.

As you run out of traditional hooks, replace them with premium versions. Investing a few packs at a time won't deplete the bait fund as much as a one-time overhaul. Of course, if you hook more fish, you'll likely waste less bait in the process. A fine point, but a valid one.

Selected Premium Hooks for Walleyes

Model numbers and size ranges (NA—not available in that style)

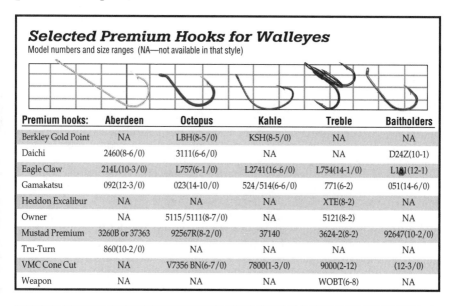

Premium hooks:	Aberdeen	Octopus	Kahle	Treble	Baitholders
Berkley Gold Point	NA	LBH(8-5/0)	KSH(8-5/0)	NA	NA
Daichi	2460(8-6/0)	3111(6-6/0)	NA	NA	D24Z(10-1)
Eagle Claw	214L(10-3/0)	L757(6-1/0)	L2741(16-6/0)	L754(14-1/0)	L181(12-1)
Gamakatsu	092(12-3/0)	023(14-10/0)	524/514(6-6/0)	771(6-2)	051(14-6/0)
Heddon Excalibur	NA	NA	NA	XTE(8-2)	NA
Owner	NA	5115/5111(8-7/0)	NA	5121(8-2)	NA
Mustad Premium	3260B or 37363	92567R(8-2/0)	37140	3624-2(8-2)	92647(10-2/0)
Tru-Turn	860(10-2/0)	NA	NA	NA	NA
VMC Cone Cut	NA	V7356 BN(6-7/0)	7800(1-3/0)	9000(2-12)	(12-3/0)
Weapon	NA	NA	NA	WOBT(6-8)	NA

SINKERS MAY BE STINKERS,
BUT LEAD IS FAR FROM DEAD

With much ado about lead and the environment in recent years and a proposed lead ban for fishing tackle, panic throughout the fishing industry led to hasty development of more environmentally friendly weights. Brass, tin, bismuth, Ultra Steel, and various other alloys and concoctions are now available in limited (and more expensive) sinker selections. Less dense materials that require larger, bulkier shapes to achieve equal sinking power may be better than lead for the environment, but until lead is outlawed, anglers are unlikely to let go of traditional lead sinkers—particularly walleye anglers, who need lead to take livebaits, jigs, spoons, and spinners down into the fish zone and keep 'em there. Without clear and documented evidence that links lead sinkers to aquatic environmental chaos, the dense efficiency and cost effectiveness of lead weights will not go out of style.

Slipsinkers give 'em the slip—Slipsinkers are the heart of livebait rigging presentations. They're used for weighting and sending baited rigs to bottom for drifting or trolling and for feeding line to finicky biters. Slide the sinker on the line, then use a barrel swivel, split shot, or bobber stop to hold it a set distance above your hook, bait, or lure. When a fish strikes, release tension; the line slides backward through a hole in the sinker, and the fish feels no resistance until you set the hook.

Northland Fishing Tackle, Lindy-Little Joe, Let m Run, Quick Change, Walleye Angler, and Cabela's all manufacture or sell some form of walking slipsinker designed to stand up under tension and to skip over rocks. Popular sizes include 1/4, 3/8, and 1/2 ounce, sometimes 1/8 ounce for the shallows or 3/4 ounce for deep water, in either plain lead or fluorescent finishes. Hot colors and easy on-off rigging to change sinker weight or color without retying are recent innovations.

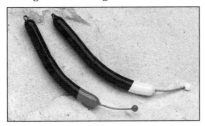

Lindy-Little Joe's No-Snagg Sinker, designed by In-Fisherman co-founder Ron Lindner, is a curved slipsinker with flotation at the top that causes the sinker to pivot and swim around most snags. It costs more than traditional slipsinkers but makes possible fishing in snag-infested waters that were once considered off-limits to conventional sinkers.

Egg sinkers are available in a wider range of sizes and are good alternatives to walking sinkers. Magnum eggs excel for drifting or trolling in deep water, strong wind, or current. Smaller eggs are great for casting and for letting the rig sit stationary while the bait wriggles to tempt fish. Retrieve a few inches before repeating. Bullet sinkers—primarily used for Texas-rigging plastic worms for bass—are also excellent for livebait rigging along or through sparse weeds or wood snags. Some even rattle, adding a bit of potential attraction.

For whom the bell trolls—Bell sinkers, bass casting sinkers, drop sinkers, pyramids, and miscellaneous pencil-shaped weights are traditional casting sinkers adapted to trolling and drifting. In most cases, they originated for casting some variation of a three-way rig from a riverbank and incorporated enough weight to remain stationary on bottom in current. The same rigs are also ideal for drifting or trolling livebait, artificials, or combos of each in strong current or deep water.

On traditional bell sinkers, a wire runs through the weight and ends in a round loop eye for tying the line or attaching a snap. Bass casting sinkers feature a molded-in barrel swivel to minimize line twist. Water Gremlin features bell sinkers with plastic quick clips for traditional attachment. These can also snap over your line and function like slipsinkers. Some have rubber band-style attachments designed to break under heavy pull and sacrifice the sinker to snags while retaining the rig.

Most anglers use traditional bell sinkers (1/2 to 3 ounces) for fishing three-way (Wolf River) rigs with livebait snells, spinner rigs, crankbaits, or flutterspoons. About 1¾ to 2¼ ounces suffice in most cases. In some areas, river anglers have opted for longer, thinner, pencil-shaped weights to minimize line twist in current and to provide enhanced snag resistance in craggy rocks. Plain dull lead finishes are standard. Ever seen a bell with a fluorescent paint job?

Magnum 3-ounce-plus sinkers may be difficult to find at retail outlets other than those in river towns where bank fishing is popular or where deep trolling is common, like the Great Lakes. The best outlets for obtaining heavy lead are catalogs catering to trollers or commercial fishermen. In a pinch, heavy pyramid or bank fishing sinkers suffice, but they're better suited for catfishing or as marker weights.

It trolls for thee—Trolling sinkers basically are in-line weights, tied in-line or attached on-line at a desired position. Traditional trolling sinkers are long, like cylindrical pencil sinkers, but slightly larger at midpoint, tapering to a smaller diameter at each end. They may have simple looped wire tie-ons, snaps or snap-swivels, or swiveling chain attachments (Bead Chain Tackle). Keel sinkers basically are trolling sinkers with finlike projections off one side that function like rudders, minimizing line twist at trolling speeds. They're available in numerous sizes from about 1/2 ounce to over 3 ounces.

Grateful for Lead

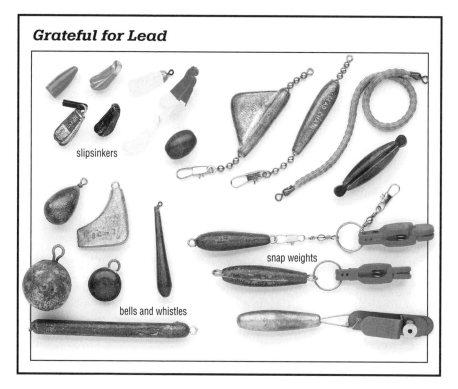

slipsinkers

snap weights

bells and whistles

Several manufacturers offer quick on-off rigging via an internal rubber grip that fits inside a slot in the trolling sinker. Insert your line into the slot, twist the ends of the rubber strip, and it grips your line without actually tying. Twist in the opposite direction to detach. Rubbercor sinkers and their imitators minimize rigging time.

Gotten to the core—Leadcore line functions like a living sinker: an outer core of braided Dacron with a thin, flexible internal filament of lead for weight. Simply reel the line and internal sinker up through the guides and onto the reel. Tie a 50-foot leader of 10-pound-test monofilament ahead of the leadcore to avoid spooking fish with heavy line and to allow your lures to achieve proper action.

Leadcore trolling line comes in 100-yard spools, with every 10 yards a different outer color to mark line. Very simply, the more line out, the deeper your lure runs. With 18-pound-test Cortland or Gudebrod leadcore—popular for walleye trolling—every 10 yards of line weighs about 1 ounce. A large-capacity trolling reel is necessary to handle the bulk of the line needed to sink crankbaits, spoons, or spinners to depths exceeding 50 feet and to hold them there. Trolling more than 30 yards of leadcore, however, tends to sink the average sideplaner. Sometimes sideplaners are trolled with a small amount of segmented leadcore—one, two, or three colors—tied into the main 10-pound-test monofilament line to reach down to 40 feet.

Snap weights—More versatile than leadcore, snap weights are easy on-off fasteners that grip the line without damaging it and hold an attached weight at a specific location, typically 50 feet ahead of a lure for most open water trolling. Run your lure out 50 feet, attach the sinker size of your choice, let out enough additional line to reach the target depth, and troll. When you get a strike, reel in until the sinker comes within reach, then reach up and pop it off the line. Fight in the fish the last 50 feet unencumbered by an in-line weight. Should you wish to change sinker size, simply clip on another snap with a lighter or heavier weight. Best for suspended fish, snap weights may pop off the line when they contact bottom.

Off Shore Tackle Snap Weights dominated the snap weight market for years. The recent addition of Church Tackle's Mister Walleye Super Clip Drop Weights add a nonslip grip clip for use with skinny superlines. Original snap weights grip mono line tightly but may require a second wrap around the clip or a backup snap-swivel attached to the line to prevent the snap weight from popping off superline during a strike.

Most kits come with pencil-shaped or standard trolling sinkers (no bead chain or swivel), but virtually any sinker works with snap weights, including heavyweight 3- to 6-ounce bell or round sinkers. Tight-gripping Wille Zonies can handle heavier sinkers of a pound or more for deep or fast trolling, or in heavy current. Redi-Rig's In-Line-Releaser grips your lure at the desired position, then slides down the line upon strike impact.

Hop, skip, and a bounce—Wire-legged bottom bouncers skip and bounce over rocks, logs, or clean bottom, and excel in situations requiring coverage or snag resistance. They're also used for slow trolling, drifting, and presentations of 3/4 to 2½ mph—fast enough to spin a spinner blade or wobble a minnow-imitating crankbait. To rig up, tie your main line to the bend in the wire form, then attach the looped end of a leader snell—plain, spinner, floater, whatever—to the snap or snap-swivel at the top of the wire arm. The leader stretches back 3 or 4 feet to your bait or lure. Anything longer than that tends to drag a bait on bottom, increasing the possibility of foul-hooking debris or snags.

While 1-, 1½-, and 2-ounce models dominate most drifting or slow trolling

Take Your Best Shot

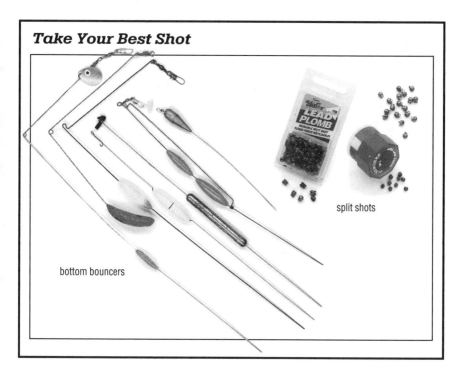

split shots

bottom bouncers

conditions, they're available lighter or heavier, from about 1/2 ounce up to over 3 ounces. Lake trout anglers fish deep water with 6-ounce Gapen Bottom Walkers. Anglers trolling Great Lakes basins for walleyes often skip heavyweight bouncers across bottom, though anything heavier than 3 ounces tends to sink planer boards when multiple lines are trolled.

Bouncers also can be fished almost motionlessly, with just enough line out to touch bottom and dangle bait in front of a fish's face. Use 'em with plain snells (no spinners or hardware) just like livebait rigs. It may not be possible to feed much line to a biting fish, but you can drop your rod tip back toward a biter while the bouncer simultaneously pivots toward the fish to create at least 6 to 10 inches of give before you set the hook.

To feed line to a fish while retaining the snag-resistant features of a bouncer, try a slip bouncer like the Quick Change Lite Bite. Much like a sliding slipsinker, the wire-legged lead weight clips into a clevis that slides down the line until it hits the barrel swivel at the end of the snell, positioning it a set distance ahead of the bait. Got a bite? Now feed all the line you want, so long as the bouncer doesn't topple and fall between cracks. And should you need a bigger bouncer, simply unsnap the first weight from the clevis and insert a heavier version. No retying.

Bouncers come in different wire lengths and thicknesses, depending on the manufacturer. Cabela's and System Tackle offer bouncers with slip-on detachable lead weights for easy weight changes. Bullet Weights and Walleye Angler add a little rattle in their lead-free bouncers so fish can hear 'em comin'. Missouri River Tackle even has bouncers with spinners rotating on the wire shaft for added attraction. Once limited to dull lead finishes from basement manufacturers, bouncers now sport fluorescent orange, yellow, and chartreuse colors from tackle companies like Bait Rigs, Lindy-Little Joe, and Northland.

Pb Freebee

Lead-free sinkers are available in various shapes, but they're less dense, more expensive, and offered in fewer versions than traditional lead.

Split the difference—From the heaviest heavyweights to the tiniest tidbits, lead provides depth control, even in the most subtle situations. For the ultimate in casting stealth, a simple split shot attached to your line about 18 inches ahead of a livebait combines slow sinking stealth with on-bottom fishing. The ultralight-weight shot minimizes snags and avoids spooking light-biting walleyes. Adjusting size and number of split shot fine-tunes the balance of slipbobber rigs, making them barely buoyant bite detectors and hovering livebaits at the desired level. A few shot up the line from a trolled minnow-imitator sends the bait a bit deeper on the troll, reaching the exact depth needed to catch fish.

Carry an assortment of split shot in sizes BB, B, 3/0, and 7/0 for fine-tuning the balance and depth on subtle presentations. Shot like Water Gremlin's removable and reusable split shot have tiny wings to bend the shot open and remove it from your line. Standard round shot is difficult to remove unless you pry it open with a pocketknife. Purists believe round shot reacts truer in shallow river drifting conditions to avoid snags and allow the most natural action. Most steelheaders carry round shot, while walleye anglers use the reusable kind. Serious light line bank fishermen of the Euro persuasion often prefer ultrasoft shot like Dinsmores (available through Cabela's or fly shops) to prevent damaging extra-light line on the pinch—not a bad idea for ultralight ice fishing for panfish. Some brands are billed as nontoxic.

Many walleye-oriented tackle companies offer sinkers in various shapes and sizes, colors, and configurations. Much of the time, however, plain old no-name lead sinkers perform just fine. Carry an assortment for adapting to conditions.

COMPONENTS, FLOATERS, AND ATTRACTORS

Versatile walleye anglers design and refine all manner of livebait rigs, customizing them to best match daily or even hourly conditions. Carrying an assortment of component parts is essential. The following guidelines reflect years of experience collected across a wide array of waters. (Spinners and related components will be covered in Chapter 6.) You'll likely develop additional favorites, color preferences, even unique selections in which you have confidence.

SNAPS, SWIVELS, AND STOPS

Barrel swivels—#10 or #12, most often used to tie slipsinker livebait snells. A swivel prevents a sliding sinker from slipping down the line to the hook. It also creates slip three-way rigs or can be tied in-line to reduce line twist.

Three-way swivels—#8, #7, or #6, for fishing three-way rigs with livebait snells, spinner snells, floater snells, crankbaits, or flutterspoons.

Snaps and snap-swivels—#2 or #3 snaps. Use plain snaps for most applications; use snap-swivels when line twist is a problem. Also use them for attaching and changing drop sinkers without retying. Snap-swivels usually are designated by swivel size, not snap size. For example, a #2 snap and #10 snap-swivel may have the same size snap, and sizes vary slightly by manufacturer. Berkley and Sampo probably dominate the upper end of the swivel market, but many imports are available, and a few specialized clips have applications.

Lindy-Little Joe Swivel Clip—Quick attachment for snells with looped ends.

Berkley Not-a-Knot Fastener—For easy attachment to monofilament without tying a knot or as a dependable attachment for superlines that require special knots. Available on barrel swivels and snap-swivels, too.

Split rings—#0 or #1, sometimes substituted for barrel swivels in livebait rigs. Split-ring pliers help detach rings.

Bobber stops—Neoprene or string bobber stops create adjustable length livebait snells and position beads and spinners a set distance ahead of a trailing livebait hook. A spinner-leech rig, like the Gopher Tackle Joe Fellegy Mille Lacs Long-Line Spinner, works best with the single hook positioned about 2¾ inches behind the beads, rather than tight against them. Don't know why, but the walleyes do.

The Component Connection

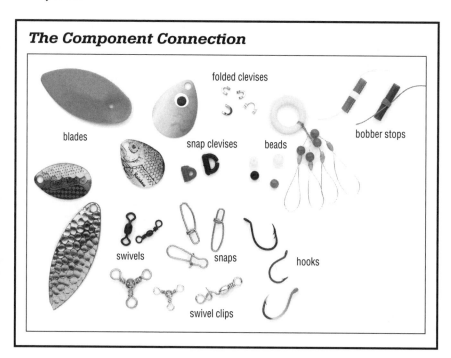

folded clevises

blades

snap clevises   beads

bobber stops

swivels   snaps   hooks

swivel clips

LINE

Extra spools of 4- through 12-pound-test monofilament line, typically thin diameter and limp, like Stren Magnathin, permit livebait to move naturally on slipsinker rigging. If you retie lots of long livebait rigs during a day's fishing, take line from the extra spools instead of from your reel, so you don't empty your reel spool quickly. For spinner rigs, use a tougher, more abrasion-resistant line like Trilene XT, perhaps as heavy as 12- to 17-pound test, unless subtlety and light-weight line are required. If so, check line wear from the clevis and retie often.

ATTRACTORS

Attractors are available in many shapes and sizes, but they can be separated into several broad categories.

Floating jigheads—These started as foam heads, moved on to cork, hollow soft plastic, and other variations. Northland Fishing Tackle's Phelps Floater is a small, soft bodied floater. System Tackle's Bandit and Rattling Bandit are larger. Lindy-Little Joe's Floating Fuzz-E-Grub floats high and is perhaps the largest common walleye float on the market. Stinger Tackle offers weedless Bohn Head floating heads.

Some floating jigheads ride hook up; others ride hook down. Put 'em in the water and check before you hook.

Most floating jigheads don't float well. It's necessary to move slowly, with pauses, in order for them to raise livebait. Many become just colored attractors and are perhaps neutrally buoyant.

Sliding floats—Common with steelheaders, variations of Lil' Corkies have been adapted to walleye fishing. Most walleye-oriented tackle companies offer sliding floats, and catalogs are loaded with options. Round sliding floats tend to

Up and At(tract) 'Em

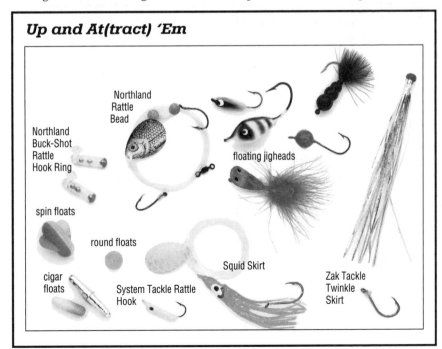

Northland Rattle Bead

Northland Buck-Shot Rattle Hook Ring

floating jigheads

spin floats

round floats

cigar floats

Squid Skirt

System Tackle Rattle Hook

Zak Tackle Twinkle Skirt

be just over 1/4 inch in diameter and come in a rainbow of colors. Cigar-shaped floats are variation on livebait rigs and slide up the line ahead of the hook. Cigars are sometimes incorporated into spinner harnesses called floater spins, adding profile and color and a slowing sink rate when movement stops. String several together (interspersed with beads) to increase flotation and profile, perhaps in color combos imitating whatever the prevailing forage is.

Spinning floats—Originating with salmon and trout anglers, these are now available on some pretied rigs and as add-on components. Triple J's Shake, Rattle & Roll is a spinning, hollow, plastic chamber with rattles. Mister Twister's Walleye Prop is pointed on one end. Apex's SpinBob has a soft, cushy, colorful body that spins.

Tiny spinners—#00 and teeny flikker spinners add a bit of flash on livebait rigs at low speed. The smallest versions of Lerass Leaderspins, placed ahead of livebait and lures, add flash and vibration, particularly on three-way rigs.

Tiny spoons—Spoons like the Bait Rigs Willospoons add a wobbling, swimming action to livebait, casting, or trolling.

Plastic or mylar bodies—Squid bodies on spinners from Quick Change and other companies add profile and action. Insert a Zak Tackle #1033 mylar Twinkle Skirt (with a bead head) to the rearmost bead position of a spinner-nightcrawler harness. Let the reflective silver trailers drape over the crawler and hooks, adding flash and lifelike movement.

Berkley's Power Crawlers are specifically designed to replace live nightcrawlers on spinner rigs, providing an alternative when bait is unavailable or when panfish tear and steal nightcrawlers. Nearly any small plastic tail can be incorporated as an attractor by threading it on a hook.

Hook enhancements—Northland Fishing Tackle's Fire Eye hooks are painted fluorescent colors. Their Buck-Shot Rattle Hook Rings add rattles to hooks, much as their Rattle Jig Rings add sound to jigheads. System Tackle's Rattling Hooker has a tiny bead in a hollow, colored chamber along the hook shank. Soft phosphorescent attractors are basically enlarged silicone bobber stops that slip over the hook shank and glow.

Attractors create a variety of effects, but in the grand scheme of things, they're icing on the cake. Active livebait, proper snell and spinner rig construction, proper sinker size and style, and size and sharpness of hooks are most important.

Prepackaged component kits are available from major walleye tackle manufacturers like Lindy-Little Joe, Northland Fishing Tackle, Quick Change Tackle, and others. Catalog suppliers often have component parts and kits. Kits are a good way to go until you become familiar with sizes and types of parts. Then order specific sizes and models.

LIVEBAIT RIGS—
WRIGGLE, WIGGLE, WOBBLE, JIGGLE

We've looked at components—hooks, lines, sinkers—myriad trinkets in shapes and sizes for specialized conditions. Now let's put 'em all together into productive combinations: popular livebait rigs with track records for catching fish. In many cases, major manufacturers of walleye tackle have taken the fuss and muss out of buying and assembling individual components; they offer pretied rigs with the correct balance of materials—the right size hook tied to the right length of not-too-heavy, not-too-light line, complete with swivel, snap, sinker, spinner, and maybe more. Pretty good choices, most of the time.

At other times, however, you may prefer to tie your own rigs to personal specifications in order to match prevailing conditions more closely or to save money. Most anglers do a little of each. The more serious you are about fine-tuning rigs to match fishing situations, the more likely you'll be to opt for assembling premium components and blending individual ingredients into a recipe for success.

SLIPSINKER LIVEBAIT RIGS

Livebait rigging is a slow, careful, teasing process. Imagine a leech, minnow, or crawler dancing in a walleye's face. You can do it, too, so long as you're in the right spot. You don't have to be a skilled rigger if fish are biting fairly well. But when fish are fussy, nibbling, or just holding onto the bait so your line barely feels heavy, finesse and skill pay off.

The sliding sinker carries your bait to bottom, drifted or trolled, and feeds line to a biting fish. Let the baited rig fall on an open bail, then grab the line with your forefinger to detect sensitive bites. Lift-drop the rig along, backtrolling or drifting, occasionally touching but not dragging bottom. When you feel or suspect a bite, release the line with your finger, allowing the fish to take the bait without feeling unnatural resis-

Selected Pretied Snells

Eagle Claw 139GE—Looped 8-inch snell features red bait holders on 10-pound test.

Eagle Claw L4277—Lazer Sharp Wedding Ring Spinner on 8-inch, 8-pound snell

Gamakatsu 05608 bait holder—7-foot, 8-pound snells in packs of 10

Gamakatsu 09708 Aberdeen snell— 7 feet long on 8-pound line

Mustad Spade-Hook Crawler Harness—3-pack of 7-foot, double-hook snells tied with 224 BLN spade-end hooks on 10-pound test

Owner Walleye Plus snell—6-pack of 6-foot leaders on 6- to 10-pound test with #8, #6, or #2 super needlepoint Feather-Lite hooks and glow-lacquer connection

Finesse rigging with single hooks or spinner rigging with tandem hooks has never been easier or more effective. Most hook companies offer pretied snells with premium hooks and leader lengths up to 7 feet long. Grabbing one out of the pack and tying it to a swivel on the main line reduces knots, saving precious time during a hot bite. Most of these snells come in a variety of line weights, hook sizes, and styles.

tance. No need to give 'em lots of line—just let a little slip through your fingers on slight tension. Then close the spinning reel, take up the slack, and set. Simple, but effective.

When walleyes are tight to bottom, go with about a 4-foot snell, probably with a plain single hook tipped with livebait. If the water's really clear or on electronics the fish appear to be a bit above bottom, switch to a 7- to 9-foot snell. This not only minimizes spooking but also allows the bait to work naturally and to let walleyes see it working. Northland's Roach Rig features an adjustable stop for adjusting snell length instantly without retying. Or make your own.

Six- or 8-pound mono should be sufficient; most commercially made snells are 6-, 8-, or 10-pound test and probably between 30 and 40 inches long. Match hook size to bait size—# 6 for crawlers; #8 for leeches; and # 1 through #4 for minnows, depending on bulk. On premade snells, choose those with the right balance of components for conditions. When fish are really fussy, however, downsize to 4-pound test and a smaller hook, generally with a longer homemade snell.

All walking-style slipsinker rigs work unless snags are horrendous. If so, switch to something more snag resistant, like a bottom-bouncer rig. If wood or weeds present snagging problems, change to a shorter snell, weedless hook, and bullet-style sinker to slither your rig between stalks and sticks. Sliding egg sinkers are good for both backtrolling and casting, while fixed sinker rigs tend to be better for casting, provided they're in castable lengths (that is, less than 3 feet long).

When livebait rigging, most people troll way too fast. Just because you're backtrolling doesn't mean you're moving slow enough. Barely creep along, giving the fish time to respond to your bait. If your leech, crawler, or minnow isn't squirming or swimming naturally, you're moving too fast. Shift into neutral, pause, and let the bait entice the fish. When you spot a fish

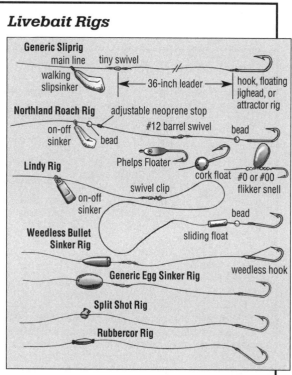

Livebait Rigs

Generic Sliprig
main line   tiny swivel
walking slipsinker   ◄— 36-inch leader —►   hook, floating jighead, or attractor rig

Northland Roach Rig   adjustable neoprene stop
on-off sinker   #12 barrel swivel   bead
bead

Lindy Rig   Phelps Floater
on-off sinker   swivel clip   cork float   #0 or #00 flikker snell
bead
Weedless Bullet Sinker Rig   sliding float
Generic Egg Sinker Rig   weedless hook
Split Shot Rig
Rubbercor Rig

Livebait rigging is used to drift or troll livebait on or near bottom, with frequent pauses to give walleyes a good look at the bait. If a fish strikes, drop the rod tip toward the fish or grudgingly feed it a little line as it swims off. A sliding sinker eliminates weight resistance and gives the walleye extra time to take the bait deeper. Heavier fixed sinkers risk spooking fish when they tentatively inhale the bait and feel unnatural pressure.

on your electronics, lift the rod tip, then pause, hovering and letting the bait rise, then flutter and swim downward, squirming enticingly toward bottom.

Feel is important for detecting light bites and for interpreting bottom conditions. It's possible to feel the difference between rock, sand, mud, gravel, and weeds if you pay attention. Walleyes often lie along edges and transitions in bottom type, so feel for edges—changes—as well as for bites.

Watch your depthfinder. Subtleties in signal interpretation reveal changes in bottom. At first, fish only where you see fish to improve your confidence and your odds. Sit on fish for a while, teasing them with a live meal.

Use a 6- or 6½-foot medium-action graphite spinning rod, 6- or 8-pound-test monofilament, and a prepackaged snell. Then fine-tune if necessary by adding components like floaters for color-action-flotation, tiny flikker spinners for flash-color-vibration, and beads for color.

THREE-WAY RIGS

Three-way rigs catch walleyes in lakes, rivers, and reservoirs, along structure, across open basins, and at different depths. Livebait, plastics, crankbaits, floating jigheads, spinners, flutterspoons, and combos thereof follow the three-way lead.

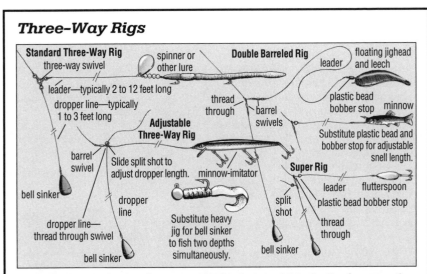

Three-Way Rigs

Standard Three-Way Rig
three-way swivel
leader—typically 2 to 12 feet long
dropper line—typically 1 to 3 feet long
barrel swivel
bell sinker
dropper line—thread through swivel
bell sinker

spinner or other lure

Double Barreled Rig
thread through
barrel swivels

Adjustable Three-Way Rig
Slide split shot to adjust dropper length.
dropper line
minnow-imitator
Substitute heavy jig for bell sinker to fish two depths simultaneously.

floating jighead
leader and leech
plastic bead bobber stop minnow
Substitute plastic bead and bobber stop for adjustable snell length.

Super Rig
leader flutterspoon
split shot plastic bead bobber stop
thread through
bell sinker

Bell sinkers in the 1-to 2-ounce range dominate weight selection for presenting minnows, floating jigheads, or twistertails in current. To troll minnow-imitating crankbaits, it may be necessary to go heavier to compensate for speed. Lake anglers often use three-ways to troll spinner-crawler rigs, but river anglers seldom take advantage of spinner techniques. They work if you hold in place in heavy current or troll upstream, but the spinner blade hangs slack when worked downcurrent, defeating the purpose of the spinner.

Some anglers use a minnow-imitator crankbait, which works equally well for hovering in strong current or trolling upstream. A shallow runner doesn't dive deep enough to snag bottom, suspending just above walleye eye level and wobbling slowly like a minnow hovering in current. Three-way rigging with minnow-imitators, spinner harnesses, or light flutterspoons also is popular on big lakes, though more weight (3 ounces) is needed as depth and speed increase.

The strength of three-ways is their ability to hold livebait or lures just above bottom, regardless of depth, current, or speed. A wide range of bell sinkers, from 1/4 ounce to 5 or 6 ounces, covers all conditions. Simply select the proper size for the job. The heart of the three-way system is the junction formed by the swivel. Three loops provide attachment points for your main line, dropper line, and leader. Varying the length of the dropper line moves a lure or bait closer or farther from bottom. Changing the snell length positions your lure or bait farther or closer to the hardware and affects how far off bottom a presentation runs. In general, the longer the leader, the farther your offering will droop toward bottom unless a float is added to increase its buoyancy. A good rule of thumb is that at normal speeds for most walleye presentations—1/2 to 2½ mph—a spinner or other lure sinks from 1/8 to 1/5 the length of the leader below the horizontal. Thus, a 5-foot leader may run as much as 1 foot below the swivel, more or less.

The strength of three-ways is their ability to hold livebait or lures just above bottom, regardless of depth, current, or speed.

Misconception #1 about three-ways is that they're not forgiving, like livebait rigs; you supposedly can't feed line to a fussy biter. Not so. When a fish strikes, just drop your rod tip back toward the fish. The whole rig collapses toward the critter, providing momentary slack until the fish pulls line directly between the hook and sinker. By then, you've had plenty of opportunity to set the hook.

Misconception #2 is that they're snaggy. Some truth to that, especially on rock or wood bottoms, but they're great for open basins. Best bet for snags is to use lighter line on the dropper. When you snag, a strong pull breaks the dropper, so you lose only the sinker while retaining the lure. Also, keep leaders short to prevent dragging bottom or wrapping around wood- or weedcover.

Misconception #3 is that three-ways work only within 2 or 3 feet of bottom. Definitely wrong. Tie the dropper as long as you wish, anywhere from a typical 1 to 3 feet (keep it short—12 to 15 inches— for rivers), up to 10 feet or more to position baits way off bottom. How to net fish with such a long dropper? Just leave the sinker dangling in the water while you net the fish.

The ultimate in versatility comes from an adjustable three-way that doesn't even require a three-way swivel. Instead, tie a standard barrel swivel between your main line and leader. Next, thread a long dropper line up through one of the loops of the swivel and clamp a split shot somewhere on the dropper line opposite the sinker and swivel. The split shot functions as a bobber stop. It sets the distance your swivel rides above bottom at the depth of your lure or bait. To adjust its level above bottom, simply slide the split shot up or down the dropper—an easy variable to tinker with. And should you snag, a firm pull will slide the split shot off your dropper line so that once again you lose only the drop sinker.

Want the ability to feed even more line with a three-way? Tie a double barreled rig. First, tie a standard dropper line and weight to one loop of a barrel swivel. Next, thread your main line through the opposite loop of the swivel, then tie it to a second swivel connected to your leader. Bingo—a slipsinker three-way rig. Feed a fussy biter as much line as you wish. Substitute a bobber stop and bead for the second swivel, and you can easily adjust leader length as well.

Combine all aspects of adjustability to make an adjustable snell-length, variable dropper-length rig. Rather than trying to explain, check the Super Rig figure.

Three-way rigs and bottom bouncers work best with about a 6- or 6½-foot casting rod, a flippin' reel, and 10-pound-test mono. Hit the thumb bar to release line, and drop the rig to bottom. Then lift you thumb to automatically re-engage the reel. No need to take your other hand off the motor to turn the reel handle.

BOTTOM-BOUNCER RIGS

Bottom bouncers combine the characteristics of slipsinker and three-way rigs with added snag resistance. Basically, they use the same snells on wire-legged sinkers that skip over rocks, climb up and down slopes and across basins, and position bait a few inches off bottom.

While most folks use bouncers with spinner snells, drifting or trolling at paces fast enough to rotate their blades, bouncer rigs also excel at slower speeds with plain baited hooks, floats, or floating jigheads, or with tiny flutterspoons. Keep snells shorter than about 40 inches to minimize snags. While most bouncers don't slip, you can simply point the rod tip back at a biting fish, then sweepset forward to give the fish a half heartbeat of extra time before you set the hook. If fish are fussy, switch to a slip bouncer like the Gopher Stik or Quick Change Lite Bite.

Unlike prepackaged slipsinker rigs, which come complete with snells, sinkers, and components, bouncers are sold without snells. For three-ways, buy prepackaged snells but construct the rigging to go with them.

SPLIT SHOT RIGS

The effectiveness of split shot rigging with livebait for shallow walleyes was popularized almost 30 years ago in *Nightcrawler Secrets*, a book published by *Fishing Facts* magazine. It's so effective and so simple that in today's high-tech fish-

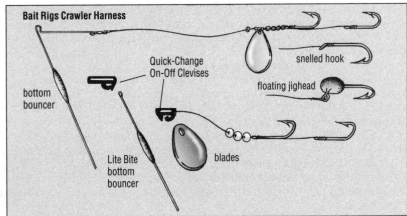

Bottom-Bouncer Rigs

Bait Rigs Crawler Harness

Quick-Change On-Off Clevises

bottom bouncer

snelled hook

floating jighead

Lite Bite bottom bouncer

blades

In general, bouncers are best for situations requiring coverage or snag resistance—slow trolling, drifting, or presentations of 3/4 to 2 1/2 mph, fast enough to spin a spinner blade or wobble a minnow-imitator crankbait, generally on or near bottom. Traditional livebait slipsinkers tend to perform better below that range. And three-ways are better for faster speeds or for presenting baits farther off bottom. Each system has its strengths and weaknesses.

Bouncers present nearly any form of livebait rig, but they should likely be shorter than 40 inches to prevent drooping and snagging bottom debris.

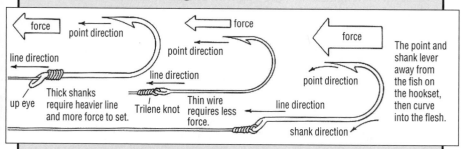

Force In Hooksetting

force
point direction
line direction
up eye
Thick shanks require heavier line and more force to set.
Trilene knot

force
point direction
line direction
Thin wire requires less force.

force
point direction
line direction
shank direction
The point and shank lever away from the fish on the hookset, then curve into the flesh.

Up-eye hooks must be snelled to create direct pull, where line and hook point move in the same direction. On straight-eye hooks, tie directly with your favorite knot.

ing environs, it's often forgotten.

Tie on a hook. Lightly crimp on a split shot 12 inches to 4 feet up the line. Done deal. Slip on some bait, and pitch, drift, or troll in a slow zigzag pattern over the shallow flats that walleyes use this time of year. Nothing can be simpler in water 10 feet or shallower.

Split shot rigs troll nicely, but depending on where fish are located, you may prefer drifting. Position the boat sideways with a drift sock to cover a wider swath. In heavy wind, try backtrolling, while in a light breeze, try trolling with the bow-mount trolling motor. In emerging weeds, pitching is an option. Split shot rigs are just as versatile as jigging in shallow water and often outproduce jigs at this time of year, especially during tough bites. In clear water with little wind, when the fish are shallow but difficult to approach, split shot rigs consistently outproduce everything else. They're the first choice whenever conditions include clear water, bright sun, or calm conditions.

Split shot rigs must be fished slower than jigs. Minnows tend to move more freely, and leeches or crawlers have time to work at a slower pace. Fish them slow, but not necessarily on bottom. With lighter shot, swim these rigs slowly off bottom over developing weeds or woodcover. Pace is the key. Move slowly to let the bait do its thing. Split shot with any bait—crawlers, leeches, or minnows—but don't inject crawlers with air at this time of year, because the idea is to swim the bait naturally off bottom most of the time.

That means balancing tackle to conditions. Heavy wind and short lines require heavier shot, maybe 1/8 ounce or more, placed 12 to 18 inches up the line. Calm conditions call for long lines, up to 100 feet or so behind the boat, with a single BB placed 4 feet up the line. Play with the weight, based on wind and depth, in order to stay close to bottom without punching bottom, swimming the bait along slowly.

The trick is to move slowly with the right amount of line out to touch bottom occasionally. If the combo's running perfectly, it should begin to drag with 2 or 3 more feet of line out. The deeper the water, the farther the split shot should be from the hook, allowing the bait to move. Place it as close as 8 to 18 inches in shallow water, and 2 to 4 feet in 6 to 10 feet of water, to give minnows more freedom to swim, crawlers more space to undulate in. On dead calm days, try feeding out the bait and trolling it without any weight at all, just the weight of the hook.

No matter the conditions, shallow water walleyes are always spookier than deeper fish. Have at least 50 feet of line out. At 100 feet, however, you lose control of the rig. Feeling out the conditions to create that proper blend of weight, distance, line strength, and leader length is a daily matter. And because shallow walleyes are spooky, light line is better than heavy most days.

Light line in this case is 4-pound test. In light wind on sunny days, it's crucial to go light. Walleyes are line shy, and more bites come on lighter line. Beef up to 8-pound line in heavy cover. But day in and day out, you get more bites with lighter line.

In the shallows, a simple bronze hook baited with something lively works best most of the time. Use the lightest wire hook possible, such as a Mustad Finesse or an Eagle Claw Featherlite. Thin wire sets much easier on light line.

Long 6½- to 7½-foot rods are key to this presentation. Split shot rods are a little softer in the tip than jigging rods. Fish must be able to take the bait and hold on without feeling you. A longer rod allows more control of bait, line, and fish. Use a medium-action and medium- or medium-light-power rod to protect 4-pound line.

OPEN WATER TROLLING HARNESSES

While open water trolling for suspended fish using snap weights or leadcore to reach desired depths, walleye pros often switch the rear single hook of a crawler harness to a larger premium treble. Sometimes they switch the front hook, too, to provide extra hooking power. So long as you're not near bottom and in no danger of snagging or picking up debris, why not? P/K Tackle's Open Water Spinner and Bait Rig's Big Water Rig offer twin treble arrangements for oversized spinners. Or make your own.

That's why it's called rigging.

DE HOOKING OF DE BAIT DEBATE

"Through the sucker? behind the collar? by the tail?" Oft-repeated questions heard daily in North America's finer bait shops. Walleye anglers everywhere use livebait or livebait-lure combinations for most of their walleye angling.

When to use livebait? How to hook it? And why? The three most often asked questions. Every rule has exceptions, but we're establishing here the basic, time-proven methods for hooking livebait.

First, make sure the bait is lively. To increase your odds considerably, search out fresh, well kept bait. For example, leeches kept in a tank with fresh flowing water almost always are more hyper on the hook than packaged leeches stored in a cooler.

Ask how long a batch of minnows has been in the tank. Check nightcrawlers for firmness. After purchase, keep leeches and crawlers surrounded by ice, and keep minnows in fresh water. In 90°F air temperatures, bait reaches a terminal condition in just a few hours.

Minnows can be fished on jigs, rigs, and spinners. For best results, carefully hook them in nonvital areas. A lively, naturally swimming bait almost always outproduces a terminally hooked bait.

A minnow hooked lightly through the lips presents the most natural profile on a jig, because it appears to swim behind the lure in a chasing fashion. Hook minnows in this manner unless repeated casting or ripping through weedcover tears them off the hook. In this case, hook the minnow up through the lower jaw and out through the top of the skull. This kills the minnow but creates a more workable bait. Change minnows frequently to keep fresh ones on the hook.

When trolling a minnow on a livebait rig, match the hook to the size of the minnow. A short-shank, light wire #6 hook allows a lip-hooked 3-inch fathead to

---

Hooking Up–Hook Size and Location

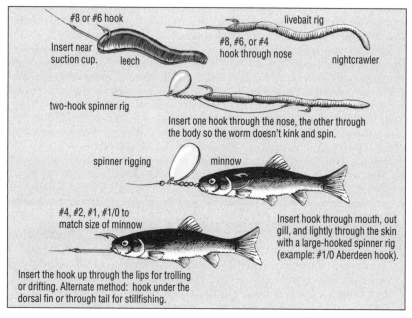

#8 or #6 hook

Insert near suction cup.   leech

livebait rig

#8, #6, or #4 hook through nose

nightcrawler

two-hook spinner rig

Insert one hook through the nose, the other through the body so the worm doesn't kink and spin.

spinner rigging   minnow

#4, #2, #1, #1/0 to match size of minnow

Insert hook through mouth, out gill, and lightly through the skin with a large-hooked spinner rig (example: #1/0 Aberdeen hook).

Insert the hook up through the lips for trolling or drifting. Alternate method: hook under the dorsal fin or through tail for stillfishing.

swim freely. To fish a bigger bait like a chub, a #4 or even a #2 may be necessary to provide sufficient hook gap. A hook too heavy fatigues the bait and rapidly diminishes its effectiveness.

When hovering or fishing slowly for walleyes, reverse-hooking the minnow just in front of the tail often triggers nonaggressive fish. When the sinker's at rest, the minnow attempts to swim away from the weight, struggling against the restraint and sending out the message that it's vulnerable to attack. This can be especially productive in late summer and fall, when walleyes tend to school in deep water.

Fast-track presentations, like power trolling a spinner with a minnow, offer several hooking options. In most cases, small to medium minnows produce the best results behind a spinner.

Lip-hook a minnow on a #4 or #2 short-shank hook for aggressive 'eyes, or increase hooking odds by using a #2 light wire Aberdeen-style (long shank) hook inserted through

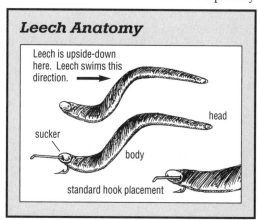

Leech Anatomy

Leech is upside-down here. Leech swims this direction.

head

sucker

body

standard hook placement

the mouth, out the gill, and nicked through the skin in front of the dorsal fin. Pull the minnow through the water next to the boat to make sure it's swimming behind the spinner, not rolling.

Properly rigged leeches often are irresistible to walleyes. Always use a short-shank #6, #8, or #10 hook, depending on leech size. Hooking a leech once through the sucker and out the back allows it to swim and wriggle. Use a similar hookup with a slipbobber to maximize the leech's natural swimming motion.

When casting a jig, try double hooking the leech by penetrating its back downward behind the sucker, threading the hook point toward the tail for 1/4 inch, then up and out the back again. This keeps the leech on the hook while still allowing free movement. While leeches can be fished on spinner rigs, we've rarely found them more effective than minnows or crawlers.

And finally, the most delicate of livebait options: nightcrawlers. "Squeeze 'em by the ears until they open their mouths"—the point being that taking the time to conceal the hook in a crawler will put more fish on your line.

For fishing crawlers on a jig, a long shank hook with a bait keeper barb is preferable. Thread the hook through the opening at the dark end (nose) of the crawler,

Reverse Crawler Rigging

Sneak up on that old trickster Al Lindner, and you may find he does some things backwards. Crawler rigging, for example. "Everyone rigs a crawler so it runs head first," he observes. "That's fine for spinner rigging and most other situations. But for straight rigging (Lindy Rigging), sometimes it works as well or better to run the hook through the tail instead of the head. The bait exhibits an entirely different action when you stop and let it sit. You need a lively crawler, of course. And add just a bubble or two of air if you're injecting the crawler; don't blow it up like a balloon."

He reminds anglers that lively crawlers can also be hooked through the ring, again to add a different action to the bait when it sits in place after being pulled forward. "Moving along with a livebait rig covers water to find fish," he says. "But walleyes most often are triggered during a pause phase that some anglers don't even incorporate into their rigging repertoire. Big mistake. I give walleyes a second or two longer to eat a reverse crawler, surmising that some fish might still nip the crawler at the head end. It's vital, I think, to add a bead ahead of the hook to focus the fish's attention there."

Experiment with different ways to hook a livebait, no matter the bait.

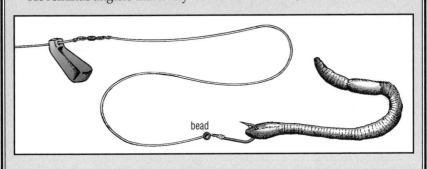

bead

bringing the hook out just in front of the collar. Then squeeze the nose end of the crawler over the bait keeper barb to hold it in place.

In short strike situations, add a single hook on a short mono line, threading and burying it toward the crawler's tail. Or break a crawler in half, using the dark end with the collar. Thread it on the jig through the broken end, leaving the more durable dark end hanging off the hook.

For livebait rigging, thread the crawler on a #4 or #6 light wire Aberdeen hook, then squeeze the nose over the hook eye, leaving only the barb protruding in front of the collar. Inject a little air to float your crawler for a stealthy presentation that will follow your line through the water rather than rolling and twisting, as lines do when crawlers are hooked off center.

Another option is a #8 or #6 short-shank hook looped through the middle of the crawler, which creates a twin-tail presentation to hover in front of a walleye's nose. Some anglers use a similar hookup when casting jigs.

When pulling a spinner with a crawler, thread its dark nose onto the customary #6 or #8 short-shank harness hook, then bury the trailer hook just far enough back to allow the crawler to stretch out straight. Set too far back or rigged on an offset nose hook, the crawler can cause a rolling action you want to avoid.

One final tip concerning hooks: the new generation of supersharp hooks allows for better penetration with smaller diameter, lighter hooks. Experience says that these premium hooks are well worth their additional cost.

Next time you go walleye fishing, pay a little extra attention to de hooking of de bait.

FINESSE RIGGING DETAILS
PUT THE FINE IN FINESSE

Livebait rigs consist of hook, line, and sinker. What could be simpler? Still, if livebait rigging is such a no-talent drag, then why do some riggers consistently outproduce the rest of the crowd?

Like everything else in fishing, attention to detail in rigging improves effectiveness and increases your catch. Fishing is a percentage game, and the more you enhance your odds a few percentage points here, a few there, the more likely you'll win the competition between angler and fish.

Details like matching snell length and hook size separate the veteran livebait rigger from the bait dragger. Don't cut corners. A balanced rig that presents lively bait on the fish's nose is a thing of beauty. A half-dead minnow towed around on heavy line, on the other hand, begs for a skunking.

QUEST FOR FINESSE

Sometimes anything less than finesse won't do. Cold fronts send walleyes into hibernation or at least reduce their enthusiasm for feeding. Fishing pressure makes them spooky—too many rigs dancing along the drop-off, too many of their buddies disappearing. Clear water accentuates the unnatural aspects of poor presentations to predatory 'eyes.

Livebait triggers strikes because it is unfettered by restrictions on its swimming motions. Baits shouldn't be towed; they should swim through the water, exhibiting natural fish-attracting traits. They should be moved slowly or held motionless, if necessary, to give them time to work their magic and to trigger responses.

Fall is a particularly appropriate time of year for livebait rigging, because deep water walleyes must be worked precisely, in pinpoint locations, with little wasted

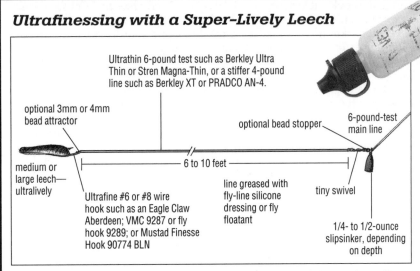

Ultrafinessing with a Super-Lively Leech

Ultrathin 6-pound test such as Berkley Ultra Thin or Stren Magna-Thin, or a stiffer 4-pound line such as Berkley XT or PRADCO AN-4.

optional 3mm or 4mm bead attractor

optional bead stopper

6-pound-test main line

medium or large leech— ultralively

6 to 10 feet

Ultrafine #6 or #8 wire hook such as an Eagle Claw Aberdeen; VMC 9287 or fly hook 9289; or Mustad Finesse Hook 90774 BLN

line greased with fly-line silicone dressing or fly floatant

tiny swivel

1/4- to 1/2-ounce slipsinker, depending on depth

A super-lively medium leech is one of the most seductive of all baits for walleyes conditioned to other baits and standard rigging systems. The key is to use rigging components that allow a superleech to do its ultralively thing. Besides the components outlined here, the key, according to Al Lindner, is a silicone fly-line dressing rubbed on the snell line to make it float slightly. Most mono sinks, making it slightly more difficult for a leech to do its thing.

effort. That's the strength of livebait rigging—lively critters down there working for you 100 percent of the time. Big livebaits often are needed to trigger big fish, and there's no better way to do it than to present large chubs or shiners on finesse snells. Stick them in the fish's face and let them wiggle, panic, entice, and trigger a bite. Patience and natural attraction are a dynamic combo, producing many of the largest walleyes of the year.

BALANCING ACT

Tailor snell length to conditions. Short 2- to 3-foot snells minimize bait mobility and reduce snags in timber or weedcover. Longer snells separate bait from sinker, theoretically enhancing the bait's natural appearance and permitting a greater range of motion. Ten to 12 feet isn't unusual for finesse presentations, but typical, easy-to-use 3- to 6-foot snells suit most conditions. Long snells allow baits dressed on floating jigheads to rise a bit off bottom, if you move slowly with frequent pauses and use sufficiently buoyant floaters on those long snells. Long snells, however, complicate hooksets and increase the challenge of landing fish with a net.

In most instances, a plain hook baited with a leech, crawler, or minnow performs best. Match hooks to bait size and type. Small octopus or baitholder-style hooks or light wire Aberdeens typically work well with leeches and crawlers—about a #6 for crawlers hooked lightly through the nose and a #8 for leeches hooked through or slightly behind the suction cup. Using larger hooks diminishes the natural action of these tempting morsels. Pause during trolling passes occasionally to let baits squiggle and wiggle—treats too good to ignore.

For coldwater fall fishing, minnows generally are en vogue; fairly large minnows, in fact, like 4- to 6-inch chubs, shiners, or suckers. Minnows require larger hooks to compensate for their bulk; the bigger the minnow, the larger the hook gap is needed to prevent the hook from sliding through a walleye's mouth on the hookset. Appropriate hooks bite and hold but don't reduce minnows' natural swimming action. Generally, hook a minnow up through both lips with a hook ranging from about a #4 through #1. Slowly backtroll the minnow along dropoffs or through concentrations of fish, using frequent pauses to allow the bait to swim and struggle, potentially triggering walleyes.

When you spot fish that don't bite on the first or second pass, try tail-hooking the minnow to tease fish into biting. Insert the point of the hook through the tail between the dorsal and tail fin. While this would result in unnatural motion if you were drifting or trolling, at rest it allows the minnow to swim away from the sinker. Hover over the fish, let the minnow attempt to swim away from the sinker, and wait for a pickup. This is a great presentation for reluctant fish that don't attack bait on the first pass.

Match sinker size and style to conditions, too. Traditional walking slipsinkers perform best in rocks or on smooth bottom, but they tend to pick up weeds. Bullet sinkers perform best along weed or timber edges, sliding through or over obstructions. Team them with short snells and weedless single hooks. Egg sinkers are good compromises of both versions, because they allow you to fish effectively in most conditions. Plain lead finishes are often best in clear water, while fluorescent orange or yellow versions add a bit of attraction in stained or dirty water. Same for hooks: dull finishes for clear water, bright finishes for dark water. Or thread a small colored plastic bead on the line ahead of the hook to

Mixing up Those Minnows

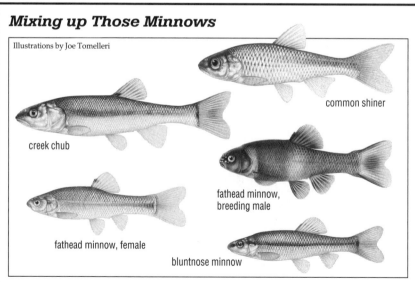

Illustrations by Joe Tomelleri

common shiner

creek chub

fathead minnow, breeding male

fathead minnow, female

bluntnose minnow

Try something different. Sometimes minnow size triggers a different response. Other times, a switch from one minnow species to another is what counts. Sometimes, too, even the sex of the minnow in question makes the difference between getting bit and not getting bit.

focus the fish's attention.

While most folks use slipsinkers for livebait rigging, bottom bouncers or three-way rigs accomplish much the same thing—particularly when rigged as sliprigs for feeding line to fussy biters. Slip three-ways can be rigged with heavy sinkers for deep water, while slip bouncers minimize snags among boulders. Heavy weights of an ounce or more generally require casting tackle and about 10-pound test to withstand the strain. Otherwise, use traditional rigging rods that fall in the medium-action spinning category, ranging somewhere from 6 to 7 feet long, depending on personal preference. Consider using softer actions if you prefer no-stretch superlines; limper rods absorb shock and prevent line breakage.

BOAT CONTROL

Don't just find the first drop-off on the lake and start trolling along it. Begin by looking for and locating fish to determine productive depths and orientation to structure. Locate prominent areas like points, humps, weededges—typical feeding and holding areas for walleyes. Then search edges with electronics, noting irregularities in drop-offs and sections that attract fish. Fall often calls for fishing deep water, and spotting fish is usually much faster than fishing for them. Once walleyes are spotted, match your presentation to their depth and location.

Ideally, slowly backtroll with a transom electric motor (or bowmount electric on larger boats), maneuvering along the edges of structure, following contours with your baits. Move slowly enough to keep your lines as vertical as possible in order to maximize control and sense of feel. You want your bait below the boat in the transducer cone, where you can see both fish and bottom. If the wind kicks up, backtroll with your tiller outboard if necessary or use a combo of a big console engine with one or two sea anchors to maintain boat control. Maintaining bottom contact and sense of feel, and interpreting changes in bottom conditions

Steep and Deep

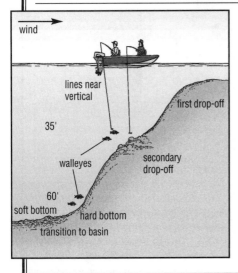

Some structures have more than one possible concentration level. Here, the secondary drop-off at 35 feet offers excellent fish-holding potential. Also try the deep transition to the basin somewhere between 50 and 60 feet.

Use electronics and your sense of feel to determine where fish are present. Then drop baited lines down to them. Keep your lines nearly vertical to maximize feel and hooksetting ability. Move slowly with frequent pauses to give walleyes time to react to the bait's natural attraction. Patience and lively minnows often trigger even the most lethargic hawgs. A great pattern for the largest walleyes in the lake!

are paramount to success.
Lift and hold your sinker slightly off bottom most of the time, keeping the bait near bottom to avoid snags. Dip the sinker down every few seconds to reconfirm that it's near bottom and to feel for changes, such as transitions from rock to sand or mud. In fall, deep fish like to lie along changes in bottom—for example, where the harder bottom of a drop-off joins the softer bottom of the basin, often as deep as 30 to 50 feet. Pay particular attention to such changes along prominent points because they gather walleyes.

Don't hurry if you see fish on your electronics. Hover in limited areas, working and reworking fish. Backtroll upwind, control drift downwind, and saturate the area with lively livebait. Change the direction of your trolling path if necessary, moving up and down the drop-off rather than back and forth along it. Show the fish something different from other rigs in the area. Patience is key. If fish are aggressive, they'll bang a minnow right away. If not, you may have to spend several minutes letting the minnow wiggle in their faces before triggering a bite. The biggest mistake is to breeze through good spots too quickly. Give 'em as much time as necessary in order to trigger a response.

Boat control is key. Boat movement positions the bait. What you do on the surface is mirrored by what occurs below.

The Beadmeister

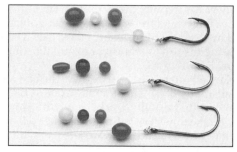

According to Al Lindner, it's almost impossible to hurt a fine-tuned livebait presentation by the addition of a bead just ahead of a bait. But the additional bead, usually in chartreuse, hot orange, pink, or phosphorescent, is often responsible for ever so barely catching a walleye or smallmouth's eye and triggering a bite. When in doubt, "bead on." The standard bead shape and size is a round 5mm or an oval 5x7mm. Experiment, though. Bead sizes range from 3mm to 8mm in a round style, 3x6mm to 7x10mm in oval. Stamina Tackle (800/546-8922) and Netcraft (800/NETCRAFT) offer beads.

OBSERVE, INTERPRET, REACT

The ability to interpret what walleyes are doing, trigger and sense strikes, and even set the hook properly complete your final connection to deep water rigging for walleyes.

When to set the hook? Depends on what you feel. A solid strike, with the fish sitting still? Probably engulfed the minnow—even a big bait. Tighten up slack with your rod tip pointed at the fish, then sweepset home.

Minor run, followed by a stop? Fish probably needs a bit of time to reposition the bait. Grudgingly feed a little line during the run by spilling a few loops of line off your index finger. Then engage the reel and begin taking up slack as you slowly follow the fish, repositioning the boat above it. Once the slack's out, set firmly.

A long fast run after the strike indicates competition; the fish hustled away before his buddies could snatch the bait. Good—more fish are around. Let some line spool off during the run, then engage the reel again, slowly motor back above the fish while taking up slack, and set the hook once you're in position. When's that? When you lift and feel your sinker slip down the line and tap the swivel. A tap or sudden weight, followed by a few reluctant chews? Chances are the walleye has the minnow by the tail. Strip off a few feet of line, regrasp it with your index finger, and feel what's happening. If nothing occurs, ever so slightly lift the rod tip to put a little pressure on the fish. Then back off. Try to trigger a reaction, causing the fish to regrasp or engulf the minnow. Repeat if necessary until you think it's OK to set.

How 'bout when the fish grabs the bait and runs from the drop-off to a suspended position? That's a tough one. You can try setting the hook during the run, but that usually works only with smaller leeches or crawlers. Big minnows take time. Try letting some line spill off the bail, then engage the reel and slowly move the boat toward the fish while gingerly taking up line. Lift, reel down, move. Repeat.

After lifting and sliding the sinker down the line a few times, you finally reach a point at which you begin lifting the sinker off bottom. Decision time. Set the hook? . . . or be courageous and continue slowly moving toward the fish, lifting and sliding the sinker down the line, even though the fish can begin to feel the tug of the suspended weight? When you feel the sinker tap the swivel or run out of nerve and fear you'll spook the walleye, sweepset the hook home. With luck, you've reduced the slack enough to get a good set.

What's a good set? When you sweep upward and are stopped by a tight connection to a throbbing behemoth on the other end. Great feeling. Some anglers prefer setting the drag to slip on a good hookset—set, pick up slack, wind down, and set again until you hear the drag slip. Use whichever method you prefer. Just don't try setting hooks in deep water immediately after a fish runs any distance, because the resulting slack reduces hooksetting force. Reducing the distance between yourself and your quarry increases the odds for hook penetration.

Details not only put the *fine* in finesse, but also put fins in the net.

WALLEYES TIMES THREE

"At times, three-way rigs absolutely work better than livebait rigs or jigs," Al Lindner insists. "It's not rare. Probably even equal to a jig as a universal walleye presentation. I *always* carry a rod rigged with a three-way. I troll first, jig or rig later. My first pass is with three-way rigging, in all conditions, any time of year. I'm startled to hear myself say it," Al says.

Why does three-way rigging work so well?

"When I see fish (on sonar) 3 to 6 feet off bottom, I can use a 4- to 6- or 7-foot dropper to the weight. I can put the bait right there in a fish's face. If they're 2 feet up, I nip the dropper down to 3 feet. With a 5-foot leader to a minnowbait, the lure dives about 1 foot. It's in the fish's face, instead of in and out of its view.

"A 2- to 3-foot dropper's standard. The lure shouldn't be pounding bottom. Up 1 or 2 feet off bottom is optimum most of the time. Unless you see fish higher than 2 feet, assume a 2- to 3-foot dropper will work."

Can you present livebait with three-way rigging?

"A three-way fishes everything. Works with spinners and crawlers. Works with floating jigs and leeches. Still covers territory faster than a bottom bouncer.

"Use the same basic rigging to present a leech on a bare hook to finicky fish. Tie the dropper to a barrel swivel and slide the swivel onto your main line. Tie another

Where Three-Way Rigging Works

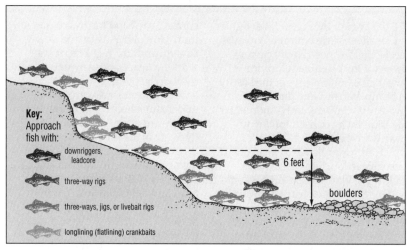

Key:
Approach fish with:

downriggers, leadcore

three-way rigs

three-ways, jigs, or livebait rigs

longlining (flatlining) crankbaits

6 feet

boulders

Three-way rigging is most effective in water deeper than 15 feet, where structure allows the rig to be walked along bottom or up and down slopes. This rigging works best for walleyes in the 6-foot zone just above bottom, including bottom-hugging fish usually considered rig or jig fish.

barrel swivel to the end of the main line to stop the sliding swivel and dropper. Tie a leader from 24 inches to 6 feet or longer to the swivel on the main line.

"Once a fish takes, give line by dropping your rod tip toward the fish before the fish feels the weight. You can even feed line to the fish, although I seldom do. Most important, you can present the bait at the fish's level whenever walleyes are within about 6 feet of bottom.

"No better way exists to present a floating jig tipped with a leech or minnow, especially when anchored or hovering in river current, with the bait bobbing up and down in the flow. Or when using a floating jighead to trigger fish on the rise. Pause, and the bait rises. Most baits rise slowly and are pinned near bottom when they're moved along on a typical slipsinker rig. But make the dropper just the right length, and the jig starts rising right in the fish's face and drifts slightly above the fish on the pause. Move the bait, and it stays right at walleye level."

Are you limited by depth?

"Yes, on the shallow end. I don't work three-ways much shallower than 15 feet. At that point, other quick coverage methods become as efficient or more so—longlining, snap-on boards, or casting crankbaits. The way I approach it, this is a middepth to deep water rigging system. Of course, you can use lighter weight, get the bait farther from the boat, slow down a bit, and do well."

Other problems?

"Rocky terrain's a problem. Running almost vertically helps because your sinker is in and out of the rocks right away. Try a breakaway sinker or a straight wire bottom bouncer rigged on a three-way."

RIGGING AND TECHNIQUE

"A 3-ounce weight works from 20 to 50 feet deep," Al says. "I can make that

Three-Ways in Rivers

The greater the current, the tighter walleyes hug bottom. Walleyes seek "dead zones" where current slows. One prominent location is where the bottom rises at the base of a hump, bar, or wing dam. Here, water hits the base and is momentarily trapped by current forcing its way over the obstruction.

Dead zones also exist just behind an obstruction, just beyond and below the lip of a drop-off, and anywhere that shore obstruction protrudes into current, causing the current to slow and reverse itself. Productive dead zones are almost always near current, as opposed to the center of a large eddy or hole— although these spots hold fish, too.

Three-way rigging can be used to walk a lure precisely up and down a slope. Hold the rod, don't holster it. Reel in on the upslope, thumb the flippin' switch going down.

Having checked for dead zones and other holding areas, plot an upstream course for forward trolling. Try to run along the same contour. Control is best when you're moving upstream. Stall the boat, hovering on spots to let current work the lure.

Or quarter, moving up and across current, back and forth across a contour. Don't hesitate to troll downstream, though. Just keep lures working near bottom by using about a 2-foot dropper.

Al wants to start with the big midchannel hole. "Start along the shoreward edge," he says. "Zigzag the edge of the hole. Then troll down through the center. Take a swing along the midstream edge. Use a few quartering passes at the head and tail of the hole, the most prominent place for walleyes to hold. Hover there with the nose of the boat pointing into current. Then slowly quarter back and forth across the face of the hole.

"Move to the gravel bar after running along the front face of the wing dam. The gravel bar offers the most habitat and the largest area to cover. Hit the eddy behind the wing dam. Make another run along the face of the wing dam. Move to the hump.

"If fish are wired tight to a spot— say, a portion of wing dam or the tail of the hole—go back, anchor, and jig. But troll first. Find the heaviest concentrations and milk them for active fish. Then jig. On some days, the jigging rod stays in the locker, even in 34°F water."

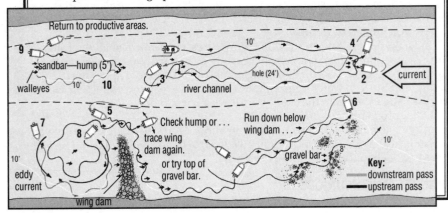

Return to productive areas.

9

sandbar—hump (5')

walleyes 10' 10

1

10'

4

3

hole (24')

river channel

2

current

5

Check hump or ...

trace wing dam again.

or try top of gravel bar.

6

Run down below wing dam ...

gravel bar

10'

8'

7

8

10'

eddy current

wing dam

Key:
downstream pass
upstream pass

30-foot up-down swing with 3 ounces without dead time. *Chunk, chunk, chunk.* Down you go, up you go. Say I fish a break that lips at 20 feet and bottoms at 50. I walk the rig right down the break without losing bottom contact or control of the rig."

Control's a matter of guiding a lure across a piece of structure without having it leave the strike zone. Watch structural layout on sonar as you run a rig that works almost vertically below the boat. The more vertical the rig, the more confident you can be that it's hitting what you see, that it's hitting the same spots the boat's going over. Otherwise, it's a guessing game. You may see fish on screen, but you have no way of knowing if the lure or bait is passing through them, especially in wind and on structure that requires lots of turns.

"Three-way rigging demands vertical control," Al continues. "You're doing it right if your line enters the water at no more than about a 45-degree angle.

"Draw an imaginary line going straight to bottom behind your transom. The surface of the water hits that line at a 90-degree angle. If your line goes down at an angle halfway between your imaginary line and the plane of the surface of the water, that's 45 degrees, about the farthest you want to extend it. If your line blows out farther (toward 60 degrees), you lose absolute control."

Line angled at about 30 degrees over 15- to 20-foot depths is, however, ideal if you intend to work deeper soon; you have a cushion before you reach 45 degrees. A 3-ounce bell sinker on 8-pound or 10-pound-test main line works. Twelve's OK, but thinner line cuts deeper quicker (less resistance).

With the weight properly adjusted, three-way rigging is the most speed-tolerant of all bottom contact techniques . . .

Too thin, though, tempts fate and results in line stretch and loss of feel.

Use lighter weights over large flats when your 1/4-mile trolling passes cross bottom varying from 5 feet deep to less. Lighter weights may also work better when walleyes demand slower, stop-and-go tactics. Still, the line should remain at about a 45-degree angle.

"The faster you go," Al says, "the heavier the weight. The slower you go, the lighter the weight. The fish tell you how fast they want it. Just keep adjusting weight to maintain a 45-degree angle."

With the weight properly adjusted, three-way rigging is the most speed-tolerant of all bottom contact techniques, which is perhaps the most important advantage of all. Speed tolerance is most appreciable when running spinner rigs.

"I've seen walleyes really go for high-speed spinner-and-crawler tactics in summer," Al says. "I mean really haulin', like 3 miles an hour or more. You can't zip it high off bottom without a three-way. If you spot a fish 4 feet up or 6 feet up, how can you put a crawler on its nose with a bottom bouncer? And when fish are tight to bottom, you can maintain control at higher speeds as well as with a bottom bouncer.

"No matter what you show the fish—spinners, spoons, cranks, livebait— always play with speed until you find the trigger speed. Then run through a spectrum of speeds by pumping the rod tip forward to speed it up, dropping it back to slow it down.

"That's another key to the effectiveness of three-ways—you're connected to the rod. You're working the rod. I like that more than jamming my rod in a holder and waiting. Hands-on is more fun and more effective. Of course, I also use a dead rod in conjunction with a handheld rod when I can.

"But the versatility of three-way rigging doesn't begin or end with speed and depth control. Switch from bait to lures or from crankbaits to spoons, without major rerigging. Backtroll, forward troll, use a controlled drift. With lures, I generally troll forward, even in very cold water. If necessary, I kick the outboard in and out of gear to maintain a slower speed."

FIND FISH

Walleyes spotted on sonar 15 to 60 feet down on structure are candidates for three-way rigging, with the exception of fish holding tight to a vertical wall. If they can be seen on sonar, they're probably active.

Say you and a friend map the areas you want to fish on a lake. Make several slow fly-bys of each spot, scanning sonar for baitfish and walleyes. If you don't see fish, don't stop. Check later.

While scanning the next potential spot, you spot fish. Say this spot is a rocky reef topping at 10 feet and dropping quickly to a basin flat at 50 feet. Say fish are scattered, most 2 to 3 feet off bottom along the edge at 18 to 24 feet.

Tie a 2½- or 3-ounce sinker on each dropper. One rod needs a 3-foot dropper, the other a 4-foot dropper. Use a 5-foot leader with a 4- to 6-inch minnowbait. Position the boat to make your first run along the 18-foot contour. Using a slow forward troll, whoever's driving fishes straight behind the transom or slightly to the shallow side of the boat, covering the 16- to 20-foot range. Your partner fishes over the deep side of the boat, covering water 18 to 24 feet deep.

The wind blows you off track as you net the first fish, but your partner hooks up even as the boat drifts deeper. Run through 'em again. As the pass reaches the break, keep your sinkers in contact with bottom. Walk the rigs down the slope, adjusting by hitting the thumb bar on your reel.

Turns can be made sharply because the rigs are vertical. Make another pass. If nothing takes and nothing shows on sonar, make a shallower pass, then another that's slightly deeper. No more takers? Come back later. By now, though, you've made five or six passes, have caught three or four fish, and you're on your third spot. If you were fishing jigs, you'd still be working your first spot.

Three-way rigging is simple to construct and simple to fish, yet it adapts to almost any presentation in walleye fishing. Still, as many ways as Al finds to modify the rig, it's hard to beat minnow plugs for finding fish. Baits like Rapalas, Bang-O-Lures, Rebels, ThunderSticks, and Rattlin' Rogues produce all year.

"Three-way rigging isn't a back-up," he insists. "It works spring, summer, fall, and winter. It's the most versatile tactic I know of. No matter what walleyes are eating—spoons, cranks, spinner rigs, livebait—covering water is one key to catching active fish. Control depth. Find the right speed.

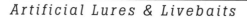

Chapter 5

The World's Most Versatile Lures

**JIGS &
DRESSINGS**

Jigs haven't changed much since Fred Flintstone used rocks to get his line down to the bassasauruses. Nuts and bolts comprised the first huge advancement in sinkers. Then some genius decided to use lead, not the heaviest or densest element, but the most commonly available and easily moldable material that isn't radioactive or in a liquid state.

Later, some genius put lead right on the hook. Now, there was a guy with some real Albert in his veins! He knew that the farther the weight was from his bait, the less control he had over what his bait was doing. Rigging with weights, he decided, compromised his sense of feel, because fish could move the bait toward the sinker without his feeling it.

Jigs are precise tools, and have offered a classic presentation for walleyes since the 1950s, when monofilament lines appeared. Today's classics, however, are even better. The advent of advanced tempering processes in the past five years has brought better hooks to the scene—thinner, sharper, stronger hooks that sink in quickly to the set and won't bend out on big fish. Thinner-diameter steel and smaller barbs allow easier penetration. Many jig makers have worked with hook manufacturers to design premium hooks for jigs.

But jigs need more than sharp hooks. Head designs have evolved through the years into task-specific tools for walleyes. Choose the right tool for the job and the process of presenting baits and hooking fish becomes much easier.

MATCHING JIGHEAD DESIGN TO FISHING CONDITIONS

Ask golfers how to hit a golf ball far, and they'll tell you to use a one-wood driver and your best swing. Balls of different design, however, perform certain ways once they're hit into the air. Some balls go longer, higher, lower, stop quicker, roll farther, or decrease slice. Some fly through wind better.

Like golf balls, jigs are universal fishing components that can be used in many different water conditions. Different head shapes have unique characteristics that you can use to your advantage. Successful jig fishing starts with selecting the right jig to match conditions. Some designs help detect changes in bottom. Others work through weeds or stumps, and help detect subtle strikes. If you can't tell what's going on with your jig under present conditions, you're probably using the wrong jig for that situation.

Round heads—The most basic jig design is the classic round head with a medium shank or medium-long shank hook. The Lindy Fuzz-E-Grub and Jack's Jigs come to mind. Northland's Fire-Ball, a short-shank version, holds bait tighter to the leadhead.

Al Lindner prefers versions of the round head most of the time. "About 75 percent of my jigging is with round heads," Al says. "The other 25 percent involves head shapes that provide an advantage in some kind of cover."

Round jigs excel for vertical jigging, cutting current, and retrieving through snags. Under most conditions, round heads are as good as any other jig design. For vertical jigging in current or deep water, use a jig heavy enough to cut through the water. But round heads are usually a poor choice in thick weed areas because the line-tie placement and head design are prone to snag and foul.

Round heads are commonly available in bulk, painted or unpainted, from numerous tackle manufacturers, retailers, and catalogs. Heads weighing 1/16 and 1/8 ounce (for shallow slack water), and 1/4 and 3/8 ounce (for medium depths or subtle current), suit most common conditions. In extremely shallow water or in situations calling for a slipbobber, 1/32-ounce jigs may be necessary to avoid spooking fish. For extremely deep water or for maintaining bottom contact in strong winds or heavy current, 1/2-ounce-plus heads may be necessary.

Modified jigs—The head design and position of the line-tie help these jigs stay down in current. They excel for vertical fishing and for casting to shore and swimming back to the boat. Most designs, however, tip over when rested on bottom, increasing their chances of snagging.

Round heads, a good compromise in any situation, expose more surface area to current than do bullet heads. Getting down quicker means more bottom coverage, and bullet-head designs like the Blue Fox Foxee dig into current a little better. The

Jig-A-Whopper Competition Jig works well with dragging retrieves.

For deep water and heavy current, narrow, deep-bodied jigs that turn a thin face into the current work best. Examples include the Lindy Jowl Jig and Jack's River Jig. The flat-sided design cuts current and can be kept close to bottom. It's a good design for vertical fishing and for heavier current conditions. The flat-sided profile provides visibility, making it effective for fishing dirty or deep water. Red Neck Tech's hydro-shaped tapered head keeps the jig from rising in heavy current and helps determine bottom makeup.

Flattened on the sides, jigs shaped like an aspirin pull out of almost any crevice they fall into—a classic example of a design well suited to a particular niche. In

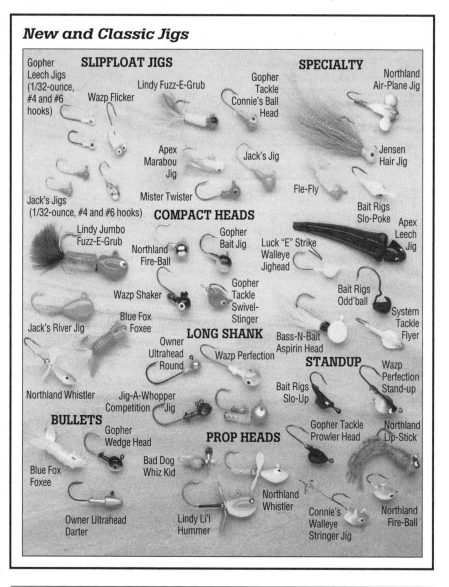

New and Classic Jigs

Gopher Leech Jigs (1/32-ounce, #4 and #6 hooks)

SLIPFLOAT JIGS

Wazp Flicker

Lindy Fuzz-E-Grub

Apex Marabou Jig

Mister Twister

Jack's Jigs (1/32-ounce, #4 and #6 hooks)

Gopher Tackle Connie's Ball Head

Jack's Jig

SPECIALTY

Northland Air-Plane Jig

Jensen Hair Jig

Fle-Fly

COMPACT HEADS

Lindy Jumbo Fuzz-E-Grub

Northland Fire-Ball

Gopher Bait Jig

Luck "E" Strike Walleye Jighead

Bait Rigs Slo-Poke

Apex Leech Jig

Wazp Shaker

Blue Fox Foxee

Gopher Tackle Swivel-Stinger

Bait Rigs Odd'ball

System Tackle Flyer

Jack's River Jig

LONG SHANK

Owner Ultrahead Round

Wazp Perfection

Bass-N-Bait Aspirin Head

STANDUP

Northland Whistler

Jig-A-Whopper Competition Jig

Bait Rigs Slo-Up

Wazp Perfection Stand-up

BULLETS

Gopher Wedge Head

PROP HEADS

Bad Dog Whiz Kid

Gopher Tackle Prowler Head

Northland Lip-Stick

Blue Fox Foxee

Owner Ultrahead Darter

Lindy Li'l Hummer

Northland Whistler

Connie's Walleye Stringer Jig

Northland Fire-Ball

fact, no other design fishes so well in broken rock. Currently, the few commercially available aspirin heads include those marketed by Bass 'N Bait and Cabela's. The Fle-Fly, which has a narrow profile, with slightly rounded sides, also fishes well in rocks.

Tear (bullet)—This head design easily slips through water, yet the length of the head and the line-tie position make it a good choice for a swimming retrieve. Tear shapes fish well in current, through weeds, and perform fairly well when fished vertically. On a tight line, they tend to touch bottom in an upright position; on a slack line, they may tip over, increasing the chance of snagging bottom. It's a good head for casting shallow or for areas where current meets calm water, using current and a gradual lift-drop retrieve to work the jig back toward potential fish-holding areas.

Longtime anglers call on the Rock-A-Roo jighead design. Also, Kalin's Weedless Darter Jig cuts current and fishes snag areas well. Removing the blade from Northland's Whistler Jig allows it to cut through current better and makes it a good choice for casting and swimming or vertical jigging.

Weedless—These styles tend to be pointed, and the line-tie is positioned at the nose to reduce or eliminate the collection point for debris. They slither through weeds and wood much better than standard heads. Those with weedguards, like Bait Rigs' Slow-Poke or Northland's Weed Weasel, or those rigged weedless with

River Retrieves

Jig designs help anglers fish a variety of conditions, but it's the way jigs are fished that causes walleyes to strike. Some anglers jig up more fish than anyone else, even though others are using the same size jig, bait, and similar equipment. They may even be fishing from the same boat. Anglers who fine-tune their presentations to match the location and mood of the fish trigger more strikes.

Vertical—Vertical jigging is one of the most effective methods for

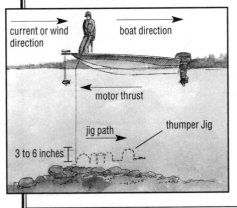

current or wind direction
boat direction
motor thrust
jig path
thumper Jig
3 to 6 inches

fishing jigs in rivers. Most conditions call for slowly slipping downstream, using motor thrust to neutralize drift speed as much as possible. Use a lift-drop-pause movement of your rod tip to give a 3- to 6-inch rise-fall action to the jig. Anchoring may be a good choice when hovering near deeper holes that concentrate walleyes.

Thumping—Heavy jigs that are not traditionally thought of as walleye jigs work well for vertical jigging in dirty water, deep water, or heavy current. Use 3/4- to 1-ounce jigs that will hold in current and fish them nearly vertical to your rod tip. Avoid a jighead with a wide, flat bottom that resists sinking and causes the jig to plane. Round, oblong, or banana shapes cut water and current, allowing jigs to drop deep and stay there. This technique works best when backtrolling, drifting, and even forward trolling into current. Bounce jigs on bottom and off rocks to help triggers strikes.

plastic tails, fish well through snags. They're a good choice for casting into flooded weeds or flooded timber along shorelines in spring, but a poor one for deep water.

The hook on the Bait Rigs Odd'ball can be fished exposed or hidden in a plastic body (including shad bodies) after cutting a slit in the belly for the hook. The unique eye on the Odd'ball is less likely to grab weeds than most other eye designs.

Standups—Standup or keel heads generally have flat bottoms. Their low center of gravity makes the jigs stand upright at rest, or at least resist tipping. On some standup designs, the line-tie is positioned toward the front of the head, making them more weed resistant. The head design and forward line-tie placement make Bait Rigs' Slo-Up jig a good bottom-walker. Its wedge-shaped head cuts current and keeps the jig upright, even on slack line. The slightly curved bottom of Northland's Fire-Ball Stand-Up jig helps it stay upright in most conditions, and the short-shank hook is a good design for walleyes. The line-tie on Jack's River Standup jig is positioned in the center of the head, which causes moving water to push the head downward, while its standup qualities are maintained. A good choice for vertical jigging or controlled drifting.

The versatile Odd'ball stays upright on bottom like a standup jig. For presenting minnows with a dragging retrieve, the Odd'ball creates a unique tipping, rocking action.

Weedless jigs work—
Weedless jigs can be cast into shoreline vegetation or brush with minimal snags. Allow jigs to follow the natural contour of the weedline or flooded timber. Use jigs that are light enough to glide over the top of cover, yet heavy enough to fall into openings. Slowly work through the cover, shaking or twitching your rod tip to maneuver through snag areas.

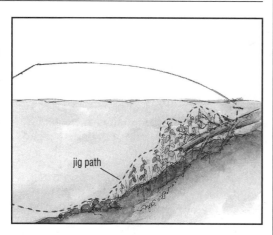

jig path

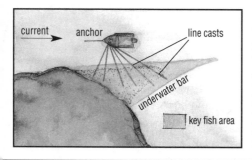

current   anchor   line casts
underwater bar
key fish area

Current breaks—Use current to fish jigs along current where fast-moving water meets calm water. Use jigs heavy enough to anchor your bait, yet light enough to drift with the current when lifted off bottom. Sharp visual taps to your line or a slightly heavier feeling to the jig often indicates a strike, so be alert.

Airplane jigs—Circling jigs, such as the Northland Air-Plane and System Tackle Flyer, are designed to swim on the drop. Typically used as attractor jigs for ice fishing, these work for walleyes, too, for several horizontal presentations.

Thumper jigs—Heavy 3/4- to 1-ounce jigs, nicknamed thumpers, work well for vertical jigging straight up and down in heavy current. They excel in strong current or where deep water demands additional weight to reach, hug, and work bottom. Thumper jigs help stay in contact with bottom, and their larger profile provides increased visibility in dirty or deep water. Bounce and bang them on bottom and on rocks to trigger strikes. Lindy-Little Joe makes a good 1-ounce thumper. Bait Rigs' 3/4-ounce Slo-Poke and Northland's 3/4-ounce Whistler jig are other heavy jig choices.

Spinner—Northland Whistler, Lindy Hummer, and Apex Whiplash Jigs add flash and vibration to jigging presentations. Casting spinner jigs into dirty shallow water in combination with a slow lift-and-drop retrieve is effective. They also work well for vertical lift and for drop yo-yo jigging in slack current. Water resistance against the spinner causes these jigs to be pushed back easily in heavy current. Use a heavier size to prevent current from lifting the jig off bottom.

Rattle jigs—Jigs rigged with rattles help attract fish, especially in dirty water. Northland's Buck-Shot Rattle Jig is a round head that comes equipped with a silicone "rattle band" shell containing rattle beads. The Apex Rattle Head Jig has a rattle inside the molded leadhead. Both are effective for attracting fish in dirty water, and for bouncing off rocks to trigger strikes.

HEAD COLORS AND PATTERNS

Jigheads are available in a rainbow of colors and patterns, and choice depends largely on personal preference and confidence, along with a few basic guidelines.

Walleyes are most sensitive to colors in the orange-yellow-chartreuse range, making these primary color choices in dark or dingy waters, in rivers, under windy conditions, or anytime visibility is reduced and you wish to make the jig more visible. Doesn't mean they're the best choices—just more visible. Fluorescent or phosphorescent paints aids visibility in dingy water or during low-light conditions. Two-tone or tri-tone jigheads offer several spots of color to trigger fishes' reactions.

At the opposite extreme, clear, still waters with good sun penetration may favor subtle shades like white, black, brown, or green, which appear more natural. Forage-imitating patterns of heads and bodies designed to resemble perch, shiners, ciscoes, smelt, crayfish, etc., lead to a variety of mix-and-match choices.

Carry a variety of head shapes, sizes, and color patterns to cover a wide range of depth, current, and water clarity. Experiment to see if fish display a preference. Sometimes color is of little importance; at other times, fish show a decided preference for certain colors or patterns. You'll never know if you don't try.

TIPPING WITH LIVEBAIT

Walleye anglers commonly tip jigs with some form of livebait, even though jigs often come preassembled with plastic, hair, feather, or chenille bodies that provide color, bulk, profile, and action. Many times, a plain leadhead (no body) tipped with livebait is a top option. Jighead styles, weights, and hook sizes should be matched not only to depth, cover, and current conditions, but also to the type of livebait.

Leeches—Slipfloats demand small jigs. Leeches are the most commonly used bait, though other baits work well under the right circumstances. A small jig allows the leech to move and swim more freely.

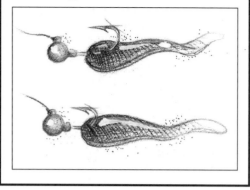

Hooking Leeches

Ideal jigs for leeches are 1/32- and 1/16-ounce sizes. The problem with jigs this small, until recently, has been hook size: a jig with a hook smaller than a #6 has too small a gap for walleyes. It bounces free on the hookset, unable to penetrate and hold in the tough mouth of a walleye. In most cases, jigs this size were designed for panfish, and had panfish-sized hooks. Others that size have collars for attaching plastics, which are a waste of lead on slipfloat jigs.

Jack's Jigs offers 1/32-ounce ballheads in eye-popping colors on #6 and #4 hooks. Gopher Tackle features the Leech Head jig with #6 or #4 Mustad Accu-Point hooks. Most of the lead on the Leech Head is below the shank of the hook, with the eye tight to the head, to further increase the gap. Collarless jigs are classics for presenting leeches on slipfloats, and larger versions of these same designs work well for pitching crawlers.

Pitching leeches on light jigs requires a relatively short shank and larger gap. A 1/16- to 1/8-ounce Bait-Rigs Slo-Poke, with its elongated head, drops slow, fishes slow, works well through weeds, and accentuates the action of a writhing leech. Many other jigs work well, too. Leeches fish better on light heads with short- to medium-shank jig hooks.

Crawlers—Jig-crawler options are almost unlimited. Tiny segments of crawlers add scent and taste to plastic combos, and larger segments work nicely in place of plastic on jigs with collars. Long-shank jigs such as the Wazp Perfection Jig and Owner Ultrahead in 1/8-, 3/16-, and 1/4-ounce sizes excel for crawlers. It's easier to hold a crawler on the jig while pitching with a long-shank hook, and the hook is far enough back to nab a few short biters. The Perfection Jig has a sharp three-way barb that does a good job of holding the crawler against the head.

Alternatives and new designs provide cues to aid in triggering finicky walleyes. The Bad Dog Whiz Kid is a vertical prop jig. Its teardrop design falls

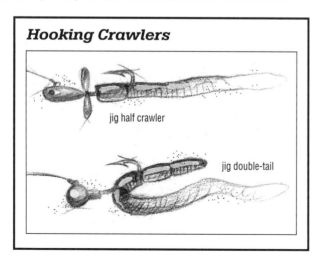

Hooking Crawlers

jig half crawler

jig double-tail

bend-first with the eye straight up. Unlike other prop jigs, the propeller turns or flashes on the drop, providing a temptingly slow target with leeches under a slipfloat. The Wazp Flicker Jighead, with its flat, wavy design, flutters on the drop, another good float-duty tool.

Minnows—Hooking minnows on a jigs requires a larger gap between hook point and jig eye to accommodate the bulk of the minnow and to permit good hooksets. Two classic styles have emerged: compact and long shank. Today, these two styles have evolved into designs specific to certain types of cover and conditions, like current.

The classic compact head is the Northland Fire-Ball. This wide-gap short-shank hook was unique to this head for years before other manufacturers jumped on the bandwagon. The design allows sufficient room for a big minnow with space left over for some segment of a walleye's upper jaw. With the hook running into the minnow's mouth and out behind the head, and the minnow pushed against the jig, the Fire-Ball typically hooks short biters without a stinger, but a special eye for attaching a stinger is supplied under the hook. The bend in the shank is so close that it holds the minnow tight to the head, creating a compact package.

Like the Fire-Ball, Gopher Tackle's Bait Jig, or short-hook jig, also allows the minnow to hinge closer to the weight of the jig. This head is slung low, with most of the weight beneath the shank, and the shorter eye creates a wider gap.

Long-shank jigs, by comparison, present a different profile. The length creates a hinge effect, which may or may not appear natural, but it lightens the business end of the package, causing the longer hook to pivot toward the inhaling fish much easier. Head shapes vary extensively. A wedge head on the Wazp Perfection Stand-Up jig, with its Eagle Claw Lazer Sharp Tri-Bend hook, works well through weededges and stands on bottom, delivering the minnow in an aggressive tail-up fashion. The Wazp Perfection Jig also stands flat on bottom, but the long-shank hook lies on the same plane as the head, laying the minnow belly to bottom, a presentation that excels with sweep-drag retrieves.

TRADITIONAL LIFT-DROP JIGGING

Be it on lakes, rivers, or reservoirs, vertical jigging with a leadhead jig is a fundamental presentation throughout the walleye world. We'll highlight subtleties to the system throughout this book, showing how to match this deadly technique to various depths, locations, and current conditions. For now, let's briefly discuss the basic system.

When vertically jigging, keep the jig as plumb as possible to maintain feel and control. In calm conditions, you can fish an 1/8-ounce jig tipped with a small (2½-inch) minnow down to 15 feet, and a 1/4-ouncer down to 30, providing you move slowly enough. Increased depth, wind, and current, however, tend to complicate the process, forcing you to make adjustments: using 1/4 ounce down to 10 or 15 feet, for example, and 3/8 ounce below. Below 30 feet, 3/8- or 1/2-ounce jigs generally become necessary.

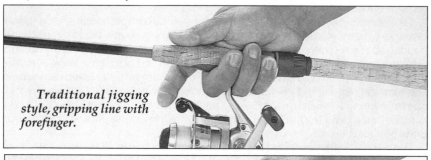

Traditional jigging style, gripping line with forefinger.

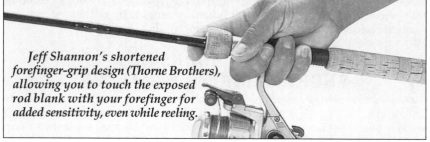

Jeff Shannon's shortened forefinger-grip design (Thorne Brothers), allowing you to touch the exposed rod blank with your forefinger for added sensitivity, even while reeling.

When using bulkier jigging combos, such as jigs tipped with large, 4- to 6-inch minnows, larger plastic bodies, or combinations of plastic bodies and livebaits, increase head size (weight) to accommodate the increased water resistance of the combo. Whatever the conditions, the basic rule is to select a jig weight just heavy enough to allow you to maintain frequent bottom contact on a short line. A short line maximizes feel and control; dragging jigs on long lines creates water resistance against the line and reduces effectiveness.

A 6- or 6½-foot, medium or medium-heavy action spinning rod spooled with 6- or 8-pound monofilament provides an excellent balance for vertical fishing. Open the bail on your spinning reel and drop the jig to bottom. Once the line stops spilling off the spool, engage the reel and take up slack, leaving out just enough line to be able to lift the jig on and off bottom, using a slow, 3- to 12-inch lift-drop of the rod tip. Grasp the line with your index finger to sense bottom contact, bottom type, and strikes. Should you move shallower or deeper, adjust line length so that once again you barely touch bottom on each lift-drop. Repeat lift-drops every few seconds, letting the jig pause barely on bottom between jigging motions.

If snags are a problem, however, lift and hold the jig 1 or 2 inches off bottom immediately after each contact in order to minimize snags.

Most days, walleyes prefer a slow drop speed. Maintaining a taut line without drastically restricting the jig's fall allows you to sense strikes on the fall, which is when most fish strike. Either then, or when the jig rests on bottom.

Some days, fish riding higher off bottom prefer a more aggressive jigging stroke. Snap the jig up to or just above the level of the fish, then follow it down again with a taut line, dropping your rod tip as the jig plummets. Once again, fish tend to strike as the jig falls, resembling a wounded baitfish. Avoid slack line on the fall, or you won't feel the strike. Walleyes may drop the jig prior to your next upward stroke, and you'll never know they were there.

When inactive walleyes are belly to bottom, as is common in cold water, a longer pause between jigging strokes may be in order. You may need to wait 10 seconds between jig movements to trigger walleyes.

Strikes can range from aggressive thumps to subtle bumps to feelings of unusual heaviness. In most cases, immediately sweepset the rod upward to get the hook point to start penetrating (in deeper water), or to actually bury the hook point (in shallower water). The key is removing line stretch and achieving hook penetration. Set several times, lowering the rod tip and reeling up slack between sets, if necessary, to remove stretch and to maintain a tight connection. Then slowly and carefully pump the fish upward, using patience to bring it to net. Don't pull too hard, or you'll bend the hook and pop it out, or risk breaking the line. Experience is the best teacher.

Some days, walleyes seem fussy, refusing to take the jig all the way into their mouths. Try a short pause before setting the hook, risking the possibility that they may sense the weight and drop it of their own accord. In cold water, or when snags are largely absent, try the following approach.

STINGER HOOKS NAB
SHORT-STRIKING WALLEYES

Winter river fishing means cold water, often fussy walleyes, and short strikes. Time and again, your jig-and-minnow comes back to the boat with the minnow's tail skin peeled off like a grape's. Gummy 'eye. The fish don't eat it; only grasp and hold the minnow lightly by the tail. When you set the hook, that momentary hint of resistance was the minnow popping back through walleye lips.

In tough conditions, nine out of ten gummy 'eyes can be converted to lip-hooks by adding a stinger to the jig. In most cases, that's a small #8 or #10 treble attached via a short section of monofilament or braided wire. Used to be, you had to tie your own, connecting the end opposite the hook either to the bend in the jig hook or to the eye of the jig. The main challenge was tying it short enough to be just forward of the minnow's tail, in perfect position to nab a short striker.

Today, most companies catering to walleye anglers offer some form of quick add-on stinger for tough conditions. Many feature a fast-snap clip that clicks into an additional eye on the jighead. Some looped connectors still slip over the hook bend or eye, requiring you to pull the mono tight to form the knot. In some cases, a neoprene stop or crimpable sleeve seals the deal.

Lindy-Little Joe rubber-coats their connectors; slip 'em over the hook point, and the rubber grips the hook shaft. (Available in Stinger Snell treble and slip-over Stinger Hook single-hook versions, plus Fast Snap treble Stinger Snells.) Northland Tackle also offers rubber-coated snelled Slip-On Stinger Hooks, plus

Stinger Hooks

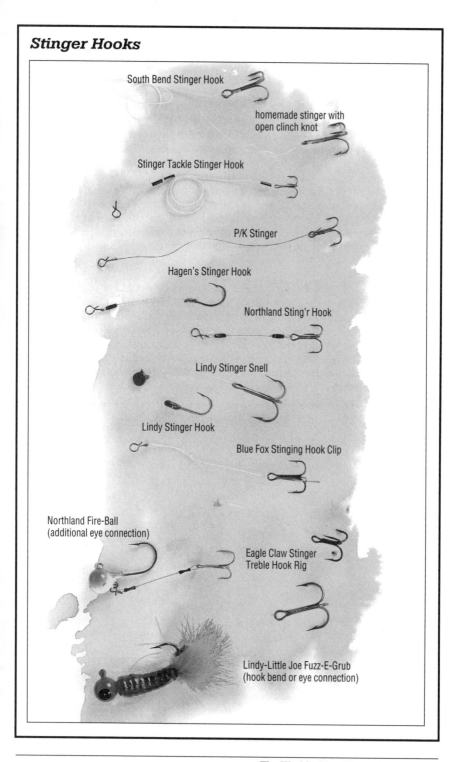

South Bend Stinger Hook

homemade stinger with open clinch knot

Stinger Tackle Stinger Hook

P/K Stinger

Hagen's Stinger Hook

Northland Sting'r Hook

Lindy Stinger Snell

Lindy Stinger Hook

Blue Fox Stinging Hook Clip

Northland Fire-Ball (additional eye connection)

Eagle Claw Stinger Treble Hook Rig

Lindy-Little Joe Fuzz-E-Grub (hook bend or eye connection)

snelled fast-snap treble and single Sting'r Hook versions.

There are two ways to use these stinger hooks. One is to let the stinger flop free, which does not restrict minnow action, so it flows up and down with each jigging motion. This method is perhaps more prone to snagging. The other is to insert one tine of a treble into the minnow's tail, just ahead of the tail fin, to reduce snags and perhaps enhance hooking. This is likely to restrict the minnow's action a bit, however. Blue Fox's Stinging Hook Clip attaches firmly to the minnow's tail. P/K Tackle's FireLine stinger features a reversed barb on one hook tine to grip the minnow but pops out easier on the hookset, allegedly improving hooking.

A few jigs feature stingers permanently attached to the jigheads. Most, however, incorporate removable stingers for times when you don't need 'em (aggressive fish), or when snags are too prevalent to permit stinger use (weeds, wood, or snaggy rocks). In most jigging conditions throughout the year, you probably won't need a stinger hook. But for gummy 'eyes in cold water, stingers reach out and stick lips, converting bumps and hesitations into 'eyes on the line.

PLASTIC FANTASTIC TIPPERS AND RIPPERS

Years ago, jigs were tied strictly with subtle bucktail, hair, or feather bodies. Natural materials still excel for slow, subtle retrieves and for the breathing action of their tiny fibers when the jig is at rest. Nowadays, however, a growing range of interchangeable plastic bodies add versatility and a rainbow of colors. Mix-and-match body shapes and colors to achieve desired results.

Plastic tails range from small, subtle profiles and actions geared to garner bites from reluctant fish, to bulky attention getters that trigger strikes from aggressive

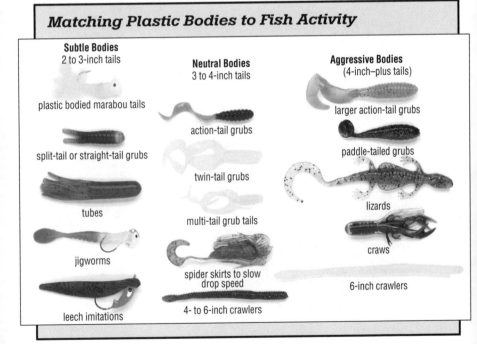

Matching Plastic Bodies to Fish Activity

Subtle Bodies
2 to 3-inch tails

plastic bodied marabou tails

split-tail or straight-tail grubs

tubes

jigworms

leech imitations

Neutral Bodies
3 to 4-inch tails

action-tail grubs

twin-tail grubs

multi-tail grub tails

spider skirts to slow drop speed

4- to 6-inch crawlers

Aggressive Bodies
(4-inch–plus tails)

larger action-tail grubs

paddle-tailed grubs

lizards

craws

6-inch crawlers

biters. In between lie a wide range of sizes, colors, and actions with different degrees of attraction. In general, the more wild and aggressive the tail or leg motion, the better they perform with rapid lure motions, unhindered by livebait. More subtle marabou-tipped and nonaction tails, however, either plain or tipped with leeches-crawlers-minnows, usually can be fished slower, depending on the desired effect. Sometimes the addition of livebait is essential; at other times, untipped plastic is fantastic. Aggressive fish may thump any tail; passive fish may require the scent and taste of the real thing or a taste- or scent-impregnated product like Power Bait. In many cases, plastic-livebait combos are the ticket, not necessarily either/or, but both, for best results.

Most plastic tails popularly applied to walleyes are tipped on jigheads and tend to be a small- to modest-sized, grub-tube-shad items. Jigheads with barbed collars grip and hold plastic bodies better than nonbarbed versions. On the upside, plastic withstands the abuse of ripping through weededges or timber better than fragile, rip-off-the-hook tipped livebait. For open water and snag-free conditions, however, livebait still dominates.

Whenever livebait runs out, or is difficult or impossible to obtain—for example, on a Canadian fly-in trip—plastics dovetail nicely with many walleye systems, particularly for active fish. We divide plastic bodies into three broad categories to match fish activity: subtle, neutral, and active.

Subtle—Small and simple, with minimal inherent action, best describes the subtle body category. Tiny 2-inch up to more typical 3-inch tails are perfect. If you have trouble obtaining actual walleye jig bodies, substitute something geared toward smallmouths, rather than largemouths.

Subtle bodies with marabou tail dressings, like Lindy-Little Joe Fuzz-E-Grubs, Northland Tickle-tail Grubs, Berkley Power Teasers, and Bass Pro Shops Crappie Grubs, entice fussy fish at actions ranging from lift-drops, to barely moving, to motionless. At rest, marabou breathes, creating the illusion of life. Bull Dog Lures' Lightning and Fuzzy Squirts, impregnated with salt and minnow parts, feature flash and marabou tails, respectively.

Flat-tail grubs like Mann's Sting Ray Grub, Mister Twister's Stinger Grub, and Bass Pro Shops' Scrub Grub don't wiggle, but they create baitfishlike or crawfishlike profiles. A Bait Rigs' straight-tailed Bergie Worm is even more subtle. An entire series of Berkley Power Bait Pro Select Tournament Strength Walleye baits, anchored by the particularly good 3-inch Jigworm, are subtle, but pack a punch. Check out the new Neonz bright color series.

Any number of hollow tube bodies, from Garland's original Gitzit, to Berkley's Power Tube, Bass Pro Shops' Tender Tube, and Northland's Gum-tail Jig-jackets slip over small jigheads for a slow falling, gentle jigging attraction. They're great for casting and swimming across shallow rocks. Hollow buoyant bodies are harder to keep on bottom in deep water or current, however. A solid-bodied tentacled tail, like Northland's Lip-Stick, might be a better choice for fishing deep.

Leech imitations like Mister Twister's Wave-E Tail or ReAction Lure's Vibra-Fin Leech fit the bill for gentle swimming retrieves that ripple thin plastic trailers. Somewhat similar are small reapers or Mojo Reefers, though they're seldom seen in walleye tackle boxes.

Also on the subtle front, hair jigs and small pork trailers are good options when subtlety is required, but livebait is unavailable.

Neutral—Slightly increase either body size or action, or both, and you cross from subtle to neutral. More aggressive 3- to 4-inch action tails, like venerable 3-inch Mister Twister Meeny Grubs, perform better with faster or irregular retrieves.

Similar offerings are the Bass Pro Spring Grub, Northland Screw-tail, Berkley Power Grub, and a host of generics at every tackle department or sport show bargain bin—the standard jigging assortment for Canadian walleye fly-ins.

Tipping livebait on single-action tails may interfere with tail action, ruining the natural action of the lure. Western anglers who commonly free-fall jigs down steep bluffs or canyon walls, however, often use jigheads dressed with twin-tail grubs, tipped with a pieces of crawler between the wiggling tails. The twin tails slow lure descent and add action and profile, while livebait adds scent and taste. Mister Twister's Double Tail or Mann's Manipulator Twin Tail Grub are perfect. Twister's Split Double Tail—actually a quadruple tail—would be better fished without bait. A spider skirt can be added ahead of the grub, like the Bass Pro's Nature's Own Caterpillar Skirted Grub or the Manns' Mann-A-Live, to achieve a similar slow falling effect.

Consider experimenting with 4- to 6-inch straight-tailed crawlers, like scent-impregnated Berkley Power Crawlers, for spinner-harness presentations, especially when walleyes are active, or when pesky panfish peck the tails off your live crawlers.

Aggressive—Beef up the bulk, increase the action, or both, and you cross into the the active and aggressive category. Action tails 4 inches and over, like Kalin's 5-inch Lunker Grub, may produce, though their noticeably bulkier bodies require heavier jigheads to keep 'em down.

Paddle-tailed grubs and shad bodies enter the fray, with larger profiles and thumping tail actions that send out vibrations to alert fish. Lures like the Mister Twister Sassy Shad, Renosky Shad, and Bass Pro Squirmin' Shad and Slice Shad, typically should be fished more aggressively to maximize their inherent action, either with distinct hop-drops or full-fledged swimming retrieves, to maximize their inherent action.

Bulkier lizards and craws aren't typical walleye fare, but they're an option when bigger and bulkier offerings are needed to tempt big fish. Or when loads of little fish nail your jig before the big ones can get at it. Remove the 3-inch tail, add a lizard, tip it with a minnow, and hang on. When you get a strike, it'll be a good one. It's a great tactic for winter tailwater trophies or dirty water conditions. Examples: Renosky Jig Minnow and Crawfish, Riverside Lizard, Nature's Own Caterpillar Craw, Kalin Salt Lizard, and the Luck "E" Strike Guido Bug.

Active walleyes may not display any hesitation in striking 6-inch Power Crawlers on a spinner harness, or at times even on a slipsinker-livebait rig. With luck, you can catch loads of fish without rebaiting on something similar to Carolina rigging for bass. Walleye anglers aren't known for using such larger or action-tail plastic worms, though. Just 'cuz they catch bass, don't make 'em walleye bait—though odds are you could toss Slug-Go imitations up onto windswept reefs or points and nail big 'eyes—perhaps worth a try sometime.

Unreal action and attraction beneath summer greenery.

COLOR

White, black, brown, and yellow are good initial choices in clear water, as are any combination of subtle colors that imitate natural forage like minnows, crayfish, and leeches. In dark water, try fluorescent orange, chartreuse, phosphorescent glow, or brighter two-tone or tri-tone patterns to increase visibility. In between lie a host of combinations that fall into the category of personal preference, matched to the degree of stain or color in the water.

In general, tails should be visible without appearing gaudy. Put 'em in the water, and if you feel comfortable with their appearance, you'll probably be confident using them. If they don't look and feel right, change. Experiment. Color sometimes makes a difference. Switching colors amidst a school of fish may take a few more after the initial flurry dies down.

DURABLE SOFT PLASTICS
TRIGGER WEEDLINE WALLEYES

In summer, the weedline angling fraternity separates into distinct and dia-metrically opposed camps, like Moses and the faithful on one side of the chasm, and nonbelievers on the other. In this case, it's the livebait faithful dutifully back-trolling breaklines and weedline edges, while the heretics—the plastic pitchers—probe the weededge.

Neither group is wrong in its beliefs; both are after the same results from different perspectives. Parallel versus penetration, slithering versus ripping and triggering. The results speak for themselves.

In summer, thick, lush, healthy green weedgrowth attracts walleyes, even in classic clear structure-bound lakes. And in shallow stocked waters, if you don't at least probe the weeds occasionally, you're likely missing the proverbial boatful.

If weeds are deep enough to leave the fish sufficient room to maneuver between stalks and beneath overhead canopies of sun-blocking cover, walleyes function well in weedcover. Weeds are the next best thing to aquatic sunscreen during summer, especially because they also attract and hold baitfish and other prey.

When working weededges with jigs, the basic idea is to maneuver parallel to the edge with your electric trolling motor, remaining within a short casting distance of the weeds. Use a combination of your depthfinder, visual sightings of weeds with polarized sunglasses, and feeling the weeds with your jig to position the boat correctly. The same approach works for deep outside weedlines (keeping your boat just outside the growth) and shallow inside weedlines (positioning the boat slightly shallower).

Cast semiparallel to the edge, dropping your jig into the weeds at the end of the cast, and remaining within them for perhaps 1/3 to 1/2 of the retrieve, until your jig comes back out to open water, in perfect position to trigger a weedline biter. Work slowly along the edge until you locate twists, turns, pockets, or some other change in the weedgrowth that may concentrate fish.

There are two schools of thought on jighead design: weedless versus open-hook jigheads. Both have their place. In sparse weeds, the traditional open-hook design frequently hangs up, delivering a better feel for density and type of weed-growth. When a jig stops falling and lodges on weeds, tighten up slack as you drop your rod tip, then use an upward wrist snap of the rod to break the weed.

Then the jig descends again until it falls onto another weed, descends to bottom, or plunges into the mouth of a striking fish. The triggering effect of ripping weeds cannot be duplicated by tickling the outer edge. And triggering is often

Jigs & Plastic

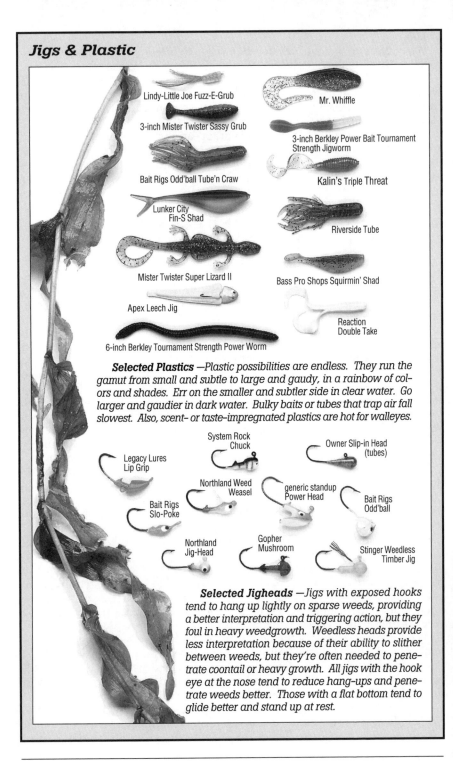

Lindy-Little Joe Fuzz-E-Grub

3-inch Mister Twister Sassy Grub

Bait Rigs Odd'ball Tube'n Craw

Lunker City Fin-S Shad

Mister Twister Super Lizard II

Apex Leech Jig

6-inch Berkley Tournament Strength Power Worm

Mr. Whiffle

3-inch Berkley Power Bait Tournament Strength Jigworm

Kalin's Triple Threat

Riverside Tube

Bass Pro Shops Squirmin' Shad

Reaction Double Take

Selected Plastics —*Plastic possibilities are endless. They run the gamut from small and subtle to large and gaudy, in a rainbow of colors and shades. Err on the smaller and subtler side in clear water. Go larger and gaudier in dark water. Bulky baits or tubes that trap air fall slowest. Also, scent- or taste-impregnated plastics are hot for walleyes.*

Legacy Lures Lip Grip

System Rock Chuck

Owner Slip-in Head (tubes)

Northland Weed Weasel

generic standup Power Head

Bait Rigs Slo-Poke

Bait Rigs Odd'ball

Northland Jig-Head

Gopher Mushroom

Stinger Weedless Timber Jig

Selected Jigheads —*Jigs with exposed hooks tend to hang up lightly on sparse weeds, providing a better interpretation and triggering action, but they foul in heavy weedgrowth. Weedless heads provide less interpretation because of their ability to slither between weeds, but they're often needed to penetrate coontail or heavy growth. All jigs with the hook eye at the nose tend to reduce hang-ups and penetrate weeds better. Those with a flat bottom tend to glide better and stand up at rest.*

necessary to garner strikes during midsummer cold fronts, when walleyes tuck to bottom inside weedcover, motionless and inactive, refusing to respond to anything that doesn't bonk them right on the nose.

Heavy weeds, too thick to effectively rip through, require a jighead of more weedless design. These are either pointed, with the hook eye at the nose to separate and deflect weeds to the sides, or feature a weedguard of some sort, or both.

They reduce sense of feel because they slither between and over weeds so well. But with so many more weeds around, the total effect is to retain some semblance of interpretation without continually foul hooking and uprooting weedgrowth. Wedge-shaped jigs, often featuring flat bottoms to stand up when they reach bottom, project their plastic tails or livebait upward in a visible attitude.

Bass anglers typically use casting gear, heavy line, and jigs exceeding 3/8 ounce to probe weeds. Walleye anglers stick to spinning gear, perhaps 10-pound line, and 1/16- to 1/4-ounce heads, matched to depth, density, and type of cover.

WHEN PLASTIC'S FANTASTIC

"Plastics seem to work best in stained or dark water," Al Lindner explains, "or in clear water at night. Plastics also work well in current, or in cover like weeds and wood, where the bait is being ripped or pulled free some of the time."

Plastics also appear to perform better in cool water, as opposed to summer and winter conditions. "The optimum range of water temperatures is from 50°F to about 68°F," Al adds. "But when compared side-by-side on the water, livebait provides better catches most of the time in water below 50°F." Anytime fish need to be cajoled, refusing to be triggered with quick, active presentations, livebait outperforms plastic.

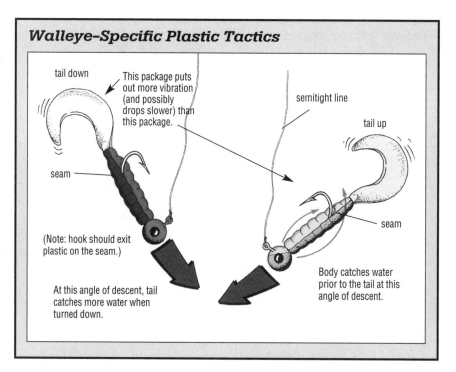

Walleye-Specific Plastic Tactics

tail down

This package puts out more vibration (and possibly drops slower) than this package.

semitight line

tail up

seam

(Note: hook should exit plastic on the seam.)

At this angle of descent, tail catches more water when turned down.

seam

Body catches water prior to the tail at this angle of descent.

Plastics also have certain depth limitations within a range of effective presentations. "They're most productive when walleyes are shallow—in 15 feet of water or less," Al says. "Horizontal to semihorizontal presentations work better than vertical ones. Plastics shine in casting or snapjigging situations, as opposed to vertical fishing in deep water, where livebait tends to be far more effective. Or at least anglers are more confident using livebait."

Shallow is better because horizontal tactics best complement the strengths of plastics. Therefore wind is a plus. Under the cover of waves and broken light, walleyes often feed more aggressively in shallow water, especially during stable weather. "The key," Al reiterates, "is finding aggressive fish. Aggressive fish can be triggered, and plastics are triggering baits."

You can start triggering plastic immediately after each cast, without fear of snapping bait off the hook. "Fish plastics aggressively," Al says, "with lots of poppin'. It's the opposite of the subtle movements and slow drop you look for with livebait. Don't pause. Don't wait. When it comes to plastic, speed kills."

Anything from a short, quick pop of the rod tip to a long, hard snap of the rod falls within the range of triggering mechanisms to use with plastics and jigs. Drop speed should be increased. If you usually use 1/8-ounce jigs with 3-inch minnows, go to 1/4-ounce jigs with 3-inch plastics. It's not a commandment, but it tends to work well.

Fishing horizontally or semihorizontally brings out the best in what plastics have to offer—their triggering qualities. Bait offers scent and live action, cues that stimulate a feeding response. Plastics should be fished quickly, allowing less time for fish to observe the bait. Force the issue. Force a decision.

With plastics, triggering starts as soon as the jig touches bottom. Anything from a short, quick pop of the rod tip to a long, hard forearm snap falls within the range of proven triggering mechanisms for plastics. The point is to fish quickly, hopping or snapping the jig the moment it touches bottom. Drop the rod tip, feel for the thunk, and hop or snap it again. Typically, one of the few times a pause works with a jig-plastic combo is during a swimming retrieve.

For fishing through wood or over broken rock, cast, drop the rod tip to 3 o'clock, keep a tight line on the drop, count the jig down until it's just over bottom or a tangle of wood, and lift the rod tip to 1 o'clock. As you drop the rod tip back to 3 o'clock, pick up slack line with the reel and repeat the process. Don't let the jig settle or drag. Keep it slowly undulating along, just off bottom, letting the action built into the plastic talk to the 'eyes. After moving the jig 15 to 20 feet, a slight pause in the procedure may trigger a following fish.

In spring, swim the jig-plastic combo over and through emerging weeds, over short weeds like skunk weed or chara, and through tops of tall weeds like cabbage and coontail. On windy days or in low light, walleyes sometimes ride up high in the weeds, where plastics tend to produce better than bait. When contact is made with a weed, rip it free. Ripping often triggers strikes. As the jig approaches the deep weededge, let it fall to bottom, then rip it through the outside edge. Don't pause when it hits bottom. Just rip it again.

THE GREAT DEBATE

Some jigheads come plain and require adding a bait or attractors of some sort. Others feature plastic bodies—curly tails, grub bodies, shads, marabou-tailed bodies. Still others can theoretically be fished plain, but are often tipped with livebait for added confidence. Simple guideline: If you need livebait to trigger strikes, add it. If you don't, leave it off. What is lost in attraction often is made up for in ease of use and effectiveness.

In recent years, a growing number of soft plastics suitable for walleyes have been scent impregnated with salt, fish oil or fish parts, natural oils, or other secret concoctions. Sometimes, they make a difference, sometimes not. Trouble is, you never know which it is, so you're forced to experiment. Aggressive fish'll hit almost anything. Fussy biters demand a limited menu.

To our knowledge, of all the plastics currently on the market, only Berkley has specifically researched formulated scented plastics for walleyes. Their Walleye Power Baits feature popular body shapes, sizes, and colors, both scent and taste impregnated, and slightly softer yet still durable forms than those typically found in bass baits.

In-Fisherman Professional Walleye Trail pro Gary Parsons goes ten steps beyond tradition: "I never use livebait in rivers."

Never? From now to eternity, as in *Forever Baitless* on the great walleye rivers of North America?

"Well, almost never. I think it's easier to fish these new jig tails from Berkley than to fish livebait. In about 80 percent of the cases where I formerly fished livebait, I can catch fish just as well if not better with Power Bait tails. Actually, I catch more fish overall with plastic, because it's not quite so soft as the real thing, and it isn't bitten off as easily. When I strike and miss, something remains on the hook to drop back to the fish. And the bites feel harder, because the plastic transmits better. No wasted time rebaiting, less cleanup, less hassle, more time spent fishing.

"The biggest mistake walleye fishermen are making right now is not using enough plastic. I don't even consider using livebait on rivers much anymore. Art Lehrman is the best river fisherman I've ever known, and I don't think he ever uses livebait. Only plastic. Walleyes in current have less time to scrutinize and are programmed to feed faster."

In-Fisherman editor Dave Csanda smiles at Parsons' comment. "I think a jig-plastic combo is a great multispecies approach along weedlines," Csanda replied. "For really ripping through weeds, it offers a durability factor. Bait won't stand up. The same goes when we're faced with plagues of panfish. Then I prefer to tip with plastic, be it on a jig or bottom bouncer-spinner-crawler combo. In Canada, as walleye pro Gary Roach points out, aggressive fish, livebait restrictions, and unavailability provide obvious reasons for taking a lot of plastic tails. During a really torrid bite almost anywhere, yes. Otherwise, I don't feel as confident throwing untipped plastic in most other situations. Yet I've seen anglers catch walleyes on pure plastic at times when I was reluctant to remove livebait."

In-Fisherman Editor In Chief Doug Stange believes it's a matter of conditioning. "Coming from the Walleye Belt, tearing away from old tried-and-true systems is difficult," he says. "Midwestern walleye fishermen still don't, as a rule, feel confident throwing plastics. Whereas out West, that's not the case, where everything is looked at from a plastics perspective. The tradition in the West was to start with plastic, even when bait was available. But when you've tipped with bait all your life, it's hard not to."

The Evolution of Shape

Mister Twister Tail—*Augering tail provides subtle vibration and an almost holographic image, suggesting a swimming minnow or leech. Developed as a catchall. Optimum length: 2 to 3½ inches.*

Mister Twister Sassy Shad—*Long, thin profile, deep from dorsal to belly, imitates shad, ciscoes, alewives, bullheads, and other key walleye prey. Thumper tail attracts with vibration, and the deep profile provides flash. Another catchall. Optimum lengths: 3 to 4 inches.*

Lindy-Little Joe Fuzz-E-Grub—*Lozenge shape designed to fish with bait, after action tails began to be perceived as overkill with minnows or leeches. Body bulks up the profile, adds color, and slows drop speed, while marabou adds a subtle, breathing trim.*

Johnson Sizzler—*An action tail that incorporates dynamic flash.*

Berkley Power Leech—*One of the first realistic leech imitations and one of the first plastics designed to stand alone (without bait) specifically for walleyes. Slow fall with subtle, fluttering action.*

Mann's Bait Company Leech—*Newest of the leech imitators. Thicker body suggests weedless rigging with specialty heads for working thick cover for walleyes.*

Berkley Power Jig Worm and Power Crawler—*Softer than most bass plastics. Designed with a thinner approach to the tail for more sinuous action. Low-action tails allow the bait to undulate, more like a true crawler. Experiments with chemical scent impregnation specifically target walleyes. Optimum length: 4 to 6 inches.*

Larew's Salt Craw—*With the proper chemical recipe, is this the shape of the future for certain applications at certain times of year?*

"Washington and Oregon prohibit the use of live minnows," says outdoor writer Keith Jackson. "We catch walleyes on plastic all year, though we often tip the combo with a piece of crawler. On the deep, clear Columbia river, we've caught walleyes on plastics as deep as 100 feet, using heavy jigs and a vertical presentation."

Jim Kalkofen, executive director of In-Fisherman's Professional Walleye Trail, says: "Parsons' statement will be debated by many old-time walleye pros. We've been saying for years that plastic is the next revolution in walleye fishing. What Parsons says is a step in that direction. What the plastics industry faces is the walleye fisherman's comfort zone. Walleye fishermen don't feel confident enough in plastics yet. But they are making a mistake by ignoring plastics in many situations."

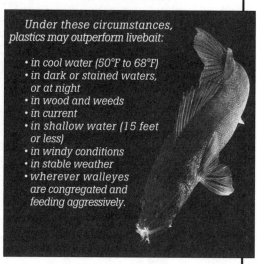

Where Plastics Shine

Under these circumstances, plastics may outperform livebait:

- *in cool water (50°F to 68°F)*
- *in dark or stained waters, or at night*
- *in wood and weeds*
- *in current*
- *in shallow water (15 feet or less)*
- *in windy conditions*
- *in stable weather*
- *wherever walleyes are congregated and feeding aggressively.*

"Plastics work best when added to a system," Csanda says. "Nobody rigs plastic alone for walleyes without a spinner harness, a jig, or something to carry it. No walleye angler places plastics alone on a hook the way bass fishermen do with Carolina rigs, weightless Texas rigs, or Slug-Gos. Perhaps that's because we've yet to see a good enough plastic imitation to stand alone in slow finesse situations—if indeed it ever happens."

To which Al replys, "I find myself using plastics more than ever before and more successfully than ever before in all environments. But I agree that it should be teamed with some form of hardware and moved aggressively. You still have to show people it works to open their eyes. Most people are relying on livebait too much and have been for too long."

Perhaps *evolution* is the right word. Now we have plastic tails in soft, durable shapes attractive to walleyes, and these can be as effective as livebait in many situations.

Include plastics as part of your component collection for walleyes. Carry a range of body colors from subtle smokes, clears, whites, and blacks for ultraclear water, to chartreuse, orange, and multicolored (generally a different tail and body color) for stained or dark water, as well as everything in between. Personal preference, confidence, and productivity dictate your choice. Put 'em in the water and see what looks and feels right. A color pattern too visible in clear water may spook fish. Likewise, if you can't see your offering in dark water, the walleyes may have a harder time locating it, too. If it doesn't feel right, change to a more effective combination.

Compromising traditional beliefs? You can always tip your jig-and-plastic tail with a minnow or half crawler. Plastics aren't quite the real thing, but they're often close enough and sometimes even better, particularly when fished on jigs.

Flashin' Passion

SPINNERS AND BOUNCERS

Spinner rigging for walleyes dates back to the late 1920s and was probably first practiced on Mille Lacs Lake in Minnesota.

Early rigs were primitive, incorporating heavy June bug-style spinners on wire leaders. These were presented on three-way rigs with bulky, homemade bell sinkers. By the mid-1940s, the trend was to lighter spinners mounted on wire, such as the Prescott Pike Hook #2 and the Mille Lacs Free Spin. The first spinner rig marketed with a monofilament leader, the Little Joe "Red Devil," appeared in the early 1960s. It combined a 30-inch, 25-pound leader with a trim, easy-turning, high-quality blade.

The success of the Red Devil led to further refinements. The trend was toward smaller, lighter blades, which spun easily at slow speeds, and lighter leaders, which gave the bait a more natural appearance. As blades and hooks became lighter, leaders became longer. What we now call finesse rigging was the result of these trends.

Spinners, therefore, date back many years as an integral system, not merely as add-on enhancements to slipsinker rigs. In fact, most spinner fishing is accomplished with either a bottom bouncer or a three-way rig—systems ideal for the quick movement that rotates blades, anchored by modest-to-heavy weights that keep livebait either near bottom or at a predetermined depth for suspended fish.

As is so often the case in walleye presentations, balancing these components is key to achieving desired results. Here's a quick checklist of popular parts that cover most spinner rigging conditions.

COMPONENTS

Spinning blades produce intermittent flashes of color or reflection and vibrate to alert walleyes of their presence long before the fish actually see the lure. If the combination of components is correct, maximizing or minimizing attention, matching preyfish or simply arousing curiosity, walleyes may be triggered to strike. Blades don't necessarily have to thump and spin hard; often a side-to-side wobble is sufficient. Experiment through a range of options to determine what matches the walleyes' aggressiveness and preference on any particular day.

Colorado blades—Carry sizes 00 through 8, although most often you'll use 3, 4, and 5. Exceptions are larger 6 through 8 for open water, suspended Great Lakes giants and tiny sizes 00 or 0 as flikker attractors on slipsinker snells. Colorados spin at a wide angle for lots of thump and vibration, even at slow speeds.

Popular colors include fluorescent orange, red, chartreuse, yellow, and lime; gold, nickel, copper, and brass. Hammered nickel (dimpled for more surface area and reflection) or silver-plated (more expensive and shiny) blades maximize flash. Northland's Rainbow Baitfish, Bait Rigs' Astro Brite, and Lindy-Little Joe's Lin-Fleck offer two-tone and three-tone colors, scale patterns, and other effects. Cupped blades vibrate harder than flatter models. Most blades are metal, but plastic is growing in popularity.

Indiana blades—Similar in sizes and colors to Colorados. They're a bit narrower than Colorados and rotate at a shallower angle, creating less vibration but producing more flash because of faster rotation. Fish them a little faster than Colorados to keep them spinning.

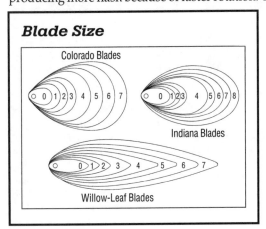

Blade Size

Colorado Blades

Indiana Blades

Willow-Leaf Blades

Willow-leaf blades—# 2, #3, and #4. Sized differently from other blades, willow-leafs rotate tight to the line, creating subtle vibration but lots of flash. They must be fished at high speeds to rotate properly.

Custom blades—In-line blades rotate around a hub in the middle, rather than the end of the blade, and create a more subtle vibration and action. French blades, like those on the Mepps spinner, are heavier and require speedy presentations.

Common Spinner Rig

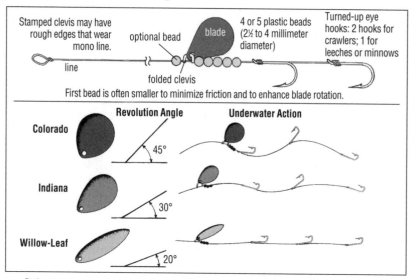

Stamped clevis may have rough edges that wear mono line.

optional bead

blade

4 or 5 plastic beads (2½ to 4 millimeter diameter)

Turned-up eye hooks: 2 hooks for crawlers; 1 for leeches or minnows

line

folded clevis

First bead is often smaller to minimize friction and to enhance blade rotation.

Revolution Angle   **Underwater Action**

Colorado   45°

Indiana   30°

Willow-Leaf   20°

Spinners are the most popular modification of livebait rigs. Spinner blades typically rotate on a clevis ahead of crawlers, minnows, or leeches. A set of beads maintains adequate distance between the clevis and bait to allow the blade to spin without striking a hook.

Action is determined by blade shape and angle of revolution. Wider blade revolutions produce more action.

Spinner blades come in three popular configurations, but others are used as well. Colorado (wide) blades have a wide angle of rotation and spin at low speeds. Indiana (intermediate) blades rotate at a shallower angle and require slightly more speed to spin properly. Long, thin willow-leaf blades rotate on a tight axis and require the most forward speed to make them spin. Willows give off the most flash, Colorados the most noticeable vibration, with Indianas exhibiting characteristics of both. Sizes #2 through #5 Colorados and Indianas are most popular.

Swing (hammered) and rippled blades have elongated shapes to achieve effects between those of Indianas and willow-leafs. Presto blades have deeply cupped ends for more vibration. Fluted blades have long depressions to add flash and vibration. Lindy-Little Joe's lopsided Hatchet Blade, available as a component or on pretied Hatchet Harnesses, creates a distinct thumping vibration.

Folded metal clevises—#1 or #2, for attaching spinner blades to line. Metal, the traditional choice, spins more easily than plastic and maximizes blade rotation at slow speeds. Plastic snap clevises, originally available from Lindy-Little Joe (X-Change) and Quick Change and now available from a growing number of tackle companies, allow for snapping blades in and out, so you can experiment without retying rigs. Quick Change offers two sizes—Quick Change (small) for blades and Weight-Change (larger) for detachable bottom bouncers and slipsinkers.

Plastic beads—Best choices come in metric sizes (2, 2½, 3, 3½, and 4 mm) or in 3/32-, 1/8-, 5/32-, and 3/16-inch versions. Use small beads as attractors ahead of the hook on livebait snells or for spacing between the hook and clevis on the tiniest spinner rigs. Larger beads add color and profile; they work best for spacing components on spinner rigs. Don't let the blade overlap the hook, which inhibits a good hookset. (Spinning bright silver blades also reflect bead color.) Carry a wide selection of sizes and colors to match local preferences or to imitate forage types (orange and green to imitate perch, white and blue to resemble smelt). Northland's new, large diameter Buck-Shot Rattle Beads add color, sound, vibration, and flotation to homemade or pretied snells. New Products Corporation packages beads in a handy plastic tube.

ASSEMBLING OR PURCHASING BALANCED SPINNER COMBOS

The first key to putting a good spin on spinner fishing is to select or assemble a properly balanced combination of components to match conditions. Every packaged combo on the tackle store rack isn't an effective tool. While many pre-assembled rigs are balanced for peak performance, others are more likely to catch fishermen than fish. Balance is the key. Spin out of control for walleyes, and you won't need a net.

The dictionary describes balance as "a state of equilibrium or parity characterized by cancellation of all forces by equal opposing forces." Also "a harmonious or satisfying arrangement or proportion of parts or elements, as in a design." A spinner rig requires a bit of both. It must spin properly (equilibrium) and look good to present livebait effectively and to hook a fish that bites (design).

Blades—Colorado and Indiana blades dominate the market, because they spin at the low to modest speeds common to walleye presentations, provide flash and vibration, impart a hint of motion to your bait, and allow you to feel the rig working. Colorados have the widest rotation, the most thump, the most distinctive flash, and the slowest rotation. Indianas rotate a bit faster, offering a different spectacle of flash and vibration. Colorados spin at slightly slower speeds than Indianas, making them good choices for the slowest spinner presentations. Indianas are the most versatile choice, though, in most instances.

Size 0 and 1 blades usually are used with tiny flikker snells to add a smidgen of attraction to slipsinker livebait presentations, chiefly in clear water, where overdoing flash may spook walleyes. But blades of such small size seldom see much use with bottom bouncers or three-way rigs, the two most popular methods for presenting spinner systems.

Size 2 is a transition between ultra-light and standard # 3 and #4 spinners found on most pretied walleye

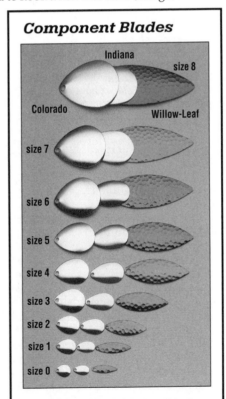

Component Blades

Indiana

size 8

Colorado

Willow-Leaf

size 7

size 6

size 5

size 4

size 3

size 2

size 1

size 0

Blade Options

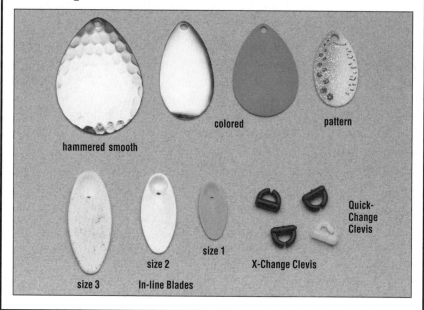

hammered smooth

colored

pattern

size 3

size 2

size 1

In-line Blades

X-Change Clevis

Quick-Change Clevis

rigs. Size 3 and #4 blades are good choices for medium water clarity and for mid-sized walleyes—that is, for average conditions. Thus most spinner combos available in stores or catalogs feature #3 or #4 blades.

Size 5 blades represent a transition to the jumbo class of #6, #7, and even #8 spinners. These whoppers are used for producing maximum attraction. Anglers often assume they get used mostly in dark or dingy water to alert walleyes to the presence of bait. Sometimes, though, they are used most successfully for walleyes running in open water, even when the water is clear—for example, for suspended fish in the Great Lakes. (Pre-assembled spinner rigs with large blades tend to be rare, so most anglers tie their own big-bladed combos.)

An apparent contradiction? Big blades in clear water? It's one of those exceptions borne of experience rather than of logic. With large Great Lakes walleyes, big blades do not appear to be deterrents. In fact, they alert and attract distant fish, and trigger strikes.

Willow-leaf blades fall into a miscellaneous category. Their narrow rotation minimizes vibration and maximizes flash. Willows must be trolled or drifted quickly to make them spin. For some reason, willow-leaf blades have their own numbering system; a #4 does not resemble a #4 Indiana, for example, which makes blade selection confusing. Most anglers don't use willow-leaf blades, but we think they deserve consideration for presentations in open water. Big willows produce a unique thump and offer a distinctive alternative to the more commonly used Colorados.

In-line blades, which spin through an integrated hub, rather than on a clevis, add yet another dimension somewhere between an Indiana and a willow-leaf. They are probably the slowest spinning of all blades.

Clevises, beads, and hooks—Clevises, beads, and hooks play prominent roles in balancing a spinner rig, although most anglers assume blade choice is the major

Balanced Spinner Rigs

The key to spinner performance is to balance all components. Properly blended components spin and wobble enticingly. Tie in components that are too large or too small, and you sacrifice performance, profile, and fish-catching ability.

	Small	Midsize	Large
Blade	0,1	2,3,4	5,6,7
Clevis	1	2	4
Beads	3	4	5
Snell hooks	6	4	2
Minnow hooks	2,1	1/0,2/0	3/0,4/0
Trebles	6	4	2
Mono line	8	10	12

factor. Metal folded clevises have been the walleye industry standard for years. (Avoid stamped stirrup clevises because their rough edges wear line; they work better for spinning on metal shafts—for example, on bucktails). Clevises rotate on the line, allowing the blade to spin.

Once again, balance is the key. A #1 clevis works best with small blades, a #2 with midsized blades, and a #4 with larger blades. Assemble the combo out of whack, and it won't perform properly. Well constructed, however, it's poetry in circular motion.

Recent introductions of plastic, snap-in clevises from Quick Change Tackle, Lindy-Little Joe (X-Change), and others offer easy blade changes. You can just snap in different colors, sizes, or shapes without cumbersome retying. They're a boon to experimentation; you can switch blades in a snap. Purists, however, note that plastic clevises don't spin as easily at slow speeds as metal folded models. A good strategy may be to use small folded clevises with tiny blades and a mixture of clevises with larger offerings.

Round plastic beads provide spacing between hooks and the whirring blade-clevis combo. They also add color and profile. A spinning blade creates an indistinct aura of flash and color, while the beads remain clearly visible, perhaps enhancing the target. Bead size and color therefore are important factors for balance and for triggering fish.

Three mm (millimeter) plastic beads work best with tiny blades, 4 mm round or 5 mm oval with midsized versions, and larger, 5 mm round or 7 mm oval beads function with larger blades. (Catalogs sometimes offer bead diameters measured in 1/32-inch increments, but millimeters are the common designation.) Bead color choices are almost infinite; select bright chartreuse or red for visibility, subtler greens or whites for reduced prominence, or other combo of colors for other results. Local preferences and personal favorites evolve on some waters.

Beads also position the blade at a desired distance ahead of the hooks, ultimately determining the length and shape of the profile. Incorporating five or six beads into a spinner rig is common, yet fine-tuning with more or fewer is just as feasible. Some folks feel that placing an additional bead ahead of the clevis enhances rotation. (We're certain it does for fishing through weedgrowth.) Others insert a 3 x 6 mm (width x length) oval bead directly behind the clevis for the same purpose. Design your own rigs, and you can try anything you wish.

With prepackaged combos, you're limited to what comes assembled on the line. Hooks must also balance with blade size, bait size and type, and bead size. In general, the larger the blade, the bigger the hook. Matching hook size to the bait is perhaps most important. Many pretied rigs come with hooks that are too small. Most anglers select a hook one size larger than they'd typically use for livebait rigging. Choose a #6 for small blades used chiefly with crawlers, leeches, or tiny minnows; use #4 with midsized blades for crawlers or leeches; and perhaps even larger #2 hooks with big-bladed models that target large Great Lakes fish.

Increased hook size isn't a deterrent when you're dealing with reaction strikes. Anglers often snell one or two trebles into the harness while trolling for large, open water walleyes. This arrangement further enhances hooking.

As a rule, use two-hook harnesses for nightcrawlers, single-hook versions for leeches or minnows. Hook crawlers through the nose and at midlength, leeches through the suction cup, and minnows up through the lips. On a two-hook crawler harness, snell the hooks 2 to 4 inches apart to ensure good spacing and to hook short striking walleyes.

As always, though, exceptions exist—a noteworthy one being an option for dragging a dead leech along and through a weededge. Weededges are feeding areas for walleyes, which prowl morning and evening (sometimes all day on rainy days).

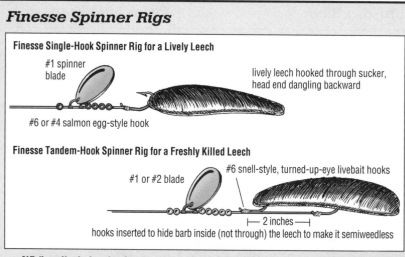

Finesse Spinner Rigs

Finesse Single-Hook Spinner Rig for a Lively Leech

#1 spinner blade

lively leech hooked through sucker, head end dangling backward

#6 or #4 salmon egg-style hook

Finesse Tandem-Hook Spinner Rig for a Freshly Killed Leech

#1 or #2 blade

#6 snell-style, turned-up-eye livebait hooks

⊢— 2 inches —⊣

hooks inserted to hide barb inside (not through) the leech to make it semiweedless

While a lively leech often works well tipped in reverse on a single-hook spinner rig, sometimes a freshly killed leech is just as deadly trolled on two-hook spinner rigging. Most two-hook spinner rigs, however, are made for trolling crawlers. The distance between the tandem hooks must be reduced to about 2 inches for leeches. It may be necessary to tie your own spinner rigs.

Leech rigging often produces in waters where most other anglers are spinner rigging with crawlers. It's also a deadly combination in waters where heavy populations of panfish make it impossible to drop a crawler in the water. A freshly killed leech is tough enough to pull away from most panfish. And it pulls more easily than a crawler through weededges.

To kill a leech and get it to exude those lovely juices, drop it onto the boat floor and step on it firmly a time or two. The dead leech won't twist and curl on your rig, a fine way to use leeches that aren't lively enough for finesse livebait rigging.

But these areas are also notorious for panfish, which quickly peck a crawler to pieces.

To make a dead leech rig, tie a two-hook harness with the hooks about 1½ inches apart. Step on the leech a time or two so it hangs straight on the harness. Doesn't make any difference if the leech is run sucker first or tail first. Insert the point of the hooks (#6s) only partway into the body of the leech, not all the way through. With a #2 blade, usually an Indiana, this becomes a semiweedless rigging that panfish can't peck to pieces. When panfish hit, just shake them off and continue fishing.

Learn to tie a uni-snell, the best knot for attaching hooks in sequence. At the forward end of the snell, you might tie a surgeon's loop for easy attachment and for changing with snaps. To prevent kinking the line, store your snells in resealable plastic bags or wind them on round storage tubes like a Tackle Tamer, Tackle Buddy, or a length of foam pipe insulation.

Of course, balancing hook size to the bulk of the minnow is also important, lest a half-hearted grab by a fish result in a miss when the hook's too small and the bait slides through the walleye's mouth. Hook gap must be large enough to accommodate a lip-hooked minnow yet still retain enough exposed bite to stick a walleye. We prefer switching from the traditional turned-up or turned-down snell hook to a larger, light wire Aberdeen, say, a 1/0 or 2/0. Insert the hook point into the minnow's mouth, out the gill, then nick it back into the minnow's

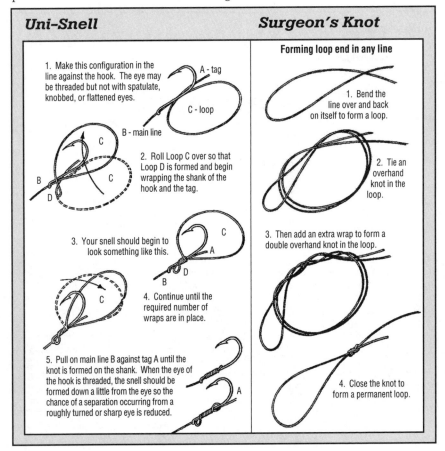

Uni-Snell

1. Make this configuration in the line against the hook. The eye may be threaded but not with spatulate, knobbed, or flattened eyes.

A - tag
C - loop
B - main line

C

B   C

D

2. Roll Loop C over so that Loop D is formed and begin wrapping the shank of the hook and the tag.

3. Your snell should begin to look something like this.

C

A

D

B

C

4. Continue until the required number of wraps are in place.

5. Pull on main line B against tag A until the knot is formed on the shank. When the eye of the hook is threaded, the snell should be formed down a little from the eye so the chance of a separation occurring from a roughly turned or sharp eye is reduced.

A

Surgeon's Knot

Forming loop end in any line

1. Bend the line over and back on itself to form a loop.

2. Tie an overhand knot in the loop.

3. Then add an extra wrap to form a double overhand knot in the loop.

4. Close the knot to form a permanent loop.

back in perfect position to set the hook.

Line and snell length—Even line choice affects spinner performance. Apologies to the light line crowd, but skinny mono and spinners just don't mix. A soft, supple 6-pound-test mono just doesn't balance with big blades. Heavier, stiffer, more abrasion-resistant line like Ande Premium or Trilene XT, holds up better, as well as allowing the clevis and blade to rotate easier. Balancewise, a tough 8-pound mono works well with small blades of #0 or #1; 10-pound's better with mid-sized blades of #2 to #4; and perhaps 12- or 14-pound test—sometimes heavier—is intended for blades exceeding #5.

Snell length determines several factors:

• visibility—separation from hardware used to present the snell, such as sinkers or swivels

•distance—how far off bottom the bait runs.

The longer the snell, the farther removed it is from fish-spooking sinkers. Longer snells also tend to droop toward bottom unless some type of float is used. A rule is that if you run a spinner at typical walleye speeds, it may dip about 1/5 the snell length below horizontal, so a 5-foot snell just drags bottom behind a bottom bouncer.

Some companies incorporate a long, thin plastic foam float into their rigs to help it resist sinking. Shorter snells, meanwhile, restrict lure motion, minimizing tangling in weeds or wood. A 2-foot snell is a better choice if weed, wood, or rock snags are prevalent.

More on blades and balance—The concept of balance brings us back to blades, where we began. Again, blades aren't the only important feature; all components work in unison to deliver a final product. But blades are important, so let's discuss colors and finishes and teaming blade size with different livebaits.

Fishing a #0 blade in front of a large minnow adds minimal attraction to an already seductive offering. At the other end of the spectrum, a leech behind a #8 Colorado is dwarfed and overpowered by the size of the blade. Both rigs are out of balance. In between lies a host of options that suit conditions far better.

Need to add subtle attraction to a leech or crawler? Sounds like a #0 to #2 blade balanced by equally small components. Want to fish a 4-inch chub behind a spinner? Try a #3 to #5 blade with larger beads and a big single hook to match the bulk of the minnow. A two-hook nightcrawler snell? Well, which is in order here—a subtle or a powerful attractant? Depending on conditions, blade size could run perhaps #2 to #6, again with balanced components to keep everything working smoothly. Size 2 to #4 would suit most conditions, with #5 to #6 more suited to open water trolling for giants.

Once the rig is properly proportioned, fine-tune the blade. Bright fluorescent blades maximize visibility. Rotating two-color or patterned blades blur or whirr out into an aura of color. Chrome blades offer a seductive flash in clear water; more expensive silver-plated blades outflash chrome. Copper or gold is perhaps more visible than silver-chrome in dark or dingy water. Dimpled blades increase blade surface area and amount of flash. Smooth blades reduce flash. Dull or smoked (held in a candle flame) blades cut flash to a minimum but retain their vibration.

With an array of combos to choose from, try to balance your selections, choosing spinners to attract and trigger fish without spooking them. Combining certain blade sizes and colors, bead colors and orientations, hook sizes and line weights outproduces many off-the-rack combos. The ability to choose correctly comes with experience.

DELIVERY SYSTEMS

Now that we have some sense of balancing spinner rig components, let's go for a spin—a quick review of popular systems for presenting spinners at a variety of depths, over different bottom contents, and in different kinds of cover.

Walking sinker livebait rig—Walking sinker spinner rigs, sometimes called flikker snells, have tiny #0 or #1 blades and 3mm beads for slight added attraction that doesn't detract from the subtlety of light line livebait rigging. Bigger blades, which require faster forward speed to rotate properly, perform best with other presentation systems. Flikker snells work well in crowds, where the fishing pressure of mass livebait rigging makes fish less susceptible to biting unless something different is offered. Relatively long (6- to 12-foot) snells may work well amid a pack of boats. This is the most subtle of all spinner presentations.

Bullet sinker livebait rig—Usually used in and around weedbeds or timber, generally with a short snell to restrict motion and minimize snagging. Substitute weedless hooks to further avoid hang-ups. Used with small to medium blades and balanced components, these rigs can slither between snags and fall to bottom during pauses. They're best used along edges where pauses are minimal.

Split shot rig—The most lightweight rig used for skimming spinners subsurface, just above weed tops, woodcover, or snaggy, rocky bottom. Longline troll or drift across shallow flats. This is an underused night-fishing technique, not a weight method for large-bladed combos.

Bottom bouncer—An old standby on western reservoirs with potential almost anywhere walleyes swim, this is undoubtedly the most widespread form of spinner presentation. The wire leg of the bouncer skips across bottom on a bump-pause-surge trolling or drifting pass, imparting a change in motion to the spinner combo. Action ranges from a fast blade spin to a side-to-side wobble to a minimal flicker-flop. The bouncer also kicks up small clouds of silt ahead of the spinner rig, like creatures rustling bottom.

Bottom bouncers are versatile because they make it easy to follow slopes or contours, adjust to depth changes, and position spinners just off bottom. Yet they also excel for drifting or trolling deep basins, and they can be used in tandem with in-line planer boards to broaden coverage. In general, use a spinner snell less than 5 feet long to prevent the spinner from sagging and snagging the blade on bottom and stopping rotation. Can be used with any size blade, although traditional #3 and #4 blades usually work best.

Three-way rigging—Ranks behind bottom bouncing as the second most popular form of spinner presentation. A versatile system in which the sinker is usually held just above bottom, occasionally dropping to reconfirm bottom content and proximity. The rig consists of a three-way or barrel swivel with a dropline and Dipsey (bass casting) sinker tied either to the drop rung (three-way swivel) or the first swivel loop (barrel swivel).

The standard drop distance is 2 to 3 feet, but it may extend to 5 or more. Excels for open basins or soft bottom conditions that swallow other sinkers. It maintains spinner position a set distance off bottom for semisuspended fish; adjust dropper and snell length to achieve the desired results.

Three-ways can be fished with long or short snells and just about any blade configuration. They tend to snag on nasty bottom, however. Anglers often opt

Classic Spinner Rigs

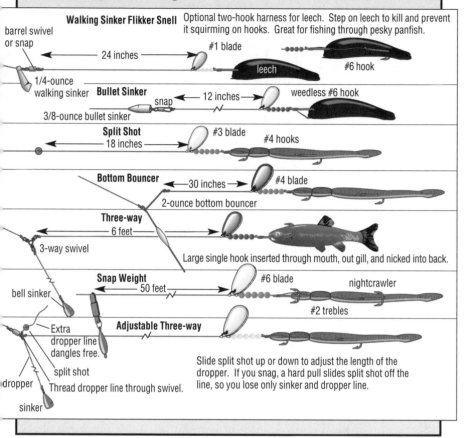

Walking Sinker Flikker Snell — Optional two-hook harness for leech. Step on leech to kill and prevent it squirming on hooks. Great for fishing through pesky panfish.

barrel swivel or snap
24 inches
#1 blade
leech
#6 hook
1/4-ounce walking sinker

Bullet Sinker
snap
12 inches
weedless #6 hook
3/8-ounce bullet sinker

Split Shot
18 inches
#3 blade
#4 hooks

Bottom Bouncer
30 inches
#4 blade
2-ounce bottom bouncer

Three-way
6 feet
3-way swivel
Large single hook inserted through mouth, out gill, and nicked into back.

Snap Weight
50 feet
#6 blade
nightcrawler
bell sinker
#2 trebles

Adjustable Three-way
Extra dropper line dangles free.
split shot
dropper
sinker
Thread dropper line through swivel.
Slide split shot up or down to adjust the length of the dropper. If you snag, a hard pull slides split shot off the line, so you lose only sinker and dropper line.

for using lighter line on the dropper than on the main line, so a strong pull breaks a snagged dropper and loses the sinker but saves the spinner snell and swivel. For a more snag-free three-way rig, clip the top wire arm off a bottom bouncer and use the remaining straight shaft wire-and-sinker combo on the dropper line.

Bell sinkers up to 5 or 6 ounces make three-ways versatile rigs for deep water. A three-way spinner rig also is a prime choice in river current, because the flow imparts rotation to the blade. Drift downstream, however, and the blade stops spinning, defeating some of its purpose. Floating jigheads, plain snells, or crankbaits may be better river presentations for three-way tactics.

Snap weighting—The current rage for open water trolling lets you position a sinker on your line ahead of the lure—say, 50 feet—without having to tie it in-line or attach it firmly in place with a Rubbercor sinker, which complicates netting a hooked fish. Instead, a simple pinch release clips to the line once your lure is running behind the boat. Then you let out additional line to reach the desired depth. To retrieve line when a fish is hooked, reel in until the sinker is a few feet from the rod tip, then reach up to pinch and disconnect it from the line, and drop it into the boat. Fight the fish unencumbered by weights.

Off Shore Tackle snap weights, Mr. Walleye Drop Weights, and Wille Zonies work with any sinker size. They take spinners to any depth and work in tandem with in-line trolling boards that feature similar pinch releases.

Snap weights are best used for suspended presentations. Large-bladed spinner rigs dressed with crawlers have excelled for Great Lakes walleyes. Anglers trolling off bottom often switch to snelled treble hooks to increase hooking efficiency.

Changes in speed or direction affect spinner depth. Move faster, and a spinner doesn't sink as much; move slower, and it

Leader Lengths for Various Riggings

Common Snell Lengths	Feet
walking sinker flikker snell	2 to 12
bullet sinker	1 to 2
split shot	1 to 5*
bottom bouncer	1 to 5
three-way	1.5 to 12
snap weight	5 to +50*
leadcore	20 to +50*
diving planer	5 to 10
downrigger	5 to +100*

*Total length of short pretied snell and leader or main line between spinner and weight.

sinks deeper. The spinner tends to exhibit a quicker or slower sink rate when speed changes, perhaps triggering fish because of a change in blade rotation.

SPEED

Whichever system is used to present spinners, at least 1/2 to 3/4 mph of forward motion is required to make most blades rotate. About 1 to 1¼ mph is the most common speed for running baits while searching for fish. A speed of 2 mph really gets spinners hummin' and sometimes works for aggressive fish.

Most anglers present spinners at a set speed, then experiment with different speeds throughout the day. Often, though, change or hesitation in set speeds is the key to triggering walleyes. One attractive hesitation mode is the natural rush-pause that pulses baits when the boat or trolling boards surge in waves, or when the boat rocks while drifting. Such motion can also be imparted by pumping the rod tip during a steady troll or drift. Complete pauses cause blades

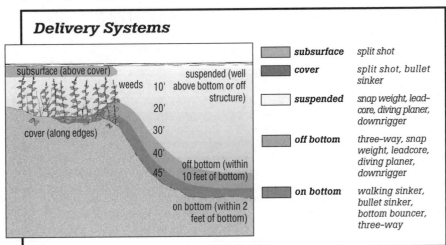

Delivery Systems

subsurface (above cover)
weeds 10' suspended (well above bottom or off structure)
20'
cover (along edges) 30'
40'
45' off bottom (within 10 feet of bottom)
on bottom (within 2 feet of bottom)

subsurface	split shot
cover	split shot, bullet sinker
suspended	snap weight, leadcore, diving planer, downrigger
off bottom	three-way, snap weight, leadcore, diving planer, downrigger
on bottom	walking sinker, bullet sinker, bottom bouncer, three-way

to stutter-stop, wobble, and then fall, a combination that can be deadly.

Spinners aren't good everywhere, every time out. But there's something special about that little bit of extra flash, color, and thump that often suits walleyes' tastes, driving them to distraction and action.

SPOOL 'EM WITH SPINESSE

"Much of the time, I've gone to an adjustable rig system to position blades farther ahead of the first hook, totally exposing the hook for better hooking," says Mister Walleye, Gary Roach, perhaps the world's most traveled walleye pro, and the one with the largest bag of rigging tricks. "To do this, I put a bobber stop on the line between the last bead and the first hook. I like standard string bobber stops, though neoprene models are also popular. Slide the stop forward or backward, depending on how far you want the spinner ahead of your bait. Sometimes I fish it close. Other times, I push the blades and beads 4 to 8 inches up the line, like a mini-cowbell for trout. The blades look like a school of minnows, while the bait lingers behind like a wounded baitfish. Walleyes, trout, or any fish like to pick off stragglers that can't keep up with the rest of the school.

"A bobber stop offers the option of threading a crawler up the line ahead of the hook, which I think provides several advantages. First, it tends to make the crawler run straight, preventing spinning and line twist. Second, a crawler can be fished on a single hook, rather than on a two-hook harness. At times, multiple hooks spook walleyes, while single hooks hidden in the crawler never do.

"I use a #4 Tru-Turn light wire hook, inserting the point into the crawler's nose,

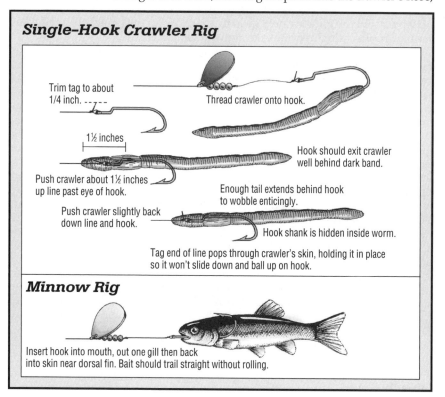

Single-Hook Crawler Rig

Trim tag to about 1/4 inch.

Thread crawler onto hook.

1½ inches

Hook should exit crawler well behind dark band.

Push crawler about 1½ inches up line past eye of hook.

Enough tail extends behind hook to wobble enticingly.

Push crawler slightly back down line and hook.

Hook shank is hidden inside worm.

Tag end of line pops through crawler's skin, holding it in place so it won't slide down and ball up on hook.

Minnow Rig

Insert hook into mouth, out one gill then back into skin near dorsal fin. Bait should trail straight without rolling.

then threading the worm up past the eye onto the line. The barb should exit the worm just past the dark band, leaving the tail of the crawler to dangle and wiggle enticingly. Yet the hook point is far enough back in the worm for a good hookup, even without a trailer hook.

"Anytime I thread a crawler maybe 1½ inches up the line, I leave about 1/4 inch of tag end when I trim my knot. This creates a stiff little tag end over which I can thread the crawler. Then, when I push the crawler slightly back toward the hook, the little tag end pokes out sideways through the crawler's skin, in effect holding it in place so it won't slip down the hook. I've done this for years, and nobody else seems to have thought of it.

"As for line, I don't use light line with spinners. Spinners create a reaction strike, so line visibility isn't a factor. The lightest line I use with spinners is 12-pound-test Trilene XT, the heaviest about 17 for bigger blades. Tough line withstands the wear of a clevis spinning on the line. I prefer metal folded clevises that spin at lower speeds than plastic clip-in clevises, because they allow my spinner to wobble or spin rather than hang limp and lifeless. If you're experimenting a lot, however, plastic clevises that allow for snapping different blades in and out without retying save time. Either way, I always run the line between my thumb and forefinger to feel for line wear where the spinner rotates. When you use a bobber stop to position the blades, just slide it up or down the line a couple inches to change the wear point, extending the amount of time you can use the same spinner rig without replacing it.

"For minnows, I prefer a larger hook, like a #2 or #1. I insert the point through the mouth, out one gill, then nick the point into the minnow's back. It tracks straight without rolling and hooks fish well. With small minnows, a short tag end of line run out the gill may help keep the minnow on the hook better. Leeches simply require a single #6 hook through the suction cup.

"Most of the time, I prefer larger blades in dingy or dirty water, smaller blades in clear water—except in the Great Lakes, where the large average size of walleyes generally calls for big blades. Colorado-style blades display more wobble at slow speeds and tend to work best in dark water. Indianas are my favorites for clear water and probably my first choice in general. They spin a bit faster than Coloradoes, with a bit less thump and more flash.

"For drifting or trolling spinner rigs, I usually use 20/8 Berkley FireLine as my main line. The thin diameter lets me reach deep with minimal line length, whether I'm fishing with bottom bouncers, three-way rigs, or trolling for suspended fish with dropweights. It's so sensitive, I can almost feel blade rotation, and my rod tip pulsates with big blades.

"I tie all my spinner rigs about 3 feet long with a small barrel swivel on the end. Then I wind them on a piece of large-diameter foam pipe insulation to minimize the coiling effect of snells stored in small bags or wound on small-diameter storage tubes. Then, if I want a longer snell, I simply tie more line to the barrel swivel and add another barrel swivel at the desired length.

"Pretie likely or proven combinations before going out, but be ready to modify components when conditions demand. Experiment. Change blade color, size, style. Lengthen or shorten your leader. Add a Northland Buck-Shot Rattle Hook Ring to the front hook for more sound. Slip a bead and mylar tail combo like a Zak Tackle Twinkle Skirt (a component of a salmon trolling squid) on your line, letting it drape over your crawler so it looks more like a silvery baitfish. Sometimes a little change takes a lot more fish, especially in a crowd."

Mister Walleye always has a better way to outfinesse—or outspinesse—Mister Walleye.

HOP, SKIP, AND A BOUNCE

Name's Bouncer. 'Course, they probably shoulda named me Skipper, 'cause I do more skippin' than bouncin'. If you want real bouncin', go see that Tigger fella with the stripes. But if you wanna see some first-class skeedaddlin' across snaggy bottom, up and down slopes, or across open basins, you done come to the right place.

While traditional livebait slipsinkers embody the ultimate in fish-catching finesse, under some conditions, bottom bouncers have a leg up on slipsinkers. These wire-legged weights skip and bounce over many underwater obstructions—rocks, logs, or clean bottom—but they don't handle heavy brush or weeds well. In general, bouncers are best for situations requiring coverage or snag resistance: slow trolling or drifting presentations of 3/4 to 2½ mph, fast enough to rotate a spinner blade or wobble a minnow-imitator crankbait. Traditional livebait slipsinkers tend to perform better below that speed range. Each system has its strengths and its weaknesses.

Bottom bouncers originated on the Plains, have been expanding both east and west in the last decade, and are now popular in a host of states. They come in many sizes, shapes, and colors. Once limited to dull lead finishes from basement manufacturers, they are now available in fluorescent orange, yellow, and chartreuse versions from large tackle companies like Bait Rigs, Lindy-Little Joe, and Northland. Missouri River Tackle offers bouncers with rotating spinners on the wire shaft for added attraction.

While 1-, 1½-, and 2-ounce models dominate most drifting or slow trolling

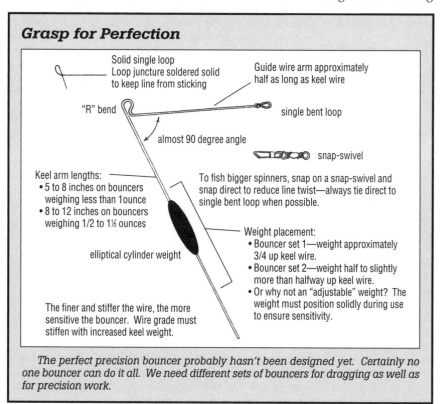

Grasp for Perfection

Solid single loop
Loop juncture soldered solid to keep line from sticking

Guide wire arm approximately half as long as keel wire

"R" bend

single bent loop

almost 90 degree angle

snap-swivel

Keel arm lengths:
• 5 to 8 inches on bouncers weighing less than 1 ounce
• 8 to 12 inches on bouncers weighing 1/2 to 1½ ounces

To fish bigger spinners, snap on a snap-swivel and snap direct to reduce line twist—always tie direct to single bent loop when possible.

elliptical cylinder weight

Weight placement:
• Bouncer set 1—weight approximately 3/4 up keel wire.
• Bouncer set 2—weight half to slightly more than halfway up keel wire.
• Or why not an "adjustable" weight? The weight must position solidly during use to ensure sensitivity.

The finer and stiffer the wire, the more sensitive the bouncer. Wire grade must stiffen with increased keel weight.

The perfect precision bouncer probably hasn't been designed yet. Certainly no one bouncer can do it all. We need different sets of bouncers for dragging as well as for precision work.

conditions, lighter or heavier models from about 1/2 ounce up to 3 ounces or more are also available. Lake trout anglers fish deep water with 6-ounce Gapen Bottom Walkers, and anglers trolling Great Lakes basins for walleyes often skip heavyweight bouncers across bottom, although anything heavier than 3 ounces tends to sink planer boards if multiple lines are run. Bouncers call for medium-weight casting tackle— 6½- to 7½-foot, long-handled rods to take the strain off your forearm (tuck the long handle under your elbow) or to insert into rod holders while trolling or drifting.

The outlandish safety pin design of bouncers triggers a host of misconceptions among the uninitiated. First, you need to figure out how to tie the darn thing on. Typically, the main line is tied to the bend in the wire form, then the looped end of a leader snell—plain, spinner, floater, whatever—is attached to the snap or snap-swivel on the wire arm. The leader stretches back 3 or 4 feet to a bait or lure. A longer leader tends to drag the bait on bottom, increasing the possibility of foul-hooking debris or snags.

Contrary to popular opinion, a bottom bouncer doesn't just drag; it also adds action via nonstop, variable motion. As a bouncer touches bottom, the wire leg sticks, and the bait momentarily stops. Then the bouncer pivots forward slightly, moving your leader and bait. Once boat movement pops the wire leg free of bottom, the bottom bouncer scoots forward, imparting a rushing motion to the bait until the sinker once again descends to bottom and stops. A spinner pulses, then its rotation slacks or ceases. Livebait dashes forward, then lags; lifts, then sinks. Bouncers react like miniroller coasters, taking livebait on an extended pogo stick ride.

Are bouncers good only for quick, nonfinesse presentations? Nothing says they can't be fished almost motionlessly by letting out just enough line to touch bottom and dangling bait in front of a fish's face. Use 'em with plain snells (no spinners or hardware) just like a livebait rig. You may not be able to feed much line to a biting fish, but you can drop your rod tip toward a biter while the bouncer pivots toward the fish, offering at least 6 to 10 inches of give before you set the hook. That's just enough time to lift the rod out of the rod holder once you see it begin to bend, before sweepsetting the hook. Bouncers are also more snag resistant than traditional livebait rigs—a particularly useful characteristic in boulder snags on rocky Canadian waters or on rocky southern impoundments.

Bottom bouncers are draggin', skippin', bouncin', hoppin', liftin', hoverin', dancin' machines.

Should you want to feed line to a fish while retaining the snag-resistant features of a bouncer, try a slip bouncer like the Quick Change Lite Bite. Much like a sliding slipsinker, the wire-legged lead weight clips into a clevis that slides down your line until it hits the barrel swivel at the end of your snell, positioning it a set distance ahead of the bait. Got a bite? Now feed all the line you want— so long as the bouncer doesn't topple and fall between crags. And should you need a bigger bouncer, simply snap the weight out of the clevis and insert a heavier version. No retying.

Want more flexibility? Well, you can get that in different wire lengths and thicknesses, depending on manufacturer. Bullet Weights and Walleye Angler put a little rattle in their lead-free bouncers to help fish hear 'em comin'.

Bottom bouncers are draggin', skippin', bouncin', hoppin', liftin', hoverin', dancin' machines. They tug and tow, high and low, whether longlined to ride up and down slopes without adjusting line length or shortlined to hold bait just above rig-eating snags. The upshot is, if you fish for walleyes, don't be without 'em. They'll put a little bounce in your walleye two-step.

ONE-LEGGED WONDERS

A good bounce to shortstop. A bad bounce up the middle. A high hopper to third. A bloop single. A ground-rule double. An inside-the-park home run. A sinker ball in the dirt. A knuckleball over the catcher's head. A foul ball off some guy's noggin'—ouch! A grand slam over the center field fence.

How many ways can a baseball bounce? About as many ways as you can bounce a crawler.

Bottom bouncers are the solution to presenting livebait at a steady pace a scant few inches above snaggy bottoms, flats, or open basins. A wire feeler arm (actually a *leg*) on most bouncers minimize hang-ups while scratching upright across rocks and rubble. Bouncers can also be fished vertically on short lines, even hovered in place, so long as you avoid slack and don't let 'em topple over and snag. While all bouncers are standup guys, all are not equal, even though they're poured from much the same mold. Slight variations in design offer different options for fine-tuning livebait presentations to walleyes.

Standard bouncers—These comprise 90 percent of all bouncers on the market. Features include a bent wire arm with a line attachment at the bend (tie direct to the wire shaft), a snell attachment (swivel or snap-swivel) at the end of the upper arm, and a fixed weight positioned about halfway down the leg. Standards skip, bounce, momentarily wedge and pause, then rock forward, pop free, and scoot ahead, imparting to bait a pulsating forward dash-pause and flutter motion. Ideal for spinner-crawler harnesses and livebait snells.

Daddy longlegs—Keeps bait farthest off bottom, but it's difficult to store in a tackle box because of excessive length unless you bend the leg over for storage and rebend it outward to use it. To position bait farther off bottom, switch to a three-way rig.

Stumpy—No wire bottom feeler, but it still has feelings. Wide-bodied weight rests directly on bottom and has less tendency to tip over when paused and allowed to rest in place. Originally developed for fishing rivers, it has applications anytime that it's desirable to pause a bait. Heavier models excel at slow, vertical fishing. Not as snag resistant as wire feeler models.

Slip bouncer—Rigged to slip, these incorporate the best aspects of snag-resistant bottom bouncers with the slip weight characteristics of livebait rigs. You can feed a little line to a tentative biting fish before sweepsetting the hook. To add finesse for fussy biters, attach an extra snap-swivel at the bouncer eye, threading the line through two swivels, then tying it to a third swivel to form the leading edge of a livebait snell.

> *Bottom bouncers are the solution to presenting livebait at a steady pace a scant few inches above snaggy bottoms, flats, or open basins.*

Because the bouncer is not tied directly to your line, it pivots instead of rocking forward when the wire feeler momentarily hits bottom. This creates more subtle motion than the rocking action imparted by standard bouncers. A Quick Change snap clevis permits easy weights changes without the need to retie knots.

Straight bouncer—Similar to a Quick Change, but it lacks the slip option. Often a three-way swivel is molded into the upper end for line and snell attachment. Imparts an intermediate action to livebait between that of standard and pivoting slip bouncers.

Adjustable bouncer—Allows easy change of weight size, position, and color. System Tackle bouncer weights slide onto the wire feeler and clip in place. Cabela's E-Z Change and Luhr Jensen Walleye Bottom Bouncers feature weights that slip onto the wire feeler and grip in place wherever you position them. Reel Feel Bouncer weights slip on the shaft and are held in place above a kink in the wire.

Odd shapes—One example is an old version of the Lindy-Little Joe Bottom Cruiser with a wide, flat weight and double wire feelers designed more for skimming and planing in the shallows than for penetrating deep water.

COLOR

Hot colors like chartreuse, orange, and phosphorescent green are the current rage, but whether or not they attract more fish than standard dull lead finishes is debatable. A video available to fishing clubs on loan from Northland Fishing Tackle demonstrates colored bouncers underwater. Viewed from the front or rear, the bouncer is difficult to separate visually from a trailing spinner, instead creating the illusion of a group of minnows or a larger wiggling target. Some bouncers feature attractors like floats or beads, which add color.

Select Bottom Bouncers

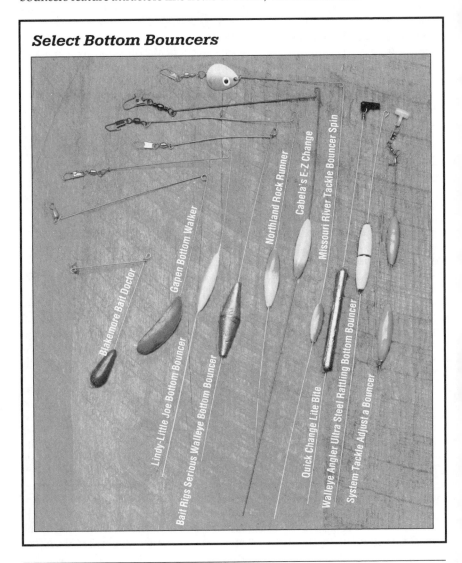

SIZES

Most bouncers are designed to present spinner rigs at modest speeds, but they also work well at slower speeds with livebait snells and floater snells and at higher speeds with flutter spoons. Some folks even use 'em with short snells and shallow running crankbaits. Weight selection, therefore, depends on a combination of depth and speed. Guidelines:

- For shallow water—less than 10 to 15 feet—use a 1/2- to 1-ouncer. Lighter models generally aren't necessary at the slow to medium drifting-trolling speeds used for walleyes.
- For medium depths—to 20 feet—use a 1½- to 2-ouncer. These cover most applications for fishing reservoir points and flats, as well as drop-offs in natural lakes and Canadian Shield waters. Available in most popular sizes.
- For use in deep water and open basins, such as drifting or trolling spinner-crawler harnesses 30 to 40 feet deep in the Great Lakes, go with a 2½- to 3-ouncer. Additional applications include river currents, holes, tips of wing dams, and bridge pilings.
- For extra deep water, heavy current, or faster presentations like trolling flutter spoons, or for precise vertical positioning to minimize snags or to trigger fish, use a 3 ounce-plus. For most conditions, this is seldom necessary. Few bouncers over 3 ounces are available. Switch to three-way rigs with bell sinkers.

Remember, bouncers are great for fishing at a steady pace across relatively clean bottom, including snaggy rocks that eat jigs or livebait rigs. They're also good for fishing livebait over scattered horizontal wood like sticks or logs, but they tend to snag in heavy brush, stumps, flooded trees, and weeds. If you give 'em slack, they fall on their faces and may snag whatever's snaggable. But if you keep 'em movin', they keep on groovin' bottom like mini plows trailering maxi walleye harvesters.

That's the way the ball (bait) bounces.

BOTTOM-BOUNCER FINESSE

Bottom bouncers help tame the toughest situations: walleyes holding tight to structure; over bottom terrain like rock, gravel, shale, and even certain types of weed flats or sparse timber.

Bottom bouncers allow for fishing the nastiest places efficiently. Efficiency means maintaining an attractive presentation in the zone as much as possible. When walleyes are on structure, they're usually tight—within a foot of bottom—especially in shallow water. Bouncers allow you to glide a bait through the zone at 'eye level.

Rather than use a presentation that measures distance from surface down, bouncers measure from bottom up, maintaining precise depth control. They also add an attraction no other device offers: bouncers bounce, thump, and scratch bottom as they move along, resulting in more noise. And noise is good. Divers on Lake Oahe, South Dakota, click rocks together to attract curious walleyes.

Bouncers also impart an erratic action to a bait. The tip of the bouncer skips and hops across bottom, transferring motion back to your bait and causing it to jerk in an erratic and enticing fashion. Traditional fixed bent arm bouncers do this better than sliding models; sliding bouncers tend to absorb some of the action because of their straight design and hinged action.

Sliding bouncers do provide some advantages, however. Bullet Weights developed a unique "swing arm" rattling bouncer that rotates 360 degrees to eliminate

Bouncer Basics

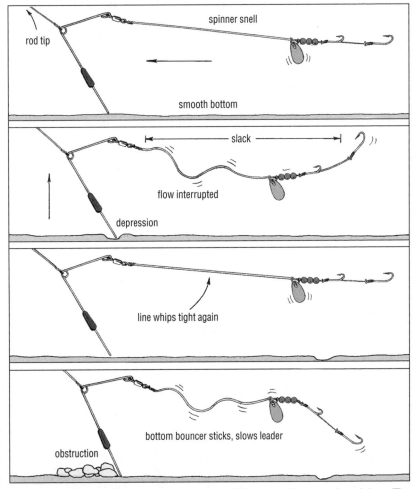

On a smooth lake floor, a bottom bouncer glides along like any other sinker. The slightest change in bottom depth or composition, however, causes the bottom bouncer to stick momentarily before plowing ahead. This unpredictable stutter-step action entices fish to strike.

tangling when the sinker is lowered. The swing arm also helps reduce the resistance felt by a striking fish, thereby keeping them hanging on longer. The biggest advantage of sliding bouncers is their ability to let soft-biting 'eyes run with a bait, giving the fish more time to engulf your offering fully.

Anytime you drop a bouncer, however, you lose snag resistance. Rather than dropping a bouncer to a biting walleye, just hold on and wait until you think the fish has fully taken the bait before setting the hook.

The most popular bouncer combo is a spinner rig tipped with livebait. A spinner pulled behind a bouncer, hopping and popping across uneven bottom, creates a quirky, jerky action. The universal favorite bait is a big, fat, juicy night-crawler dressed on a multiple-hook harness. An extra hook inserted toward the tail of the bait improves your strike-to-landed ratio.

In snaggy conditions, however, multiple hooks also mean more hang-ups. In this case, switch to a single hook, but not the standard salmon egg hook found on most pretied snells. Instead, use a #6 or #4 light wire crawler hook and thread the crawler as far onto the hook as possible, then position the hook toward the back of the bait. Rather than tying the leader directly to the hook, tie in a small Berkley Cross Lok Snap and slide the head of the worm over the clip. The clip helps pin the crawler in place, providing a straight bait that won't twist the line. Also, a snagged hook usually unbends before the leader breaks, and the clip helps to change a damaged hook quickly. A steady pull on the rod returns the rig for rebending and rebaiting the hook.

Try adding a float to help keep your rig out of snags. A small float provides sufficient lift to keep the bait off bottom, but in the zone. Keep your snell short—maybe 3 feet or less. Spinners with small floats still drop when paused, and more snell length means more drop. Increase trolling speed, if necessary, to prevent dropping.

Leeches, minnows, and plastic tails are effective rigging options. Leeches hooked through the suction cup help nail short biters because of the leeches' smaller size. Minnows are effective at times and can be hooked several ways. One hook, inserted up through the bottom lip, keeps a minnow alive longer. Some anglers hook a minnow through both eyes to help it stay on the hook better, but dead minnows hooked in this fashion don't ride upright. Or try a larger, 1/0 to 3/0 Aberdeen light wire hook inserted into the mouth, then out one gill, with the hook point nicked into the body near the anal vent. It's an effective rigging that resists snags.

Plastic baits are highly overlooked rigging options. Dress a Berkley Power Crawler on a two-hook harness just as you would a real crawler. Lake Erie charter captains use them to minimize rerigging time between fish. Mille Lacs Lake, Minnesota, is often overrun by small perch. Walleyes want crawlers, but perch invariably beat them to the crawler, peck-peck-pecking and tearing up crawlers in short order. When we started using plastic to eliminate bite-offs, the perch still hit, but we could pull our bait away intact.

While bouncers are most commonly used for trolling spinners, they can also be fished like livebait rigs.

While bouncers are most commonly used for trolling spinners, they can also be fished like livebait rigs. A light bouncer with a plain hook or floater is a finesse rig that can be fished to a standstill. A bouncer allows you to rig in snaggy areas previously thought impossible to fish. Use a bouncer just heavy enough to stay in contact with bottom. Use as short and vertical a line as possible to retain snag resistance.

Bouncers normally aren't associated with weeds, but in the 1998 In-Fisherman Professional Walleye Trail (PWT) tournament at Lake St. Clair, Michigan, anglers found plenty of walleyes buried in massive cabbage weed flats. Isolated pockets of walleyes were spread amidst thousands of acres of plush weedgrowth, and the only way to locate them was to fish through the weeds. The problem was finding a presentation that would quickly fish through the weeds without snagging. The answer was a 2-ounce bouncer-spinner combo. The bouncer plowed a path through the weed tops, allowing the spinner to come through without constant fouling. Run just deep enough to tick the tops of the weeds, bouncers turned an almost impossible situation into a fishable one.

Bouncers don't work in every situation. They don't lend themselves to muddy bottoms, and they lose their effectiveness when fish are suspended high off bottom. But they effectively handle a surprising number of applications, from the Great Lakes to natural lakes and rivers to big reservoirs of the South and West— and they deserve a prominent spot in your walleye arsenal.

BOUNCING BIG TIME AT MODEST SPEEDS

"Most folks fail to discern the difference between 'dragging' and bouncing with finesse," says Al Lindner. (Al, who hails from Minnesota, where anglers are permitted to use only one rod at a time, tends to rationalize most multiple-rod trolling tactics as "dragging.") "Dragging is like speed trolling with a crankbait. You're trying to cover water—searching for fish or looking for scattered fish. It isn't much of a precision thing. You don't need a lot of sensitivity in the rigging; the bait's usually way out there behind the boat somewhere. And you're usually using a moderately limber longer rod. Granted, you need to know where the rig is, relative to bottom. But most of the precision in dragging comes in changing spinners, sizes, and so on.

"Spinner rigging can be precise if you couple the right spinners with the right bouncer rigging. Fishermen—and manufacturers, too—should understand that bouncers are different, just as crankbaits and other fishing tools are different. Different cranks, for example, present different profiles. They offer different running depths. They vibrate differently.

"Same basic idea with bouncers. Some bouncers are better precision instruments. Bouncers that drag well have a hunk of lead hanging way down low at the midpoint on the wire or at or near the bottom of the wire. Lead placed low anchors the rig—stabilizes it. It's what's needed to keep a big Colorado spinner running true. But lead down low deadens the rig. The lead thumps along bottom instead of tippy-toeing along.

"The most sensitive bouncers are those with the lead higher up on the wire. A well-designed and properly used bouncer is perhaps the most sensitive instrument for telling you what's happening below. A bouncer does that job better than a slipsinker livebait rig and at least as well as a jig. You can't effectively drag a jig except on gravel and sand. Most of the time, you have to lift it and let it fall. But a bouncer keeps constantly tipping along on a wire toe.

"Unfortunately, manufacturers disregard the quality of the wire. But the wire's a lot like a fishing rod—the stiffer the rod, the better it transmits signals. Same deal with the bouncer wire. Sure, wimpy wire works to drag baits. But precision bouncers need stiffer wire. It's the wire that tips bottom and sends a signal up the line.

"The lead should be positioned at least half and as much as three-quarters of the way up the wire. That gives the wire room to work—to twang as it bumps rocks, to tingle as it drags sand.

"The wire acts as a resonator. And to do the job right, the wire stiffness has to be relative to the amount of lead it carries. Most companies, though, don't change the grade of wire as they increase the amount of lead. Most heavy bouncers are a wimpy lot only fit for dragging. But it doesn't have to be that way.

"Sensitivity depends on a combination of elements. The wire has to be right relative to the amount of lead. The lead has to be positioned properly. And you must tie directly to the bouncer at all points, both the rigging connection and the main line-to-bouncer connection.

Dragging

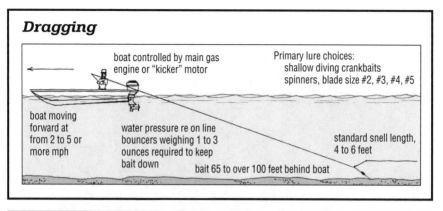

boat controlled by main gas engine or "kicker" motor

Primary lure choices:
shallow diving crankbaits
spinners, blade size #2, #3, #4, #5

boat moving forward at from 2 to 5 or more mph

water pressure re on line bouncers weighing 1 to 3 ounces required to keep bait down

bait 65 to over 100 feet behind boat

standard snell length, 4 to 6 feet

Bouncers for Dragging

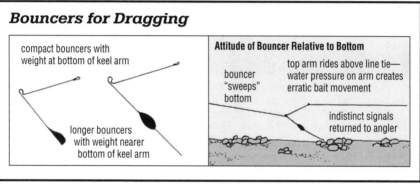

compact bouncers with weight at bottom of keel arm

longer bouncers with weight nearer bottom of keel arm

Attitude of Bouncer Relative to Bottom

bouncer "sweeps" bottom

top arm rides above line tie— water pressure on arm creates erratic bait movement

indistinct signals returned to angler

Precision Bouncing

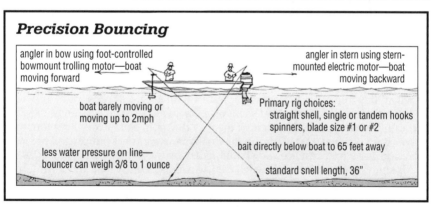

angler in bow using foot-controlled bowmount trolling motor—boat moving forward

angler in stern using stern-mounted electric motor—boat moving backward

boat barely moving or moving up to 2mph

less water pressure on line— bouncer can weigh 3/8 to 1 ounce

Primary rig choices:
straight shell, single or tandem hooks
spinners, blade size #1 or #2

bait directly below boat to 65 feet away

standard snell length, 36"

"That means no snaps or snap-swivels at the head of the bouncer or trailing the bouncer leading to the snell. Tie direct. And the bouncer should have a single wire loop or an 'R' bend, not a circled wire. It's tough to tie directly to circled wire. Come to think of it, even the single twisted wire loop causes problems, because your line can get stuck in the bent loop. The best thing going's an R bend.

"Use stiff line—a tough-skinned line like Berkley XT instead of Berkley XL, or perhaps even FireLine. Stick with 8-pound test most of the time—10 maximum— unless there are lots of snags. And wind it on a small casting reel. A casting

Bouncer Line-Tie Options Compared

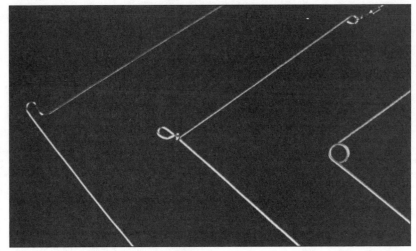

The line-tie portion of a bouncer must allow for tying direct. The most common line-ties have (from left to right) an "R" bend, a single bent loop, and a double bent loop.
Double-looped wire creates excessive line stress, which the light line necessary for precision bouncing can't handle. Be careful with single looped wire, too, because line often sticks in the loop crease, weakening the line.

combo's the most versatile option for a range of bouncers from less than an ounce to more than an ounce. Spinning tackle's fine for light bouncers.

"The type of rod and rod-and-reel combo's vital. Lighter means more sensitive. The rod and reel must be as light as possible, so we're also talking the smallest possible reel—no need to hold much line because you're presenting bait near the boat.

"For hand holding bouncers, I prefer a high-modulus graphite rod—as fine a rod as is available. That's just the opposite of the run-of-the-mill rod folks think of when they think about dragging spinners with long, soft rods.

"You need a 6½-foot rod that's stiff as an arrow at least 75 percent of the way through—maybe even 85 percent of the way through. Stiffer rods are more sensitive. But you need a bit of play in the tip to maneuver the bouncer and to avoid telegraphing your presence and spooking fish on the strike.

"If I need slow precision, I switch back to a slipsinker livebait rig. Sliprigging presents livebait naturally. You know exactly where the sinker is, though not exactly what the bait's doing. And you must move slowly in order to let the livebait do its thing.

"When fish are really off, sliprigging remains a fine option. And remember that a lively sliprigged bait often covers mistakes fishermen make when trying to present other baits. Just let the livebait do its thing. But get good with a bouncer, and you can do just about anything with it that you can do with a sliprig.

"Too many good fishermen get stuck in the same trap I was stuck in. Rigger's mentality. Someone says 'walleyes,' and they think slipsinker rig. They think a bouncer's primitive, that it won't work where they fish. This thinking runs rampant in the heart of the old walleye belt in Minnesota, Wisconsin, and Michigan.

Precision bouncing can accomplish almost anything that a slipsinker rig can accomplish and more, often at a quicker pace.

"The jig, on the other hand, well, nothing will ever replace the jig. Jigs fish precisely. The lead and the hook are one, right there on the end of your line. When you lift, the bait lifts. You control exact size, color, and profile. You control speed precisely—and depth. Jigs are the choice most of the time in situations calling for absolute control.

"A precision bouncer rigging is almost as exact, and you can move faster while still presenting livebait naturally. You can present the bait with an attractor like a small spinner, too.

"I'd say I use a jig about 50 percent of the time these days. I rarely want to fish slower than I can fish with a jig. And when I want to go a bit faster while still maintaining control of my livebait, I choose the bouncer—oh, say, another 25 percent of the time. That leaves 25 percent of my time for dragging spinners, speed trolling crankbaits, sliprigging, slipfloating, and so on. But most of my time is split between jigging and precision bouncing."

PRECISION BOUNCING

"Precision bouncing isn't so much different from jigging," Al continues. "The bouncer's almost always directly below the boat. I keep a tight line to the bouncer and use the combination of slight water pressure on my line and the bouncer to balance the toe of the bouncer on bottom as I move forward.

"I choose bouncer weight based on the speed I want to move and the depth of the water. I carry bouncers weighing 3/8 to just over 1 ounce for precision work. Most of the time I use bouncers that weigh 3/8, 1/2, 5/8, or 3/4 ounce. Three-eighths ounce fishes about right, from 10 down to 15 feet. A half ounce works well down to 25. Fishing deeper than that usually requires switching to a sliprig or a jig. Faster fishing calls for a heavier bouncer at the same depths.

"The simplest presentation maneuver is to hold your rod tip perfectly still as you move forward (sitting in the bow of the boat and using a foot-control, bow-mount electric trolling motor) or backward (sitting in the back of the boat using a transom mount electric). The toe of the bouncer just tips along bottom.

"You generally feel a distinct *thump* when a fish hits. As the boat continues to move slowly forward or backward, ease your rod tip back to the fish at the same speed the boat's moving. Let the fish hold in place momentarily. The only thing that's really moving is the boat. The fish doesn't feel the weight of the bouncer or

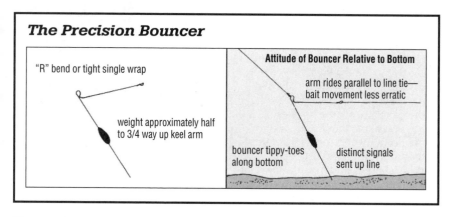

The Precision Bouncer

"R" bend or tight single wrap

weight approximately half to 3/4 way up keel arm

Attitude of Bouncer Relative to Bottom

arm rides parallel to line tie—
bait movement less erratic

bouncer tippy-toes along bottom

distinct signals sent up line

you, for that matter, because the bouncer's perfectly balanced with its foot on bottom and water pressure and your rod are holding the bouncer up. The rod's fast tip has just enough give to let the fish move slightly. Once your rod tip drifts back a foot or so, set the hook.

"The bouncer wire tipping bottom adds an action to the bait that can't be duplicated. It's a kind of *tip, tip, tip* . . . the bait darts slightly. And I'll tell you something else: I'm convinced the noise of the wire pinging along attracts fish. Some manufacturers slip a bead chamber—a rattle chamber—on some of their bouncers. A noisy rig if there's both a rattle chamber and a twanging bouncer wire.

"Another fine maneuver is to sweep your rod tip slowly forward from a position 45 degrees back from perpendicular. Then set the bouncer on its foot (toe) while the boat continues to move. Let the bait sit until your rod tip drifts back 45 degrees, then sweep forward again.

"The bait skitters and jumps, then pauses—skitters and jumps, then pauses. And you're still maintaining perfect control and bottom contact.

"A long snell distracts from the precise qualities of the rig. A 3- to 4-foot snell's just about right. Five's too long—spinners begin dragging bottom.

"I use a neutral-colored line—something clear, green, or gray—2 pounds lighter than my main line. Tie the snells at home and wrap them on something like a Tackle Tamer. I use #6 Mustad livebait hooks with a leech, small crawler, or a small to medium minnow—a #4 hook with anything larger. And of course I often use tandem-hook rigging with crawlers.

"When fishing without spinners, I often add a chartreuse or orange bead ahead of the hook for a speck of attraction. For more attraction, I might go with a Northland Phelps floater. I like the stinger model coupled with a small crawler. Lots

Bouncer Testing

Compare two bouncers weighing the same and with the same wire stiffness, one with the lead positioned higher on the keel wire, the other with the lead positioned lower on the keel wire. Hold the bouncers loosely on the line-tie ring.

Test 1: With the wires at a 45-degree angle to a table, bounce the tip of each keel wire on the table. Which bouncer is more sensitive? (The lower the position of the lead, the more rubbery the bouncer feels.)

Test 2: With the wires at a 45-degree angle to a flat surface with things on it, drag the tip of each bouncer along the surface. Which bouncer transfers messages about the surface of the table better? Which bouncer maintains more consistent bottom contact? (The lower the position of the lead, the more consistent the contact. Higher lead position allows the "leg" to resonate messages.)

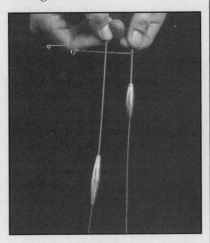

of companies are making good floating jigheads, though.

"I use small spinners, too—#1 or #2 Indianas or Colorados when moving slowly, almost like slipsinker rigging. Bigger blades and willow-leaf blades are for dragging. Keep things laid back for the most part when you're precision bouncing.

"Same deal with colored bouncers. They look great. They attract attention. I think they can play a role when you're dragging, trying to find fish. But most of the time I use a plain lead (no paint) bouncer ahead of a precision rig. At times when the fish are active, you want to attract attention as you move along a little quicker. Then I might use a colored bouncer. Most of the time, though, naah."

Keeping a Bouncer Balanced

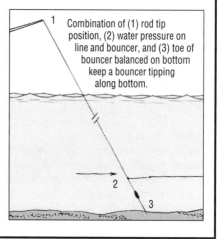

Combination of (1) rod tip position, (2) water pressure on line and bouncer, and (3) toe of bouncer balanced on bottom keep a bouncer tipping along bottom.

TO EACH HIS OWN

Note that Al's perspectives on bottom bouncing are those of a traditional northwoods livebait rigger and jigger, who through his travels learned the deadly effectiveness of bouncers, spinners, and other tactics if used under the right conditions.

Pivot Distance

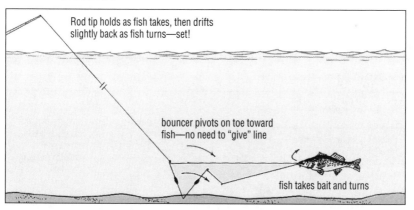

Rod tip holds as fish takes, then drifts slightly back as fish turns—set!

bouncer pivots on toe toward fish—no need to "give" line

fish takes bait and turns

Novice anglers worry that once a walleye takes, it will feel them and the bouncer—one of the reasons for the popularity of the slipsinker livebait rig. Makes perfect sense to drop the line and let the fish run.

Rarely, though, is it necessary to do more than allow the fish a moment to turn ever so slightly before setting. Once a fish takes, hold the rod tip still or let it drift slightly back toward the fish as it moves. Even a 2-inch move by the fish increases the chance of a clean set in the corner of its mouth. The bouncer will pivot on its toe as your rod tip drifts back toward the fish.

When bottom bouncing, he still prefers to use baited hooks or smaller spinners, lighter bouncers, and perhaps moves less quickly than western anglers, who cut their 'eye teeth drifting or trolling spinners and bouncers at higher speeds. And he obviously still doesn't relish that "dragging thing."

The fact is, many walleye anglers use multiple rods stationed in rod holders to present several baits simultaneously, move at swifter speeds, often enhancing their effectiveness with these tactics. Long, soft rods placed in holders bend on the strike, betraying a walleye's presence before it realizes it's about to be hooked. Multiple rods spread lures to the sides, covering more water and several depths with each drift or trolling pass. Swifter speeds and larger spinners also have their time and place, requiring heavier bouncers (1½ to 3 ounces). So there's a lot to be said for multiple rod trolling, alias dragging, with blades ranging from small to extra large.

In the end, everyone has his own comfort zone. Even Al. We've seen him fish multiple rods, but he's admittedly more comfortable with a handheld, sensitive rod than waiting for the big soft one in the holder to bend on a bite. He's a hands-on guy at heart, but he'll do whatever it takes to get bit. Even if it means draggin' an extra line and a big flashy blade tipped with livebait.

SPINNER RIGGING WITH BOUNCERS VS. THREE-WAYS

Every trend has a countertrend. As lines get thinner, blades smaller, and hooks lighter, fish become conditioned to such subtle rigging. Then a 180-degree turn occurs in tactics, and "western bold" rigs are in—big baits behind #6, #7, or #8 blades. Bigger can be better. More flash draws big, aggressive fish from a greater distance. And a heavier thump is easier to locate in dark or cloudy water.

Standard rigging tends to work anywhere rigs are catching walleyes. But tweaking the presentation can lead to better catches. At certain times and places, it's best to deviate from the norm.

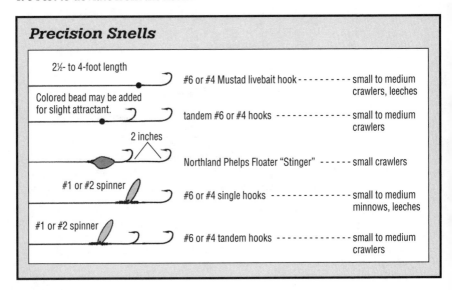

Precision Snells

2½- to 4-foot length

Colored bead may be added for slight attractant.

#6 or #4 Mustad livebait hook - - - - - - - - - small to medium crawlers, leeches

tandem #6 or #4 hooks - - - - - - - - - - - - - small to medium crawlers

2 inches

Northland Phelps Floater "Stinger" - - - - - small crawlers

#1 or #2 spinner

#6 or #4 single hooks - - - - - - - - - - - - - small to medium minnows, leeches

#1 or #2 spinner

#6 or #4 tandem hooks - - - - - - - - - - - - small to medium crawlers

SLOW-DOWN FINESSE RIGGING

From *Webster*: *finesse* (fi-nes´) *n* **1** Artful restraint and delicacy of performance. The philosophy behind slow-down rigs is that finicky fish often respond best to less speed, less flash, and less attraction and instead key on subtler movement, scent, and quality of livebait. Finesse spinner rigs are lighter, smaller, slower, and longer. In order to slow down with a spinner rig, you need to trim down the weight of every component. Hooks should be the thinnest gauge of steel, so they don't drag the rig down. Blades must be smaller and lighter to turn at slower speeds. Leaders should range from 4 to 12 feet long to keep the rig on or near bottom and to emphasize natural movement of the bait.

> The philosophy behind slow-down rigs is that finicky fish often respond best to less speed, less flash, and less attraction and instead key on subtler movement, scent, and quality of livebait.

Slow-down rigs sport #00 to #2 Indiana or Colorado blades (willow-leaf blades drag bottom at ultraslow speeds). The subtle flash and vibration of fingernail-size blades is just enough to entice fish that may be turned off by the thump of larger blades.

"The ultimate tandem-hook finesse spinner is rigged with plenty of space (about 4 inches) between hooks to allow a crawler to contract and expand," says Gary Parsons, two-time PWT Angler of the Year. "Slow-down rigging works best when trolled at about 1/2 mph. Speed change, not flash and vibration, is the key to the slow-down rig. It needs to be fished in conjunction with a Dakota-style bottom bouncer that stutter-steps along bottom."

Finesse rigs strike a compromise with moderately light monofilaments. Heavy monofilament provides the advantage of thickness, which resists dropping as fast on the pause and provides an added buffer against damage to the line by a revolving metal clevis. Light mono allows the bait and rigging more freedom of movement and is potentially less visible to fish. The best compromise is probably 8-pound, abrasion-resistant line, as described earlier by Al Lindner.

A bottom bouncer with a finesse rig offers several advantages. It snags less, holds the rig higher off bottom, and imparts a unique action to the rig. "Four factors—speed, snell length, blade shape and size, and rig weight—affect a rig's action behind a bottom bouncer," according to Parsons. "The main focus in slow-down rigging is to enhance the horizontal jigging motion provided by the bottom bouncer. Because the wire catches and sticks on bottom, it creates a stutter-step action. Unpredictable speed and behavior are the basis of the system."

When the wire catches bottom at these slow speeds, the spinner flutters, the bait falls. At the higher speeds necessary to revolve larger blades, this herky-jerky action is lost or minimized. The bouncer becomes a means to hold the spinner off bottom. Not only does the slower, jerkier action trigger more fish, but it also catches more fish. Immediate hooksets are the norm, as opposed to waiting and hoping that the fish has the bait.

If longer is better, three-time PWT winner Steve Fellegy does it best. For his ultralong 12-foot snells, he generally uses the more traditional three-way rig and tends to troll faster—3/4 to 1 mph—with a 2- or 2¼-ounce bell sinker. For fishing rocks, he switches to a bottom bouncer, but he feels the three-way offers more versatility.

"My rule for rigging three-ways is that for every 4 feet of leader, the rig drops about 6 inches. To swim the bait in the fish zone (in the bottom 2 inches, occasionally glancing off bottom) with a 12-foot snell and a 12-inch dropper, the sinker

Fellegy's 8 to 1 Ratio

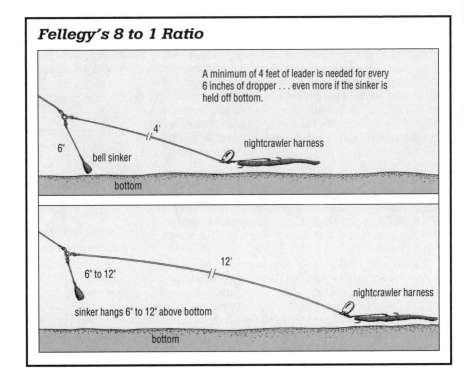

A minimum of 4 feet of leader is needed for every 6 inches of dropper . . . even more if the sinker is held off bottom.

4'

6"

bell sinker

nightcrawler harness

bottom

12'

6" to 12"

nightcrawler harness

sinker hangs 6" to 12" above bottom

bottom

must be lifted about 6 inches off bottom and held there. For every walleye you see on sonar, there are 50 you don't see, their fins pegged to bottom. To catch those fish, the blade has to turn in their eyes."

Fellegy almost always uses a 12-foot snell on a spinner rig, and he likes to keep his sinkers off bottom whenever possible. He believes dragging a sinker along bottom spooks fish, which is quite possible in some—maybe most—environments. Ultralong snells increase distance between the bait and any unnatural movements or sound created by a sinker.

THUMPERS

Bigger blades are thumpers. Anything bigger than a #3 could be called a thumper. A thumper fairly screams, "Make no mistake about it, this here's a meal." Thumpers require speed. Moving .8 to 1½ mph keeps thumpers up and turning. Colorados provide more thump than Indianas, and Indianas thump more than willow-leafs.

Obviously, thumpers and finesse rigs can't be fished in the same boat at the same time. Someone has to change systems. And if you're searching for fish or picking up scattered fish across a large flat, the person changing systems better be the one with the finesse rig. By simply moving faster, standard rigging and western bold rigging make contact with more fish.

Experimentation with different aspects is key—just ask Fellegy. "We've done a lot of testing over the years," he says. "The true test is to put all your options in the water at the same time through the same school. We did that when we ran a charter service on Mille Lacs. With 6 to 16 lines in the water at the same time, we did lots of testing. On Mille Lacs, day in and day out through years of experimenting, a #3 Indiana produced better than other sizes and styles."

On most waters, most days, Fellegy uses #3 silver- or gold-plated Indiana blades produced by Lakeland, Inc., of Isle, Minnesota. "Where you get your blades makes a difference," Fellegy says. "Lakeland's blades are thinner, with less of a cup than other Indiana blades, so they turn better at slower speeds. Say what you will, walleyes want things slow most of the time—the slower, the better."

Even so, Fellegy used a #8 blade to win the PWT event on Saginaw Bay in 1993. "It's like preparing steaks," he explains. "If you're feeding the Minnesota Vikings, you serve 20-ounce sirloins. If you're feeding a bunch of fifth graders, you choose 6-ounce rib eyes.

"In a typical walleye environment, the fish average about 18 inches or less. A 2-inch blade spooks those fish. But in the Great Lakes and in some western impoundments, fish average 4 pounds or better. Hey, that's a Viking! Offer him a petite fillet, and he'll go next door. Break out the #8 blades."

Trolling spinners for suspended walleyes often calls for different systems, like snap weights and planer boards, to match the conditions. When you troll above suspended fish and know the rig is in front of them, pop the motor into neutral and push the rod tip back toward the fish, letting the spinner flutter down. Large Indiana blades spin better than Colorado blades on the drop. Walleyes hit on the drop or just as you start pulling forward again.

The concept of western bold rigs developed on fisheries like Fort Peck, Starvation Lake, and the Columbia River, where populations of walleyes grew to massive size before most anglers realized they were even there. Big fish, big blades—western bold.

Fluttering

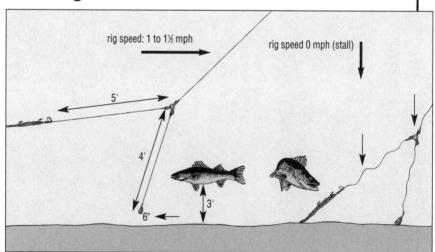

When you spot aggressive fish above bottom with your electronics, wait until the rig reaches the fish, then stall the boat and push the rod tip toward it. The rig goes into free fall, and the blade spins and flutters on the drop, often attracting or triggering active fish. Just before or as the rig touches down, re-engage the engine, and the rig moves forward. Strikes often occur at this point.

But if you're hitching up the team for a western pilgrimage sometime soon, don't leave your standard rigging at home. Ed Iman, well-known walleye guide on the Columbia River in Washington-Oregon, typically uses #3 and #4 blades on most of his rigs. "Standard sizes have always worked," Iman says. "No real trend to larger or smaller blades has appeared on the Columbia. The most consistent producer for me is a #4 Indiana. If I had to rig all year with one blade, that would be my choice."

Which is not to say other combinations won't improve the seasonal catch. "Bigger blades, like a #6, work on occasion in August and on into fall when forage size increases. American shad start running in August, and walleyes key on them. But sometimes rather than increasing the size of the blade, I just add a blade. I run three beads down to a #2 Indiana, then three more beads down to another #2 Indiana. It adds vibration, but it's different, not the same as the thump of a larger blade. Some days, the rod rigged with tandem blades is the only one getting bit, until everybody wants a rig 'just like that one.'"

Tricks are fine. Everybody has them, and they work on occasion. Consider designing your own standard spinner rig based on fishing pressure, the average size of fish in the neighborhood, the speed of the troll, and a few clues from great anglers who are willing to help. Use the most appropriate presentation system, be it three-ways, bottom bouncers, or trolling with sideplaners.

Interview 50 top anglers, and you'll get 50 different answers on the best way to rig spinners. "You can argue over blade size, snell length, color, and weight," Iman says, "but it all comes down to meaningless drivel without this: *Don't forget the worm.*"

Chapter 7

Artificial Lures & Livebaits

Heavy Metal Magic

SPOONS, BLADES, WEIGHT-FORWARDS, AND VARIATIONS

A variety of metallic concoctions have metamorphosed out of the original basic rig-jig format, broadening the scope of heavy metal walleye lures. Some incorporate livebait or plastic tippers-trailers, while others are best fished unfettered by clutter or bait. Most, by their heavyweight nature, excel in deep coldwater jigging. Others are year-round winners from inches of water to the depths.

Jigging spoons—Traditional, wide-wobbling spoons like Dardevles are designed for shallow swimming retrieves. Most jigging spoons are narrow, thick, and heavy, designed primarily to sink quickly and to be vertically jigged in deep water. A thin, wide spoon for vertical jigging sinks slowly, wobbles

dramatically, swings wide to the side as it descends, and offers much more water resistance. Traditional spoons are difficult to fish deep because the slightest drift or current causes them to plane behind the boat and rise off bottom.

Open water jigging spoons for walleyes usually weigh between 1/2 and 1 ounce, with 3/4 ounce a popular choice. Lead bodies predominate, though slower falling tin (Hildebrandt Bun-G-Blade) and zinc models are available. Silver, gold, and fluorescent are the most popular colors, but a wealth of shades and realistic finishes (Luhr-Jensen Crippled Minnow) are available. Adding colorful Witch-craft reflective tape enhances attraction.

Drop speed and action, two of the most important characteristics of jigging spoons, are primarily determined by shape and weight. Flatter, wider spoons, like the Hopkins, Bass Pro Shops Strata Spoon, Cordell C C Spoon, Acme Kast-master, and Bullet Spoon (zinc, for a comparatively slower drop speed), provide the most wobble and descend the slowest. Narrower lures with a distinct bend, like the Bay de Noc Swedish Pimple, sink a bit quicker, vibrating more than wob-bling. Bomber's Slab Spoon and Bait Rigs' Deep Willospoon are nearly oval in shape but quite heavy, combining a quick drop with a flutter. Slender, minnow-shaped spoons, like the Luhr-Jensen Crippled Herring, Horizon Pirk Minnow, and Bull Dog Feather Jigging Spoon, tend to drop quickly with less side-to-side action. Match these aspects to the aggressiveness of the fish—faster and more prominent for active fish, slower and more subtle for inactive fish.

Drop a spoon to bottom, then engage the reel, taking up slack until the line is tight and the spoon is touching bottom. Beginning with your rod tip pointed down at an angle (about 8 o'clock) toward the water, lift your forearm slightly while mod-estly snapping your wrist upward to about 11 o'clock. The combination flexes the rod tip and pops it upward about 18 to 24 inches, a lift that transmits a bit less to the

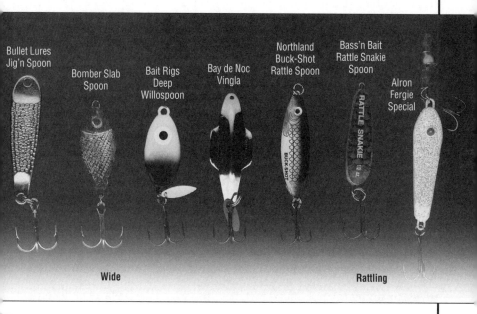

Bullet Lures Jig'n Spoon

Bomber Slab Spoon

Bait Rigs Deep Willospoon

Bay de Noc Vingla

Northland Buck-Shot Rattle Spoon

Bass'n Bait Rattle Snakie Spoon

Alron Fergie Special

Wide

Rattling

spoon because of line stretch. The lure scoots upward with little vibration, eventually coming to a momentary rest at the top of the arc.

As the lure begins to descend again, follow it downward with the rod tip. Maintain slight tension in order to feel strikes. You'll simultaneously feel the wobble and vibration of the spoon as it flutters to bottom. It'll either hit bottom or be stopped by a fish. Any doubt? Set the hook.

Both the hook rattling against a spoon's body and the natural throb of displaced water create sound, but recent success with additional sound suggests the direction of future modifications. Bass 'N Bait's Rattle Snakie features enclosed rattles. Alron's Fergie Special—a flat spoon with a rattling bead-and-brass combo on a wire leader at the head—produces phenomenal deep-water reservoir catches in the Plains states.

Traditionally, jigging spoons are used mostly during the cold weather months for deep water walleyes. Primary reservoir points, for example, are favorite vertical spooning areas during winter. Yet spoons also produce year-round, particularly where walleyes are near schools of open water suspended baitfish like ciscoes, shad, smelt, or alewives. Apparently, a fluttering, shiny spoon imitates an injured, easy meal.

Ice spoons and lures—Ice fishermen typically use lighter jigging spoons than do open water anglers to achieve a slower, more subtle drop and slighter action in cold water. Spoons can be lighter because they're fished from a stationary platform—no drift. The Swedish Pimple is a good example. It's lighter than the average open water jigging spoon, but heavy enough to fish through the ice.

Let's divide ice jigging spoons into four categories: (1) swimming lures that move in wide circles beneath your ice hole, like the #5 Jigging Rapala, #3 Nils Master, System Tackle Walleye Flyer, or Northland Air-Plane Jig; (2) straight, wide spoons for slow descent and flutter action, like the Acme Kastmaster or small Hopkins; (3) narrow or bent spoons for intermediate drop speeds and moderate flutter action, like the Bay de Noc Swedish Pimple, Ivan's Slammer, Northland Fire-eye Minnow, or Rocker Minnow; and (4) thin, wide-bodied bent spoons like the Blue Fox Tingler or Reef Runner Slender Spoon for ultraslow descent and maximum flutter. Fluorescent orange, yellow, and chartreuse colors, silver and gold, and prism tape finishes in silver, chartreuse, blue, and green are popular. In general, tip the hook with a minnow head to add scent and taste.

Even a light, wide spoon like the Reef Runner Slender Spoon can be vertically jigged beneath the ice, combining abundant action with a slow descent—perfect when fish are fussy and you have the patience to wait 'em out. Narrow spoons display less inherent action, sink quicker, and typically are better choices for ice fishing, however. An intermediate choice like a Luhr-Jensen Krocodile—a medium-width, medium-heavy, curved spoon often used for open water trolling—occasionally produces through the ice, particularly when fish are aggressive.

Trolling spoons—Thin metal flutterspoons, like Silver Leaf Spoons, Luhr-Jensen Diamond Kings, Sutton Spoons, Arbogast Thin Doctors, and others associated with Great Lakes trolling for salmon, trout, and steelhead, are often excellent walleye lures. They lack sufficient weight for casting but can be trolled with planer boards, downriggers, diving planers, or on weighted lines to achieve the proper combination of depth and speed. While not so popular as crankbaits in most walleye trolling fisheries, they do provide the added dimension of speed. Spoons trolled up to about 4 mph, and sometimes a bit faster, take walleyes under certain conditions, and water can be covered quickly.

If you fish the Great Lakes or bodies of water with silver suspended baitfish like shad, alewives, ciscoes, smelt, or shiners, be prepared to experiment with spoons. Select sizes and shapes that match prevailing baitfish, typically in flashy silver, gold, or fluorescent colors. Multispecies spoon catches of steelhead, salmon, lakers, and walleyes are common in various Great Lakes ports and on numerous reservoirs, too.

Tiny flutterspoons like walleye Willospoons also work with bouncers or three-ways, plain or tipped with livebait or plastic.

If you fish the Great Lakes or bodies of water with silver suspended baitfish like shad, alewives, ciscoes, smelt, or shiners, be prepared to experiment with spoons.

Casting-swimming spoons—Miniature standard spoons, like the Acme Little Cleo, Eppinger Dardevle Midget, Northland Fire-eye Minnow, or #8 Len Thompson, provide an additional casting option for shallow water walleyes. Small spoons (1/8 to 2/5 ounce) cast well on 8- to 10-pound test, swim over weeds nearly reaching the surface, and flutter downward a few feet on each pause. Hold the rod tip high while reeling. If the treble hangs up, give a quick wrist snap to pop and flutter the lure free, triggering potential strikes. Spoons can be surprisingly effective on fertile prairie lakes with dark water and patchy weedcover, where fishing is concentrated in less than 4 feet of water.

Narrower spoons like the Mepps Syclops (light) and Luhr-Jensen Krocodile (heavy) defy description because they're versatile enough to function as vertical jigging, trolling, and casting spoons.

For heavier, faster-moving casting, try some of the 1/2- to 3/4-ounce jigging spoons mentioned earlier. Cast, swim, pop, and retrieve 'em across sand-rock-gravel flats, across weed tops and down into pockets, or down sloping shoreline

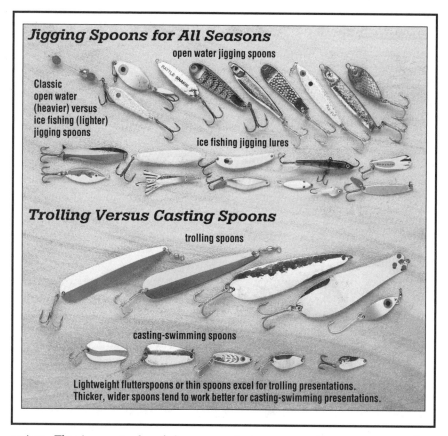

Jigging Spoons for All Seasons

open water jigging spoons

Classic
open water
(heavier) versus
ice fishing (lighter)
jigging spoons

RATTLE SNAKIE

ice fishing jigging lures

Trolling Versus Casting Spoons

trolling spoons

casting-swimming spoons

Lightweight flutterspoons or thin spoons excel for trolling presentations.
Thicker, wider spoons tend to work better for casting-swimming presentations.

points. They're great when fish are spread across expansive areas—even when they're suspended. On a long cast, pop the rod tip up, then reel up slack while dropping the rod tip, repeating all the way back to the boat. Spoons come through weeds somewhat easily if you jig and retrieve simultaneously, keeping the spoon just above the weed tops. If snags are abundant, try a small version of a more weedless Johnson Silver Minnow, Mepps Ultra Lite Timber Doodle, or Normark Rapala Minnow Spoon, using a slow, swimming retrieve.

Straight-shaft spinners and spinnerbaits—Spinners, like spoons, are considered more of a multispecies than a walleye lure, but they produce walleyes under the right conditions. Straight-shaft spinners, like the Mepps Aglia, Panther Martin, Worden's Roostertail, and Blue Fox Vibrax or Vibrax Minnow Spin, excel at straight retrieves just beneath the surface, skirting over the tops of weeds, rocks, or submerged wood. Storm's Pygmy Spin features a snap clevis with interchangeable blades. Spinners are ideal for shallow riffles in rivers, and they're great for smallmouths and trout. They don't flutter well, however, and treble versions snag easily when they contact cover. Stick to small to midsized models with #2 or #3 blades.

Safety pin spinnerbaits are primarily bass-pike lures, but will, under the right conditions, produce walleyes in cover like reeds, cane, or flooded wood. Stick to smaller 1/8- and 1/4-ounce models, primarily tandems, for straight retrieves. Examples: Northland Reed Runner, Strike King Mirage, Hart Throb, or Horizon

Straight-shaft Spinners vs. Safety Pin Spinnerbaits

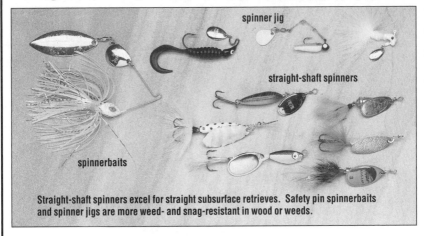

Straight-shaft spinners excel for straight subsurface retrieves. Safety pin spinnerbaits and spinner jigs are more weed- and snag-resistant in wood or weeds.

Ghost Minnow. Or try a spinner jig, like a Johnson Beetle Spin, Blakemore Road Runner, or Bass Pro Shops Stump Jumper.

Bladebaits—Bladebaits, like the straight-bodied Heddon Sonar, Bullet Blade, Cordell Gay Blade or Silver Buddy, and the curved-bodied Reef Runner Cicada or Rippletail, are thrumming, vibrating metal baits that sink at rest. Work them like spoons for casting or vertical jigging. The main difference is that they vibrate hardest on the upward surge and less so on the fall. Spoons tend to exhibit less action on the rise but flutter and flash as they fall.

Avoid a slack line drop to increase your sensitivity to strikes. Lower the lure with your rod tip, choosing a drop speed anywhere from almost a free fall to a slow lowering. Touch or bounce bottom, but avoid laying the lure on bottom to minimize snags. About 7-foot medium-heavy spinning or casting gear spooled with 10-pound-test mono works best.

Bladebaits are available in colors like those of spoons. Half-ounce 3-inch versions in metallic colors from dull to chrome, often with prism tape, are popular.

Bladebaits and Tailspinners

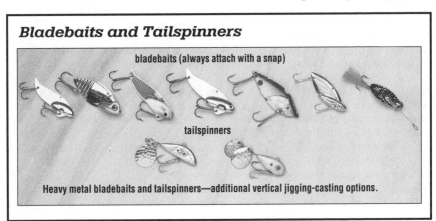

Heavy metal bladebaits and tailspinners—additional vertical jigging-casting options.

Weight–forward Spinners and Variations

weight-forward spinners

Lindy-Little Joe Flippin' Harness

Thread an entire nightcrawler onto the large hook on weight-forward spinners.
Rig the Flippin' Harness more like a two-hook crawler harness.

Most bladebaits have multiple line attachments (holes) along the backs, which require the use of a small snap being tied directly to the metal body. Changing the attachment point varies wobbling action.

Seldom used for walleyes as casting lures, bladebaits nevertheless have applications for swimming or lift-dropping retrieves to cover large areas. Mann's Mann Dancer, a unique bladebait with a flat lure body turned horizontally rather than vertically, makes a great swimming as well as vertical jigging lure. Heddon Sonars are available with added rattles.

Tailspinners—Tailspinners like Mann's Little George are ignored options for walleyes that deserve more attention. Their heavy lead bodies range from 1/4 to 1 ounce, with belly-mounted treble hooks teamed with blades that spin on a clevis at the tail. The combo creates aggressive, vibrating, flashing lures for casting and vertical jigging.

For vertical jigging, work them as you would spoons and bladebaits. Tailspinners vibrate hardest on the upward surge, though their blades flutter and flash on the drop. For casting, let the lure drop to bottom on a taut line and hold the rod tip at about 10 o'clock. Once it touches bottom, sweep it toward you by raising the rod and retrieving line. Hold your rod tip high to skip the bait over bottom and to minimize frequent snags, which are characteristic of this style of lure.

Weight-forward spinners and variations—Weight-forward spinners are versatile lures good for long-distance casting, fishing over shallow weeds or rocks, or for a countdown method that strains the depths from subsurface to perhaps 40 feet. They incorporate a weight, leader, spinner, and large single hook onto which an entire nightcrawler is threaded. They originated on Lake Erie for casting. Count down to the desired depth, then retrieve for suspended fish. Strain different depths on consecutive casts without having to change lures. Once you find the approximate depth of active fish, it's easy to zero in with the right combination of sinking time and lure size (from 1/4 to 1½ ounce).

Storm's Hot'N Tot Pygmy, the Erie Dearie, Single Spin Lure Company's Walleye Lure, and numerous generics abound around Lake Erie, but they're often difficult to obtain in other areas. Silvers, chartreuses, and greens predominate, matching the colors of light-colored, suspended baitfish.

Lindy-Little Joe's Flippin' Harness and Single Spin Lure's Walleye Wiggler (mayfly imitator) are weight-far-forward spinner variations designed by Lake

Erie charter skipper Jim Fofrich, Sr., for use on spooky fish in the clearer water that has followed the filtering effect of zebra mussels. They look like a trolling or drifting rig for use on bottom and could, of course, be fished that way. But their primary function is as casting rigs, much like weight-forward spinners, except that their weight is separated from the spinner harnesses by about 20 inches of mono. The result is often a better reaction from fussy walleyes suspended high in the clear water column. Fish apparently strike the rig more aggressively or are able to inhale the harness easier when they don't have to engulf the lead weight.

The Pa's Lure is a lipped, heavy lead spinner rig somewhat similar to a weight-forward spinner but commonly used as a trolling option for presenting crawlers to big suspended 'eyes on Saginaw Bay of Lake Huron.

SPOONFEEDING WALLEYES
—JIGGING AND CASTING

The recent effectiveness of vertical jigging with spoons has led anglers to re-examine casting spoons in shallow water. In general, lighter jigging spoons work best in the shallows, though wide, medium-weight models are also effective. So are traditional casting spoons that combine a subtle swimming action with a fair pause and flutter.

For subtle swimming retrieves, cast a light spoon like the Bait Rigs Willospoon on a light line. Add a leech, partial crawler, or small minnow to increase casting weight. Or dress it with a gitzit tail by inserting the spoon inside the plastic tube body. Rig with 6-pound line, and retrieve slowly with frequent flutters for a stealthy presentation.

MATCHING CONDITIONS

Drop speed and action, two of the most important characteristics of jigging spoons, are primarily determined by shape and weight. Match these aspects to the aggressiveness of the fish—faster and more prominent for active fish, slower and more subtle for inactive fish. Shape and weight also affect castability and fishability in deep water.

Drop speed and action, two of the most important characteristics of jigging spoons, are primarily determined by shape and weight.

"Spoon size should match the size of the forage walleyes are feeding on," notes walleye pro Daryl Christensen, "not unlike matching the hatch when fly-fishing for trout. If the main walleye forage base is smelt, I go with a long, thin spoon. If it's gizzard shad, I use a short fat spoon. If it's emerald shiners, I fish a thin, short spoon."

Christensen continues: "During postspawn, walleyes tend to be shallow in most environments, feeding over shallow sandbars, rocky shorelines, or emerging weed flats. Cast a spoon with a large profile because most forage— alewives, shad, perch, whatever—tend to be large adults, not juveniles.

"But most large spoons are too heavy for shallow water. They must be fished too fast to keep them off bottom. Try a spoon like the Bullet Lures zinc spoon. It's large but weighs less than lead or nickel spoons.

"One summer at Lake Oahe, South Dakota, I found walleyes feeding on smelt in the backs of deep bays. I fished a 1-ounce, long-profile spoon to simulate smelt. I picked up only a few fish with this practice. Something was missing. Local anglers were cleaning fish one evening, and I discovered the walleyes were eating smelt, but the smelt were only about 3 inches long. My bait was too large. I

Shape Versus Performance

Spoons Imitate Forage

long, narrow

smelt

medium length, wide

gizzard shad

short, narrow

shiner

Typical Jigging Spoon

CURVATURE

treble or large single hook
narrow to medium width

straight—minimum wobble

slight curve—medium wobble

bent—heavy wobble

WIDTH

heavy, sinks quickly

thick body

narrow—falls quickest

medium—falls intermediately

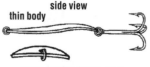

wide—falls slowest

Traditional Spoon

top view

wide body

side view
thin body

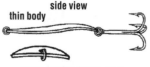

cross-section (back view)
usually cupped

returned to the same bays the following day and scaled down to a 3/8-ounce spoon to match the size of the smelt. After that, I limited each day."

JIGGING VERSUS CASTING

Jigging spoons are often an alternative, or at least a supplement, to rigging and jigging with livebait. They can be cast and vertically jigged. When fish are suspended or spread on flats or shallow cover, use a horizontal presentation—in this case, casting—to cover water. When they're bottom oriented in deep water or concentrated along distinct edges, use a vertical presentation—in this case, vertical jigging—to keep your lure in the fish zone.

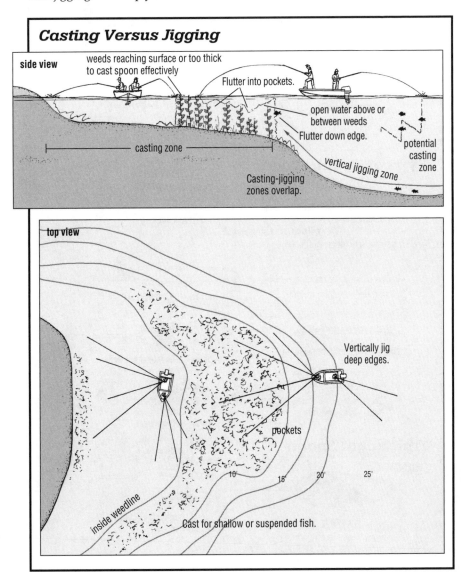

Casting Versus Jigging

side view — weeds reaching surface or too thick to cast spoon effectively

Flutter into pockets.

open water above or between weeds

Flutter down edge.

casting zone

potential casting zone

vertical jigging zone

Casting-jigging zones overlap.

top view

Vertically jig deep edges.

pockets

10'   15'   20'   25'

inside weedline

Cast for shallow or suspended fish.

Christensen suggests: "Say you mark fish along a shelf, from 20 to 30 feet deep and within three feet of bottom: vertical jigging, not casting, makes sense. If you mark fish at several different depths along the shelf, though, cast. Flutter a spoon to bottom on a long cast, then retrieve by pulling the rod tip back, reeling up slack, and letting the spoon fall to bottom.

"Whenever you find fish on a deep break, cast into the nearby shallows, too, especially to weedlines. Even spoons rigged with a treble come through weeds well. A sharp snap of the rod tip frees most weeds, often triggering strikes from following walleyes. When working a spoon over weeds, jig and retrieve at the same time, keeping the spoon just above the weeds.

"Deep stumps or timber can hold lots of walleyes, but casting a spoon into them results in expensive deep water decorations. Such areas are perfect, however, for vertical jigging. I use a light wire hook. If I get snagged, I pull the spoon free.

"I also vertically jig along current breaks in rivers, since most rivers are littered with trees and other snags. If the river has a deep sand cut, however, I cast a spoon to or over the bars and jig the spoon back to the boat."

When rivers get really cold, like 33°F in midwinter, it's natural to stick with even slower, more subtle techniques like minnow-tipped jigs. But jigging spoons are even more effective than jigs at times—no surprise, since jigging spoons work so well for walleyes through the ice. Carry one rod rigged with a jigging spoon the next time you're on a river.

PRESENTATION TIPS

Vertical jigging with spoons is similar to fishing with jigs, except it's more aggressive. Jigs are more subtle, requiring only lifts and drops, perhaps an occasional jiggle. Spoons, however, require a bit more momentum to get them up and moving.

Drop a spoon toward bottom. Engage the reel, taking up slack until the line is tight, with the spoon touching bottom.

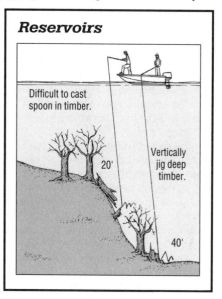

Reservoirs

Difficult to cast spoon in timber.

Vertically jig deep timber.

20'

40'

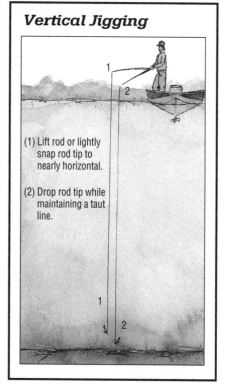

Vertical Jigging

(1) Lift rod or lightly snap rod tip to nearly horizontal.

(2) Drop rod tip while maintaining a taut line.

Beginning with your rod tip pointed down at an angle toward the water, lift your forearm slightly while snapping your wrist slightly upward. This flexes the rod tip and pops it upward about 18 to 24 inches, transmitting a bit less lift to the spoon because of line stretch. The lure scoots upward with little vibration, eventually coming to a momentary rest at the top of its arc.

As the lure begins to descend, follow it down with the rod tip. Maintain slight tension so you can feel strikes. You'll feel both the wobble and vibration of the spoon as it flutters to bottom. Plunk. It hits bottom, and the line goes slack.

Use your sense of feel. Is bottom hard, soft, snaggy, clean? Did something disturb the vibration on the way down? That's a fish. Set the hook. Don't wait for 'em to jerk the line. Set at any hint of activity, even when you first drop the spoon to bottom.

Suspended walleyes usually feed on flashy baitfish, and a spoon falling to bottom looks good enough to eat. If you get hit on the way down, jig the spoon at the depth you spot fish on the depthfinder. Or jig it on bottom, then reel up a few feet, and jig several times. Repeat until you get bored or bit—whichever comes first.

The deeper you fish, the faster you drift, the more current you face, the heavier the spoons you need. Adjust lure weight and amount of line out to match conditions. In general, fish as vertically as possible to enhance feel and to maintain control.

Experiment with lure style and color. Try different jigging motions, some aggressive, others subtle. Spoons by their basic nature are flashier and louder than jigs. Fish in the area become aware of them. They'll even attract fish from a

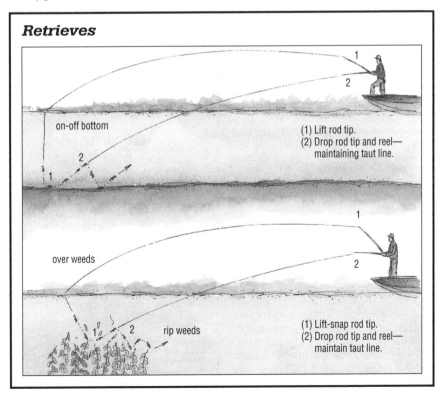

Retrieves

on-off bottom

(1) Lift rod tip.
(2) Drop rod tip and reel—
maintaining taut line.

over weeds

rip weeds

(1) Lift-snap rod tip.
(2) Drop rod tip and reel—
maintain taut line.

distance. If you're not catching fish on spoons, either they're not there or the combination of speed, flash, and vibration isn't productive. Try another combination.

"Casting jigging spoons isn't much different than casting jigs," Christensen says, "with one exception. Since spoons are heavier than most jigs, it's possible to cover a lot of water in a short time. With two anglers in the boat, one casting to deep water, the other working the shallows, spoons are great fish finders as well as fish catchers.

"Work the spoon all the way back to the boat, then vertically jig it a few times, in case a walleye's following. Then reel up, cast again, and repeat the process all the way down the break. Never jerk the rod tip hard, causing the spoon to move too fast and too erratically for fish to strike easily. Also, the hook may foul on the line, wasting the cast.

"I never rig a heavy jigging spoon with livebait for casting because the buoyancy of the bait destroys the built-in action of the spoon. Plus a bait only hangs on for one or two casts before it falls off, feeding fish instead of catching them.

"When I'm vertical jigging, I tip a heavy spoon with a minnow tail or small minnow, or perhaps a piece of crawler. This creates a slower drop speed, and the bait is likely to stay on the hook, because I'm fishing only the bottom 2 or 3 feet of water."

Some anglers prefer long-handled casting rods between 6 and 6½ feet long, believing they offer better control and hooksetting; line length can be increased simply by pushing a button. Others prefer spinning tackle with lighter line. Some use both.

"I like to fish spoons on calm days," Christensen says, "but calm days are rare on big waters. The stronger the wind and waves, the heavier I go for better lure control. I use a Quantum 6-foot baitcasting Tour Rod for spoons over 1/2 ounce, and a 6-foot medium-action spinning Tour Rod for lighter spoons. I rig my reels with 10-pound-test line.

"Use a Cross-Lok snap in order to change spoons quickly. Also, a spoon flutters and drops better with a snap. And tying a spoon direct (no snap or split ring) can wear line in a hurry. Spoons need a split ring to give them better action.

"I prefer spoons in hammered gold or silver finishes, because they reflect and flash like injured baitfish. Match a #4 or #6 Mustad treble hook to the size of the spoon, even for fishing weeds.

"Color can be important, sometimes critical," Christensen says. "Of spoons cast for walleyes in shallow water one year at a Saginaw Bay tournament, gold outfished silver 4-to-1 during the first day of competition. On the second day, silver was the ticket. Day one was cloudy; day two, sunny. Also, on day one, a 3/4-ounce spoon was best, but the second day, with a slight cold front passing through, I had better results with a 1/2-ounce bait that had a shorter profile."

Fishing jigging spoons takes patience and practice. So does trolling crankbaits, fishing livebait rigs, or casting jigs-and-minnows. Spoons aren't magic baits, but on some days, they outfish other presentations, even livebait. Try them on ice and in open water.

SHAKE THEM RATTLIN' JIGGIN' SPOONS

We've got the shakes. Can't count the times we've picked up Northland Tackle's Buck-Shot Rattle Spoon, positioned it between thumb and forefinger like a throwing dart, and began shaking it near our ears like a miniature maraca.

Using every means possible to help fish find your lure sometimes helps attract and catch more of them. Lures designed with rattles would seem to be proven fish attractors. A few winters back, through the ice on Mille Lacs, Minnesota, the Rattlin' Snakie spoon by Bass'N Bait proved itself to many walleye ice anglers by seemingly outproducing spoons without rattles.

On Northland's lead jigging spoon, a rattle tube is embedded on the exterior of the backside, leaving half the chamber uncovered to achieve maximum volume from the rattle. The length and width of the spoons (1/4, 3/8, and 5/8 ounce) match baitfishes' proportions. A lifelike, holographic 3-D baitfish image and Northland's "match the hatch" paint job add realism and flash to the spoon.

Dan Ferguson's Alron Fergie Special, another rattling variation, does the trick on huge walleyes at Lake McConaughy, Nebraska, when other anglers are catching nothing.

Jigging spoons have been successful for a long time, but Ferguson has added sound to his spoons. Two glass beads sandwiched around a brass bead slide up and down a thin wire when the spoon is jigged. Ferguson is convinced the noise makes a difference, especially when fish are deep and visibility is low.

At McConaughy, for instance, divers say that at 35 feet, it's like going into a closet and turning out the light. Yet Ferguson has caught walleyes as deep as 72 feet. Can the fish see his spoon at that depth? A walleye's lateral line detects vibrations as the lure flutters, but we also know that walleyes can hear.

"When walleyes are aggressive," Ferguson says, "I don't think the beads are necessary, because I can catch them on any spoon. But when I go deeper than 30 feet, I notice a 3-to-1 difference between a regular spoon and one with noise."

Ferguson first used a superline like Berkley FireLine when he began probing depths of 50 feet or more with his spoon. "I thought the zero stretch would work well, especially in deep water," he says. "But these spoons fall so erratically that the FireLine tends to wrap around them. So I've gone to Berkley Big Game or a low-stretch monofilament like 20-pound Berkley XT. I fish 12- or 14-pound line in shallow water, going to 20-pound line to eliminate stretch for deep water."

The spoon comes in two sizes. The 1 ounce is 2½ inches long, the 1/2 ounce, about 2 inches. It has two treble hooks—one at each end. "It's a long, thin spoon with a flattened front that makes it flutter," Ferguson says. "When the spoon is snapped hard, then allowed to flutter down, the head of the spoon always goes down first. The stinger hook catches walleyes who strike the head, as they usually do."

Ferguson snaps the spoon 1½ or 2 feet on each lift and doesn't drop his rod tip back until the slack goes out of his line. This indicates that the spoon's on its way back down. Then he drops his rod tip to control the fall of the spoon. If the spoon stops or slack remains, Ferguson immediately sets the hook hard.

"I let the spoon down on what I call controlled slack," Ferguson says. "I don't want the line so tight the flutter of the spoon is ruined. Drop too fast and the spoon flutters away, and you don't feel a fish. With controlled slack, you can see the fish smack the lure. The line jumps, or you feel the hit."

A jigging spoon may not be the best presentation to search for fish. But when you've found them at the tip of a point, along a drop-off, or on structure like submerged trees, spoons are deadly. Drop one down in front of a walleye's nose and flutter it a few times. The fish can't resist it.

A note of caution: when jigging in deep water, bring the fish up slowly, or its air bladder will expand and kill it. "The fish I release head straight down again," Ferguson says. "But I bring them up slowly, forcing myself to take time. Then I get the fish off the hook and back into the water as soon as possible."

SPOONS DOWN DEEP

The sonar shows a cloud of shad extending several feet deep. Thick black lines can be seen streaking through the shad. "There, that's what we're looking for," Tom Bruno says. "You see those big hooks below the shad? Walleyes."

Bruno and Terry Wickstrom are taking advantage of one of the most predictable and repeatable patterns in western walleye fishing, a pattern that materializes in almost all western prairie plateau reservoirs with significant shad populations. In October and November, as the water temperature in these impoundments drops below 60°F, shad become stressed, especially young-of-the-year. When stressed, the shad congregate in large schools—safety in numbers. These large schools of vulnerable baitfish present a feeding opportunity for large predators looking to fatten up for winter.

On this particular day, they're fishing Pueblo Reservoir in south-central Colorado. The large black streaks on sonar running through the shad are wipers (hybrid stripers). While the wipers make vicious passes through the school of baitfish, the walleyes prowl below, munching away.

You might think this condition presents a "can't miss opportunity" to catch walleyes. Some specific keys are needed, however, to catch these fish. Among the most important are the lure and the presentation. These walleyes become so focused on dying shad fluttering down from these large schools that they ignore almost anything else.

By far the most effective presentation is a jigging spoon. While various brands and models will work (Hopkins Spoon, Kastmaster, Swedish Pimple, among others), one particular spoon has been a standout—a long, slender, 1-ounce spoon made by Fle-Fly of Texas. The unique shape and highly reflective prism finish imitate a crippled shad.

By far the most effective presentation is a jigging spoon.

Just as important as the spoon is how it's presented. Drifting around using a simple lift and drop won't catch many fish. Fish as vertically as possible. Either anchor or hold the boat in position with your front electric motor. Then, with your spoon about 6 inches off bottom, sharply pop it upward about 3 to 5 feet. Snap the rod tip so the spoon turns from hanging vertically to lying in a horizontal position. Then follow the spoon back down with your rod, allowing it to fall on slack line. The strike will usually come as the spoon flutters down. If your line stops before it's down to where it started, set the hook. If you don't get a hit on the fall, pause for a moment. At times, a walleye will hit the lure as it settles on bottom after the fall. And you won't know you have a fish until the next time you snap upward.

The other key to this pattern is location. Shad tend to school in water from 25 to 50 feet deep, at the mouths of feeder creeks. Other spots with high potential are deep areas near underwater humps and points. While the shad don't seem to be relating to the structure, having a hump or point nearby seems to concentrate them. Spend time looking with your electronics, and if you don't see schools of baitfish, don't stop to fish. Once you find concentrations of shad, the fishing can be incredible.

Use a 6-foot 6-inch trigger-style rod and a baitcasting reel with a flipping switch, spooled with 10- or 12-pound-test line. If you use spinning gear, try a reel with antireverse to eliminate reel handle slap. Use a rod with a fairly heavy backbone. Too whippy a rod makes it difficult to snap the spoon up fast enough to turn it over. Also, a heavy rod is needed to get a good hookset in deep water. Tie a ball bearing swivel about one foot above the spoon to prevent line twist.

THE SONAR STANDARD

A wee lad watches as his father and grandfather catch phenomenal numbers of trophy walleyes on the Mississippi River near LaCrosse, Wisconsin. It's the mid 1950s, and the family patriarchs are using a revolutionary new jigging presentation—the Heddon Sonar, a weighted metal blade sporting twin treble hooks. By the late 1950s, the lad has grown to become an avid angler himself, part of the river revolution with bladebaits. He and his family have nearly abandoned livebait in favor of vibrating blades—a progressive attitude for those times.

Heddon Sonar

Blitz Blade

Fast forward to the present: the lad is now a grown man with nearly 40 years' experience fishing rivers and lakes with Sonars. His name is Wally Moser, and along with partner Phil Caldwell, he has become a legend in Pacific Northwest walleye circles, with many top tournament money finishes to his credit.

Almost as amazing as Moser and Caldwell's tournament tally is the fact that they did it with just one method—jigging Heddon Sonars. This violates the versatility standard other walleye anglers live and die by. But on river systems, it's tough to argue against the Sonar standard.

Reef Runner Cicada

"So Wally, whatcha gonna use?" It's a normal question for most fishing buddies, but not for this pair. With these two, the question is facetious, cheeky, and downright funny.

THE LURE

Metal bladebaits of various designs hang in most well-stocked tackle stores: Heddon Sonar, Reef Runner Cicada, Luhr-Jensen Ripple Tail, Blitz Blade, Silver Buddy, and more. Moser and Caldwell use the term "Sonar" for actual Sonars and the several look-alikes currently on the market.

Luhr-Jensen Ripple Tail

To achieve optimum profile, vibration, and drop speed, they recommend 1/2-ounce blades roughly 3 inches long. They prefer straight blades over concave versions. "Concave blades don't have the drop speed and vibration I like," Moser says. "For colors," he affirms, "we like all the metallic colors from dull to chrome. Also, yellow and the full range of greens from dark to chartreuse."

The key to getting strong vibrating action is to snap a tiny Duolock into the forward line hole (the Sonar has three attachment holes, each providing a different action). Onlookers have speculated that these guys modify their lures with secret bends and such. They occasionally put small bends in the blade, but only to make a poorly vibrating lure respond better, like tuning a crankbait.

JIGGING MOTION

Anyone who has fished a bladebait knows that the best way to get strong vibrations is to jig a bit more aggressively than with ordinary leadheads. Caldwell describes this special Sonar jigging action this way: "Both flicking and pulling strokes are used, with something in between a flick and a pull being generally the most effective. A flick is done mostly with the wrist; a pull, mostly with the elbow. Typically, I do more pulling on the raise stroke, and Caldwell does more flicking. Of course, if Phil's flicking is outcatching my pulling, I adapt."

The drop is at least as important as the upstroke. These blade masters usually avoid a slack line drop, preferring to lower the lure with their rod tips. This allows them to choose drop speeds anywhere from almost free fall to slow lowering. In essence, they're versatile in the way they choose drop speed. This tight line dropping motion also enhances sensitivity to strikes, an important factor when using metal artificials, because walleyes quickly spit out a solid piece of metal after the initial hit.

Because bladebaits are susceptible to fouling—the hooks catch your line—they're most often fished just off bottom.

"Detecting a subtle hit on the drop is one of the main keys to success," Moser stresses. "If the hit is detected on the drop, an immediate hard hookset can be made. If, on the other hand, the fish isn't felt until the upstroke, it's much harder to make a good, quick hookset. If you feel the fish on the upstroke, it's automatic to stop the usual stroke, then react with another hooksetting stroke. We call this double clutching, and the percentage of hookups is much lower than with a single-stroke hookset."

Because bladebaits are susceptible to fouling—the hooks catch your line—they're most often fished just off bottom. Let the lure touch bottom, and it's easier for the hooks to grab the slackened line. Moser and Caldwell, however, are less concerned with fouling than with catching fish. Each jig stroke concludes with what they call "the bounce." They let the lure bounce bottom, sometimes even allowing it to linger for a couple of seconds before starting the next stroke. To maintain sensitivity and to reduce fouling, they barely touch down, not letting the lure lie on its side on a slack line.

GEAR

Fishing 1/2-ounce metal lures in river current is not a game for standard medium-action walleye rods. According to Moser, "The sense of feel needed to fish Sonars requires a stiff, sensitive rod." Caldwell and Moser prefer a medium-heavy or heavy 7-foot rod. For lightness and strength, both anglers have chosen Lamiglas Certified Pro models.

Though they agree on rod action, Moser and Caldwell prefer different rod styles. Moser likes a spinning rod, because, he says, "It's easier on the arm, elbow, and shoulder. Bouncing Sonars all day can be a lot of work, and a spinning outfit hangs naturally in the fingers. It also allows me to feel the line with my fingers for increased sensitivity. On the other hand, Phil prefers a casting rod and reel because the flipping switch is handy for adjusting line length to differing depths. He also prefers to play fish on the casting rod. The winchability and smooth drag

Heavy Metal

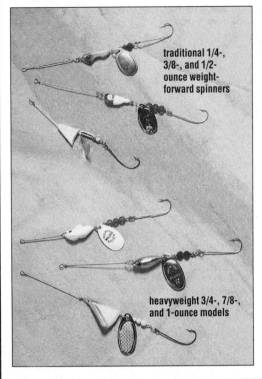

traditional 1/4-, 3/8-, and 1/2-ounce weight-forward spinners

heavyweight 3/4-, 7/8-, and 1-ounce models

on a casting rod make it hard to argue with this logic."

These bladebait purists are fussy about the line they use. "For feel, a low-stretch, high-conduction line is best." Though it sounds like they're describing Berkley FireLine or SpiderWire Fusion, they actually use Berkley Tri-Max, with 8- and 10-pound test as standard.

POWER DRIFTING

Nothing tricky or fancy in their means of presentation. They drift downstream using the electric to pull them along slightly faster than the current. You could call it "power drifting." So, unlike leadhead jigs, which are generally fished by chasing the jig downcurrent at about its natural drift speed, they determine the speed and direction, dragging their heavy metal along behind them. It's a semivertical presentation. If they're fishing along a slope, a drop, or a ledge, they S-curve the boat up and down the area of depth change while simultaneously power drifting downcurrent.

During warmer seasons, Moser and Caldwell power drift faster. They also vary their drift speed, based on walleye mood. Hot fish get a faster presentation, and vice versa.

Wally Moser and Phil Caldwell vary jigging action, drop speed, bounce time, and boat speed to create a versatile system of bladebait fishing—the Sonar standard.

The next time you chase walleyes in a river system, "Whatcha gonna use?"

WEIGHT-FORWARD SPINNER TACTICS FOR THE 21ST CENTURY

The zebra mussels that now strain Lake Erie's waters have led to drastically clearer water in the Western Basin. Early in the year, when water clarity is reduced by run-off and spring winds, fishing the top 10 feet is still one dynamite tactic for Lake Erie walleyes, as it can be almost any time of year when weather and water conditions draw suspended walleyes near the surface.

Once the water clears and sunlight penetrates the crystal depths, walleyes tend to stay down. Fishing below 20 feet becomes the norm, and catching walleyes as deep as 40 feet or more isn't unusual. Fish don't come up on the reefs or rise to the surface as regularly as they did in the 1970s and early 1980s, when the water sported an emerald green midsummer tinge. Fish the shallows at night, in wind, or during rain or cloudy weather, but modify your approach for most daytime fishing most of the year.

With walleyes remaining deeper, trolling tactics have begun to gain popularity on Lake Erie. For old-timers who grew up casting weight-forward spinners in the Western Basin, this is a tough pill to swallow. Casting weight-forwards is a wonderfully effective, as well as an up-close-and-personal tactic for catching walleyes.

Strain different water levels without changing lures by letting lures sink to a different depth on each cast before beginning your retrieve. Best of all, strikes can be felt—an instant, intimate connection to the marble-eyed brute on the other end of the line. Four, five, even six fish on at a time per charter boat is possible. A three-ring circus. Nets dip. Lead flies. Spinners flutter. Anglers cry, "Fish on!"

Those days aren't gone. But conditions have definitely changed. Change along with them, or don't expect consistent catches with weight-forward techniques, plain and simple.

The key to continued success with weight-forward spinners in Lake Erie's Western Basin is refining and fine-tuning your approach to the clearer water. Used to be . . . smaller, lighter lures; heavier line; short, stubby, inexpensive rods; short casts off the ends of the boat; and heck, even spinners dragged on a short line behind the boat as you drifted amidst packs of charter boats floating above schools of suspended walleyes. Nowadays, you can't cut corners, get sloppy, or succeed with ho-hum equipment. Stay away from other boats whenever possible, because they spook fish. And don't expect to drift over areas several times with as much success. Fish react to our presence; we must react to their response.

ADAPTATION

Walleyes are spookier, dashing out from the sides of the boat at greater distances when the boat's shadow appears overhead. Make longer casts, preferably off the bow and transom. This creates a swing effect as the boat draws parallel to and begins to pass the lure, causing it to speed up, rise, pulsate, and change direction. It's a classic triggering mechanism for Lake Erie lead slingers.

Because six anglers on a charter boat can't fit their casts into those two small, magical zones off the bow or transom, some must cast far downwind and work their lures back to the boat while drifting toward their spinners. Practice is necessary to match retrieve speed to wind velocity correctly, so the blade on the lure can spin, flash, and wobble while the lure and the boat approach each other on a collision course. This technique has become vitally important for catching spooky walleyes with casting techniques in the clearer water of the early 21st century.

To achieve this long-distance control, longer rods and lighter line are vital, like 6½-footers of high-quality graphite, spooled with 8-pound-test premium monofilament. These combos cast farther, telegraph strikes better, and set hooks with authority, even at long distances. Jim Fofrich uses custom rods made on G. Loomis IMX blanks, designed by Tom Cooney of Rod-Craft in Chicago—#783 for spinning gear that casts 1/2- to 3/4-ounce midsized lures, and #784 for casting rods designed to pitch heavyweight 3/4- to 1-ounce models. Consider using a colored line like Berkley Solar to help detect strikes visually. Tie on 20 feet of clear line between the end of the main line and the lure to diminish visibility to the fish.

In order to fish deeper and cast farther, use heavier lures than those popular in the past. Today, 3/4-, 7/8-, and 1-ounce weight-forward spinners with easy rotating blades often are necessary. You can zing them a mile, and they sink faster and deeper, retaining a degree of control that lighter lures forfeit. Work them like smaller weight-forward spinners, swimming them at the fish's level, crawling them just off bottom, or even using a pump-and-flutter to skip across bottom without catching too many zeebs (zebra mussels). The key is to do this successfully at 30, 35, 40, or 45 feet—the big-fish zone most of summer and fall.

Fishing the Downdrift

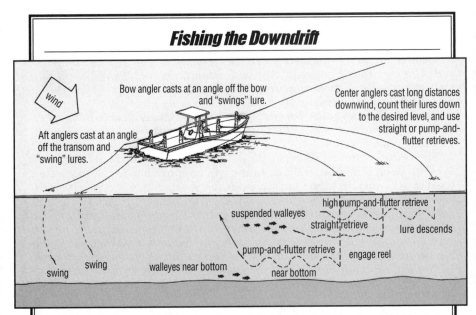

The center anglers fishing nearly straight downwind (the downdrift) must fire casts far enough downwind to reach fish that aren't spooked by the approaching shadow of the boat. Lures must then descend to the appropriate level and be worked back to the boat with the right combination of speed and rod action to trigger fish, creating a sort of vertical pump-flutter version of the swing without the benefit of casting off the bow or transom.

Count your lure down to the appropriate level (determined by experimentation or by spotting fish on electronics), then engage the reel and firmly pop the rod tip upward to eliminate slack and start the blade spinning. Then retrieve it fast enough to continue feeling the blade vibrate, even while drifting toward the lure. Experiment with straight retrieves, pump-and-flutters, and combinations. Try different lure weights, color combinations (blades and lure bodies), even different blade styles.

When you hit on the right combo, walleyes often pop the lure with authority or nail it on the descent. Yet at other times, they barely lip the crawler, so pay attention. If you get a bump and miss the fish, immediately drop the rod tip back to let the lure flutter momentarily, then resume your retrieve. Walleyes sometimes return for a second whack—or else another nearby fish takes the bait.

Clearer water in Lake Erie has resulted in several major changes on the weight-forward front. First, separating the weight from the sinker rig seems to amplify the rig's effectiveness. Lindy Little-Joe's Flippin' Harness is a sort of weight-far-forward rig designed for this purpose; it also triples as a great

Fishing the Swing

L ake Erie anglers use weight-forward spinners to strain the water column, searching for the right combination of depth, retrieve speed, lure action, and color to trigger walleyes. Depending on lure weight, a weight-forward spinner with a whole nightcrawler threaded onto the large single hook will sink a certain distance per second.

Heavier lures obviously descend faster, light lures more slowly. Test different sizes and models to determine how fast each drops, but for demonstration purposes, we'll assume it's 1 foot per second. Count "One thousand one, one thousand two, one thousand three . . ." after your lure strikes the water to estimate how deep the lure is before you begin your retrieve.

Used to be you could make relatively short casts (*A*) and still catch fish. But with clearer water and increased walleye wariness, longer casts (*B*) are more in order.

Anglers casting to *B-1*, *B-2*, and *B-3* can incorporate a triggering mechanism called *the swing* into their retrieve. Basically, the lure runs along a slightly curved path (*1-2-3*) until the drifting boat draws parallel to it (*4*). At that point, the boat begins moving ahead of the lure; tightening the line; increasing lure speed; making it change direction and rise toward the surface, "thrumming" the blade as it ascends (*4-5*). This easy-to-feel change—the swing—triggers following fish. So many fish fall for this technique that it should be used whenever possible.

Trouble is, everyone can't fish off the bow or transom. Someone has to fish downwind (*B-4*, *B-5*, and *B-6*).

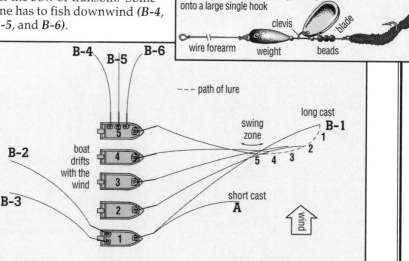

drifting or trolling rig. Second, a boom in mayfly populations causes walleyes to key in on them times almost to the exclusion of other forage, making spinner fishing difficult. A variation of the flippin' harness, Single Spin Lure's Walleye Wiggler, sports a smaller blade, a hackle, and a smaller hook. Tipped with a piece of nightcrawler instead of an entire crawler threaded onto the hook as with traditional weight-forwards, it more closely resembles smaller insect forage.

Fine fish can be caught on weight-forward spinners all summer if you match tactics to conditions. Travel east of the Catawaba Peninsula in summer, and you can catch fish on weight-forwards in 50 to 60 feet of water if you do it right, thus retaining the unique magic of catching big-water walleyes on the casting techniques that Erie is so famous for.

At some point, however, it becomes more effective, number-wise and odds-wise, to switch to a trolling approach in order to keep your lure in deep water nearly 100 percent of the time rather than in the air or the unproductive upper layers of water. The T-Word is still a dirty word to many longtime Erie anglers, but experience has shown that trolling is too effective to ignore when walleyes go down and dirty.

Weight-forward tactics have changed over the last decade, but they're a long way from dead in the water. They'll always be the king of Lake Erie walleye tactics. Long live the king, and the queen of walleye fisheries, Lake Erie.

Crankin' and Spankin'

**CASTING AND
LONGLINE TROLLING
CRANKBAITS**

Bass fisherman call 'em crankbaits; you cast 'em out and crank 'em back in again. But amongst walleye anglers, hard baits, body baits, and, yes, even crankbaits aren't just for casting. Depending on region, trolling may prevail. But wherever hard baits see action, the action's mighty good—especially for big walleyes.

Speaking of action, the various shapes of crankbaits create a range of wiggles and wobbles that trigger strikes from many species of gamefish. The most popular and widespread models are the fat, round-bodied lures originally referred to as alphabet lures—Big O's, Little N's, Model A's—named for letters of the alphabet. While these hardwobbling lures catch loads of bass and definitely produce some walleyes, crankbaits of other general shapes tend to outproduce fat alpha baits when the specific target is walleyes.

MINNOW-IMITATORS

Foremost among walleye trolling baits are long, thin, straight-backed lures generically referred to as minnowbaits or minnow-imitators. They resemble long, thin forage like minnows, shiners, ciscoes, or smelt. Classic examples, in no particular order, include Rapala Floating Minnows, Storm ThunderSticks, Smithwick Rogues, Bomber Long A's, Arbogast's Snooker, Poe's Cruise Minnow, Rebel Spoonbill Minnows, Bagley Bang-O-Lures, Cordell Red Fins, Bass Pro Shops Pro Qualifier Minnows, and Rebel Minnows and Fastrac Minnows.

Foremost among walleye trolling baits are long, thin, straight-backed lures generically referred to as minnowbaits or minnow-imitators.

Most are short-lipped, shallow runners, achieving only 1 to 2 feet of depth when cast and retrieved, perhaps 3 or 4 feet when trolled on an unweighted line. A few deep-diving versions, like Storm Deep ThunderSticks, Rebel Spoonbill Minnows, and the larger Bomber Long A's, may dive into the 20- to 25-foot range when longline trolled. Otherwise, adding weight ahead of the lure takes minnow-imitators down into the 30- to 70-foot levels—the staple walleye presentation for open water trolling on the Great Lakes and on large inland lakes and reservoirs.

A recent offshoot of the minnow-imitator family could be described as *humpies* or simply *bent minnows* because of the pronounced humpback bend in their otherwise minnowlike bodies. The Reef Runner Deep Diver, Ripstick, and Little Ripper, Fenwick Wobbl'n Minnow, and Yo-Zuri Wobbl'n Minnow fall into this category. Place them in the water side by side with traditional long, thin minnow-imitators, and you'll notice that humpies display more action. Walleyes notice it, too. Not that humpies are consistently better than minnow-imitators—they simply provide a different action that sometimes triggers more fish.

Whether constructed from balsa or injection-molded plastic, minnow-imitators typically exhibit a shivering wiggle as opposed to the wide, side-to-side

Minnow-Imitators

Mann's Stretch Series

Normark Rapala

Smithwick Super Rogue

Storm ThunderStick

wobble of rounder-bodied baits. On the average, walleyes tend to prefer reduced action over more aggressive wobble. Perhaps this explains the general preference for solid minnows over jointed, *broken-back* counterparts that possess more inherent wiggle. Yet even within the minnow-imitator category, variations exist—a Rapala is thinner than a ThunderStick and a ThunderStick is thinner than a Rebel Minnow, for example. The rounder-bodied Nils Master Invincible, often hard to find in America despite outselling the Rapala in Europe, is also effective on walleyes. Action can be fine-tuned simply by shifting lure families while staying withing the same basic size and color pattern.

Some lures rattle; others are relatively subtle and silent. In general, open water trollers seem to prefer a bit of added sound and vibration, while anglers trolling shallow water at night lean toward stealth and reduced noise. Once again, experimentation is the best selection method. Let the fish tell you what they want.

Color patterns vary among lure manufacturers, but those that imitate natural forage predominate among walleye lures. Dark-backed, flashy (silver-sided) lures produce best for open water trolling in clear water and at night in the shallows. Daytime fishing in clear water calls for matching lures to forage like perch, shiners, crayfish, rainbow trout, or white bass. Select lures with a splash of orange or chartreuse for added visibility in murky waters.

SHADS AND SHAD-OWS

Ranking second on the walleye crankbait front and most popular among casters targeting structure like rock points or reefs are shad-bodied crankbaits like Normark Shad Raps, Rebel Shad-R's, Bagley Shads, Cordell C. C. Rattlin' Shads or Wee Shads, and Storm Thin Fins and Lightnin' Shads. Closely resembling tri-angle-shaped shad forage, shad baits are considerably deeper bodied than minnow-imitators, but still thin. This creates the illusion of a shad- or alewife-shaped baitfish profile. Shad baits have a fairly subtle action compared to that of rounder-bodied baits; once again, subtle action predominates for walleyes. Shad baits are also great bass lures for times when reduced vibration and action are preferred. They're available in shallow and deepdiving versions that run from 1 or 2 to perhaps 6 feet on a cast and retrieve. They are underutilized as trolling lures, even though they perform well wherever shad or alewife forage predominate.

Lightweight balsa shads are difficult to cast on heavy line, so most anglers toss them with 8-pound-test monofilament and spinning gear. Plastic-bodied shads, particularly those with rattles like the Rebel Mystic Shad-R, are heavier

Shad-Minnow Crossover

Normark Risto Rap

Mann's Wally Track

Lindy-Little Joe Shadling

Cordell Walley Diver

and easier to cast long distances or into the wind. Some, like the Shad-R and Excalibur Shad-R, are available as both floaters and suspended lures.

These relatively flat sided baits are sensitive to speed when you're casting or trolling; too much speed, and they go out of balance, ruining the retrieve or trolling pass, unless the lure is properly tuned to run above 2 or 2½ mph. Anglers fishing eastern shad-based impoundments often troll shad baits at high speeds—3 to 5 mph—just beneath the surface for suspended walleyes and muskies.

Shad-ows are hybrids of shad crankbaits and minnow-imitators. They're rounder bodied than minnowbaits, and often have a bit of a hump or a curvature. Lures like the Mann's Stretch Series, Lindy-Little Joe Shadling, Cordell Wally Diver, Mann's Wally-Trac, Rebel Shad-R, and Luhr-Jensen Power Dive Minnow fall into this loose category. Most come with a fairly substantial diving lip, so they're good casting lures for banging bottom or ripping weed tops and for fish preferring more action than minnow-imitators or shads provide. Shad-ows tend to dive 7 to 10 feet on a cast, and beyond 15 feet when trolled on an unweighted line.

Most of the time, shad-ows are about as aggressive as you want a lure to be for walleyes. But not all the time, as the category that follows demonstrates.

AGGRESSIVE WOBBLERS

Historically, this class of lures dates back farther than traditional diving crankbaits, to lures like the Flat Fish and Lazy Ike, which are still around and still productive. Generically referred to as banana baits because of their humpbacked profile, they wiggle side to side, even when they make little forward movement. They lack a diving lip, achieving what little depth they do strictly by means of the angled nose of their bodies. Thus they're predominantly trolling lures—longlined in shallow water, generally at night, or trolled near bottom in deep water with a weight a few feet ahead of them. Their aerodynamically challenged shape and light weight defeat casting efforts.

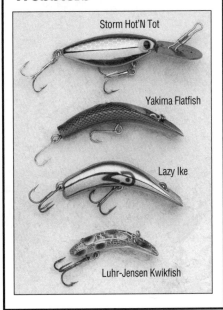

Banana Baits & Wide Wobblers

Storm Hot'N Tot

Yakima Flatfish

Lazy Ike

Luhr-Jensen Kwikfish

Banana baits have either treble hooks or sets of gang hooks—small trebles attached with wire spreaders. The old theory was, the more hooks, the better the hooking. This was particularly true when gang trebles got twisted in a landing net. What the old-timers did, and it's still productive today, was to tip one set of hooks with pieces of nightcrawler, which added scent and taste without stifling the action. A similar tactic on a shivering minnow-imitator might kill its wiggle altogether.

Also included in this category are wide-wobbling diving lures, the most famous being the Storm Hot'N Tot, a trolling lure of wide repute. Tots can be trolled on unweighted lines down 10 to 25 feet. Beyond

Rattling Crankbaits

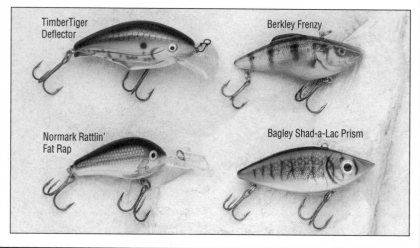

TimberTiger Deflector

Berkley Frenzy

Normark Rattlin' Fat Rap

Bagley Shad-a-Lac Prism

that, add snap weights or other lead to sink 'em farther. Once again, the wide-wobbling body accepts tipping the hooks with a piece of crawler. You might include Storm's Wart series and Luhr-Jensen's Hot Shot in this category as well. And when walleyes are feeding on crayfish, try Reef Runner's Scooter, Rebel's Crawfish, Luhr-Jensen's Crankin' Klawdad, and Arbogast's Mud Bug. Otherwise, traditional, round-bodied alpha baits in crayfish patterns fit the bill.

LIPLESS RATTLEBAITS

Lipless rattlebaits like the Bill Lewis Rat-L-Trap, Cordell Spot, Normark Rattlin' Rapala, and others lack an external diving lip, and use the angled nose of the lure body to promote diving. Most depth, however, is achieved by the weight of numerous lead or copper BBs rattling and shifting throughout the hollow plastic lure body, which also creates a loud commotion. Cast and retrieve 'em fast, just under the surface. Pause in your retrieve, and let 'em sink to the desired depth, then retrieve again. Vertically jig them like bladebaits. Lipless rattlebaits are versatile lures.

Most walleye anglers probably use rattlebaits either to cast and burn above shallow weed tops or to cast into the wind while shorecasting at night. Both are excellent adaptations, providing their noise doesn't spook fish. The Cordell Suspending Spot is a neutral buoyancy version.

ENHANCEMENTS

Internal rattles have been a hit on the walleye scene in recent years, particularly with open water trollers. Various lures have different volumes, ranging from that of a single BB bouncing around inside an internal rattle chamber to a host of BBs slam dancing against the body walls. It's impossible to say what works better, best, or worst for any situation until you try. In some cases, noise is great; in others, a turnoff.

Slow-sinking lures like Normark's Rapala Countdown series, which have been around for years, are used primarily to achieve added depth on short retrieves. Rebel's Trac Down Zone Minnow adds another sinker to the collection. Gaining

Shad Baits

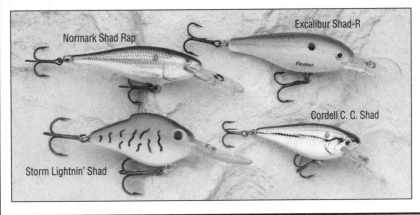

Normark Shad Rap

Excalibur Shad-R

Floater

Cordell C. C. Shad

Storm Lightnin' Shad

popularity in recent years are almost neutrally buoyant crankbaits that can be paused and hovered beneath a fish's nose to tempt a strike, like the Smithwick Suspending Rogue, Normark Husky Jerk, Rebel Mystic Shad-R and Suspending Zone Minnow, and Mann's Loudmouth Jerkbait. Great for shallow water shore-casting in a few feet of water. And heavy enough to cast into wind.

Storm's adhesive lead tape SuspenDots and SuspenStrips offer the ability to fine-tune the buoyancy of lures by adding enough weight along the belly to cre-ate anything from a slight floater, to a hoverer, to a slow sinker. It's a versatile addition to any tackle box.

In general, today's crankbaits sport far better treble hooks than those of a few years ago. The new wave of ultrasharp hooks—Heddon Excalibur, Mus-tad Accupoint and Triple Grip, Eagle Claw Lazer Sharp and Kahle Treble, VMC Barbarian Outbarb, and similar premium models—hook and hold like never before.

Colors and lifelike finishes are constantly improving and expanding. Excalibur's LiveShad scalelike finishes and Rapala's metallic finishes are two prominent examples.

A much greater selection of crankbaits are targeted toward walleyes these days. Manufacturers are conscious of the growing market and want to cash in on sales with appropriate lures. Because many situations suitable to walleye crankbaits call for trolling, weight is often added to the line to achieve greater depth, because not very many diving models have yet appeared, compared to such designs for bass.

Classic case: maybe a manufacturer offers a shallow and a deep diver in a wall-eye crankbait series rather than several different sizes of diving lips that cover a wider range of casting depths, as they'd do with lures targeted for bass. Mann's Stretch series is an exception—it offers numerous models designed to cover trolling conditions from just beneath the surface to 30 feet deep. Shad Raps, a multispecies lure, come in various sizes with diving lips designed to perform within specific casting (and trolling) depth ranges down to around 15 feet. Consider these when stocking your crankbait box.

Hardbaits for walleyes are tailored to a wider variety of situations than ever before. And they catch walleyes from the shallows to the depths.

CRANKBAIT ACTIONS—WALLEYE REACTIONS

"For every action, there is a . . . reaction."—Sir Isaac Newton

Time was, hardbaits didn't make much of a wave for walleyes. But the initial ripple turned into a walleye chop, building and evolving in recent years to a tidal wave of popularity and success. Big walleyes love crankbaits—the right crankbaits, under the right conditions.

As more folks learned where, when, and how to use them, certain styles of crankbaits achieved prominence and dominance on the walleye scene. Long, thin minnow-imitators like Rapalas, ThunderSticks, Rogues, Rebels, Bomber Long A's, Reef Runners, and other stickbaits produce a shivering, wiggling, rolling wobble.

This less flamboyant wiggle of minnow-imitators appears better tailored to triggering walleyes in several situations:

- *shallow water*—a minnow-imitator, cast and retrieved or longline trolled along shorelines, atop shallow flats, or across shallow reefs, is deadly for triggering fish in skinny water, particularly at night.
- *open water trolling*—the rolling wiggle presents a fairly consistent profile that is easy to locate and target in the vast expanse of nothingness surrounding the bait. Lures with dark backs and bright, flashy sides create flash-flash-flash patterns every time the bait pivots, alternately revealing side-back-side, flashing like traffic lights to gain attention.

Lures range from small to large, most of them from 3½ to 5 inches. Some feature standard forage patterns. Others sport wild colors for added visibility in dark water. Some rattle for extra attention, while others slide and glide through the shallows with a whisper. Balsa, wood, and foam models tend to be more subtle than plastic ones. Plastic baits often contain rattles, and their durable construction takes a lickin' and keeps on stickin' walleyes amidst rocks and wood.

Big walleyes love crankbaits—the right crankbaits, under the right conditions.

Shad-shaped lures like Normark Shad Raps, Bagley Shads, Arbogast Shadeauxs, and Cordell C. C. Shads have flat sides that restrict wiggle to a minimum, but present higher bodied shad profiles than their skinny, stickbait cousins. Shad baits, with their diving bills of different lengths, appear more popular with casters than trollers, but they've proven their effectiveness when trolled through the shallows or plumbed in the depths. Like minnow-imitators, they tend to function best at low speeds—trolled at 1 to 2 mph and then retrieved just fast enough to wiggle the lure. Generally of a more fragile design and construction, they may fracture upon repeated contact with rocks or brush.

For every action there is a reaction, and for every generality there are exceptions. While minnow-imitators and shad baits undoubtedly dominate crankbait selection when trolling for suspended fish and when casting and retrieving above cover or bottom, other baits excel when banged and bounced off rock or wood. These work best for walleyes relating to rock riprap in rivers and reservoirs or to natural rock outcroppings in lakes and rivers. Crayfish abound in such locations, and walleyes definitely key on them.

Crayfish have a rounder body shape than minnow-imitators and shad baits, so lures with rounder profiles may be better choices. These lures take a pounding, whether cast or trolled, and need to withstand the punishment of repeated contact with rock. The most durable molded plastic baits have diving lips that are molded into the body rather than inserted and glued. River anglers often select baits like Bomber Model A's, Reef Runner Scooters, Lindy Shadlings, and Cordell Wally Divers. Call 'em shad-ows.

Lipless rattlebaits like Cordell Spots, Normark Rattlin' Raps, and Bill Lewis Rat-L-Traps excel at shorecasting into strong onshore winds and at loud, shallow retrieves in dark or dingy water. Heavily weighted with internal BBs, these lures rattle when retrieved and sink when paused. Hold your rod tip high and use a steady retrieve to run them inches beneath the surface or just above bottom and cover. Pause your retrieve to flutter the lure into pockets or along cover.

Wide wobblers, like Storm Hot'N Tots, and banana baits, like Lazy Ikes, Flat Fish, and Brooks Reefers, defy traditional tight-swimming action for walleyes. These lures offer aggressive wobbling actions and comparatively little forward motion. They're generally trolled rather than cast, and one hook is sometimes tipped with a piece of nightcrawler to add scent and taste. Most are trolled with weighted lines for additional depth, but they're also trolled in shallow water, particularly at night.

Sir Isaac was right. For every action there is a . . . reaction. Choose a crankbait with the right action to provoke a reaction from walleyes.

CASTING THAT OLD MOVIN' MAGIC

Nothing magic about it. Just seems that certain anglers never fail to score monstrous walleyes. Lots of them, along with scads of lesser fish. Today, with walleye populations across the country in their best shape ever, crankbaits—arguably the best lure style for producing big fish—deserve a critical look during the finest of all seasons for consistently catching big walleyes.

Although particulars may vary, during fall, walleye anglers across the country generally use minnowbait-style crankbaits in one of several classic approaches. Shorecasters work from piers jutting into Lake Erie, in harbors, and at the mouth of rivers. The other Great Lakes host similar fishing, although some of the best spots haven't yet been discovered.

Meanwhile, shorecasters on reservoirs look for the fishing to heat up in tailwater areas below dams, while anglers fishing rivers concentrate on the mouths of creeks where they empty into the main river. And anglers in natural lakes stand at the mouths of feeder creeks or work necked-down areas that funnel current between lake areas.

Minnowbaits are critical to longline trollers who run lures across shallow shoals, usually at night. Or they may run the same baits in deep water, searching for walleyes holding on basin flats. Shallow shoals and deep basins tend to attract walleyes in rivers, lakes, and reservoirs, large and small.

A QUESTION OF SIZE

Simply said, bigger baits rarely intimidate walleyes, particularly during fall. The surest sign of a novice walleye angler is an insistence on choosing baits several sizes too small for the job.

A lure is a presentation package. The most important factors in the package are depth, speed, and vibration pattern. Size is secondary, an indirect factor affecting depth, speed, and vibration. A walleye can feel a moving bait much more critically than it can measure exact size. Once a walleye feels a lure approaching, lure size helps the fish locate it easily. And once the fish tries to eat the lure, there's more bait for him to strike.

Most of the time, fishermen could use a size or two (or more) larger bait and catch at least as many or more walleyes as well as many more big ones. That's because walleyes—big walleyes in particular—are usually more attracted by the slightly wider and more distinct wobble offered by bigger baits.

But how big is big? Baits the size of the #13 Floating Rapala key walleyes during fall. The #13 Husky Rapala is the same length as the regular #13 but offers a beefed-up body size that pushes more water to give off an even more distinctive vibration pattern. A bait the size of the #13 Husky Rapala is the smallest you should consider for an evening of trolling at a river mouth on the Great Lakes. A #18 is probably even better. Baits the size of the #11 Floating Rapala, a standard size in spring, are too small in fall.

The #18 Rapala, a 7-inch-long bait that immediately intimidates most walleye anglers, turns almost as many fish during fall. A bait that size often becomes preferred bait at night on waters where bigger fish are common. Baits the size of the #18 Rapala aren't popular among shorecasters fishing shallow water at the mouths of feeder streams in fall, because the bait runs too deep to be retrieved effectively. But such baits should be critical for shorecasting anglers on piers of the Great Lakes, where depth isn't a critical factor. Add Storm SuspenStrips to baits this size to cast them farther. You need a sturdy spinning rod, preferably 7 or 7½ feet long, coupled with a wide spooled reel loaded with 12- or 14-pound line.

Remember, though: speed and depth remain the critical elements in any presentation.

Critical Size Range of Minnowbaits During Fall

One approach to determining vibrations walleyes prefer is to choose from among a spectrum of baits—one type of bait from one manufacturer. Become familiar with each model and the slight variations in vibration that result from size.

As you expand your versatility by adding new lines of baits, you'll need a well organized tackle box.

Floating Rapalas

#18

#13 Husky

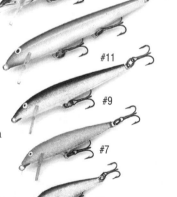

#13

#11

#9

#7

#5

GOOD VIBES—HEART AND SOUL OF THE CRANKBAIT EQUATION

Most walleye anglers know that vibration and sound are important, yet rarely is the vibration (and sound) pattern of a lure one of the top reasons for choosing a lure. How a lure looks is vital, but vibration and sound, not vision, are the first indication of food and danger to a walleye. In most situations, fish feel the presence of a crankbait before they see it. Logically, then, a vibration pattern must be compelling enough to entice walleyes to respond positively once they finally see the crankbait.

Most fishermen, however, overlook the importance of sound. Instead, they believe that walleyes can detect subtle shades of color and that they respond better to one visual pattern than to another. They play incessantly with color and color patterns. They may even consider taste, smell, and lure profile. But rarely do they consider vibration as more than an incidental part of the continuing experiment that is fishing. And that's a mistake during fall, when crankbaits are so important to success.

Vibration Patterns

Lures produce underwater vibrations that fish detect with their lateral line. Even lures that don't seem to vibrate, like flat spoons or jigs, send out waves that trigger neuromast organs along the fish's side.

A crankbait's bill causes the lure to wobble and produce vibrations that a walleye may feel several boat lengths away. Some vibrations startle fish; others attract them; but most are ignored.

Successful fishing depends on efficient vibration control as well as more familiar controls like speed and depth. Retrieve or trolling speed and lure design are factors anglers can tune for vibration patterns.

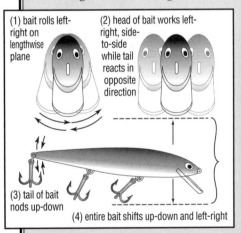

(1) bait rolls left-right on lengthwise plane

(2) head of bait works left-right, side-to-side while tail reacts in opposite direction

(3) tail of bait nods up-down

(4) entire bait shifts up-down and left-right

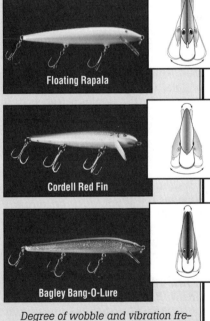

Floating Rapala

Cordell Red Fin

Bagley Bang-O-Lure

Crankbaits produce four basic movements that result in vibration patterns unique to each bait style. (1) Baits roll back and forth on a lengthwise plane running through the center of the bait. (2) As the bait rolls, the head of the bait also works back and forth, left-right, left-right. The tail makes opposing movements in response. (3) Because the baits are buoyant and work head-down and tail-up, the tail of most baits also subtly rocks up and down. (4) Finally, the entire bait shifts left-right, right-left, up-right (knuckle-ball-like) in response to water pressure on the bait as it moves forward.

Degree of wobble and vibration frequency are positively correlated with retrieve or trolling speed. Shape of lure, lure bulk, and bill design also affect vibration frequency and intensity. Bait styles such as the three pictured here each offer unique vibration patterns.

Change the way you think about vibration; place it at the heart of the presentation equation, along with depth and speed. It will change your fishing perspective. We make fun of fish calls, but that's what a crankbait is. As you fish, you're constantly calling fish, constantly signaling them with vibration, or sound and vibration, to move toward the call. You're constantly signaling that something's coming, enticing the fish to see what this thing is and to eat it.

But what vibration pattern, and when and where? How to decide which style of crankbait to use to produce the right vibration pattern? What vibrations do different natural baits give off? How do vibrations differ among the same baits of different sizes?

Change the way you think about vibration; place it at the heart of the presentation equation, along with depth and speed. It will change your fishing perspective.

BAIT SPECTRUMS

Stock up on proven crankbaits of several designs, each in several proven sizes. Don't simply stock up on one of these and two of those and a fistful of others. This is too often the case in many walleye anglers' tackle boxes.

A typical inventory of crankbaits for a fall run of serious longline trolling would include six #13 and six #18 Floating Rapalas, and nine #13 Husky Rapalas in three basic minnow patterns—gold, silver (or shad), and rainbow trout. As a group, Floating Rapalas produce a relatively tight vibration pattern. Each succeeding size pushes more water and produces more distinct vibrations. (PRADCO F20, F30, and F40 Rebels can be substituted for Rapalas.)

Add to your selection of Rapalas a spectrum of Storm ThunderSticks. ThunderStick Juniors are too small for this duty, so carry nine regular ThunderSticks (4½ inches) in the same basic color patterns as the Rapalas. ThunderSticks work a little harder at vibrating than Rapalas, and they also offer built-in rattles. Super Rogues are a bit larger—about 5½ inches, so you'll want some of those, too.

Two more lure spectrums, and you're nearly set. You need six 4¼-inch and nine 5-inch Bagley Bang-O-Lures. Bang-O-Lures produce a lazy swimming wobble different from the Rapala's tight wobble and the ThunderStick's harder wobble.

Finally, add six Reef Runner Little Rippers and nine Reef Runner Rip Sticks, a humped-back bait with a hard-working, almost lopsided wounded wobble that offers a wobbling action different from our other choices. Note that the Little Ripper looks too small for fall, but it wobbles enough to create the illusion of being larger.

Worry first about depth, speed, and vibration. Bait size is not a factor except as it bears on vibration. Color is secondary to depth, speed, and vibration. Get those right, and walleyes generally will attack a lure no matter the color. Color is only a matter of fine-tuning. Fire-tiger (chartreuse), blue back, and silver are common hot colors on most waters.

Sift through the various vibration patterns offered by different bait styles and sizes. Some nights, walleyes will eat almost anything you drop in the water, so long as it's running at the right depth and speed. But on some waters in certain situations, certain bait sizes and styles far outproduce other offerings. The #13 Husky Rapala has been a top producer for us across the country, both for shorecasting and for longline trolling. But sometimes the Bang-O-Lure outproduces other options, as do other baits.

SPEED

Once you've chosen a spectrum of lures and targeted a certain depth range based on fish location (suspended, basin, shallow cover, shorelines, creek mouth), retrieve or trolling speed becomes the next critical factor. The rule of thumb has always been to move baits slowly for walleyes, whether they're livebait or artificial lures. So casting or trolling crankbaits at 1 to 2 mph, particularly in cold water, makes sense. At these speeds, action ranges from a bare wiggle to a slow rolling wobble that sends out low frequency vibrations to alert distant walleyes.

Shorecasters often use a slow wobbling retrieve with occasional pauses to hover lures in front of a fish's face. But the argument can be made that walleyes prefer slow, steady movement, because such retrieves make the lure easier to track and attack in the darkness. If so, then why do longline trollers fishing shallows at night tend to trigger strikes better with occasional pump-forward, drop-back motions of the rod tip, which cause the lure to rush ahead, then stop? Argue with time-tested tradition, but you won't win. You'll have to try both to find out which works best.

The same holds true with open water trolling with minnowbaits on lines weighted with leadcore or snap weights to reach depths of 20 to 60 feet for suspended walleyes and for fish roaming across deep basins. Steady trolling speeds don't seem to trigger as many strikes as when wave-struck passes impart a rush-pause-rush to planer boards, thereby varying the speed of trailing crankbaits or spinners. Something as simple as turning the boat, which causes the inside lines to slow down and the outside lines to speed up a bit, usually results in strikes on one or the other presentation. These aren't massive speed changes, but they're evidently noticeable to walleyes. Once again, not a hard and fast rule, but one to be aware of and to experiment with.

Because we're talking fall and cold water, which slow fishes' metabolisms, we're also talking slow motion. A little earlier in the year, during the warm water of summer, expanding the throttle window up to 3, even 4 mph or more may trigger strikes amidst the season's wealth of surrounding food. Speed-trolling crankbaits through schools of suspended shad—ripping, burning, vibrating such lures through like a runaway rocket—may cause fish to strike. But as autumn deepens, such tactics are likely to become poor calls.

RATTLING CRANKBAITS

Whether or not to use crankbaits with built-in rattles, and when, are curious concerns among most serious walleye anglers. No definitive answer exists for the variety of situations in which crankbaits apply during fall, but we can offer observations that may help you decide whether or not to use them in the waters you fish. If your approach to this question is, "Can't hurt," the answer is, it probably can. On the other hand, if your answer is "Can't help," the answer is, it probably won't—but could. Simply said, rattling makes sense in some situations, but not much in others.

Most baits make a little noise beyond the basic vibration they give off when they move through water. Vibration is felt through the fish's lateral line instead of heard through its inner ear. At a minimum, hooks rattle against the bodies of some baits, particularly plastic baits. Balsa baits are almost silent, however, except for their vibration pattern. So anglers do possess choices along a spectrum of noisiness ranging from nearly silent to loud.

The question remains, though: how critical are baits with internal rattles to making walleyes bite? That rattles work for walleyes during fall is accepted knowledge among walleye anglers fishing the Great Lakes, especially those fishing from the piers of Lake Erie, where shorefishing for walleyes began in recent times.

The Quest for Neutral Buoyance?

Much written about and seemingly much in demand, especially for casters, is the elusive quality termed *neutral buoyance*. Gaining popularity in recent years are near neutrally buoyant crankbaits like the Smithwick Suspending Rogue, Normark Husky Jerk, Rebel Mystic Shad-R and Suspending Zone Minnow, and Mann's Loudmouth Jerkbait, which theoretically can be paused and hovered beneath a fish's nose to tempt a strike. Great for shallow water shorecasting in a few feet of water.

In reality, we see little magic in the quest for neutral buoyance in most key walleye situations during fall. Shorecasters should retrieve lures slowly and steadily, rarely in stop-and-go fashion, so walleyes will more likely track baits and not miss them when they strike. Even with stop-and-go retrieves, neutral buoyance isn't required.

A shorecaster's objective is to make long casts effectively, often into the wind. Adding adhesive Storm SuspenDots or SuspenStrips along the belly increases the weight of floating minnowbaits and allows them to be cast farther, simultaneously creating anything from a slight floater to a hoverer to a slow sinker. The right combination is a weight that allows decent casts and still allows the lure to run at the right depth and at a steady slow speed. Neutral buoyance may or may not be an incidental result of adding the strips.

Longline trollers, meanwhile, usually add lead shot from 12 to 36 inches in front of their lures to get them running at the right depth. Snap weights, which run 35 to 50 feet in front of the baits, are the most popular means to take these baits into deep water in basin areas. Again, neutral buoyance isn't required.

Slow-sinking lures like Normark's Rapala Countdown series, which have been around for years, are used primarily to achieve a little depth on a short retrieve or to cast farther into wind. Rebel's Trac Down Zone Minnow adds another sinker to the collection.

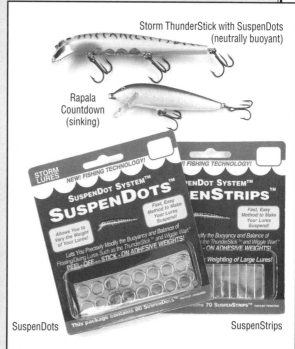

Storm ThunderStick with SuspenDots (neutrally buoyant)

Rapala Countdown (sinking)

SuspenDots

SuspenStrips

Anglers there rely on classic bass rattling baits like the Bill Lewis Rattle Trap.

Baits like the Rattle Trap are unlikely fare indeed. Walleye baits have often been big and bold (like the #18 Floating Rapala), but never so oddly shaped and noisy as bass baits like the Rattle Trap. Besides their size and noise, bass rattlers must be cranked at a relatively fast pace, which makes them the antithesis of leisurely retrieved, traditional minnowbaits fished during fall in most classic walleye waters.

But bass rattlers make a bit of sense for Lake Erie, where mobs of big walleyes feed competitively in clear water for most of their lives. Lake Erie is every walleye angler's dream—lots of bigger fish feeding hard. On a good night on Lake Erie, anglers probably cast or troll past more big fish than many of the rest of us encounter in an entire season. The added weight of all those internal BBs in bass baits helps to toss them farther out into the face of screaming onshore winds.

So, big, bold, and gaudy on the noise side fit the situation. We've always thought, though, that anglers on the Great Lakes should discard their bass rattlers in favor of traditional walleye crankbaits that rattle, like the Storm Thunder Stick or Reef Runner Rip Stick.

At times, rattles can be too much of a good thing. Many fine shorecasters and longline trollers, for example, attest that rattling for walleyes isn't a good idea when fishing from shore or when trolling over small reefs and bars on natural lakes. Vibration alone seems to key such situations, not the combination of noise and vibration. Apparently, hooks tickling the sides of baits supply just enough noise. We just haven't done well with rattling minnowbaits in such situations. But we haven't fished everywhere—and in certain situations, rattles may work. Actually, we'd bet on it. Lots of walleyes in the lakes you fish? A good population of larger fish? Do they feed competitively as they roam large areas much of the season? Then maybe rattles will be good for you and the fish.

Rattling baits for walleyes in large reservoirs generally deserve serious attention. Rattling baits for walleyes in large reservoirs generally deserve serious attention. When walleyes are hot in the tailwater areas of big dams like those in the Dakotas, rattling minnowbaits like the Rapala Husky Jerk usually produce more fish than silent baits. Several seasoned anglers have also documented success with rattles the past few years at Lake Thompson, South Dakota, a relatively new reservoir peaking right now for walleyes. Again, lots of bigger fish. These same anglers, however, agree that rattles are often too noisy in most of the natural lakes they've fished for some 30 years.

So what are we saying?—that rattles work on bodies of water with lots of walleyes, particularly lots of big walleyes that range a long way (often in open water or in basin areas) in search of forage? And that by comparison, minimal sound works better in waters where fish are confined to smaller areas and are usually tougher to trigger? Read on!

On the In-Fisherman Professional Walleye Trail, virtually no one trolls Rapala Floating Minnows or Bagley Bang-O-Lures for open water walleyes during the day, preferring plastic-bodied baits with a bit of rattle instead. This holds true for all the big water tournament sites we fish throughout North America. Yet subtle balsa lures like the Rapala and Bang-O-Lure dominate night-fishing for walleyes nearly everywhere that minnowbaits get thrown or trolled after dark.

Thousands, maybe hundreds of thousands of hours of fishing experience can be distilled down to clear, powerful concentrates: general observations and basic assumptions that you can use while you're finding your own answers on the waters you fish.

'EYES ON SUSPENDIN' BAITS

For years, we've heard about flatline trolling at night for big walleyes. But anglers ahead of the game on Mille Lacs and other major walleye waters are dropping the trolling motor and pitching on those same 5- to 7-foot flats, fancasting with suspending minnowbaits and cranks. The results will change the way you approach night-fishing during early summer.

The typical scenario is to find pods of walleyes moving shallow at different times of night. Weeds are high, but still developing. Troll through the inside once or twice, clean weeds off your key lure, and find a pod of biters. What are the odds you're going to turn around and get back on 'em? Pitchin' is a much higher-percentage game. You hit more fish from each aggressive pod, and by the end of the night, you total more fish.

By pulling a suspending bait forward, dropping your rod tip back and letting it sit, then pulling it forward again, you're calling walleyes to the spot.

It's not like fishing smallmouth with these baits—it's not a pitch-'n-rip game. The key presentation is a long cast, followed by a series of slow pulls and pauses. By pulling a suspending bait forward, dropping your rod tip back and letting it sit, then pulling it forward again, you're calling walleyes to the spot. They'll find it. Just pause for varying lengths of time to determine the most effective trigger. Even when your lure's suspending and not moving, walleyes can find it.

Rapala Husky Jerks and other suspending baits offer greater depth control, and they get a little deeper. It doesn't matter if the water's dark, stained, or ultraclear—lots of walleyes are in 4 to 8 feet of water at night, which is perfect for casting these baits.

The biggest Husky Jerk gets down to 6 feet on a cast, and walleyes rise for them at night. The biggest three sizes are key for fishing various depths while staying above the weeds on most flats. On deeper flats, recently developed suspending crankbaits get down to 10 feet, making it possible to cover sharp breaks and the edges of flats better, too.

If you know where the hot spots are, just pitching to 'em is most efficient now. It's a new wrinkle: you're fishing walleyes that have never seen this presentation. And at night in most areas, it can work better than trolling.

Medium-action, medium-power spinning rods in the 6½- to 7-foot range, 8-pound-test line, and a moderate- to large-reeled spool for distance are all you need. Work into the wind or breeze, and cover those same necked-down areas and edges of weedy flats that produced in the past. Fancast in all directions. Key colors are probably the same countershading—dark on top, light on bottom—that work for trolling.

Compared to trolling, this tactic maximizes covering high percentage spots. Downtime from snags and fouled lures is shorter. And because walleyes travel in groups, this method is seen by more fish in each group. You spend more time working each pod of fish you find. Everything is slightly more efficient.

By midsummer, cabbage weedlines that hold 15 to 20 fish in a small area are easy to find. Your chances of hitting numbers of fish by pitching suspending baits are better than by trolling. Trolling may intercept more aggressive fish during a slow bite, but most nights, nothing works better than pitching suspending baits. Because so many walleyes suspend at night, this tactic is a perfect match. Work the boat in a lazy S-pattern back and forth across the weededge, and fancast. Casting to deeper water produces, too.

So much emphasis has been placed on these baits for largemouth and smallmouth bass that people are only beginning to experiment with them for walleyes—and they're doing extremely well. It's one more wrinkle that fish haven't seen, and that translates into a big advantage for you. Don't wait until you hear about it a second time. If you fish at night for walleyes, this is something you've gotta' try right now.

COUNTDOWN LURES FOR RIVER WALLEYES

In late winter and early spring, when snowmelt or rain raises the water level in rivers, creeks, and tiny streams, walleyes appear where they're hardly expected: flowing water that may support carp, catfish, bullheads, or nothing at all, most of the rest of the year—marginal walleye water, at best.

That walleyes (and saugeyes) move upriver now is no mystery; no mystery, either, that barriers along the way concentrate these fish, providing opportunities for shore-bound anglers to catch them. Fifty percent of not many walleyes, all gathered in a few small areas below barriers, can provide some nifty fishing.

Small dams on rivers with known walleye populations are obvious places to check. Or try small dams on small tributary rivers that feed slightly larger rivers with known walleye populations. Thousands of these spots can be found across North America.

First, the water must be about as clear as it can be. Second, water temperatures must be at least stable—better yet, in a slow upswing. These two conditions combine to produce aggressive fish willing to chase instead of just grub.

Countdown lures like the Countdown Rapala can be killers under such conditions. Even though the fish must be aggressive to respond to presentations with this bait style, the bait should still be fished as slowly as possible, swung on long, slow, deep sweeps across the back of tailout pools, as opposed to simply cast out and ratta-tat-tatted back in. The objective is to get the lure deep and just barely wobbling, while it probes water where walleyes might be holding.

Besides the tailout of pools, other productive spots to present countdown lures include current breaks, especially where current swings back into shore, then breaks with half the water moving back upstream along the shore and the other half moving downstream. The fish are facing into current, so the idea is to stand wherever you can make a cast that swings the lure with the current, instead of moving it in a straight line.

The best two bait sizes have never varied. Given one choice, it would be a #7 Countdown Rapala. Second choice is a #5. River conditions that favor bigger baits usually include dirty water, which disqualifies this bait style from consideration.

• Stock mostly minnow-patterned baits in gold or silver. Experiment with firetiger and other bright patterns, but again, the river conditions that require firetiger generally disqualify this bait style. Instead, switch to a jig-and-minnow.

• Use a small Berkley Cross-Lok snap, not a snap-swivel, to allow the bait to wobble effectively and to facilitate changing lures.

• Eight-pound-test line works best, although 6-pound test is better if you're fishing with #5 baits only. These baits cast best with a rod at least 6 feet long, better 6½ feet, with a limber tip.

Losing a few is inevitable. But when the fish are cracking, when conditions are just right, if you're pinching pennies by fishing with fifty cent jigs, you'll be a half-dozen fish behind before you know it.

If you enjoy shorefishing, find a small dam or two—these will probably produce fish year after year at this time of year for the rest of your life.

A Day and Night Difference

During the day, especially during calm conditions, nonaggressive walleyes inhabiting flats often drop down into available cover like remnant or developing weeds or timber, lying under or amidst overhead cover. If overhead cover is unavailable, look for fish along transitions in bottom content, atop rises or dips in bottom, or amid cover like boulders.

With fish typically tight to bottom and unwilling to move far to chase lures, presentations must be placed close to the fish to trigger a response. For example, select a diving crankbait that occasionally ticks the tops of cover rather than a shallow minnow-imitator that runs only 1 foot beneath the surface.

Probe the cover with jigs, working them as deeply as possible amidst weeds or wood, reaching bottom whenever possible with a slow presentation that pauses frequently to trigger fish. Where clean bottom predominates and substantial cover isn't a factor, bump bottom occasionally to make sure you're in the fish zone.

At night or when walleyes become active, they typically rise above cover or out to the edges, patrolling for food. They may also move right up to the shoreline. In these conditions, they often strike free-running lures like a minnow-imitator cast or trolled subsurface. Typically, it's not necessary to fish as tight to cover as during the day.

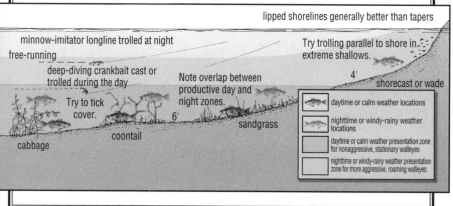

lipped shorelines generally better than tapers

minnow-imitator longline trolled at night
free-running

deep-diving crankbait cast or trolled during the day

Try to tick cover.

Note overlap between productive day and night zones.

Try trolling parallel to shore in extreme shallows.

4'

shorecast or wade

cabbage

coontail

6'

sandgrass

daytime or calm weather locations

nighttime or windy-rainy weather locations

daytime or calm weather presentation zone for nonaggressive, stationary walleyes

nighttime or windy-rainy weather presentation zone for more aggressive, roaming walleyes

CASTING VERSUS TROLLING THE SHALLOWS

Searching for walleyes on large flats without obvious pockets of weedgrowth or other structural elements requires coverage techniques like longline trolling minnowbaits and drifting with minnow-tipped jigs—methods not as precise as pitching jigs to weedy pockets.

Day or night, longlining is an efficient search tool, as well as often being the best way to trigger walleyes. One important difference between longline trolling by day and by night is depth. At night, an unweighted, shallow-diving minnow-imitator (like a #11 Floating Rapala or a 4-inch Bagley Bang-O-Lure) can be trolled slowly through water from 4 to 6 feet deep, running 1 or 2 feet below the surface.

Shallow Water Walleye Crankbait Spectrum

Crankbaits provide one of the best options for fishing flats. They cover water either quickly or slowly, dive to predictable running depths both cast and trolled, and simulate attractive baitfish profiles in a variety of actions and color patterns. Although all crankbaits are similar, different models can be tailored to individual conditions, enhancing the productivity of your presentation.

For example, for casting or longline trolling shallow water at night, the best options are shallow diving minnow-imitators that run only 1 or 2 feet below the surface. To make them run a bit deeper, pinch a split shot or two 18 inches up the line. Because shallow walleyes often rise up above cover and roam at night, they'll strike free-running lures.

Rapalas provide a subtle shivering wiggle; Bang-O-Lures a bit more rolling wobble; and rounder-bodied Red Fins a more aggressive, hard-working wobble. Fine-tune both lures and speed, though the general rule is that walleyes prefer a slow, steady movement at night, cast or trolled.

Neutral buoyancy lures like Suspending ThunderSticks and Husky Jerks add the ability to pause the retrieve, allowing the lure to suspend, thus providing a tempting target. They're great for shorecasting. The ThunderStick offers a rattle for a bit of noise. More heavily weighted lures like the Rogue are easier to cast in wind and have more rattles for added sound. Countdown Rapalas and heavy lipless rattlebaits like Rat-L-Traps are easy to cast into wind and run shallow at higher speed—another shorecasting option.

During the day, select lures that dive sufficiently deep to either rustle cover or occasionally bang bottom. Walleyes typically hold deeper and tighter to bottom or cover during the day, though faster retrieves and trolling speeds can be used to cover more water, compared to slower lure movement at night. Slightly shad-shaped lures like Shad Raps and Shadeauxs display subtler actions than more rounded baits like Wally Divers and Stretch 10s. As always, experiment with depth, speed, lure action, and color patterns. Prime colors are perch, shiner, and shad in clear water, fire-tiger in dark water.

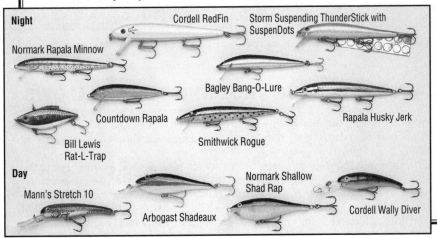

Night

Normark Rapala Minnow

Cordell RedFin

Storm Suspending ThunderStick with SuspenDots

Bagley Bang-O-Lure

Countdown Rapala

Rapala Husky Jerk

Bill Lewis Rat-L-Trap

Smithwick Rogue

Day

Mann's Stretch 10

Normark Shallow Shad Rap

Arbogast Shadeaux

Cordell Wally Diver

Or a lead shot-weighted minnowbait can be slowly trolled through water from 6 to 10 feet deep. During the day, by comparison, walleyes often hold slightly deeper or tighter to cover, so they more often prefer crankbaits that dive to their approximate depth. These diving baits can be trolled faster during the day than at night. Where shallow prairie lakes predominate, trolling at speeds approaching 3 mph may be the rule. Anglers on other waters should try trolling faster to trigger strikes, just as anglers using jigs occasionally use snapjigging.

Longlining requires about 100 feet of line to free-run lures in the shallows. For deeper water, fine-tune line length to place diving lures near bottom. We prefer to hand hold rods in order to monitor what's happening with the lures, which increases our ability to interpret subtle changes in bottom content, cover, or depth. Often we impart a pump slowly forward, drop slowly back motion to the rod tip, which causes the lure to surge forward, then slow. Following fish respond when the lure slows after the pump-forward movement.

For broader coverage on large flats, add a second set of lines with similar lures behind in-line planer boards. To minimize snags, set these lures to run slightly shallower than the lures on handheld rods. Then troll, using sweeping S-shaped trolling runs to cover different depths and to impart speed changes to lures. When you locate a pocket of concentrated fish, anchor or redrift the area, fancasting with jigs or crankbaits. Or switch to slipfloats, and drift minnows or leeches through the area.

SHORELINE OPTIONS

On darker waters, walleyes often move across flats all the way to shore. The best shorelines typically have a rocky lip where the shoreline drops quickly into 1 or 2 feet of water, instead of gradually sliding into the depths. This creates a wall against which walleyes trap baitfish. Moderate wind blowing into such a shoreline attracts walleyes, while heavy wind moves them back out. Modest wind roils the water just enough to give walleyes a visual advantage over prey. Too much wind disrupts the process in dingier lakes.

In clear and moderately clear lakes, walleyes may also move all the way in to the shoreline after dark. Both shorecasters and anglers in boats should first check current areas—feeder creeks or necked areas between sections of lakes—for active walleyes. Rocky outcroppings or points that jut from shore into flats are other top spots. Walleyes may move into and out of these areas all night, but prime times are usually the hours before and after sunrise, especially if wind is blowing into such a structure.

The plan at night is to longline troll for fish scattered across flats or along steep shorelines. As the horizon begins to lighten, head toward a rocky, windswept point for the final hour before sunrise. Anchor, and fancast lures like a #7 or #9 Countdown Rapala toward the shoreline. A minnow or a leech suspended on a jig below a lighted slipfloat is an option that often produces more, but perhaps smaller, fish.

Shore-bound anglers can catch just as many walleyes as anglers in boats during this period, but shore anglers must tailor their tactics and timing more carefully to available options. Most of the best fishing is at night, except in some prairie lakes.

Shorecasters often rely on almost neutrally buoyant, shallow-running minnowbaits, coupled with long rods, wide-spooled reel, and 10-pound line, for long casts and precise depth control. Years ago, anglers doctored these lures to reduce buoyancy by drilling into the wood plugs and inserting lead shot. This still works, but lures like the Storm Suspending ThunderStick and the Rapala Husky Jerk perform just about as well without the hassle. Also, adhesive Storm SuspenDots placed along the belly of lures make them less buoyant. Make long casts, and

Tuned Lures Catch More Fish

Many new crankbaits don't run true. Even a perfectly tuned lure can become a sidewinder after it has bumped rocks and logs or hooked a big fish. A bait that rides to the side won't reach proper depth and will foul weeds more easily—no fish. A properly tuned crankbait is essential.

To tune a crankbait, first make sure all hook attachments are on straight and that nothing is obviously out of balance. Next, inspect the eyelet. On some models it will be an imbedded wire in the nose or lip. On others, a screw-eye is threaded in the plastic.

If the lure (see drawings) runs to your left, move the eyelet ever so slightly to the right. If the lure runs to your right, move the eyelet to the left. If the eyelet is made of imbedded wire, nudge it with needlenose pliers. But be careful with the screw-eye types. Carefully bend the entire screw-eye.

Don't turn it.

It is better to undertune the lure several times than to overtune it. Bend the connection too much and you can loosen it and ruin the bait. Some lures can't be tuned if imbalance is due to a manufacturing defect. Return them or write them off as a bad investment.

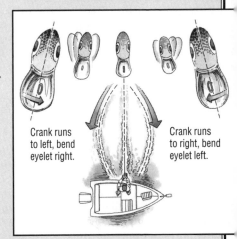

Crank runs to left, bend eyelet right.

Crank runs to right, bend eyelet left.

retrieve the baits slowly and steadily along rocky shorelines, through current areas, or over rock-rubble points.

Jigs also can be used for shorefishing at night, but instead of tipping them with a minnow, tip with a plastic shad body. Slightly bigger is better at night, so 4- and 5-inch plugs and 3- and 4-inch shad bodies on 1/4- or 3/8-ounce jigheads are the rule. Four- or 5-inch minnows presented below lighted slipbobbers also work well at night, but for larger fish, they're less efficient than casting plugs or shad-bodied jigs.

SUPERTUNING CRANKBAITS

Stray neither left nor right, but follow the straight and narrow path to success. Good advice for getting the most from crankbait presentations.

Tuning in to the fish requires establishing a preferred lure speed, color, action, size, shape, and sound. Selecting crankbaits is relatively simple. First and foremost, choose lures that run at the exact depth of a structure or a school of fish. Then tune them to provide optimum tracking and action at any speed. Finally, to maximize strike-to-catch ratio, consider altering or upgrading your hooks, turning bumps, swats, and shake-offs into hookups. The result isn't just a tuned bait, it's a supertuned bait.

If walleyes are 12 feet deep, you need a lure that runs at 12 feet. In areas with bottom snags or slimy algae, however, select a crankbait that runs just above bottom. How do you know how deep a lure runs? Pick up a chart or field guide to crankbait running depths.

Crankbaits by Mike McClelland and *Precision Trolling* by Dr. Steven Holt and Tom Irwin list carefully tested depth characteristics for hundreds of lures. Their data are more accurate than the suggested depth zones listed on lure packages, which seldom distinguish between trolling and casting depth. Trolled lures usually attain

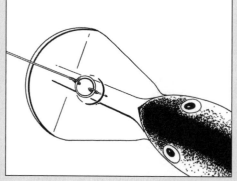

The O-Ring Connection

An O-ring or snap allows a crankbait to achieve its full range of motion. Tight knots, however, stifle bait action.

about twice the depth of the same lures cast and retrieved. These books take the guesswork out of selecting lures.

To achieve the exact running depth listed and to produce optimum action, lures must run absolutely straight when they're pulled through the water. First, tune the lure if it needs it. If it runs slightly right, grasp the eyelet with a long nose pliers and bend it slightly left. Bend the eyelet right if the lure runs to the left side.

Changing boat speed and sweeping the rod forward, then dropping it back, changes the lure's speed. Bouncing off obstructions slows a lure first, then causes it to dart forward to catch up. If a lure doesn't perform at higher speeds, it may repeatedly veer to one side when it careens off bottom. You may even experience "blow out"—shooting so far to the side that it pops upside down, often rising to the surface. Tune and test lures carefully so they perform even at the highest speeds.

Check all hook hardware and split rings to make sure they don't bind in the eyelets. If a hook or split ring occasionally wedges where excess paint has clogged a hook hanger, it can no longer swing free to allow proper lure action. Use the tip of a small pocketknife to remove these "wedgies." If necessary, switch to split rigs of thinner wire.

Line attachment is important for maximum lure performance. If the line attaches at an angle,

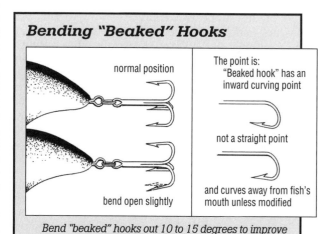

Bending "Beaked" Hooks

normal position

bend open slightly

The point is:
"Beaked hook" has an inward curving point

not a straight point

and curves away from fish's mouth unless modified

Bend "beaked" hooks out 10 to 15 degrees to improve hooking success.

off-center knot problems occur. Professional Walleye Trail angler and trolling expert Mark Martin often ties his knots low on the eyelet of minnow-imitators to change lure action subtly, but not for high speed presentations.

Most manufacturers recommend either centered knots, split ring ties, or better yet, a small snap to allow the lure to wobble freely. Not a snap-swivel, but a round end, light wire snap like a Duo-Lock or Cross-Lok. Bass Pro Shops sells these under the name Fast-Lock Bass Snaps. Choose the smallest size snap that your fingers can operate—larger sizes alter lure action.

Pellets or BBs inside a plastic lure cause imbalance when they become stuck. Sharply rap lures against a hard surface to free the rattles. Tighten loose eyelets with a screwdriver or a Super Glue-type product like Fishin' Glue.

HOOKS

A walleye can strike a crankbait's nine barbs and still get away. When a fish grabs a lure, as many as five or six hook points may touch flesh. On the hookset, pressure is divided among them. It's more difficult to bury all those points than to bury a single hook on a jig or rig.

At the very least, bend the hook points slightly outward and hone them for maximum sharpness. Many manufacturers have upgraded their hooks to straight point styles, avoiding beaked models that angle away from the fish's mouth.

Replace old dull hooks with the new superhoned models. Sticky-sharp trebles, available from major hook manufacturers, grasp and penetrate easier. This reduces the old "swing, two headshakes, and a miss."

Popular premium trebles include VMC Cone Cut, Mustad Accu-Point, Owner Tournament Trebles, Gamakatsu, and Eagle Claw Lazer Sharp. Heddon's Excalibur, a rotating treble designed to impart a cam-action twist on the set, helps a second or third point grab after the first one buries.

Crankbaits are fine walleye offerings that few anglers use to their full potential. Supertuning, premium hooks, and running at precise depths are a triple threat that can improve your catch.

TROLLING STUCK IN YOUR CRAW?

Crawfish supposedly aren't good walleye baits, but maybe we simply haven't learned to fish them effectively. Walleyes, after all, don't ignore easy meals—especially when crawfish go soft in early summer.

On inspecting stomach contents of walleyes in Leech Lake, Minnesota, we realized that during a month-long period from mid-July to mid-August, crawfish comprised a significant portion of walleyes' diet. This period coincides with the crawfishes' softshell phase, when they shed their hard outer shells, becoming more vulnerable to predation by walleyes and other gamefish.

Craws seem to remain relatively dormant at this time, hiding in and around protective rocks, which shield them from exposure to flashing teeth and jaws. Even the best refuge isn't perfect, however. Walleyes locate and prey on craws until their shells begin to harden. Once this occurs, walleyes

Hard baits—soft touch. Lures resembling softshell crawfish enhance productivity.

appear to desert shallow rocky areas in favor of areas offering different forage. Experimentation on rock humps revealed that walleyes roam the rocks at all levels—not just along the outer edge or right up on the crest. For fish spread out like this, crankbaits are often the best presentation.

You'd think you'd have to bounce bottom for best results, but it's unnecessary. A bait running relatively close to bottom garners strikes. More important is color pattern. Walleyes feeding on craws may ignore chrome, fire-tiger, and other forage patterns. In fact, certain crawfish patterns outproduce others 5-to-1. Models that closely resemble the vivid softshell crawfish remains found in fish stomachs are what you're after: Storm's 1/4-ounce Hot'N Tot and Normark's #8 Shad Rap and #7 Fat Rap produce well, the key factor being bright crawfish color patterns closely imitating the natural forage.

Walleyes feeding on craws may ignore chrome, fire-tiger, and other forage patterns. In fact, certain crawfish patterns outproduce others 5-to-1.

Lure choice depends on the depth at which most active fish are found. Fat Raps often produce best along the shallower tops of rockpiles; deeper diving Shad Raps work better along sloping edges. Yet fish can often be found along relatively flat areas as well, so long as bottom content is suitable to attracting and holding crawfish. Minor inconsistencies in bottom tend to concentrate more walleyes than consistent flats.

Use *Crankbaits "In-Depth"* or *Precision Trolling* to determine crankbait running depths on select lengths of 10-pound-test monofilament line. Once you determined the proper length of line needed to reach the desired depth just above bottom—generally somewhere between 80 and 160 feet— mark your line with an indelible Magic Marker to make repetitive trolling passes easier. Or use a line counter reel for easy reference.

Working between 1¾ and 2½ mph in the warm water triggers fish that slower presentations may miss. Plastic-lipped lures perform better at faster speeds, while metal-lipped Hot 'N Tots function better at lower speeds, where their exaggerated, wide wobble is most apparent.

Anglers can easily adapt to longline trolling and discover productive combos and depths in a few hours. Watch your line and rod tip to make sure the bait's working properly. No wiggling? Chances are you've picked up a weed or a snag that's throwing the lure off balance.

Consider trolling into the wind to help keep forward speed down, which is fine for weaving along and hugging tight contours. On some structures, it's hard to keep the lure in the fish zone without tight maneuvers. On large flats, however, planer boards spread lines across a wider area; trolling downwind minimizes tangles. Extremely shallow flats may demand planer boards that position lures away from the boat to minimize spooking. Fortunately, walleyes are accustomed to boats often drifting and trolling over their heads in 4 to 8 feet of windswept water.

Double the end of the 10-pound mono and use a spider hitch—the poor man's version of the saltwater Bimini Twist—to tie on a Berkley Cross Lok snap for attaching to the lure. This lets the bait wobble better than a direct tie, and the doubled line ensures against a pike cutting through both of the strands. Use premium sharp hooks from VMC, Gamakatsu, or Mustad. Or sharpen other hooks to make sure they bite and hold.

Don't be intimidated by wind, which turns walleyes on in big, windswept lakes. If you troll downwind, letting the rush-pause-rush of the waves add action to your lures, don't move too fast. Troll above, around, and near shallow and mid-depth rocks, even above weed tops. To troll the open water above weeds, either

Crank + bait = Crankbait
Crankbait x bait = Crankbait²

Norb Wallock field-tested a crawler-enhanced Risto Rap to a $40,000 tournament victory on the Risto Rap's maiden voyage.

shorten your line or use heavier line like 14-pound test so that lures run shallower, occasionally ticking the growth without fouling. If you occasionally hang up, give the rod a quick forward snap to clear the lure. If it begins running properly again, it's clean. If not, it's still fouled. Retrieve the lure, remove any weed strands, and reset your line.

The same trolling principle applies along weedlines and drop-offs. Depth changes typically are easiest to troll; just pick out a lure and line length combo that dives to the target depth, then weave the boat along the drop-off, making occasional contact. Move out deeper if the lure begins to pound, shallower if it runs free for more than a few seconds. When trolling weedlines or timberlines, lightly brush the outer edge, then weave out again, letting the lure run free for longer periods than when trolling hard bottom. Still, you want your lure to be close to the cover. You risk hang-ups, particularly when the contour turns outward, but after a few hours of practice, you become better at anticipating depth and cover changes and react quickly by changing trolling direction before your lure begins to foul.

These tactics work all summer long, and not just with crawfish patterns. Minnow, perch, sunfish, or shad patterns may be more appropriate to the waters you fish, better matching the available forage.

But don't ignore the crawfish option. During summer, when excuses abound for not catching walleyes because the weather's too hot or fish are losing their teeth, you can experience some of the year's best fishing by trolling crawfish-colored crankbaits through the shallows for walleyes feeding on soft craws. To walleyes, they go down smoother than soft-serve ice cream on a sunny summer day. Some like it soft, so we give it to 'em hard—a soft disguise for a hardbait surprise.

TIPPING THE TABLES—AND TREBLES —WITH LIVEBAIT

Back in the olden days—gotta be over 25 years ago—North Country anglers used what now seems an unusual tactic to catch walleyes. Since then, the tactic's largely fallen into disuse across most of the walleye range. But methods recycle once their effectiveness is rediscovered.

The presentation in question is trolling crankbaits tipped with livebait. Walleye buffs old enough to remember the prehistoric days perhaps recall drifting or trolling with banana baits like the Lazy Ike, Flat Fish, or Brooks Reefer. Shallow-running bananas could be longlined through the shallows, but to get any depth, sinkers were tied in-line a few feet ahead of the lures. To sweeten the package, the front treble of the two trebles was tipped with a piece of nightcrawler. In the event the lure sported a wire arm supporting gang trebles, a couple of pieces were added to keep things balanced.

The wide wobbling action of bananas allowed them to retain their action despite

A Bunch of Bananas

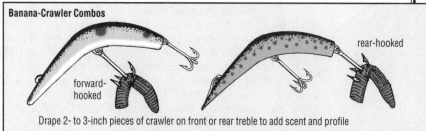

Banana-Crawler Combos

forward-hooked

rear-hooked

Drape 2- to 3-inch pieces of crawler on front or rear treble to add scent and profile

B anana baits could be described as lures that move a whole lot without really getting anywhere—lots or side-to-side wobble despite little forward progress. You could say the same thing about nightcrawlers. It's only natural to try teaming them together.

Dress small bits of nightcrawler on either forward or rear trebles. Older lures originally came with gang trebles—two hooks front and back attached via floppy wire spreader arms—that theoretically increased hooking

Yakima Flat-Fish (With Trebles)

Yakima Flat-Fish (With Single Hooks)

Luhr-Jensen Beno

Luhr-Jensen Kwikfish

Lindquist Brothers Canadian Wiggler

Bagley Smoo**

PRADCO Lazy Ike

Heddon Tadpolly*

*Discontinued in recent years, but some may still be available in tackle stores.
**Discontinued but still available directly from Bagley.

ability but created nightmare snags in landing nets.

the extra bulk and weight. Unlike the action of bananas, the action of up-and-coming subtle wigglers like Rapalas was killed by adding sections of crawler. As minnow-imitators rose to prominence, bananas sank to the bottom of the tackle box, seldom to see the light of day again.

Today's adept open water trollers, however, are bringing back the crankbait-bait concept to trigger suspended hawgs. One example is Norb Wallock's victory at a major Lake Erie tournament. Field-testing the new Normark Rapala Risto Rap before its introduction to the open market, Wallock and his associate Rick Olson spent time determining whether or not the new, large-bodied shad bait would catch walleyes and how deep the lure would run—22 feet on 100 feet of

FireLine, 27 feet on 200 feet. While prefishing, they decided to try tipping the bottom hook of the forward treble with a nightcrawler. The results were amazing.

"The lure caught fish," Wallock recalls, "but not like when it was tipped with a crawler. In fact, once we were on a school of fish, if we went more than 20 minutes without a strike on one of the lines, we considered it an indication that the crawler had come off, and we reeled in to rebait.

"I think the crawler not only adds scent and profile but also enlivens the action instead of reducing it. The weight of the crawler hanging down on the front treble positions it so it doesn't tangle with the rear hook when the worm trails straight back. The bulk of the crawler seems to enhance the action. Rick and I used a whole crawler, not just a piece. By the end of the tournament, most of the top finishers were fishing this way with some form of lure, but we were the only ones who had access to Risto Raps.

"We also trolled the lures similar to old banana bait presentations, tying a 2-ounce weight in-line 5 or 6 feet ahead of the lure, using mono line to make it easier for our amateur partners, who were unfamiliar with superlines. We placed those lines on outside board lines and sometimes ran anywhere from 3 to 7 colors of leadcore on our inside lines, depending on how deep the fish were. The Tennessee Shad pattern produced best on sunny days, the gaudier parrot pattern on cloudy days or during early morning. Once we zeroed in on fish, it was lights out. Nothin' like the real thing, even when an artificial lure is being used."

While shown to be most effective in summer conditions, tipped hardbaits can also be experimented with in spring. How about vertical fishing a banana bait on a three-way rig below a dam this winter, letting it wobble in place in current? or longline trolling a banana through the shallows in open water in early spring? or trolling a crawler-tipped shadbait along riprap at spawning time?

Tip the odds in your favor.

PULL THE PLUG (OR, THE JIG IS UP)

Temperatures have been cold enough for lakes to freeze, but you say you prefer open water fishing? Hit a river—a deep river—to steal one more open water excursion from Old Man Winter.

To fish walleyes in style, talk to Harry Stiles, one of the nation's premier river guides and a highly successful tournament angler. Anyone logging more miles than Harry on deep rivers like the Mississippi and St. Croix would have to be part river otter.

Walleye fishing can be temperamental this time of year, but we can make it simple. "Either troll crankbaits or work jigs," Stile says. "No rigging. No slip-bobbers. No trolling boards. No downriggers. Just trolling."

Knowing which presentation to go with is even simpler. "First troll to find fish. Though they're fairly bunched in late fall, it's still necessary to be mobile. Fish may be on a flat, a point, or a bar. But they're so tight to bottom that electronics won't help much. So we troll."

For a very distinct reason, Stiles' bread-and-butter bait is a Storm Thunder-Stick. "You need a plastic stickbait like a ThunderStick for fish in cold water," he explains. "Wooden baits are fine in summer when you can troll at or above the 1½-mph mark. But now I troll down to no more than 1/4 to 1/2 mph. A bait with

Three-Way Rigging Crankbaits, Stiles-style

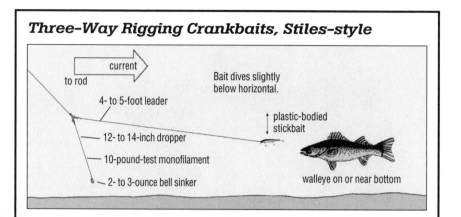

a slow, distinct wobble at a slow speed is the only way to go." Stiles sticks with natural colors—chrome-black, silver-blue, gold-black—although he occasionally pulls a fire-tiger pattern.

For Stiles, the best way to get a floating minnow-imitator down in pockets and drop-offs is with a Wolf River-type setup. "The three-way dropper system is versatile, yet it's easy to master, even for a beginner. You can work any depth, all the way down to 60 feet, with an assortment of sinkers from 1/2 ounce to 4 ounces. Use the same basic rigging, just exchange sinker weight."

Stiles doesn't like bottom bouncers for this type of coldwater river rigging. He thinks bell sinkers yield a more solid bottom contact than the fine-diameter feeler wire of a bottom bouncer. "I can't exactly explain it, but a bell sinker performs better off a 12- to 14-inch dropper."

Tie the crankbait to a 4- or 5-foot leader of 10-pound Trilene XT, place your casting rod (6½- to 7-foot medium-action) in a rod holder, and watch for the rod tip to pulsate as it occasionally ticks bottom. And cover some ground. First search for active fish—in the St. Croix, that's 25 to 30 feet with nearby access to deep holes—while looking for baitfish on the sonar. Stiles doesn't stop to fish until he sees baitfish on the screen.

Trolling direction doesn't matter much. "The current is way down, so it's not a big factor. I prefer trolling cross-current if the structure allows for it. For some reason, a crosscurrent presentation appeals to the fish."

Once you locate walleyes, switch to jigs. "It just makes sense to sit on top of them with a jig instead of making long trolling passes to concentrated fish. I usually try to stay as vertical as possible, but occasionally I longline a jig cross-current." Most days, 1/2- to 3/4-ouncers are the ticket—1/2 ounce if the wind's down, 3/4 when it's breezy.

Finally, how you fish the jig can determine success or failure. "I don't hop, drag, or jiggle," Stiles reveals. "I find that I catch more fish by hovering the jig. Remember, the water's cold, so the fish won't expend energy if they don't have to." Hovering is simply finding bottom, then reeling the jig up no more than 2 inches, occasionally dropping it again to reconfirm bottom. No jigging wizardry here. Keep it basic.

One final suggestion: Tip the jig with a large fathead or a small sucker minnow. You won't need to add a stinger if you perfect the hover technique. "When a fish clamps onto it," Stiles claims, "you'll usually hook it. He wants it pretty bad."

So the jig is up. It's time to pull the plug.

Bob, Bob, Bobbin' Along

SLIPFLOAT SETUPS & STRATEGIES

Picture an office worker drudging on past the dinner hour, pounding keys in front of a computer screen, suddenly enticed by a steak on a string. A sizzling, steaming, peppercorn-encrusted work of art from a mesquite-laden grill slowly descending from a hole in the ceiling to dangle in his face.

Aroma takes command of the room. He's alone. Sweat beads up on his forehead. Will he bite? He'll bite it and be happy to take the bait.

Such is the severe temptation brought to bear by float rigs. The bait hovers there and hovers there until a walleye just can't withstand the urge. Floats are one of the simplest, yet one of the most dynamic walleye techniques. The bait dangles, writhes, and squirms, suspended in the face of a slobbering walleye for as long as it takes. To put the bait precisely there, at the right speed and right depth, requires the right float.

Primary situations call for a float hovering on a spot-on-a-spot, such as a patch of boulders on the end of a point or reef, and covering a limited area by letting the float drift with the wind or current.

Match float shapes to depth, wind, and other conditions. Shape and size determine how the float is affected by wind and waves, how much weight is needed to balance it, how the float is affected by current, how far it casts, and how much resistance a walleye feels when dragging it under.

The most basic rule when choosing a float is to use the smallest size possible. In heavy wind or waves, a larger, more buoyant float becomes a wise choice. But when the wind dies, switch to a smaller float that fish can't easily see or feel, especially in shallow water.

Wind sweeps the line as well as the float, making speed difficult to control. Floats that attach only at the bottom, such as the waggler and several of the night floats, hold the line underwater, where it can't be lifted and swept along. But for covering territory across the top of a reef or hump in a light breeze, choose a tall slipfloat with the body in the middle of the stem and the line rising from the top—a design that catches more wind.

Float fishing is inherently a slow technique, popularly used in shallow water and somewhat limited by increasing depth. Somewhere in the neighborhood of 30 feet, the activity becomes tiresome, though it's possible to fish much deeper. The zone between 15 and 30 feet has untapped walleye potential.

SLIP SLIDIN' AWAY

Floats provide subtlety, finesse, and a hair-trigger indicator separating you and a light biter, with success hanging in the balance. They're ideal for presenting livebait above and around cover that would foul or snag lures. They also fine-tune depth control within an unlimited choice of depth ranges as no other system can.

Floats can be classified into two primary categories—fixed and slip. Both perform well in shallow water, though fixed rigging becomes unwieldy or uncastable if it's set more than about 4 feet deep. Even sweeping sidearm casts with a long rod cause fixed rigs to cartwheel and sometimes to tangle. Distance, accuracy, stealth, and effectiveness plummet.

Sliprigging, meanwhile, eliminates casting difficulties, creating an aerodynamic package that sails toward a target and enters the water with minimal noise, allowing the bait to descend to a desired level and hold there. The longest casts are with classic slipfloats and long rods. Short, classic slipfloats produce the least wobble in flight. The design of a new related model, the Wing-It, adds casting distance and accuracy. A "cut out" of a short classic, the Wing-it offers less air resistance because of its shape—almost like an arrowhead.

Walleye anglers rely chiefly on about five basic styles of slipfloats, plus the following equipment, to fish both deep and shallow.

Float stops—Two elements are elementary to sliprigging: (1)The float slides freely on the line between your bait and an adjustable bobber stop, and (2) the adjustable bobber stop positions the float a desired distance above your bait or bait-and-jig combo.

When casting, the float rests atop split shot or the jig. Once in the water, the weight

Slipfloat Shapes

Classic slipfloats have a line-through-stem design for quick, efficient passage of line. Pencil-style slipfloats (Thill), one of the five basic float groups, offer advantages in some conditions. The slimmer profile is less obtrusive in shallow water over spooky fish (especially in natural wood tones). This shape slides under quicker on the strike, offering less resistance to the fish.

The Carlson Wing-It has a compromise shape. The clefts carved into the body of the float (creating the wings) allow it to slip under water almost as efficiently as the pencil style, yet it casts better. It retains many qualities of the more buoyant, classic, round body floats.

Standard slipfloats with short, squat shapes (Thill) ride waves better, are easier to control in wind, and ride at a reasonable pace in higher winds. Tall, standard slipfloats (Strictly Walleye) catch more wind and move at a more acceptable pace in a breeze for covering flats or the tops of reefs.

Balanced, weighted versions of any design (Thill) should require no weight on the line for slower, more enticing drop speeds. The Thill Center Slider is the most stable design when weighted properly. For optimal balance in buoyancy on most floats, the waterline should mimic the line separating the two colors on the float's body, as on the Center Slider. This is a good design for actively jigging with bait, plastics, or bladebaits.

The Thill Minnow Ring Slider is a good tool for drifting active baits like minnows across flats in a breeze. This design differs from the classics. Line moving through two rings outside the float passes less efficiently, making it a poor choice to jig lures but more versatile to rig.

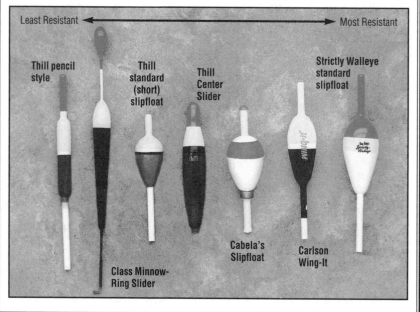

Least Resistant ← → Most Resistant

Thill pencil style

Thill standard (short) slipfloat

Thill Center Slider

Strictly Walleye standard slipfloat

Class Minnow-Ring Slider

Cabela's Slipfloat

Carlson Wing-It

of a bait or lure pulls line through the float until the stop strikes the top of the float, halting the lure's descent. To adjust depth, grasp the stop between your forefinger and thumb, then gently slide it up or down the line to reset the depth of your bait.

Stops are made from neoprene, spring wire, plastic strips, and pretied string knots. Thread 'em onto your line prior to adding the float. Or you can tie your own knot. Make a five-turn uni-knot on your line with a portion of the same test-rated line as your main line. Tighten and trim. String and neoprene versions slide easiest to avoid kinking and weakening light line.

A tiny bobber stop prepositioned on your line reels up through rod guides onto the reel, then casts out again without affecting accuracy or distance. Some fit an array of line diameters. Various-sized neoprene stops, however, work best within specific line ranges (6- to 8-pound test, for example).

Floats—The words *float* and *bobber* are interchangeable, but fishermen often equate bobbers with round bodies and floats with thinner versions. Common walleye slipfloats tend to be long and thin, rather than big and round, to minimize resistance when a tentative biter inhales the bait. The easier the bobber slips beneath the surface, the less the fish feels the line, and the less the chance of spooking it.

Long, thin floats are most sensitive. Even a light touch by a walleye makes the float sink slightly when it is pulled downward, or rise slightly when a fish moves up, inhales the bait, then remains motionless, temporarily neutralizing the lure's ballast beneath the float.

Many strikes, particularly in ice fishing, are so subtle that only a slight variation in the buoyancy of the float can be seen—most easily detected on thin floats because they react more dramatically than the round variety. Walleyes, however, tend to be a bit more aggressive, pulling the float downward or swimming along with the float following behind and breaking the surface. In shallow water, a fish may have nowhere to go but sideways.

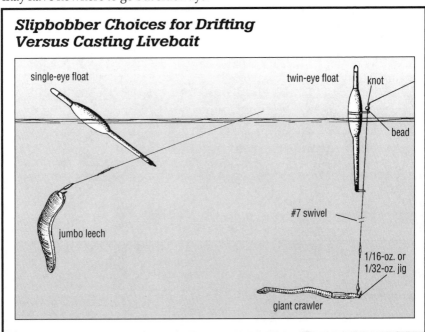

Slipbobber Choices for Drifting Versus Casting Livebait

single-eye float

twin-eye float

knot

bead

jumbo leech

#7 swivel

1/16-oz. or 1/32-oz. jig

giant crawler

River Floats

River floats have bodies near the top of their stems—precisely the opposite of the waggler style. Bodies are carried high on the surface film, which travels slower than current 2 or 3 inches below (friction with air slows the surface of a river). Because it tries to match current speeds near bottom (which are slowest), this style is the most efficient, but it still requires manipulation.

Check the float by holding it back briefly (just a second or two) to keep the bait moving at current speed near bottom for a more natural presentation that can trigger even neutral or inactive fish. The slowest design here is new from Fishpol, Inc. The Silver Dollar Float shows little surface area to the current, is sensitive, and is easily manipulated to slow the drift in fast water. Long wooden floats, like the Thill River Master and Grayling Ultra, are more durable and just as efficient in lighter current.

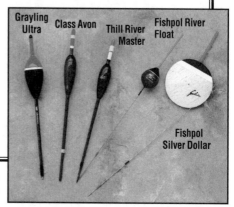

Grayling Ultra   Class Avon   Thill River Master   Fishpol River Float

Fishpol Silver Dollar

The most common slipfloat design is a generic version in which the line passes through a hollow stem extending through the float. Place a small plastic bead on the line between the bobber stop and the top stem of the float to prevent the stop from becoming wedged in the stem.

In another version, the line passes through a single hole at the base of the float stem, which is beneath water. This eliminates freezing and minimizes most wind effect on exposed line. When you twitch or retrieve, however, the float tends to collapse toward the surface, sometimes momentarily disappearing from view. At night, you may temporarily lose sight of a lighted or luminous float of this style. The benefit, however, is your increased ability to twitch and work a bait, imparting considerable action.

A less common version, referred to as a double-ringed slider, features two rings, one at the base and another along the side of the float, through which the line passes. This version, sort of a hybrid of the previous two styles, is designed as a float for rivers and can be a good option for drifting presentations to cover water in lakes. Twitching, however, doesn't impart as much action as it does with the single-eye float.

The bulkier the float (common, cigar, or center-slider float designs), the more weight it can support. The more action a jig or bait attains with twitches of the rod tip, the less likely the bait is to remain in roughly the same location. The smaller or thinner the float (pencil floats), the less weight it can support. The more sensitive it is, the easier it is for rod tip movements to move the float and bait location.

When a large portion of the float is exposed to the air, it catches more wind and drifts faster. The more the bulk of the body is positioned beneath the surface (waggler floats), the less wind affects it, and the slower and more natural the drift.

Current has the opposite effect. In fixed floats designed for current, the stem portion beneath the surface is thin (Thill River Master or Thill Turbo Master),

Wagglers

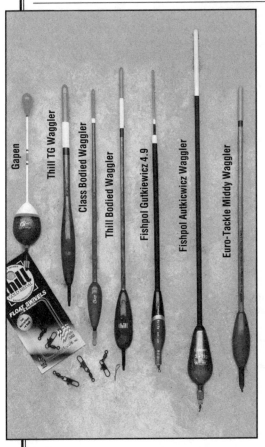

Wagglers, when properly weighted and rigged, hover a bait in place over key spots in wind. The body is low on the stem, submerging the largest mass out of the wind and surface currents.

Thill offers special loop-shaped snap-swivels designed to clip to the bottom of the stem on any waggler. Run the main line though the other end of the swivel, and the float slides. Peg it with two tiny split shot on either side of the swivel. With no attachment at the top of the float, line is held underwater, away from wind and surface currents. Additional weight is added on the line with split shot spaced about 1 foot above the bait.

Properly weighted, only the colored portion (the top third or so of the stem) of the waggler is visible above water. Some wagglers (like the Middy) are adjustable, with screw-on weighting systems that allow for a more natural, slow-dropping presentation.

minimizing drag, while the bulk of the body remains just at the surface.

The growing popularity of thinner, more finely balanced float systems has had a growing influence on fishing for walleyes, panfish, and other species. In essence, the finer the balance, the more precise the presentation.

RIGGED AND STEADY

You're rigged with an on-line float stop, plus a slipfloat of the approximate size necessary to balance your bait. Next, you add the business end of the equation—something with a hook. Might be just that, a hook. But it could also be a lightly weighted hook, a weedless hook, or a lightweight jighead.

The choice depends on bait size and style, cover, and water clarity. Generally, adding a hint of color via a jighead may offer an advantage in dark or dingy water or where wind and waves diminish visibility. Fluorescent orange, yellow, chartreuse, or pink heads stand out, focusing the strike at the head of the bait.

The hook must balance the bulk of the bait and the strength of the line. Walleye anglers use 6- or 8-pound-test mono to minimize line visibility while maximizing castability for lightweight presentations. But in extremely clear, calm water, 4-pound line is an option. So is 10-pound in and around snags. This line range demands small, light wire, sharp hooks for easy penetration. Setting the hook with a wide sweep of the rod starts the hook point penetrating. Yet the hook must be substantial enough to hold a walleye; a tiny panfish hook may not suffice.

In most walleye waters, minnows hooked behind the dorsal or in the tail for maximal action become the best option in temperatures below 50°F. For minnows, hook size depends on bait size. Match hook gap to the bulk of the bait, ensuring a sufficiently exposed hook to grab a walleye's jaw. That could be anywhere from a #6 to a 1/0. Traditionally, minnows are lightly hooked through the back near or slightly behind the dorsal fin, well above the spine. This allows them to struggle against the bobber, signalling distressed and vulnerable bait.

Kahle or wide-bend hooks have unique bends that are great for float fishing, particularly for vertical hooksets through ice.

Leeches are the preferred bait from the time the water temperature exceeds 50°F through the temperature peak at midsummer. For leeches hooked through the suction cup end, we usually use #6 or #8 lightwire Aberdeen or stouter octopus-style hooks (the same style used for livebait rigging). The hook must be sufficient to hook and land a walleye, yet avoid overweighting the leech and stifling its action. Properly rigged, the pointy nose end of the leech attempts to swim away from the hook, wiggling enticingly. Leeches hooked at the opposite end tend to ball up.

Nightcrawlers enter the picture when water temperatures exceed 60°F. For nightcrawlers hooked through the collar or at midpoint, we usually use the same models as for leeches but in #6 or #4 sizes. Let both ends of the crawler dangle and wiggle.

The same principles apply to hooking livebaits on jigheads, with the possible exception of hooking a nightcrawler through the nose, inserting the hook point at the end, and threading the crawler on a half inch or so. Jigheads range from tiny 1/32-ounce glimpses of color, through 1/16- and possibly even 1/8-ounce heavyweights for deep water or strong wind. Most of the time, smaller sizes are best.

Kahle or wide-bend hooks have unique bends that are great for float fishing, particularly for vertical hooksets through ice. Due to the larger amount of steel in Kahle hooks, we downsize by one from traditional hooks when livebait fishing for walleyes. Hooks often outproduce jigheads in the cooler water of spring because there's less hardware to spook walleyes. But once the water warms and visibility is reduced by plankton and algae, the added attraction of colored jigheads usually outproduces plain hooks.

THE BALANCING ACT

Walleye anglers often fish in big waves. Wave action causes heavily weighted or thin floats to dive beneath the surface as each wave rolls in, sacrificing visibility and control. So big water floats tend to be a bit bulkier than those for calm water. Also, line must be weighted to reduce the force necessary to sink them, but not to the same hair-trigger status as for calm water rigs.

European float specialists often spread several split shot along a section of line, causing the line to sink and then begin unfolding near bottom, eventually allowing the near-weightless hook to drift the bait downward. Shot are positioned several feet up the line from the bait to minimize visibility, with the largest at the top, the smaller near the bottom.

Slipfloat Elements

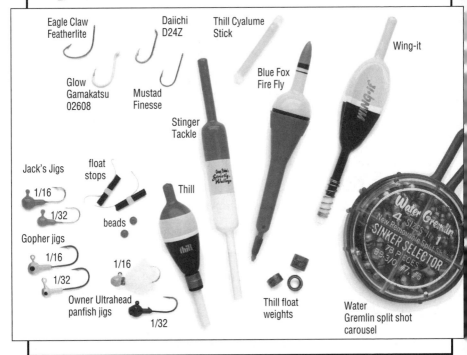

Eagle Claw Featherlite

Daiichi D24Z

Thill Cyalume Stick

Wing-it

Glow Gamakatsu 02608

Mustad Finesse

Blue Fox Fire Fly

Stinger Tackle

Jack's Jigs

1/16

1/32

float stops

beads

Thill

Gopher jigs

1/16

1/32

1/16

Owner Ultrahead panfish jigs

1/32

Thill float weights

Water Gremlin split shot carousel

Walleye anglers seldom require such precision. Often, a simple jighead is enough to pull the line down through the slipfloat and maintain a position near bottom. Yet adding a split shot or two a couple feet up from the bait feeds the line through the float more quickly into the fish zone, while simultaneously fine-tuning the buoyancy of the rig.

Split shot are available from small BB, B, 3/0 to 7, with 7 often too large and BB on the small side. Carry a selection. Squeeze 'em onto your line 18 to 24 inches above your bait, but avoid clamping, which could damage line. Reusable split shot with tiny wings are easy to squeeze and remove for adjustments or for future use. Non-reusable shot create less line twist. Generally, use enough shot in combination for near buoyancy in calm water, greater buoyancy in waves.

SETTING DEPTH

To set bait depth, either estimate the depth or attach a clip depthfinder weight onto the hook, lower it to bottom, and adjust the bobber stop accordingly before reeling up and removing the dephfinder weight. In calm water, setting a bobber stop to hover a bait just a whisker off bottom is easy. But in waves, the rig begins rising and falling, and how far up and down it travels depends on the rigging.

Say the water's 5 feet deep. How deep do you set the stop in 2-foot waves? With a traditional hook and shot setup, the hook lacks sufficient weight to return to vertical after every passing wave. Instead, it flutters near the level of the lowest shot on the line, twitching after every wave-trough combination. To keep a bait right near bottom, compensate by setting the depth a bit deeper. Ideally, set

The Fine Points of Float Fishing

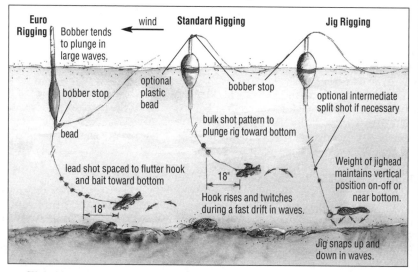

Euro Rigging — Bobber tends to plunge in large waves.
wind
Standard Rigging
Jig Rigging

bobber stop

bead

optional plastic bead

bobber stop

optional intermediate split shot if necessary

lead shot spaced to flutter hook and bait toward bottom

bulk shot pattern to plunge rig toward bottom

18"

Hook rises and twitches during a fast drift in waves.

Weight of jighead maintains vertical position on-off or near bottom.

18"

Jig snaps up and down in waves.

Slipbobber hooks should penetrate with little pressure on light line. Light wire Aberdeen styles are ideal, as are wide-bend Kahles, which contain a bit more steel but have excellent biting and holding characteristics. Octopus-style hooks, standard for livebait rigging, are excellent too, in bronze or black for low visibility in clear water, gold, red, blue, yellow, or silver to add color in dingy water. Weedless hooks help deflect snags in weeds and wood.

Jigheads in the 1/32-, 1/16-, and 1/8-ounce categories cover the bases for slipfloat walleyes. Round heads move up-down; planing heads flutter and swim. Try bright fluorescent yellow, chartreuse, or orange in dark or muddy water or in windy conditions. In clear water, black or plain lead may excel. At night, phosphorescent jigs may be the hot ticket.

the lowest split shot to occasionally brush bottom on the drift—basically at the depth of the wave troughs.

With a jig, the heavier weight tends to make the bait plunge back nearly to vertical after every wave cycle, giving it a snap upward as each wave passes overhead. Set depth to position the jig just about at the depth of bottom during each wave trough.

"I don't use a plain hook when fishing in big waves," says veteran Mille Lacs, Minnesota, guide and two-time In-Fisherman Professional Walleye Trail tournament winner Ron Anlauf, "because the bait tends to ride up off bottom, and it should stay down in the fish zone. I use a jig and set the depth to at least occasionally drag bottom, which slows its drift through good areas.

"In essence, I'm reducing drift speed to less than that of free floating in the waves. The bait spends more time in fish-holding pockets. It also tends to fall into crevices between boulders, where walleyes are. I snag more than when my bait's set off bottom, but I catch more fish.

"Every good shallow walleye spot has humps or bumps. I want to know where my bait is. If my jig drags bottom, the bobber lies down. When it's off bottom, the bobber stands up. I can tell what it's doing and what bottom's like. I never use weighted bobbers—those with lead wrapped around the bottom of the float—because they stand upright whether the bait's cruising above or resting on bottom."

Set the depth of your bait to begin brushing bottom slightly before it reaches the shallowest crest of a reef. When casting up onto a shallow spot and drifting back out deeper, the bait should immediately begin dragging bottom, then free float at some point as the combo drifts downwind. When casting to a shoreline and letting the bait drift in, it should begin brushing bottom at just about the depth where the fish are.

Fishing near weeds and wood is trickier. Interpret the depth of the tops of the cover, and estimate its density. Is the objective to float the bait just over the top or to brush it occasionally? To fish down between the weed stalks or wood clumps, risking an occasional snag? Switching from an open-hooked jig to a weedless jig fine-tunes the system and minimize snags.

CLEAN SWEEPING REEFS

The main way to fish floats on windswept rock reefs is to anchor a cast length upwind of the peak or spine of the reef, cast out, and let the wind drift the float into the spot where walleyes move up on top of the rocks. Anchor position is critical, along with a heavy sea anchor and long rope—generally 100 feet of 1/2-inch nylon—to fine-tune position. Invest in a good anchor that will hold in big waves. Fluke-type anchors with at least 100 feet of rope usually suffice.

Drop the anchor well upwind, then drift downwind, feeding rope, until you're

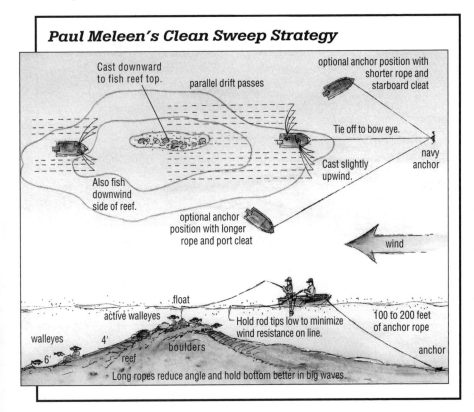

Paul Meleen's Clean Sweep Strategy

Cast downward to fish reef top.

parallel drift passes

optional anchor position with shorter rope and starboard cleat

Tie off to bow eye.

navy anchor

Cast slightly upwind.

Also fish downwind side of reef.

optional anchor position with longer rope and port cleat

wind

float

active walleyes

Hold rod tips low to minimize wind resistance on line.

100 to 200 feet of anchor rope

walleyes   4'

boulders

anchor

6'   reef

Long ropes reduce angle and hold bottom better in big waves.

in the right spot. Then tie off to the bow and begin presenting baits so they drift past prominent structural features on the upwind side of the reef, where active walleyes are likely to move shallow.

Use a short cast downwind, giving the bait sufficient time to descend before reaching the prime spot. Feed line on the drift, and fish mostly behind the boat.

"I do things differently," says professional walleye angler and Mille Lacs Lake guide Paul Meleen. "Casting straight downwind limits my ability to cover an area. Instead, one angler fishes from each side of the boat, casting out not just downwind or perpendicular to the boat, but quartering upwind. I retrieve a little line as the float drifts down alongside the boat, then feed line as it drifts farther downwind. Adjusting line length minimizes line bow and creates long, straight drifts. Start with short casts to either side, going longer on successive tosses, allowing the rig to drift down a slightly different path each time.

When one bobber goes down, other anglers in the boat should drift their bait into the same spot.

"When walleyes move onto shallow rocks, they're schooled. When one bobber goes down, other anglers in the boat should drift their bait into the same spot. Chances are that one or more additional walleyes will come from the same spot.

"Running your outboard in shallow water can spook fish. I use an extra-long anchor rope—225 feet—which allows retying at different lengths and angles without running the motor. Moving the tie-off point to different cleats around the bow of the boat changes the angle of the boat to the waves, causing it to swing wider or narrower to the wind. I can fish a 60- or 80-foot circle without reanchoring.

"Also, I sometimes catch fewer but bigger fish on the downwind side of a reef. I move to the downwind side, then slowly motor up on top into as little as 2 feet of water, drop anchor, shut off the engine, and drift back out to 6 feet or so. I cast upwind to the reef top, retrieving line as the float drifts back alongside, feeding line as it drifts past the boat.

"There's also a mistaken belief that walleyes only move atop reefs in wind. Sometimes they're right up there amidst the boulders on bright calm days, even in clear water. I can see them with polarized sunglasses, lying between or moving amidst the crevices. That's why I study reefs when weather's calm, looking for the biggest boulders or other features that draw fish. Then I can sneak up within a long cast and pitch a slipbobber rig or even a baited jig to the fish. They're spooky, but sometimes I catch some mighty nice fish by sight-fishing."

Meleen continues, "When the water's calm, however, I start fishing the outer perimeter of the reef first, while looking up into the shallows. Say a reef tops out at 5 feet, sloping to 8 or 9, before dropping off to 12. I troll slowly around the outer edge with the electric motor, using a heavily weighted slipbobber rig to keep the bait down vertical while moving. One angler simultaneously casts shallow, looking for fish on top. Once we identify shallow concentration points, I creep up a bit shallower and make long casts to potential sites.

"Likewise, if conditions change from windy to calm, the fish are still around, but they're spookier. Keep your float away from the boat to catch 'em."

Fishing shallow points involves a similar strategy. In wind, anchor and drift your float in to the primary tip of the point or to some irregular feature like an inside turn, boulder, or cover. When it's calm, use an electric motor to position within casting distance, then pitch in shallow. Let the float sit awhile, then twitch it, retrieve a little, let it sit, then retrieve again. Wiggling, tipping, and dancing jigs in calm weather add slight action to an already lively livebait.

Force-Feeding Fish

Chris Carlson "force-feeds" fish with floats. He uses this method for adding action to the bait when wind or current aren't doing it for him.

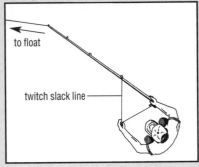

to float

twitch slack line

Cast out and take up slack. Pull line from the reel with the hand that isn't holding the reel handle. Twitch the float by snapping the slack line you're holding. Try moving it 6 to 8 times. Then let it sit. Maybe reel the float into a different position and repeat the snapping sequence.

Carlson often gets hard strikes when he uses this sequence, a good reason to hold slack line in your hand. "When a fish pulls the bait under hard," he says, "slack gives it the chance to bite before I set the hook. If the line's tight on a hard bite, resistance can pull the bait out of the fish's mouth."

For fishing over weeds and wood, or between or along the edges of cover, try to position the bait as close as possible to the top or sides of cover. Let it drift in close, then stop letting out line, holding the bait in place along the edge.

Where cover is widespread and sparse, for example, on an emerging weed flat, use a sweeping or fancasting pattern from an anchored position to strain the area. Where cover's specific, for example, flooded shoreline trees in a flowage or river, cast, drift, or generally work tight to the edge.

RIGGING FOR BIG WIND VERSUS CALM CONDITIONS

"The windier it gets," says Mille Lacs guide Chris Carlson, "the slower the float rig should move across the water. In big winds, I spread my shot rather than bunching them. I put the first one on about 10 inches above my hook, then spread several small shot a foot or more apart. That slows the rig as it moves through key zones." Waggler-style floats hold position well in high winds.

The windier it gets, the closer to the hook Carlson places his first shot. "I want to keep my bait down in the fish zone," he says. "The more I weight it down, the less the bait bounces up and down."

To impart action to the float, especially on flat water, cast out, take up slack, pull more line out of the reel, snap the float maybe six or eight times, and let it sit. Repeat the snapping sequence. Carlson calls this "force-feeding" fish. "Hold slack line in your hand. Twitch with your rod tip on a tight line, and a strong bite can pull the bait out of the fish's mouth. A lot of times when I pop the cork, I hear *ker-ploonk* as a fish pulls it under."

SETTING THE HOOK

"Use at least a 9-foot spinning rod for big water and wind," Meleen advises. "It offers an extra 4-foot sweep to tighten the line. When you see your bobber dip, dive, or move to the side, tighten up slack by reeling while dropping the rod tip. Then, when you sweepset the hook, keep an eye on the line. If it doesn't tighten sufficiently, reel up and sweep again. Once you get the hook point started, the bend in the rod ensures that the hook begins penetrating. Even if the fish runs toward you, a long rod is forgiving; you can keep the pressure on without risk of breaking light line."

When a walleye bites near cover in calm conditions, lower the rod tip toward the submerged float, reel a bit to tighten the line, then sweepset the moment you feel the fish. Put sufficient pressure on the fish to lead it away from the snag. Once you've removed the fish from cover, fight it more gingerly. Let the long rod do the work.

For dingier waters or woodcover, switch to a more visible or abrasion-resistant line like Trilene Solar XT. The tradeoff is that more abrasion-resistant lines typically are stiffer and more difficult for casting lightweight floats.

WHERE AND WHEN

Float fishing applies any time of year. In spring, postspawn areas include the rock riprap of dams and causeways; atop shallow emerging weeds where perch (walleye forage) spawn; along flooded shoreline wood in river backwaters; in back bays of flowages where shoreline and midbay woodcover is abundant; and creek mouths or bridges (anytime). In many cases, such areas can be effectively fished from shore.

In summer, try the tops of or alongside main lake weedbeds in natural lakes; rock points sticking out to deep water; the tops of rock reefs; shallow roadbeds in reservoirs; the edges of standing timber along creek or river channels. For the shallow night bite, look almost anywhere.

Also try floats along the edges of deep structure in clear lakes, even in main basins, where fish feed on insect larvae on or emerging from soft bottom. Float opportunities are endless. Especially at night.

SPRINGTIME SLIPFLOAT COMMANDOS

In spring, look for walleyes in areas either adjacent to or somewhere along the trail from nearby spawning areas. Walleyes set up shop on the first classic shallow reefs and flats they come to after spawning, typically keying on spawning perch. Perch usually spawn in 3 to 7 feet of water, in last year's weedbeds, though immature perch may seek better protection in the rocks.

Depths of 8 to 12 feet are productive for walleyes when water temperatures range from just under 50°F to just over 60°F. Walleyes move shallower under cover of murky water, high winds, and low light. From evening until after sunrise at this time of year, look for walleyes in 2- to 6-foot depths. Key spots are projections off shoreline-oriented rockbars and reefs, gravel patches, or rockpiles on shallow flats, weedlines, and inside turns on bars near the sharpest drop into deeper water.

Use a #10 or #8 bronze or black hook in calm, clear conditions, especially during early postspawn, when water temperatures are still cool (45°F to 50°F). Try red, chartreuse, or glow hooks in cloudier water. Small jigs in the 1/32- to 1/16-ounce range produce better in windy conditions, when water temperatures rise to 50°F and above. In both situations, weight the line with split shot 12 to 18 inches above the hook to balance the float. Place the shot all together in a bulk pattern for a quick drop. The float should ride high enough to be seen, yet be neutrally buoyant enough to slip under quickly, providing the least possible resistance to a biting walleye.

In shallow water and fairly calm conditions, opt for a weighted slipfloat. A lead ring around the stem below the body balances the float and allows a light jig to fall into the strike zone in a slow, enticing manner. When the float is moved, the jig arcs higher and falls slower. The package hits the water with less noise, too. In all cases, use sharp, thin wire hooks with small barbs for better hooksets.

In early spring, use small minnows. Leeches are best once the water tops 50°F. Hook minnows through the lips or lightly under the skin along the spine. Hook leeches once through the sucker end for the liveliest action, changing bait when it becomes fatigued.

Pitch In

When casting to shorelines or shoreline cover, use the standard drift-in approach if conditions permit. Hold the float just outside the cover or shoreline edge, steer it along flooded wood in a river, and generally use your rod tip to probe nooks and crannies with the float.

In calm conditions, if possible cast past or at least up to the edge of visible cover, then let the float sit awhile. Then twitch it a little, followed by a pause. Reel a little. Wait. Let the action of the lively livebait tempt fish up and out of the weeds or wood. Adding a little rod tip action, however, often entices more bites.

For casting across boulders, wood, or weed flats, twitches interspersed by pauses are key to covering water and triggering fish in calm conditions. Set your bobber stop to either suspend bait just above thick cover or down between sparse clumps, depending on what's available. If the wind comes up, simply switch to a cast-and-drift sweeping approach.

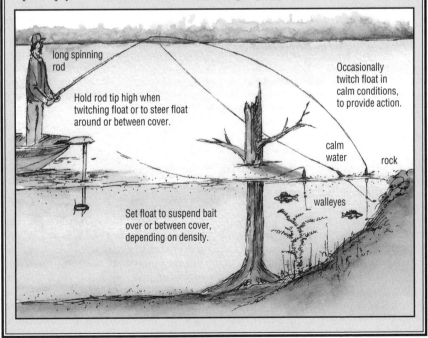

long spinning rod

Hold rod tip high when twitching float or to steer float around or between cover.

Occasionally twitch float in calm conditions, to provide action.

calm water

rock

Set float to suspend bait over or between cover, depending on density.

walleyes

BEACONS IN THE NIGHT

"Let the strike develop," cautions the guide to his squinting customer, sage advice garnered over decades of introducing anglers to the night walleye bite. Peering into the inky blackness, his trained eyes follow the tiny red light until it slips beneath the surface. "Now." The rod bends, and the faint glow begins to dart and bob a foot below the calm veneer. Fish on.

When the sun sets, a world of sensory stimulation, tension, and discovery pits visually dependent anglers against expert nighttime predators—walleyes on a moonlight prowl. Developing strikes and other key habits will help you master the art of catching walleyes at night.

WHY FISH AT NIGHT?

Some lakes have reputations as tough places to fish during the day, yet they give up their secrets after nightfall to a devout few anglers plying the tranquil waters. Perhaps recreational traffic is high, with jet skis and water skiers ruling the waters until sundown. In clear water judged excellent for swimming, sandy beaches may draw summer vacation crowds to the resorts and summer cabins rimming the shoreline. In these situations, catching walleyes—particularly big walleyes—can be tough during the day.

Catching large walleyes becomes more feasible after dark, when daytime crowds leave the lake and life above the surface settles to a quieter pace. Once you locate them, fish that are programmed to feed intensely during prime feeding periods can reward you with fast action. Pull up to a rockpile after dark, and you can often catch a quick limit of fish where none were present during the day.

Successful night-fishing is no accident, however. Rehearse every step beforehand so all you need do is step onto the stage and play your part after the lights go down.

SUMMER LOCATION

While large, clear bodies of water with cisco or smelt forage bases tend to produce the greatest numbers of big walleyes, nearly any lake, large or small, can offer good night-fishing. Veteran guide Greg Bohn believes that most natural lakes with rockbars or weed flats draw a substantial number of walleyes into the shallows at night during summer.

In the lakes and flowages that Bohn fishes in northern Wisconsin, the places where he finds fish during the day—shoreline woodcover, logjams, sandbars, stumpfields, docks, creek mouths, and fish cribs—tend to be less productive after dark than key weeds and rocks.

In summer, however, areas of weeds and rocks can play major roles for walleyes at night, yet few anglers explore these options. Fish little lakes out in the boondocks, and you may be the only boat on the water after dark. Even on popular waters, you'll likely have the best spots to yourself.

EQUIPMENT

Lighted slipbobbers teamed with livebait blend stealth and control for fishing those key spots that concentrate fish after dark. Rig during daylight to be ready when the sun sets.

Eight-pound-test mono is a good all-around choice. After placing a bobber stop and a slipfloat on the line, Bohn ties a small barrel swivel to the end of the main line. Then he attaches a 6-pound-test leader that will break first if he snags solidly, preventing the loss of the lighted float. Check the line above the float by running it between your fingers occasionally. Cut off frayed sections and re-tie as often as necessary.

Slide the adjustable bobber stop up or down to set the desired depth. Bohn uses chartreuse string stops that are easier to see at night than red or orange ones. Knots pretied on small plastic tubes thread onto the line for quick replacement.

Lighted floats have bright red diode lights powered by lithium batteries. To prolong battery life, unscrew the cap, remove the battery, turn it upside down, and reinsert it in a nonconductive position even during 15-minute trips between spots. Typical battery life of 12 hours often can be extended to 30 hours by conserving power. Floats incorporating disposable cyalume light sticks provide a single night's glow.

Bohn uses small, lightweight Slip Bobber Jigs from Stinger Tackle for float fishing at night. They hang vertically, hook down, in the water, and their bright, two-tone coloration is visible to walleyes. Bright colors entice walleyes to strike directly at the jigs, improving hooking percentages by directing the strike toward a larger hook than is usually found on such small jigs. Balancing buoyancy with split shot allows you to fish lightweight jigs—1/32, 1/16, and 1/8 ounce—which minimize spooking walleyes that mouth the livebait.

Bohn sometimes adds a 1-inch glow-in-the-dark soft plastic curlytail grub to the jig as a teaser. It creates a larger glowing target to focus the strike and offers him extra confidence that fish will see his bait.

ROCKBARS—NIGHTTIME WALLEYE MAGNETS

The top of a good nighttime rockbar usually extends shallower than 15 feet and is surrounded by water at least 20 to 30 feet deep. It may be completely surrounded by deep water, or it may be the high point on the tip of one of those underwater extensions often referred to as a *finger*. Variations in the slope of the drop-off or bottom content—large rocks mixed with smaller rock and gravel, for example—generally improve its potential. For some reason, big rocks often attract big fish.

Before attempting to fish a shallow rockbar at night, study a lake map and become acquainted with the water during the day. This is safer than running an

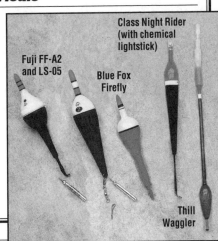

Night Floats

Most night floats are battery operated. Reverse the battery and leave it in the unit when not in use. Chemical lightsticks last one night and are a good option for transforming floats you already own into night floats, with something like the Rod'N Bob's accessory item (shown on the waggler). Both chemical and electrical night floats can be seen from a long distance, which is good for anchoring near a reef in the dark. Shape, style, and size are determined by conditions.

Fuji FF-A2 and LS-05

Blue Fox Firefly

Class Night Rider (with chemical lightstick)

Thill Waggler

unfamiliar lake in the dark, and you'll be more productive if you're comfortable with the layout and can find prime spots easily. Locate potentially good rockbars, determine where or if weeds intersect areas of hard bottom, and where walleyes are likely to hold during the day.

During the day, examine the outer edges of each bar with your electronics to detect irregularities that may concentrate walleyes, such as where deep water swings clos-est to the rocks, or where fingers project off the edge of the bar. Then motor slowly toward the top of the bar and note the minimal depth at the crest. Toss out a floating white plastic marker with a line and weight to mark the exact top where you plan to fish after dark. Walleyes usually move as shallow as possible under cover of darkness. Arrive before sundown at the first bar you intend to fish after dark, and set the depth of your slipfloat rigs before prime time arrives.

Clip a depthfinder weight to the jig. Sitting directly above the spot you intend to fish, lower the rig into the water and adjust (slide) the position of your bobber stop

Rock Tops

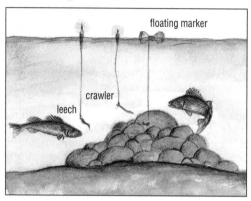

Before sundown, mark the tops of rockbars with lighted markers or white plastic bottles containing Cyalume lightsticks. Anchor your boat about a cast length upwind and set your slipfloat to suspend the bait about a foot or so off bottom.

along the line so your jig sits about 1 foot above bottom as it hangs beneath the float. When the weight pulls your float 1 foot below the surface during the setup procedure, your bait is correctly positioned. Remove the weight. If you run your boat up on top of the bar after dark to accomplish this procedure, you'll spook the fish—a common mistake novices make.

Anchor in deeper water about a half-cast upwind of the marker. Wave action works your float and bait up and down, drifting them to the fish. Walleyes also are less spooky when a little wind riles the surface. If it's safe to do so, anchor broadside to the marker using two anchors to keep the boat from swinging, thus ensuring a good cast-and-drift path to the marker. With no wind, use your electric motor to hover within casting distance.

Inexperienced anglers often try to do too much when they begin night-fishing, running multiple lines or covering too many areas. Use a single rod and line as effectively as possible to minimize tangled lines and missed fish.

Jumbo leeches are the most common livebait for slipfloat fishing after dark, though nightcrawlers are worth a try, too. On nights when walleyes tear crawlers in half on the strike, switch to leeches or half-crawlers to present smaller targets and prevent short strikes.

Minnows are fine night baits for walleyes and may offer a slight advantage in the cooler water of spring and fall. Three- to 4-inch fatheads, chubs, roaches, or shiners are all lively excellent choices. Tail-hooking lets them dart and dive toward bottom, an action that triggers strikes.

ROCKBAR RENDEZVOUS

Walleyes actively feeding on rockbars at night may have been making similar movements up to the same spot for hundreds of generations, lying in adjacent deeper water until just before dark and then suddenly moving shallow along an established route. Fish approach prime areas from the same direction each time. This is where allowing strikes to develop may illuminate more about walleye behavior.

Peering at a lighted float through inky darkness, then suddenly seeing it plunge downward, creates a reflex urge to set the hook immediately. Let some of these strikes go without setting the hook, or at least wait before setting the hook. Watch the direction a walleye swims after inhaling the bait. In most cases, it will move in the direction it came from, helping you retrace the migration route it followed from deeper water. This helps pinpoint where walleyes first contact the bar. You may be able to position your boat more precisely on future trips, within better casting distance of the contact point.

A strong strike in which the float plunges rapidly downward usually indicates many walleyes feeding atop the bar. Expect to catch more fish right away. If the float goes under 2 or 3 inches and hangs there, however, there's probably little threat of competition, suggesting few fish up on top.

Set up on a prime spot about one hour before dark. Expect walleyes to move up just before full darkness and to find the strongest feeding activity for up to two hours. After that, expect sporadic activity as the night wears on. Moving to other spots may produce a few fish from each area.

CARPETED WEED FLATS

Low sparse weeds are easy to fish with floats in spring. Once weeds grow tall and to irregular heights, there are usually better ways to fish large weedy areas. The key to summer float fishing in weeds is to select areas where weeds only rise to a consistent height, preferably not too far off bottom.

Bohn practices this tactic on low-growing sandgrass carpets rising about 1 foot off bottom in 8 to 12 feet of water. Many such areas lie adjacent to shallow bays where heavier weedgrowth reaches the surface. Focus your nighttime attention just outside the outer fringe of sparse tall weeds that don't quite reach the surface, in the transition zone between weedy bays and deeper, weed-free mudflats, where low-growing weed carpets border the outside edge of tall weeds. In gradually tapering areas with fairly uniform depth, weeds top out at a consistent level, making it easier to suspend a bait in the strike zone just above the weeds without snagging.

Set your lighted slipfloats to suspend bait about 2 feet off bottom—1 foot above the low-growing weed carpet. Drift or slowly backtroll over the flat, just outside the deep weedline, using your electronics to remain in the proper depth range. Watch for sparse weeds near bottom.

When you hook a walleye, immediately toss out a floating marker and cast all remaining lines toward that spot. Flood the area with bait. If nothing happens, reel in, cast upwind, and let the breeze drift bait through the area for an additional chance at fish. Continue moving along the weed carpet until you contact walleyes.

SEASONAL SECRETS

Weed flats begin producing walleyes in late spring and continue attracting them until after fall Turnover. Gradually, however, walleyes abandon weeds as the water temperature drops and vegetation begins to die off. They typically shift deeper onto adjacent silt, mudflats, or distinct rocky structure. Depths of 20 to 40 feet are common in October and November.

Fishing Deep Weed Carpets

Key areas to try lighted slipbobbers are bays with low-lying weed flats or the outer edges of heavy weed flats where the growth switches to a low-lying carpet of sandgrass or other short vegetation. The ideal situation is an 8- to 12-foot carpeted flat with scattered clumps of coontail or cabbage to concentrate fish. Set float rigs to suspend bait 2 feet off bottom, 1 foot above the weeds.

Drift the area with lighted slipbobber rigs until you contact fish. Bohn and his clients fish three lines: two lines approximately 50 feet long at either end of the boat and one line approximately 20 feet long down the center.

Without wind, slowly backtroll with an electric motor. Reduce to two lines to prevent tangles. Once you catch walleyes, anchor immediately and saturate the area in all directions by casting bobber rigs and working them back to the boat with frequent long pauses to let the bait settle and wiggle enticingly.

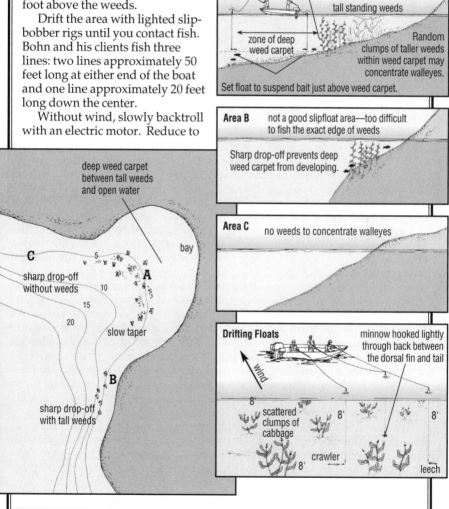

Area A deep weedline — Slow taper allows weed carpet to form and rise to a uniform height. tall standing weeds. zone of deep weed carpet. Random clumps of taller weeds within weed carpet may concentrate walleyes. Set float to suspend bait just above weed carpet.

Area B not a good slipfloat area—too difficult to fish the exact edge of weeds. Sharp drop-off prevents deep weed carpet from developing.

Area C no weeds to concentrate walleyes. Sharp drop-off prevents deep weed carpet from developing.

deep weed carpet between tall weeds and open water. bay. C. 5. A. sharp drop-off without weeds. 10. 15. 20. slow taper. B. sharp drop-off with tall weeds.

Drifting Floats minnow hooked lightly through back between the dorsal fin and tail. wind. 8'. scattered clumps of cabbage. 8'. crawler. 8'. leech.

Rockbars may continue to produce fish into October. Even then, walleyes may use rocks at almost any time, witnessed by ice fishermen contacting walleyes in these areas at first-ice. The most consistent nightly movements to the tops of rockbars, however, occur during summer and early fall.

A BIG NUTHIN' AT NIGHT

If opposites attract, then fishing structure for walleyes also has its antistructural counterpart in the web of aquatic life. The opposite to something with a distinct shape and substance logically must be something shapeless, unseen, unknown. The closest parallel we see in the walleye world is fishing for walleyes that are either suspended over or roaming across open basins. Taken one step farther, we can also explore the antipattern in its extreme form—fishin' in the middle of a big nuthin' at night. "Night-fishing is a common occurrence on Mille Lacs Lake," says former guide Joe Fellegy, the acknowledged sage of all things historical regarding mid Minnesota's premier walleye fishery. "But it's chiefly practiced on shallow structure, either longline trolling minnow-imitating crankbaits along shallow rock points, or anchoring and casting lighted slipbobbers and leeches atop shallow rock reefs poking toward the surface. In recent years, more anglers have begun night-fishing the edges of deep midlake mudflats, soaking their leeches in deep water along twists and turns in the drop-off at the 20- to 30-foot range. This new breed of midlake basin anglers has rocked the boat of traditional fishing logic—especially at night."

"A handful of launches and a growing number of anglers in small boats have been fishing the soft basin areas lying outside the glacially deposited areas of table-top flat humps locally referred to as mudflats," says Mike Gannon, a launch driver and fishing guide operating out of Twin Pines Resort. That in itself isn't unusual, considering that anglers in many areas now troll such areas for suspended fish. "The big difference," Gannon continues, "is that we do it at night, using lighted bobbers and livebait, far from structure of any kind. Baitfish, more than bottom changes, key the areas of best productivity.

"We started fishing this way by probing the edges of the flats at night, then began exploring off the edges, drifting across the adjacent basin. We found that soft bottom areas where insects or baitfish were present also attracted walleyes. We had a hard time catching any walleyes there during the day, but when we started fishing for them at night, we found the pattern consistent, easy, and lots of fun.

"Basically, we begin at the edge of one of the larger mudflats. Then we scout the adjacent open basin with our depthfinders, looking for the presence of baitfish.

Wherever we spot schools of fish, we toss out the anchor, then set our slipbobbers to dangle a small fluorescent orange or chartreuse jighead, baited with a leech, just above bottom. Or we use a split shot, a red hook, and a chartreuse bead, also with a leech. Then the whole guide party toss out their bobbers and start fishing. Sometimes it's necessary to pick up and move a few times to get in on the hot action. Generally, if we anchor within 50 to 100 yards of a school of baitfish, we find walleyes."

Does the same thing work with insect hatches like the mayfly or fishfly hatches in early summer that can make daytime fishing so notoriously difficult? "It seems that where insects are hatching out of the basin, baitfish generally are there, too," Gannon says. "The two seem to go together. And, yes, the night bite remains consistent throughout. Last year, the pattern lasted until late October, well past the time when insect hatches ended. We still caught nice midlake 'eyes at times when a hot night bite also kicked in on shallow rocks in fall, when ciscoes moved up shallow to spawn. No one expected the pattern to last so late in the year.

"We fished mostly within 1/4 mile or so of one of the big mudflats, at around 32 to 36 feet, because we were successful there and usually didn't have to move much. But when activity tended to slack off in an area after a few weeks, we found similar conditions sometimes as far as a mile or more out into the midbasin, usually in the deepest water in the area. Peak activity seemed to occur between about 11 p.m. and 1 a.m., which is when our guide parties typically conclude. I've stayed out later, though. Calm nights seem best; wind either makes bobbers jerk up and down too much, or causes walleyes to feed more during the day.

Calm nights seem best; wind either makes bobbers jerk up and down too much, or causes walleyes to feed more during the day.

"We had a television crew come up to investigate the pattern. They felt launches were using lights to attract walleyes at night, which is illegal in Minnesota. Well, we weren't shining lights in the water, just using a few lights on the boat to help anglers bait up and fish. Sure, some light trickled down into the water and attracted insects. But I can't say we ever saw walleyes in the water near the surface. And we caught all of our fish right near bottom."

SLIPBOBBERS BEAT THE BUG BITE BLUES

At times, walleyes feed almost exclusively on insects. They can be as picky as trout, indifferent to any prey other than the particular insect they're feeding on. When this occurs, during May and June and throughout summer, it creates some of the most difficult walleye fishing. Ruin an outing for walleyes? Yes!

Mayflies typically are the culprit. Studies confirm that mayflies make up the bulk of insects consumed by walleyes. And of the estimated 700 mayfly species in North America, burrowing mayflies are most important to anglers. Burrowing mayflies hatch in hordes, and their large size can quickly fill walleye stomachs. The nymphs are super-abundant, and they swim with an enticing wiggle that fish can't resist. They're also easy for fish to catch and digest.

Burrowing mayflies derive their name from the burrows their nymphs dig in bottoms consisting of mud, silt, and clay. Clay is critical to maintaining the shape of burrows. A silty bottom cannot support many burrowing mayflies.

Most mesotrophic and oligotrophic lakes, as well as many large rivers, support huge hatches of burrowing mayflies. They cover buildings, blanket parked cars, and pile up thickly enough on roads and bridges to create traffic hazards. Such hatches seldom occur in eutrophic lakes or polluted rivers because their bottom

To go the distance, you gotta slip, bob, and hook.

sediments lack adequate dissolved oxygen.

Walleyes primarily feed on mayfly nymphs when they emerge from their burrows. Most feeding takes place within a few feet of bottom, although some walleyes and other predators feed in midwater, following nymphs as they wiggle toward the surface. Walleyes also sip adult mayflies as they alight on the surface to deposit eggs.

The duration of feeding periods depends on the intensity of the hatch. *Hexagenia limbata*, the common yellow mayfly found mainly in lakes, begins to hatch when the water reaches 53°F. But the hatch doesn't peak until the water warms to the low 70°F range.

During early and late stages of the hatch, walleyes may consume mayflies throughout the day. When the hatch peaks, however, walleyes gorge for an hour or less around dawn and dusk, not bothering to feed much at midday.

Hexagenia bilineata, the most common mayfly in big rivers, hatches later than *Hexagenia limbata*. It begins to hatch at 66°F, with peak hatch at about 75°F. Hatching often occurs during May in the central part of the United States, contributing to the common name *mayfly* of this insect order. Hatches, however, may begin in late March in Georgia and extend into July in Canada. They usually begin in late afternoon, peak before midnight, and continue until daybreak.

Windrows of spent husks in the morning indicate a heavy mayfly hatch. And as veteran walleye anglers know, coaxing an insect-stuffed walleye to grab a bait is like tempting the winner of a pie-eating contest with one more slice. But it can be done.

TEMPTING PRESENTATIONS

"A few years ago," biologist Dick Sternberg recalls, "I'd been catching limits of walleyes on a large mesotrophic lake near my cabin in west-central Minnesota, so I invited a friend to join me for fast action over the weekend. Walleyes had been stacked on two points projecting from a weedy bar. I had no doubt that we'd catch lots of fish.

"Conditions were perfect as my friend arrived—overcast skies, a light chop, and a storm front moving in from the west. I figured we'd catch our fish in a couple hours and get off the lake before bad weather arrived. I graphed the area where I'd been catching fish. There they were.

"We baited our livebait rigs with crawlers and dropped them to bottom, then backtrolled to control the boat as we moved our baits through the school. After a few passes, nothing. Something was wrong. I could see walleyes piled three deep on the graph, but no takers.

"Soon it started to rain, and we took cover on an island. When I beached, I spotted windrows of spent mayfly husks. Our problem was a major mayfly hatch. After the rain passed, we countered with a different strategy—slipbobber rigs baited with small leeches. We anchored just upwind of one of the points and tossed out corks. Within seconds, both went under. And during the next hour, we caught 30 walleyes."

When mayfly nymphs emerge from the mud, they're an easy target. As they slowly wiggle their way toward the surface, walleyes leisurely pick them off.

They're in a lazy feeding mode, not as willing to chase a bait as when they're feeding on minnows. Thus the need to switch to leeches and a slower presentation.

Hook a leech through the sucker end on a 1/16-ounce jighead. Use leeches no more than 2 inches long. They work better than jumbos because they're closer in size to a mayfly nymph and move with a similar wiggling action. If you don't have small leeches, try a half crawler.

Set the bobber stop knot so the bait works about 2 feet off bottom. Fish detect the bait more often if it's above their head than at eye level. But continue to try different levels if the 2-foot level doesn't produce.

Anchor upwind of the area you intend to fish. If you anchor to the side, it's difficult to cast cross-wind to drift the spot. Wind and waves put a big bow in your line, speeding the bobber's drift. A faster drift may be advantageous when walleyes are active, but when they're feeding on insects, a slower presentation works better.

FLOAT ME ALONE

Enthusiasm for floats varies among top anglers, from "I'd rather wait in line at the boat ramp," to "There's no better way to catch fish in certain situations." "Floats offer advantages to less experienced anglers," says Dave Genz, ice-fishing innovator. "Bite indication is one advantage. It's not easy for inexperienced anglers to feel light bites on a jig or livebait rig. It's easy with a float. If it goes under, it's usually a bite."

"Float fishing is the best way for fishermen to learn," says Mick Thill, float fishing's biggest champion, a man who grew up in England, where he became a professional match fisherman and served as coach of Team USA in international competition.

"Floats make fishing visual. A balanced float allows even a neutral or negative walleye to get your bait all the way to its mouth. When fishing's tough, a float is the difference between catching nothing and catching a few fish.

"Float fishing needn't be complicated. It's fun to learn what different floats will do and when to use them. Then choosing one and rigging it becomes quite like a trout fisherman choosing the right fly— part of the sport."

Bottom Connections

Minnow Master

Waggler

Fixed float is held in place with shot.

Thill Float Swivel

Thill Float Swivel (for quickly changing floats)

bead

float stop

main lines underwater, out of wind

With lines underwater, baits can be held in place over key spots. Fished without jigs, these floats allow the bait to move freely.

bulk patterns

12"

drop shot

colored bead

6"

minnow

leech

Organized and Accessible

TACKLE BOXES AND STORAGE

During a short period between the Super Bowl and the earliest open water walleye foray, anglers' attention refocuses from ice fishing and TV football to the upcoming open water season. It's a narrow window of opportunity to reorganize. Chances are that after your last open water fishing trip, you tossed your boxes and bags in a pile in the garage and leaned your rods (with lures attached) in a tangle in the corner. You probably need to change some end-of-season line and to lubricate several reels.

Now's your chance. If you wait until the last minute, you'll enter the new season like an athlete skipping preseason training—theoretically ready to pick up where you left off, but in reality facing rusty hooks, gear that's physically out of shape, and hot new tackle that you bought at the sports show but can't seem to locate now. Preseason is preparation time. Time to replenish your supply of components, from sinkers and swivels to bobbers and lures. Time to take stock of which hooks in which sizes you still have; which packets are lost or in a jacket pocket somewhere or filled with water and rusted into a multipointed tetanus tarantula. A good time to replace old hooks with premium sharp ones.

And those lost crankbaits? or the tangle of cranks in a cardboard box, missing hooks or hook points, sporting oval-shape split rings or broken bills? Buy replacements. Add color patterns. New body styles. Replace dull hooks with sticky-sharp new trebles that grab and hold anything that dares to breathe on the lure.

River fishing's coming fast. Betcha need to replace a buncha jigs—head sizes, shapes, and colors. Stinger hooks, rattles, plastic bodies and more?

Open your tackle boxes. Unless you're a neatnik, you'll find quite a few crankbait trebles tangled together, soft plastic bodies melted into the paint of lure bodies, minirat's nests of old snells and hooks, and little bitty components that have migrated to compartments where they're not supposed to be. Plus a broken hinge or latch here and there. (Plastic boxes tend to fracture under the extended load of heavy lead, particularly in cold weather).

Preseason is preparation time.

Did you take anything out of your open water tackle collection and toss it in with your ice fishing gear—pliers? nail clipper? eyebuster? minnow scoop? Doesn't have to have a hook on it. You'll miss it first trip out if you forget to replace it.

Sunscreen, insect repellent, rags? ropes, fenders, life jackets, throwables, flares? lake maps and GPS cartridge chips? air horn or whistle? tool kit? spare trolling motor parts? extra engine oil? minnow bucket? bait coolers? rain suit and boots? the other glove?

Best bet is to lay everything out on a table, check its condition, and visualize where you store it in the boat. Picture yourself in different conditions. Forget anything? Now is the time to take care of it. Not when you need it and it isn't there.

Admittedly, organizing everything in an unheated garage during midwinter in a cold climate may not be pleasant. That in itself is incentive enough to let everything slide until the last moment. Best bet is to bring a little at a time into the house so the task won't become overwhelming or boring, to avoid overrunning your work space, and to eliminate a hooking risk to spouse, children, and pets. Nothing loses points faster than hook points that show up in the carpet, particularly when affixed to someone's sock.

Winter's the time to work new lures into your storage system and to modify or replace your tackle storage. Numerous component box and wrap systems on the market fit into Cordura storage bags with shoulder straps. They make it easy to mix and match tackle to anticipated conditions, let you beef up on expected needs, and leave the unnecessary weight at home. Organized in a stack on your shelves or workbench, of course.

Pretty well set? Then you have time to pretie livebait rigs and spinner snells. Store them in envelope wraps or wound around cylinders. Spinners are clumsy and time-consuming to tie in the boat while bouncing in waves. The task is much easier at the kitchen table.

Planer boards need screws, clips, or flags? missing a detachable rod holder? livewell or bilge pump burned out? trolling motor on the fritz? fire extinguisher? Take care of it now before you forget. Numerous little things can come back to haunt you in the form of one big thing. General rule: The farther you get from shore, the

---

more things go wrong, and the harder they are to correct, especially if you're unprepared for the unexpected. The unexpected is exactly what you should anticipate.

Luck is what happens when preparation meets opportunity. Tacklewise, the better you prepare, the luckier you'll be. You're prepared and organized, in position to switch presentations or to fine-tune tactics without wasting time trying to find something in a tackle box. That's assuming the thing's even in there, and that you brought the box along in the first place.

Prepared is forearmed. Preplanned is preorganized. That's precisely what preseason is all about.

MODULAR TACKLE STORAGE SYSTEMS

Owning a first tackle box is like owning a first home: by the time it's broken in, it's already too small. At first, a walleye fisherman needs a small box. It holds what he knows how to use with plenty of room left over for things to experiment with. But each stage of expertise requires a bigger, more complex box.

Every pursuit in the angling world has its clinkers—things that won't fit in standard tackle boxes. For walleye fishermen, bottom bouncers and big leader spools rate right up there among the hardest things to store. Then there's the tiny stuff that demands a separate container, like swivels, clevises, hooks, and beads. Lures, meanwhile, keep piling up, and no matter which box you try, it fails to accommodate some essentials. A new box is outgrown by the time it's full.

For advanced anglers and clever beginners, the end game for this confusing cycle could be a new component tackle storage system. Component or modular systems are basically tackle bags designed to carry utility boxes. One advantage to storing tackle this way is that techniques, too, become modular. Each utility box (standard sizes are about 13½ inches long by 8½ inches wide by 1¼ inches deep) can accommodate a different angling method. For instance, bottom bouncers, spinner rigs, beads, blades, and hooks all fit in one utility box. If bottom bouncing isn't on the agenda, pull that box and replace it with one full of jigs, cranks, or rigs.

All of a beginning angler's cranks may fit in one utility box. While growing through stages of development as an angler, each utility box becomes more specialized. Cranks, for instance, can eventually be separated by type or size. All the minnowbaits (like Rapalas), small to large, in one box, deep minnows (such as Deep ThunderSticks) in another, deep diving shad-style baits (like the PRADCO Mystic Shad-R) in another, and so on. Or boxes can be arranged by season. An early spring box would contain small to medium-sized minnowbaits, while a late-fall box would hold medium to big models. Choose which utility boxes to bring on each trip. As you acquire more tackle, add more utility boxes.

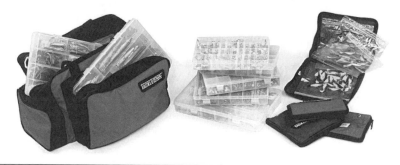

Most manufacturers include big pockets on the sides of bags for storing accessories and extras like smaller utility boxes, leader spools, or spare reels. The Plano Tackle Logic system has zippered pockets designed to hold soft pack binders. These soft packs, called Wraps, hold plastics, blades, hooks, and sinkers in individual plastic sleeves. Wraps are color-coded for quick visual identification.

Like many multispecies anglers, we have lots of stuff, large and small, for just about any freshwater fish that swims—hopefully large, preferably not too small. We try not to overdo it, but we carry at least a representative selection to cover all bases. We don't (can't) carry everything at all times, and we don't always need everything, but some components are so universal that we carry them on just about every trip.

A couple of bags are pretty much walleye-oriented, but we can pop certain plastic boxes from them to take when we fish for bass, pike, or crappies. We can also insert boxes of particular items from other bags if we need them for the day. Best of all, the system is quick and easy to use. When rigging, for instance, leave the component box out on the deck where it's handy, and everything else gets tucked away. If components are handy, it's easier to experiment. If they're buried, the tendency is to continue to fish with the same old thing.

Bags come in all configurations for various sizes of plastic boxes. Bags aren't necessarily waterproof, but plastic boxes are. Some manufacturers offer matching luggage and reel bags with adjustable compartments large enough to carry depthfinders or cameras. Pretty spiff. Some guys like to look their best when they step off the floatplane, hopefully onto the dock.

We come from the John Madden school of down-and-dirty functionality. We just want our stuff to work, to hold up to normal use, and to be easy to use. Doesn't have to be aquamarine, mauve, or one of those frilly California trout colors. Give us blue, green, red—basic colors and fabrics that will stand up to nightcrawler bedding, northern slime, and the tyrannosaurus tread of Ronald J. (Jurassic) Lindner.

Plastic boxes come in all shapes and sizes with various compartment configurations. Select combinations that suit the items you wish to carry. Boxes with infinitely adjustable dividers allow you to set them up exactly the way you want.

You need tiny compartments for livebait rigging gear. Crankbaits require larger sizes, and it's no fun when compartments are 1/8 inch too small for your ThunderSticks. Adjustable dividers solve the problem. Shatter-resistant boxes with good quality hinges, latches, and adjustable dividers cost more than inexpensive boxes with fixed compartments, but they're worth the long-term investment. If you can flex them slightly between your fingers without cracking the lid, chances are they'll stand up to below-freezing cold without breaking.

We love component systems for flying in to Canadian waters. In the past, we had to set up special boxes for each trip by stealing things from all our standard tackle boxes. It not only took time, but things never really got back to pre-trip organization after we returned. Component boxes solve the problem. Take the boxes you want, and leave the others at home.

STOCKING YOUR TACKLE BOX

Nothing new in the world of walleye tackle? Hawg wash! Seldom has such a revolution in tackle and technique occurred over so short a time. If you've been pullin' a Rip Van Winkle the past ten years, then your competitive skills may as well R. I. P. The new breed of versatile walleye angler will consistently outfish you—even on your home waters.

The past decade has witnessed an explosion in walleye fishing and related equipment. Lakes, rivers, and reservoirs demand subtle adjustments in presentation. Whole new trolling systems flourish. Rigging and jigging refinements abound. Crankbaits add speed and vibration. Heavy metal lures plumb the depths. Artificials rival or trounce livebait systems under the right conditions. Wispy superlines refine presentation techniques. Holy backlash, Baitman! It's Buck Perry turned Buck Rogers going into the 21st century.

In other words, it's time to get with the new program. Summer reruns of old fishing tactics don't draw ratings anymore. Tune in to the trends, or be left out in the cold.

WALLEYE STOCKING

Let's stock a walleye tackle box for the coming season. We plan on fishing varied conditions ranging from lakes to rivers to reservoirs, from the vast Great Lakes to the smallest weed- or wood-filled waters. Such a task requires the ultimate in versatility, and a wide range of tackle to match the conditions, your experience, and your imagination.

After 10 or 20 years, we may all be carrying a few extra pounds, and tackle boxes are no exception. With the many advancements in walleye fishing over the last decade, the average walleye angler is far more versatile and carries much more tackle. Thus the trend is away from a single box in favor of tackle bags or boxes containing smaller component boxes. Also, the prominent growth of crankbaits in walleye fishing demands much more storage space, as do the awkward shapes of bottom bouncers.

Walleye tactics require mixing and matching components. One time you team a jighead with a plastic grub, another time with a minnow, next time with both. You may rig a plain hook or floating jighead on a three-way rig, then decide to substitute a minnow-imitator crankbait for livebait. You change spinner blade sizes and colors, or switch from single-hook minnow rigs to tandem-hook crawler harnesses. Or vary trolling depth by clipping a different size snap weight to your line. It's not simply changing colors or shapes, as in bass fishing; it's integrating component lure families into productive systems. The combinations are endless. Therefore, everything has to be handy for easy experimentation. If something's hard to get at, you won't bother experimenting, and productivity ultimately suffers.

Anglers who prefer traditional large plastic tackle

boxes should select models with adjustable trays or compartments to accommodate a variety of component and lure sizes. Some feature removable component boxes, similar to tackle bags. Others require opening the entire box to get at the contents. Boxes also tend to take up more floor space than tackle bags. Some are waterproof. Others aren't.

Tackle tip—Resealable plastic bags and empty film canisters make handy containers for small items like hooks, swivels, and beads. Large or odd-shaped items like bottom bouncers or tools may fit better in a Tupperware-style single-compartment container, which also stows easily in a tackle bag.

The following categories each feature a brief summary of prominent tackle items mentioned earlier in this book, plus recommended selections, sizes, and storage options.

JIGS

Jigs are universal components, applicable from the shallowest cover to the greatest depths. Size, shape, and design tailor some jigs to specific conditions, but others perform well almost everywhere. Popular walleye jigs range in size from 1/32 to 1 ounce, though most conditions can be covered with 1/16, 1/8, 1/4,

or 3/8 ounces. Extremely shallow or subtle presentations require light jigs; deep water or current demand heavy versions. In general, increasing jig weight is accompanied by an increase in corresponding hook size.

Tackle tip—Tiny walleye jigs (1/32 and 1/16 ounce) should still have sizable hooks (#1 or #2) to handle big fish. When tipped with minnows or plastic tails, a jig hook must offer sufficient gap and strength to hook and hold large fish.

The versatile round head excels for vertical jigging, cutting current, and retrieving through weeds and snags, although the position of the hook eye atop the head tends to collect weeds and debris. Perfection or other oblong-shaped heads are modifications of the round head.

Standup heads generally have flat bottoms and low centers of gravity to make the jig stand upright at rest or resist tipping over. The hook eye tends to be positioned toward the front of the head, improving weed resistance but detracting from vertical fishing ability. It's primarily a good casting jig.

Weedless jigs tend to be pointed, with the hook eye at the nose to reduce or eliminate a collection point for debris. They slither through weeds and wood much better than standard heads. Those with weedguards or rigged weedless with plastic tails fish well through snags.

Spinner jigs like the Northland Whistler and Apex Whiplash add flash and vibration to jigging presentations—something different when fish don't respond to standard fare. Northland's BuckShot Rattlers feature removable rattle chambers for added attraction in dingy water.

Jigs were once tied only with subtle bucktail, hair, or feather bodies. Today, interchangeable plastic bodies are more versatile. Mix and match body shapes and colors to achieve desired results. Subtle tails with marabou dressing entice fussy fish. Aggressive wobbling tails perform better on faster or irregular retrieves. White, black, brown, or yellow are good in clear water. In dark water, try fluorescent orange, chartreuse, glow, or two-tone to increase visibility. Jigheads with barbed collars tend to grip and hold plastic bodies better than barbless versions.

Jigs were once tied only with subtle bucktail, hair, or feather bodies. Today, interchangeable plastic bodies are more versatile.

Stinger hooks provide a better hookset when fish simply nip at the tail of the jig—a common condition in cold water, particularly when the jig is tipped with a minnow. Many walleye jigs today come with attachable treble stingers that clip onto an eye, hanging back in perfect position to hook short strikers. Insert one barb of the stinger into the tail of the minnow.

Tackle tip—Avoid placing too much weight in one component box or bag. Chances are that you'll need more than one jig component box, anyway. Consider placing your most used small- to average-sized jigs in one box and your ultraheavy jigs in another—perhaps with jigging spoons or bladebaits. Tiny slipbobber jigs may be handier in a slipfloat box. Component plastic bodies may require a box all their own or a tackle bag pocket filled with individual resealable bags for different bodies.

LIVEBAIT RIGS AND COMPONENTS

Hook, line, sinker. Nothing fancy. A hook and snell present livebait unfettered by hardware. A stop of some sort positions the hook and bait a predetermined distance from the sinker. On the strike, you have the option to feed a little line to the fish; with the line sliding through the sinker, there's nothing unnatural to fool the fish. Whether you pretie your own livebait rigs, purchase prepackaged rigs, or tie 'em up on the spot, livebait rigs all share several important characteristics.

Slipsinkers are the heart of livebait rigging, so carry a fair selection without lugging too much lead. Weight your selection to 1/4-, 3/8-, and 1/2-ounce slipsinkers, with a few 3/4-ouncers for fishing deep water or for fishing with large minnows. Plain lead finishes are standard. Some folks, however, believe fluorescent-painted sinkers attract fish in certain conditions.

Shoe-shaped walking sinkers are traditional favorites, designed to skip over rock and soft bottom with equal effectiveness. Egg sinkers perform similarly. Pointy-nosed bullet sinkers, meanwhile, slither along timber and weededges with few hang-ups.

Size 10 or tiny #12 barrel swivels provide the most common link between your main line and snell. Lindy-Little Joe sells a swivel clip that allows for attaching looped end snells with a quick connection. Northland Tackle incorporates a slipbobber stop and bead on the main line behind the sinker for easily adjusting snell length. Simply pinching a split shot on the line positions the sinker the desired distance from hook and bait.

Snell length varies according to conditions. Thirty to 40 inches of 8- or 10-pound-test mono is standard. Long snells of 6 to 12 feet in 4- to 6-pound test excel for finesse presentations. Where snags are abundant, 6- to 18-inch snells restrict bait motion and reduce hang-ups. Purchase or pretie snells in advance or carry components to tie snells on the water.

Plain hooks are best in most conditions. Match hook size to the size of the

"I did it my way . . ." —Frank Sinatra

We can't quite picture the Chairman of the Board sitting home nights tying spinner rigs, but lots of folks 'cross walleye land do just that. It's the equivalent of

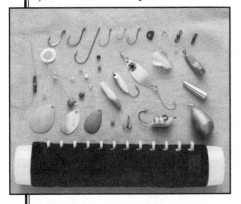

going to the grocery store, buying the ingredients, and whipping up your own concoctions. Cheaper than restaurant fare, home cooking can be suited to personal tastes. So can spinner rigs and snells. Just the right blend of line length and weight, hook size, and attractor suit that special walleye palate. In essence, your component parts collection is the spice cabinet of your walleye presentation cookbook.

Magnifique! Four-star dining versus generic TV dinners! Store-bought rigs are good choices, but they won't fool all of the walleyes all of the time. Fish that see a steady menu of burger-and-fries presentations might respond more ravenously to a house special.

bait—typically #8 for leeches, #6 for crawlers, and #4 through #1 for minnows. The lightweight hook must match the bulk of the livebait without overpowering its natural action yet must offer enough gap to penetrate deep and hold without bending under pressure. While a variety of hook styles are adequate for most livebait conditions, hooks typically referred to as octopus, salmon egg, or simply walleye hooks offer a desirable blend of characteristics for livebait rigging. A select few are available in bright colors for added attraction, but most anglers seem to prefer bronze. Where barbless hooks are required, slip a tiny piece of plastic worm past the hook point to keep livebait on the hook.

Tackle tip—If you're just starting out, start out right. Invest in ultrasharp hooks to maximize hooking and minimize wasteful sharpening time. Walleye veterans should consider updating their hook collection, too.

Attractors add some variety of enhancement to slipsinker-livebait presentations. It may be as simple as slipping a tiny colored bead on the line above your hook to add a spot of color. At times, some form of floater—on-line float or floating jighead—adds color, buoyancy, and action. Move slowly with frequent pauses, and a sufficiently buoyant floater will lift a small bait off bottom, increasing visibility, reducing snags, and perhaps triggering fish. Inflate crawlers with a worm blower for added buoyancy. Even small spinners—#00 or #0—can be used to add a hint of attraction to an otherwise natural livebait presentation.

One component box should hold all or most of your slipsinker-livebait rigging gear, unless you prefer to carry lots of sinkers or an abundance of pretied snells.

THREE-WAY RIGS

Three-way swivels are the heart of this versatile rigging system, the critical junction of main line, snell, and dropper. A #8 swivel is about right—lightweight but sufficiently strong. A snell of variable length tied directly to the swivel is used to present spinners, crankbaits, spoons, or plain livebait on a hook. Except for pretied spinner snells, snells generally are constructed on site to create the right snell length for conditions.

The dropper line connecting your sinker and swivel can be short (12 to 18 inches) to present offerings near bottom, long to position them off bottom, or anywhere in between. You can even hold the entire rig far off bottom to troll for suspended fish. Where snags are a problem, tie the dropper from line that's slightly lighter than the main line. In the event of a snag, heave on the line and you lose only the sinker, not the entire rig.

Tackle tip—Stealing line off your reel to retie long snells and droppers depletes your spool in a hurry. Carry extra line in different sizes for tying leaders or respooling reels.

Nearly any sinker style works with three-way rigs, but most anglers prefer bell sinkers, which come in a variety of sizes from 1/4-ouncers to over 4 ounces. The range of weights allows for covering nearly any depth or current condition, though 1 to 3 ounces takes care of most walleye situations. Carry a selection of the most frequently used sizes. Don't overstock on beefy heavyweights unless you think you'll need 'em, as when trolling deep lakes and fast flowing rivers. Store spares in a boat storage compartment rather than lug 'em around.

SPINNER RIGS AND COMPONENTS

Wide Colorado blades have the widest rotation, most thump, least flash, and slowest rotation. Narrower Indianas rotate a bit faster, enhancing flash but sacrificing a bit of vibration. Colorados spin at slightly slower speeds than Indianas and so are good choices for the slowest spinner presentations. Sizes 2 through #5 cover most conditions.

Willow-leaf blades have a narrow rotation, minimal vibration, and maximum flash. Willows must be trolled or drifted quickly to make them spin.

In-line blades that spin through an integrated hub rather than on a clevis add yet another dimension, something between an Indiana and a willow-leaf.

Rotating two-color or patterned blades blur or whir into an aura of color. Bright fluorescent blades maximize color. Chrome blades offer a seductive flash in clear water; more expensive silver-plated blades outflash chrome. Copper or gold are perhaps more visible than silver-chrome in dark or dingy water. Dimpled blades increase blade surface area and amount of flash. Smooth blades reduce flash while retaining wobble and vibration.

Clevises, beads, and hooks play prominent roles in balancing a spinner rig.

Clevises, beads, and hooks play prominent roles in balancing a spinner rig. Clevises rotate on the line, allowing the blade to spin. Metal folded clevises have been the walleye industry standard for years. Avoid stamped stirrup clevises because their rough edges wear mono line. (Stiffer, more abrasion-resistant line, like 10- or 12-pound-test Ande or Trilene XT, holds up better and allows the clevis and blade to rotate easier.) Plastic snap-in clevises from Quick Change Tackle (Quick Change Snap) and Lindy-Little Joe (X-Change) offer easy blade changes: just snap in different colors, sizes, or shapes without cumbersome retying.

Round plastic beads provide spacing between the whirring blade-clevis combo and the hooks, as well as add color and profile to your rig. Three mm (millimeter) plastic beads work best with tiny blades, 4 mm with midsized versions, and 5 mm with larger blades. Bead color choices are infinite. Select bright chartreuse, orange, yellow, or red for visibility; subtler greens or whites to reduce prominence; or any combo of colors to achieve desired results.

Hooks must also balance with blade size, bait size and type, and bead size. In general, the larger the blade, the bigger the hook, though matching hook size to the bait is perhaps most important. As a rule of thumb, select a size larger hook than you'd typically use for livebait rigging—about a #6 for small blades with crawlers, leeches, or tiny minnows; #4 for midsized blades with crawlers or leeches; perhaps even #2 with big-bladed models for Great Lakes trophy 'eyes. Increased hook size doesn't appear to be a deterrent when dealing with reactive strikes.

Use two-hook harnesses for nightcrawlers and single-hook versions with leeches or minnows. Hook crawlers through the nose and at midlength, leeches through the suction cup, and minnows up through the lips. On a two-hook crawler harness, snell the hooks 2 to 4 inches apart to ensure good spacing and hooking of short striking walleyes.

Hooks should have turned-up or turned-down eyes to accommodate a snell

That Was Then...This Is Now

What a difference a decade makes. Portions of a modern walleye angler's arsenal still closely resemble the assortment pictured in In-Fisherman in 1986 (left), because classic presentations like jigging and livebait rigging never go out of style. Today, though, even these old standby systems are considerably more refined and versatile. Perhaps the biggest differences in walleye tackle, however, are the advent and acceptance of open water trolling systems and the rising popularity of artificials like crankbaits, jigging spoons, and bladebaits. Where the average walleye angler's tackle assortment was once heavily weighted (pun intended) toward livebait rigging and artificial-livebait combos, with a handful of crankbaits and spoons for experimenting, it now also features an extensive and versatile lineup of artificials (below).

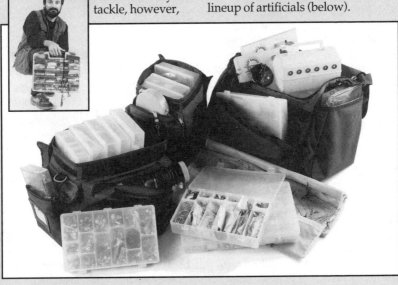

knot for attaching hooks in sequence. At the forward end of the snell, tie a surgeon's loop for easy attachment to snaps.

When using minnows, balance hook size to bulk of the minnow. Hook gap must be large enough to hold a lip-hooked minnow and still retain enough exposed bite to stick a walleye. When fishing with minnows, some anglers prefer switching from the traditional turned-up or turned-down snell hook to a larger, light wire Aberdeen—say, #1/0 or #2/0. Insert the hook point into the minnow's mouth, out the gill, then nick it back into the minnow's back.

Tackle tip—Balanced spinner construction is an art form. Subtle refinements can pay big dividends. You'll likely prefer carrying many components, particularly blades, but threading and tying components in a bouncing boat are difficult. Whenever possible, tie spinner rigs in advance.

Many walleye tackle companies offer pretied, prepackaged spinner rigs, generally in small resealable plastic bags. Toss bags in a larger component box or bag. After tying or using your own rigs, consider winding them around a tubular storage device like a Tackle Buddy. This keeps numerous spinners or livebait snells at the ready, including pretied, treble-hook spinner snells. You can pop off the end cap and store sinkers, hooks, swivels, even blades inside the tube.

Many walleye tackle companies offer pretied, prepackaged spinner rigs, generally in small, resealable plastic bags.

BOTTOM BOUNCERS

While spinner rigs are often trolled behind three-way rigs and can easily be trolled on weighted lines for suspended walleyes, the most common delivery system undoubtedly is a bottom bouncer. Bouncers also excel with plain or floater livebait snells, small shallow-running crankbaits, tiny flutterspoons—nearly anything you would run on a three-way rig, only closer to bottom.

Bottom bouncers range from 1/4 ounce up to about 3 ounces, with 1, 1½, and 2 ounces commonly used in most walleye conditions, and heavyweight 3-ouncers for deep water or fast trolling.

Generic fixed bottom bouncers are available from myriad basement tackle manufacturers. A few companies offer longer or shorter legs, detachable adjustable weights, and different colors, but the function is basically the same. Like slipsinkers, some anglers prefer colored bouncers for added attraction, while others like plain lead finishes. Add a snap swivel at the junction bend to form a slip bottom bouncer for fussy fish.

Tackle tip—The unique shape of bottom bouncers makes them one of the toughest but most essential tackle items to store. Some folks rubber-band a bunch together and toss 'em in the bottom of a tackle box or boat. Others lay them in a flat Tupperware-type container. Nebraska Custom Tackle offers a handy roll-up Bouncer Tote for holding bottom bouncers and spinner rigs.

SLIPFLOATS AND COMPONENTS

Slipfloats suspend bait above bottom or cover or periodically brush bottom on a drift or retrieve. They're great for fishing shallow, snaggy bottoms or cover and for situations in which a subtle, almost stationary presentation is necessary.

Walleye slipfloats are slender to minimize resistance and to avoid spooking when a fish pulls on your bait. Most are made from balsa, some from plastic. Glorified night-fishing versions are phosphorescent or battery powered. Standard floats are inexpensive and easy to use.

A bobber stop sets the depth at which your bait suspends. The two best forms are string ties and neoprene stops . . .

A bobber stop sets the depth at which your bait suspends. The two best forms are string ties and neoprene stops, which thread onto your line, then slide up or down to position your float. Once the stop and optional bead is on the line, thread on your float, tie on a hook or jig, add split shot if necessary, bait up, and cast. The weight of the jig or split shot pulls line through the float until it reaches the stop. On the retrieve, the tiny stop winds up onto your reel.

To set depth precisely just above bottom, first attach a clip-on depthfinder weight to your hook, lower it to bottom, then slide the stop to the appropriate spot on the line that positions bait just off bottom. Reel up, remove the depthfinder, and bait up, generally with a leech or minnow.

Carry several sizes of split shot to weight your line precisely in order to minimize resistance and to barely suspend the float. Sizes BB, B, 3, and 7 cover all the bases.

Small, light wire Aberdeen or salmon egg hooks excel for float fishing. Some specialists prefer equivalent-sized Kahle hooks, feeling they perform better on the hookset. Tiny 1/32-ounce jigheads add a spot of color for attraction in dark water. Some tiny jigs with thin, swimming-style bodies are designed specifically for bobber fishing.

Long, fragile balsa floats pretty much demand their own component storage box, with a selection of bobbers stops, beads, split shot, hooks, and tiny jigheads mixed in.

HEAVY METAL

A lightweight jigging spoon is a versatile and mobile ice fishing lure. Spoons also are good in heavier versions for open water, from 1/2 to 1 ounce, with 3/4 ounce being an all-around size. Silvers, greens, golds, prism finishes—take your pick. Most are used for aggressive vertical jigging, though they're also productive casting lures under the right conditions. Treble-hook versions are most popular, but single-hook spoons have their devotees. Tip the hook with a minnow head or piece of crawler to add scent.

Flat, wide Hopkins-style spoons and imitators display wide fluttering actions on the drop. Narrower, thicker versions fall faster, offering less action. Bent spoons wobble more than flat ones. Bass 'n Bait Rattle Snakies have internal rattles.

Bladebaits wobble most on the upsweep, less on the drop. Half-ounce versions in a variety of color patterns are popular among river anglers. Bladebaits require round-bend snaps that fit through tiny attachment holes in the metal body. Toss a few snaps in with your bladebaits so they're handy.

Great Lakes trollers fish flutterspoons for walleyes, but they're worth experimenting with elsewhere. Carry a few thin, silvery flutterspoons for trolling. Tiny flutterspoons like Willospoons also work with bouncers or three-ways, with or without livebait.

Carry a small selection of 3/8- to 1½-ounce weight-forward spinners and flippin' harnesses, perhaps with your bladebaits and spoons. They're good for long-distance casting, fishing over shallow weeds or rocks, and using a countdown method to strain the depths from subsurface to 40 feet. Beef up your selection for Lake Erie or other areas where casting weight-forward spinners is a primary tactic. Silvers, chartreuses, and greens predominate.

CRANKBAITS

Crankbaits have become an essential lure category that requires significant storage capacity as well as the largest boxes. No problem—cranks are lightweight and easy to carry. Walleye crankbaits fall into several families that vary by shape and resulting action. Carry a selection of each. Don't cut corners, because sometimes subtleties in action make a big difference.

Crankbaits have become an essential lure category that requires significant storage capacity as well as the largest boxes.

Minnow-imitators like ThunderSticks, Rapalas, and Rogues are long, thin crankbaits with a narrow, rolling wobble. Shallow runners excel for casting across flats, longline trolling with split shot on the line ahead of the lure, or deep trolling with weighting systems. Deep-diving minnow-imitators can be trolled unweighted down to about 20 to 25 feet. Constructed from either balsa or plastic, different brands offer slightly different actions. In some cases, rattling baits outproduce nonrattling versions, or vice versa.

Neutrally buoyant suspending minnow-imitators excel for shallow night-fishing. To make a lure neutrally buoyant, add sufficient adhesive lead Storm SuspenDots or SuspenStrips along the belly of the lure to reduce natural buoyancy.

Shad baits like Shad Raps have deeper bodies than minnow-imitators with shivering wiggles. Many are made from balsa, others from plastic. Perhaps used more in casting situations, they also excel for trolling.

Shad-ows like plastic Cordell Wally Divers are a bit rounder bodied and wider wobbling than shad baits. They're good for casting or trolling.

Wide wobblers like Hot 'N Tots and banana baits like FlatFish and Lazy Ikes are popular trolling lures. Some anglers tip one treble hook with pieces of nightcrawler to add scent. Banana baits require weighting the line to achieve significant depth.

Lipless rattlebaits like Rat L Traps excel for long-distance casting from shore or from a boat, retrieving over the tops of shallow weeds or rocks, adding noise in dark water or at night, and fluttering down into holes in weedbeds. Plastic lipless rattlebaits contain numerous shot in a rattle chamber, creating abundant noise and making them heavy enough to sink when you pause your retrieve.

Select families of cranks you have confidence in and carry models with different diving lip sizes that run at different depths. Stock different color patterns as well. Baits with shiny sides and dark backs excel for open water trolling or wherever silvery suspended baitfish predominate. Patterns in orange and chartreuse tend to perform better in dark water and where perch are the primary forage.

Tackle tip—Rather than keeping all your snaps or split rings in one box, spread a selection throughout your crankbait boxes so you can find them without having to search. Small #2 snaps allow crankbaits to achieve better wobble than direct ties, and they facilitate changing lures. Keep a hook-sharpening file handy, along with replacement razor-sharp trebles if necessary. Many walleye pros replace existing trebles with premium hooks.

Because of their bulky nature, crankbaits may claim up to half your component storage space, but they add little weight.

WEIGHTING SYSTEMS

Fifteen years ago, leadcore line was in regional use and segmented leadcore was coming into popularity. Snap weights did not exist. Today, these form the fundamental depth control systems for deep-water trolling.

Off Shore Tackle snap weights, Mr. Walleye Drop Weights, and Wille Zonies incorporate a pinch-on release that attaches a sinker to your line, typically 50 feet ahead of your lure. Preassemble sinker-clip combos, then snap different weights on and off to take crankbaits, spinners, or spoons to any depth. When fish strike, reel in slowly, detach the sinker, and fight the fish to the net unhindered by weight. Snap weights are best used for suspended presentations; bottom bouncing may detach the sinker.

Typical trolling sinkers are long and relatively thin, though any sinker style will work. Carry a healthy selection from 1/4 to at least 3 ounces. This is also a good place to store fixed sinkers like Bead Chains, which tie in-line, or Rubbercors, which attach to the line via an internal rubber grip.

Tackle tip—Carry a component box of snap weights and releases in the same tackle bag as your crankbaits. The weight prevents a lightweight crankbait bag from blowing out of the boat in rough weather.

Leadcore line accomplishes what snap weights do, but large-capacity trolling reels are needed to accommodate the bulk of 18-pound-test Dacron, which has an internal lead filament that weights the line. Tie a mono leader between the lure and leadcore to minimize spooking.

Leadcore lengths exceeding about 30 yards tend to sink planer boards. Anglers typically incorporate a segmented leadcore approach with planer boards, using 10-pound mono backing, 10 to 30 yards of leadcore spliced into the line, and a 50-foot mono leader.

PLANER BOARDS AND BULKY TACKLE

A topic that will be explored in the next book, planer boards (for example, Off Shore Side Planers, Wille Side Planers, Cannon Rovers, and Mr. Walleye Planer Boards) attach to and detach from your line via snap releases similar to those used on snap weights. They spread lines to the side of the boat while trolling, cover a wider swath with multiple lures, and reach fish spooked to the sides by the boat's passage. They have become fundamental items for all big water trolling applications. We recommend carrying at least two left-running and two right-running models. Because of their bulk, they are best stored in a separate duffel bag or small cooler, along with diving planers, spare reels, and extra spools of line.

Diving planers, like Dipsy Divers, Kastaway Divers, and Diver Disks, tie into the main line 4 to 6 feet ahead of the spinner. Their angled diving surface causes the diver to dig deep when trolled, taking a spinner, shallow-running lure, or spoon down with it. Some models can be set to sweep out to the sides of the boat as well as down. On the strike, an internal release trips and straightens the planing surface, allowing you to retrieve line without resistance. Most divers other than Doelcher Fish Seekers offer considerable water resistance, requiring the use of 17- to 20-pound-test line and heavy trolling gear.

Speaking of line, carry extra reel spools to change line weight or to replace bad line. Where spare reel spools are not practical, carry extra filler spools of mono, leadcore, or the new superlines. Stren offers a handy storage box that holds six spools at the ready. Tackle America's Leader Keeper holds individual spools and features a handy line-cutter for constructing snells.

Finally, releases, weights, and miscellaneous component tackle for planer-and-mast systems and for downrigging generally remain on the boat and aren't carried. We don't mean to minimize their importance to big water trolling, but they aren't included in our traveling tackle assortment.

Tackle tip—Somewhere in your storage system, add long-nose pliers, hemostat, nail clipper on a lanyard, small scissors for cutting superlines, a file for sharpening hooks, and perhaps a small fillet knife—perhaps in an easy-to-reach side pocket of one tackle bag.

RIGGED AND READY

Time to open up the old tackle box and re-evaluate your preparedness for this coming spring. If it hasn't changed much in recent seasons, you're lagging and sagging behind the times. You'll still catch your share; unfortunately, your share is exponentially shrinking. Well-equipped and versatile walleye anglers will fish rings around you.

The preceding collection should fit into a couple of shoulder bags that contain 10 or 12 component boxes—perhaps more if you troll crankbaits in open water for suspended fish. Fill additional component boxes with spare or seldom-used items, and substitute or bring them along when conditions dictate. The system is efficient, handy, and versatile. Minimal duplication exists from box to box, other than handy items like snaps or hooks, which take up little space. And all the little nit-picky mix-and-match components so critical to walleye fishing are at your fingertips.

Keep up with the times, but avoid the space jam. Restock. Replace. Rejuvenate. Reacquaint yourself with the latest changes in presentation systems for walleyes. Rebait for today.

THE $200 CHALLENGE:
OUTFITTING A NOVICE

Several recent letters have challenged the *Walleye In-Sider* staff to gear up a novice, a brand spanking new, completely unequipped walleye fisherman, for $200 or less. "Betcha' can't," they said. Gauntlet cast. Challenge accepted.

Some readers suggested heading to a Wal-Mart or K-Mart or to a mail-order company like Cabela's or Bass Pro to meet the $200 limit. Good idea, but we chose a custom tackle store (Thorne Brothers in Minneapolis), where a beginner is guaranteed to get expert advice from people who fish hard.

According to these folks, along with our input, that first walleye rod should be a 6½-foot, fast-action, medium-power graphite stick because it "walks the walk" for most tactics. With jigs, it performs reasonably well for making short casts, excels on medium to long casts, and can handle longer casts when balanced correctly. Slightly longer rods are optimal for rigging with livebaits, but a 6½-footer is nearly perfect for casting or trolling crankbaits and minnowbaits, and it fares well enough with slipbobbers in still water.

A two-piece is optimum for travel and trunk duty. Rods like the Falcon FS-3-266 ($64.95), Fenwick GLC ES66M-2 ($39.95), Quantum TS664F ($79.95), and St. Croix Premier PS 66 ML2 ($64.95) are two-piece rods that fill the bill nicely.

We looked for a slightly larger than average walleye reel with a bigger spool for longer casts. That first reel is critical, requiring durability and a smooth drag to compensate for a rookie's mistakes. We chose reels that would balance well with our rods, like the Daiwa Regal S RG-S2500T ($34.95), which has a long-cast spool and holds about 180 yards of 8-pound test. The Silstar Millenia MER30 ($44.95—130 yards of 8-pound) is another good choice, as is the Shimano TX2000 ($34.95—130 yards of 8-pound) and the Quantum E2-2 ($34.90—120 yards of 8-pound).

The reel should come with a spare spool, but we outfitted our rookie with a third spool, too. We filled each spool with a different weight line, ranging from 6- to 10-pound test. For open water and clean bottom, we chose a limp line (Berkley Trilene XL or Stren Ultracast). For rocks, wood, and heavy weedcover, abrasion-resistant lines like Ande Premium or Super Silver Thread are necessary. (Having it spooled at the tackle shop was the cheapest way to go, costing roughly $12 for three spools.)

A first tackle box is like a first house—too small. If you like the sport, you'll buy a bigger one. If you don't like it, you'll be happy you bought an inexpensive one. We chose a Flambeau 1628 three-tray ($11.99), which is plenty big for the meager supply of tackle carried by a first timer, with room left for expansion. A Plano 2300 is a comparable choice.

CONTENTS

Jigs—1/8-, 1/4-, and 3/8-ounce Fuzz-E-Grubs (six of each size), $1.80 (bulk). *Cranks*—two Rapalas ($10), four ThunderSticks (various sizes—$13.50), two #5 Shad Raps, and two #7 Shad Raps ($20). *Plastics*—mixed bag of 3-inch twister-tail grubs (various colors) at the u-pick-'em bar ($2.70 for 18), and one bag of 3-inch B1PR (bleeding shad) Mister Twister Sassy Shads ($3). *Hooks*—Eagle Claw walleye assortment, sizes #8, #6, and #4 octopus (snell) and baitholders ($2 for 12 hooks—so, say, $6). *Terminal tackle*—one 12-pack each of barrel swivels and crankbait clips ($3). *Floats*—three generic slipfloats in various sizes and a 10-pack of stops ($5). *Weights*—two Systems Tackle bottom bouncers (1 to 3 ounces, extra weights $5), a bulk pack of Lindy foot sinkers ranging from 1/8 up to 3/4 ounce ($4), split shot assortment ($1.99), and a handful of egg and cone sinkers that also can be used on bottom bouncers ($2). *Harnesses and spinner rigs*—four various styles, two each ($8). *Sunglasses* ($10).

With the Fenwick rod and Daiwa reel combination, the total comes to $194.90. Hey, we did it! Keep in mind, we might choose different lures, rods, reels, and terminal tackle depending on where our novice lives. On or near a big river, a beginner would need heavier jigs and weights, maybe a stouter rod, and a bigger reel. Tackle choices should be determined, to some extent, by areas fished.

And, obviously, these are essentials only. But outfitted as described, a novice can jig, rig, crank, and pull three-way rigs or bouncer rigs for walleyes in 80 percent of the world's walleye waters. Betcha' can!

SCENT 2000

Still have some room in that tackle bag? For some 30 years, scientists, anglers, and salesmen have continued to develop, use, and promote scent products to improve fishing success. The initial introduction of scented lures spawned high interest among the angling community. While some anglers spoke of improvements, others were unsatisfied and proclaimed scent applications a hoax. The scent market drained just about as fast as it had flooded, with many scent companies dropping their scent product line or going out of business.

Fishing scent products have, however, retained a niche in the marketplace. Several companies continue their commitment to developing scents or scented products to help catch more fish. Some strive to develop an artificial scented bait that can match or outproduce livebait.

Scent products fall into three categories: liquid, paste, or impregnated.

Liquids—Liquid and spray scents are designed to be applied as a few drops or squirts of the formula. Liquids, however, don't remain on a lure for long and must be continually added to a bait to keep it scented.

Paste—Paste scents have a tacky property designed to hold longer when applied to a lure. A small dab under a crankbait lip disperses more slowly than liquid scents.

Impregnated—These products have scent incorporated into them at the factory. Impregnated baits eliminate the hassle of applying scent—no mess and no extra effort. Most of today's impregnated plastics are designed to maintain their scent without sacrificing bait action or durability.

To our knowledge, Berkley is the only company to research and develop a scientifically formulated impregnated bait targeted specifically for walleyes. Pro Angler Gary Roach says, "I think Berkley hit it right on the head. Visually witnessing the effectiveness of Walleye Tournament Strength is convincing." Berkley Tournament Strength Power Bait Walleye Formula is available in a variety of popular shapes, sizes, and colors.

Does scent make a difference? Do scent products trigger more bites? Following are opinions from fishermen who have used scents and have witnessed them evolve.

Senior Editor Dave Csanda—I've seen scented plastics make a difference when times are tough. At times, applying scent has helped; other times, it didn't make a difference either way. Scented plastics are durable and hold up better than livebait when small fish or panfish are present or for ripping through weeds, when they can save time on rerigging. Fish seem to attack a scented bait more aggressively and to hold onto it longer. I just feel more confident having scented plastics on a jig, much more than plain plastic.

I have a hard time believing that scent plays much of a role when fish are caught on a reflex strike, such as with crankbaits. But again, I doubt it hurts or prevents a fish from striking. I see guys spraying WD 40 on crankbaits, which gives them confidence; it probably doesn't hurt, and might just help.

The word *confidence* is a part of the decision to scent your bait. If you feel more comfortable knowing that you've added scent to your bait and have covered your own scent, then you'll fish with more confidence for better results.

Contributing Editor Steve Hoffman—I use no artificial scents, ever. I use all natural, either livebait or cutbait. I

remember people saying, "It can't hurt." I think it can hurt. I think more harm than good can come from adding an unnatural scent that the fish aren't familiar with. I go completely natural or use no scent at all. I believe it makes a difference when the presentation is slow—through the ice, backtrolling or vertically jigging—and in tough-bite situations.

In-Fisherman Co-founder Al Lindner—I can remember going into a drug store to load up on anise to scent down my baits some 30 years ago. Commercial scent has evolved into today's impregnated baits, which are easier to use, more efficient, and much more effective. Some companies are getting so close to developing effective scented baits that I wonder if they'll surpass livebait. I keep moving farther and farther away from depending on livebait.

Fish hold on impregnated scented bait longer once they decided to take it. Walleyes actually swallow baits like Berkley Power Baits and Mann's PROtein Leech. I don't have as much confidence in spray or paste scents, but I do believe they mask human scent. Used day in and day out, every single time, I think scent makes a difference.

But it's necessary to compare scented and unscented products to discover what effect the scent is having on the fish. It's a confidence thing.

In-Fisherman Co-founder Ron Lindner—I remember chopping up leeches in my wife's blender . . . but that's another story. All species are attracted to or repelled by scent. If walleyes are in a neutral or negative mood, scent products work. Taste and scent are a tie, as far as which is the more important factor. I've noticed that fish tend to hang on longer once they've decided to strike on impregnated plastic baits. As far as scent applications triggering fish into striking on reflex, I believe it probably doesn't make that much difference either way.

Editor Steve Quinn—In almost all cases, scent helps. Fish use their sense of smell for social purposes and for escaping predators. I use either a natural scent such as tipping with a minnow, impregnated scented baits, or scent applications. The distance scent has to penetrate to motivate fish to approach a lure is unknown. I've noticed a positive difference when the bite is tough. When fish are hot, they'll bite with or without scent. Also, the slower the presentation, the more important scent becomes. Gel scents stay longer on hardbaits like crankbaits or suspended minnows and seem to help on jerk and pause presentations.

Editor In Chief Doug Stange—Back when there was a big scent push in the early '80s, everyone had the scent that was going to catch more fish . . . and many or most of those scents now are off the market. When I'm fishing for walleyes, adding scent or using scented products is secondary to the use of livebait.

Studies on L-serine produced and excreted through our skin indicate that it's an attractant for catfish and carp. Meanwhile, it repels salmon and trout. And we don't know what effect it has on walleyes. We know taste is a factor, and in that regard, a scented product probably helps once a fish bites. But we really don't know whether scent plays much of a factor. I'd feel uncomfortable with gasoline present on a lure. But so far as anyone really knows, it might just be an attractant.

I've given up tipping my swimming lures with a minnow head when ice fishing, which I used to do for scenting purposes, simply because I'm confident the fish are hitting the lure because of action and movement. But most fishermen probably have to go through the process of discovery to determine if adding scent makes sense.

Editor Matt Straw—I learned a long time ago that scent products do mask human scent, but I can't say whether they help trigger fish. Of all fish, of course, steelhead and trout can smell as well as blood hounds, detecting parts per million of certain scents. If it's a negative scent to the fish, they may turn away at the last moment, just before striking a lure.

The best example I have is based on a 5- to 6-year period when I didn't tell my fishing partners I was scenting with anise while trolling for king salmon. By not telling them what I was doing, my partners were my control factor. We all fished out of the same type boat with like motors, used the same rods, the same pound-test line, and the same type lures in the same areas. Day in and day out, week to week and year after year, I outfished them. What else could it have been? But then, that wasn't walleyes.

With all the scents on the market today, anglers have a choice of matching scent with the bait or imitation bait. To imitate a smelt, I'd suggest using a smelt paste. If your using a crawdad lure, use crawdad scent.

I don't think scents can hurt. Walleyes feel, hear, or see a bait first, then move in to investigate. That's when they may smell or taste the offering. Using scent helps ensure that you're not giving one more negative cue that will prevent a fish from striking. Many anglers testify that impregnated baits cause fish to hold onto the bait longer once they've decided to strike. But I feel that no scent product available today will outperform the scent or taste of livebait.

But that could change tomorrow.

Scent Versus Taste

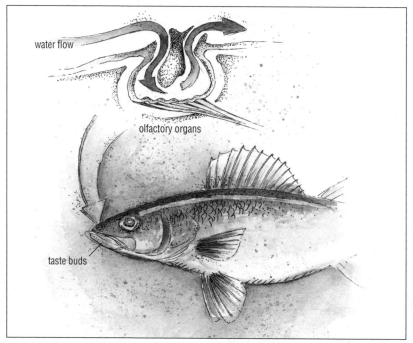

water flow

olfactory organs

taste buds

Fish have olfactory and taste organs that are important for detecting substances. Olfactory organs, located on the snout, are more sensitive than taste organs. As water passes into the nostrils and through and over the olfactory organs, the fish is able to sample a large volume of water for odor cues. Walleye taste buds are centered around the mouth and lips. Because taste is a close range or contact sense, walleyes may have to mouth a substance in order to taste it.

Technology 2000

STATE-OF-THE-ART SYSTEMS—A PREVIEW

Fifteen or 20 years ago, a versatile walleye angler might have read this book and proclaimed it a pretty good analysis of anything and everything happening in walleye presentation: primary livebait rigging and jigging systems, plus secondary crankbait, slipfloat, spoon, bladebait, and miscellaneous tactics. Simply having the right rods, reels, and tackle, however, is no insurance for walleye success. You must be able to correctly place lures and baits in the water to be effective. That's where boat control comes in. In walleye fishing, trolling is paramount to success, because in most instances, the angler controls the boat, and the resulting boat movement positions lures and baits.

Traditional walleye trolling systems incorporate various maneuvers, from slow backward movement into wind, waves, or current (backtrolling); to rapid forward movement to cover larger expanses of water at increased speed (forward trolling); to controlled drifting with the wind. Beyond these critical systems, walleye anglers also anchor and cast when fish are concentrated in limited areas, or cast while maneuvering the boat with an electric motor. Thus the ability to properly cast lures and livebaits also comes into play.

Versatile boat control, therefore, becomes the primary emphasis of the next book in our walleye series. It details the step-by-step use of traditional backtrolling, forward trolling, controlled drifting, anchoring and casting techniques, and shows how to blend them together into effective presentation systems.

Also looking back 15 or 20 years, anglers fishing traditional inland lakes and rivers felt that these boat control maneuvers pretty much covered the bases.

The goal of this book has been to familiarize you, the walleye angler, with a broad scope of traditional presentations and tactics from across the walleye world that are adaptable on lakes, rivers, and reservoirs.

But a revolution was brewing on big waters. Open-water trolling for suspended or basin-hugging fish lay on the horizon. The evolution to bigger boats, high-tech electronics and GPS mapping, planer boards and snap weights, downriggers, diving planers, leadcore, and other deep water, offshore tactics had begun. Systems rooted in offshore salmon and trout fishing were adapted to big water walleyes.

A radical change was occurring in thinking and perception, too. Walleyes had once been considered fish nearly glued to structure like points and humps, but now anglers began to realize that it just wasn't so. Tracking studies and angler experience on big waters—now safely accessible via improved boats and navigation aids—revealed walleyes to be mobile, migratory, versatile critters, equally adept at suspending and using structure. Thus the hunt for walleyes—particularly big walleyes—took on a new dimension: no longer was it strictly a search along contour edges and drop-offs. Now, in some cases, it became a three-dimensional exploration of deep, open water, with virtually every cubic inch of a lake considered likely habitat at one time or other.

Trolling multiple lines teamed with crankbaits, spinner-crawler harnesses, or spoons became hot tactics in the '90s as anglers began pursuing suspended walleyes in earnest. Seasonal migrations and baitfish movements took on new importance, providing clues about walleye location and behavior. Big walleyes began to be caught in numbers at times of the year—notably in midsummer—when the dog days blues traditionally had set in.

Here at the beginning of the 21st century, we see a blending of the old and the new. "Old" traditional tactics like livebait rigging and jigging will never go out of style. They are the meat and potatoes, the core presentations of walleye angling, excelling at subtle precision and extracting fussy fish from classic structure. Meanwhile, "new," open water trolling systems are catching on like wildfire, the flames fanned by every new catch. Walleye anglers today carry boxes and boxes of different crankbait profiles, sizes, shapes, and color patterns, plus the additional trolling equipment necessary to run lures at the desired depths. Heresy to some. Simply a logical evolution of technique to the broad-minded.

The goal of this book has been to familiarize you, the walleye angler, with a broad scope of traditional presentations and tactics from across the walleye world that are adaptable on lakes, rivers, and reservoirs. The information is invaluable and provides a solid base upon which to build walleye fishing success. Even if you never move one iota beyond the ideas set forth in these pages, you will still experience consistent success with the versatile approaches detailed here.

But . . . knowing that there's something out there, those mysterious schools of huge suspended fish, probably gnaws at your conscience. Equipped merely with rigs and jigs, good as they are, you're at a severe disadvantage whenever the local word comes back that the big bite is occurring in open water, and that trollers have the hot sticks. Suddenly, your favorite traditional techniques seem puny and ineffective when faced with fishing far offshore in the great void, attempting to pursue open water predators in a suspended environment.

Thus the dire need for the following book, the fourth in our walleye series, which details advanced trolling systems, state-of-the-art electronics, the logistics and principles of big water pursuit, and which aims at dispelling misconceptions and fears about venturing offshore, away from comfortable contours and traditional structural edges.

Book #4, Walleye Presentation— State-of-the-Art Systems, will acquaint you not only with traditional walleye boat control tactics, but also with the use of high-tech electronics and with the principles, tackle, and psychology of open water walleye pursuit.

Change isn't easy, and for long-time structure fishermen, the whole concept of fishing for suspended fish is tough to swallow. For those who balk at the prospect, we assure you that we're not trying to replace traditional presentations—just add the new dimension of open water trolling systems to the mix. Our aim is to blend the old and the new into one big brew of walleye options, which, in 20 years, we predict will be the prevailing perspective. By then, average walleye fishermen will be equally comfortable reaching for a livebait slipsinker rig on a 6-foot spinning rod or an 8-foot trolling rod rigged with a crankbait, snap weight, and planer board. Because that's what today's top walleye anglers are able to do now. They don't play favorites—just reach for the system best matched to current conditions.

For now, however, even if you're unfamiliar with off-shore trolling, you have the opportunity to be among the trendsetters. Book #4, *Walleye Presentation—State-of-the-Art Systems*, will acquaint you not only with traditional walleye boat control tactics, but also with the use of high-tech electronics and with the principles, tackle, and psychology of open water walleye pursuit. Tactics that may at first be intimidating but that progress into comfortable familiarity as you become more adept in their use and begin catching fish. You'll also find instances where the tactics work equally well on small inland waters, not just on huge portions of the Great Lakes. Another good reason to stay at the forefront of current trends.

Something old. Something new. In walleye fishing, there's always something new. Even new things someday become old hat, but many never go out of style. Ideas are forever generated, and the learning never stops. As fellow walleye fishermen, we keep learning and progressing through our own efforts and the experiences of others. We're glad to share our collective knowledge, making you a better angler in the 21st century.

Index

A

Anlauf, Ron, 201-202

B

Barnes, Dale, 21
Binkelman, Bill, 5, 6, 74
Bladebaits, 148-149, 158-160
Boats
　control of, 82-83, 237-239
　　three-way rigs, 87-88, 191
　1990s, 10
　open water and, 239
　wooden rental, 5
Bohn, Greg, 207
Bottom bouncers, 10, 64-65, 74,
　　125-142, 227
　action of, 126
　adjustable, 127
　balancing, 13
　color, 128
　daddy longlegs, 127
　dragging and, 132-133
　finesse, 129-132
　history of, 125
　rigging with, 126-132, 138-140
　size, 129
　slip, 127
　standard, 127
　straight, 127
　stumpy, 127
　techniques, 129-138
　　dragging, 133
　　precision bouncing, 133
　testing, 136
Bruno, Tom, 157

C - D - E

Caldwell, Phil, 158-160
Cameras, underwater, 12
Carlson, Chris, 204-205
Christensen, Daryl, 150, 152, 155
Cooney, Tom, 161
Crankbaits "In-Depth", 53, 54, 185

Csanda, Dave, 107, 109, 233

Depthfinders, 6, 7, 9, 12
Dingell-Johnson Act (U.S.), 9

F - G

Fellegy, Joe, 4, 212
Fellegy, Steve, 139-140
Ferguson, Dan, 156
Fine, Michael, 43
Fishing Facts, 5, 6, 74
Float fishing
　current, 197-198
　depth of water, 200-202
　mayfly hatches, 213-215
　mud flats, 212-214
　night, 207-209
　　livebait for, 109
　　technique for, 209-210, 212-213
　seasons, 205-206, 207
　weed flats, 210-211
　wind, 204-205
Floats, 194-215
　shapes, 195
　sliding, 68
　slipfloats, 195, 197
　　lighted, 207-208
　　wagglers, 198, 204
　rigging
　　for casting, 196
　　for drifting, 196
　　for reefs, 202-204
　　for rivers, 197
　　hooks for, 199, 228
　　jigs for, 199
　　livebait, 199
　　sinkers for, 199-200
　　split shot for, 228
　spinning, 69
　stops, 194, 196
Fofrich, Sr., Jim, 150, 161

Gaddis, Gadabout, 6
Gannon, Mike, 212-213
Genz, Dave, 13, 215
GPS navigation, 11, 12
Glorvigen, Marty, 47-49
Glorvigen, Scott, 47-49
Great Lakes, 65, 129, 146, 173
    Erie, 7, 9, 49, 131, 149, 150, 160-161,
        163, 172, 178, 189
    Huron, 9
    Michigan, 9
    Ontario, 9

H - I

Hoffman, Steve, 233-234
Holt, Bruce, 21
Holt, Stephen, 185
Hooks
    crankbait, 170
    eyes, and force in hooksetting, 75
    fluorescent, 69
    light line, 61
        circle hook, 61
    livebait, 76-79
    parts of, 60
    selecting, 61
    slipbobber, 201
    spinner, 111
    rattle, 69, 124
    stinger, 98-100, 223
    super, 60-61, 186, 187
    trebles, 46, 61, 232

Ice fishing
    electronics, 13
    Ice Fishing Guide, 13
    ice line, 44
portable shelters, 13
Iman, Ed, 142
In-Fisherman magazine, 7
    Ice Fishing Guide, 13
    Walleye Guide, 11
    Walleye In-Sider, 11
Irwin, Tom, 185

J

Jackson, Keith, 109
Jigheads
    floating, 68, 232
    scent-impregnated, 107, 109, 234
Jigging, 97-98
    bladebaits, 159-160
    in reservoirs, 153
    lift-drop technique, 97
    slipbobber, 201-202
    spoons, 143-152, 150-158, 228
    snapjigging, 106
    vertical, with spoons, 153-155
Jigs, 89-109, 222-223
    designs
        airplane, 94
        ballhead, 95
        bullet, 91
        compact head, 91
        long shank, 91
        prop head, 91
        modified, 90
        rattle, 94, 222
        slipfloat, 91, 208
        specialty, 91
        spinner, 94, 147, 148, 222
        standup, 91, 93, 96
        tear, 91-92
        thumper, 94
        vertical, 95
        weedless, 92, 93, 95
    rods for, 155
    tipping with livebait, 94-96

K

Kalkofen, Jim, 109
Kavajecz, Keith, 46
Knots
    arbor, 56
    back-to-back uni-knots, 55
    blood, 56
    improved clinch, 54
    palomar, 54
    simple loop, 55
    snell, 55
    spider hitch, 56
    surgeon's, 55, 118
    surgeon's loop, 55

Trilene, 54
uni-knot, 54
uni-snell, 55, 118

L

Lakes
Erie, 7, 9, 10, 49, 131, 149,
150, 163, 172, 178, 189
Huron, 9
Lake of the Woods, 10
Lake St. Clair (Mich.), 131
Leech (Minn.), 186
Michigan, 9
Mille Lacs (Minn.), 4, 7, 8, 131, 140,
156, 179, 201, 204-205, 212
Okoboji (Ia.), 6
Ontario, 9
Winnebago (Wisc.), 8
Lehrman, Art, 107
LORAN navigation, 10
Lowrance, Carl, 4, 8
Lindner, Al, 5, 6, 7, 44, 78, 83, 84-88, 90,
105-6, 109, 132, 234
Lindner, James, 50
Lindner, Ron, 5, 6, 7, 220, 234
Lindy Tackle, 5, 7
Lines
abrasion resistant, 38, 44, 50, 52, 53, 68,
119, 133, 156, 191, 205, 232
applications, 41
bottom bouncing, 133-134
crankbaits, 52-54
Dacron, 2, 4
fluorocarbon, 40
history, 39
knots, 54-56
leadcore, 64, 230
limp, 38, 68, 232
monofilament, 2, 4, 38, 41, 43-45, 133
basic characteristics, 40, 51
low-stretch, 43, 156
stretch ratio, 51
nylon, manufacturing of, 38
spooling, 56-58
superline, 27, 41, 42
depth, 52-54
superbraid, 42-44, 49, 51
fused, 19, 42, 45, 46, 47, 49, 50, 51,
52, 53, 124, 133

with casting rods, 48
with spinning rods, 48
Livebait
bottom bouncers, 131
crawfish, 186-188
jigs, 94-96
leeches
hooking, 76-78, 80, 95, 117-118, 131
minnows
hooking, 76-77, 80-81, 96,
118-119, 131
nightcrawlers, 78-79, 80, 95-96
slipfloat rigs, 198-199
spinners, 117-120
Lures
1950s, 2
bladebaits, 148-149, 158-160
crankbaits
mono vs. superline, 52-54
rattling, 176, 178
shallow water, 182
speed of, 176
tuning, 184-186
humpies, 166-167, 175
minnow-imitators, 5, 88, 166, 167, 171,
172-173, 175, 177, 178, 181,
182, 183, 186, 190, 229, 232
night-fishing, 181
vibration of, 174-175
planer-divers, 26, 38
plugs, 8, 88, 169, 172, 175, 178, 181,
182, 183, 198
banana baits and wide lures, 168-170,
172, 175, 187, 188, 229
Shad baits, 8, 167-168, 170, 171, 177,
182, 187, 188-190, 229, 232
Shad-ows, 168, 171, 182, 229
spinnerbaits, 147-148
spinners
blades, 114-115
Colorado, 112, 114, 140
Indiana, 112, 114, 140
custom, 112-13
willow-leaf, 112, 114, 140
beads for, 113-114, 116-117
cleavises for, 113, 115-116
straight-shaft, 147
weight-forward, 7, 149, 160-163
spoons
casting-swimming, 146, 147

Lures (cont.)
    ice, 145, 146
    open water, 2, 69, 143, 144, 145
    rattling, 156-157, 176, 178
    tailspinners, 149
    trolling, 146

M - N - O

Martin, Mark, 50, 186
Mayfly hatches, 213-215
McClelland, Mike, 185
McKinnis, Jerry, 6
Meleen, Paul, 202-203
Morlan, John, 43-44
Moser, Wally, 158-160
Motors
    electric trolling, 6
    outboard, 6

Navigation
    GPS, 11, 12
    LORAN, 10
Nelsen, Wayne, 21-22
Nightcrawler Secrets, 5, 74

Olson, Rick, 189

P - Q

Parsons, Gary, 46, 107, 139
Perry, E. L. "Buck", 4, 10
Planer boards, 230-231
    diving, 230
Plastic bodies, 10, 100-109, 232
    aggressive, 102, 232
    bottom bouncers, 131
    color, 103
    neutral, 101, 102
    scent-impregnated, 107, 109, 234
    subtle, 101
    water conditions, 105-6
    weedlines, 103-105
Precision Trolling, 54, 185

Quinn, Steve, 234

R

Reels
    casting
        antireverse, 32
        ball bearings, 32
        bottom bouncing, 33
        flippin' switch, 32
        line capacity, 32
        line counter, 33
        magnetic brake, 32
        retrieve ratios, 32
        thumb bar, 32
        trolling, 33
        with superlines, 48
    spinning, 2, 29-33, 231, 232
        antireverse, 31
        drag, 30
        gear ratios, 29
        line capacity, 30
        retrieve ratios, 31
        spools
          longcast, 29, 31
        with superlines, 29, 48
    spools
        lining, 56-58
Reservoirs
    Fort Peck (Mont.), 141
    jigging in, 153
    McConaughy (Neb.), 156
    Oahe (S.D.), 46, 129, 150, 152
    Pueblo (Col.), 157
    Thompson (S.D.), 178
    Western, 10
    Plains, 10
Rigs
    bottom-bouncer, 74, 120, 129-132,
          139-140, 227
    Lindy Rig, 5, 7
    livebait, 69-72, 223-224
        beads, 83
        bullet sinker, 120
        finesse, 79-82
        slipsinker, 70-72, 223
          and plastic bodies, 102
        split shot, 120
        walking sinker, 120, 223
    open water trolling harnesses, 76
    slipfloat, 193-215
    spinner, 4, 10, 67, 69, 111-124, 225-227
        balanced, 226-227

finesse, 117-120
history of, 111-112
single-hook, 123-124
weight far-forward, 149-150, 163
weight forward tactics, 160-164
split shot, 74-76
three-way, 72-73, 84-87, 224-225
rigging, 85, 87, 225
speed, 122-123
technique, 86, 140-142

Rivers
Columbia, 10, 141, 142
Missouri, 10
Mississippi, 6, 190
St. Croix, 190
Roach, Gary, 50, 107, 12-124, 233
Rods
action, 17
bladebait, 159-160
bottom bouncing, 18-19, 25, 133-138
casting, 16, 20
crankbait, 18, 20, 21, 25
downrigger, 27
fiberglass, 16, 23
graphite, 7, 16, 23
modulus, 21-22
guides, 19, 35
handles, 34
jigging, 18, 20, 24, 155
livebait, 19, 24
manufacturers, 16, 21-22, 23,
161, 231, 232
noodle, 27, 28
planer-diver, 26
power, 17-18
quality, 21
slipbobber, 26
slipfloat, 19, 26
spinning,16, 20
three-way rigging, 25, 191
tip, 19
trolling, 18, 26, 27
with mono, 19
with superlines, 17, 19, 27

S

Saugeye, 9
Scent
impregnated plastics, 107, 109, 232, 234
liquid, 233

paste, 232
walleyes and, 235
Shorecasting, 183-184
Sinkers, 62-66
bell, 62-63
bottom bouncers, 64-65
egg, 5
Rubbercor, 64, 121, 230
shoe-shaped, 5, 232
slipsinkers, 62
split shot, 66
and slipbobber rigs, 66
rigs, 74-76
snap weights, 64, 121-122, 229-230
SuspenDots, 177, 183, 229
SuspenStrips, 173, 177, 229
trolling, 63-64
walking, 5, 62
Spoons
casting-swimming, 146, 147
ice, 145, 146
jigging, 10, 157
open water, 2, 69, 143, 144, 145
rattling, 156-157
tailspinners, 149
trolling, 146
Sport Fish Restoration Act (U.S.), 9
Stange, Doug, 107, 234
Sternberg, Dick, 214-215
Stiles, Harry, 190-191
Storage, 223, 224, 227, 229, 230, 230-231
tackle storage, 219-220, 226, 231
Structure fishing, 4
Superline
fused, 19
Swivels
barrel, 67
bobber stops, 67
clips, 67
snap-swivels, 67
three-way swivels, 67

T - U - V

Tackle boxes (see Storage)
Thill, Mike, 215
Tournaments
In-Fisherman Professional Walleye
Trail, 11, 131, 201
Manufacturer's Walleye Council, 9
Masters Walleye Circuit, 9

Tournaments (cont.)
  Mercury Marine National Walleye
          Tournament, 8
  Silverline Tournament, 6
Trolling, 237-239
  backtrolling, 5
  flatline, 179-180
  on shallows, 181-183
  open water, 239
  precision, with crankbaits, 1878-188

Van Dorn, Harry, 5

W - X - Y - Z
Walleyes
  clubs, 6
  fishing history, 1-13
  tournaments
      In-Fisherman Professional
        Walleye Trail, 11, 131, 201
      Manufacturer's Walleye Council, 9
      Masters Walleye Circuit, 9
      Mercury Marine National
              Walleye Tournament, 8
      Silverline Tournament, 6
Wallock, Norb, 188-190
Ward, Virgil, 6
Wickstrom, Bruno, 157
Wickstrom, Terry, 157